D1615477

ALEXANDER ZEMLINSKY:
A LYRIC SYMPHONY

From Zemlinsky's early success as a composer and widely recognized achievements as a conductor to his eventual descent into obscurity, this new biography places Zemlinsky against the backdrops of Vienna, Prague and Berlin and illuminates his relationships with figures like Johannes Brahms, Alma Schindler, Gustav Mahler and Arnold Schoenberg. Moskovitz's exploration of Zemlinsky's songs, operas, choral works, chamber music and symphonic compositions follows the composer's search for a distinctly personal sound, revealing an artist caught up in the music of his time yet unwilling to abandon his nineteenth-century roots.

Alexander Zemlinsky: A Lyric Symphony includes an Afterword by conductor James Conlon and a complete discography of Zemlinsky recordings.

Marc D. Moskovitz is principal cellist of the ProMusica Chamber Orchestra of Columbus, Ohio, and has written for various music journals and the *New Grove Dictionary of Music and Musicians*.

Alexander Zemlinsky in his study, 1930

Alexander Zemlinsky

A Lyric Symphony

Marc D. Moskovitz

THE BOYDELL PRESS

© Marc D. Moskovitz 2010

All Rights Reserved. Except as permitted under current legislation
no part of this work may be photocopied, stored in a retrieval system,
published, performed in public, adapted, broadcast,
transmitted, recorded or reproduced in any form or by any means,
without the prior permission of the copyright owner.

The right of Marc D. Moskovitz to be identified as
the author of this work has been asserted in accordance with
sections 77 and 78 of the Copyright, Designs and Patents Act 1998.

First published 2010
The Boydell Press, Woodbridge

ISBN 978 1 84383 578 3

The Boydell Press is an imprint of Boydell & Brewer Ltd
PO Box 9, Woodbridge, Suffolk IP12 3DF, UK
and of Boydell & Brewer Inc.
668 Mount Hope Ave, Rochester, NY 14620-2731, USA
website: www.boydellandbrewer.com

A CIP catalogue record for this book is available
from the British Library.

The publisher has no responsibility for the continued existence or accuracy of URLs
for external or third-party internet websites referred to in this book, and does not
guarantee that any content on such websites is, or will remain, accurate or appropriate.

This publication is printed on acid-free paper.

Designed and typeset in Bauer Bodoni with Kabel display and Prisma initials by
The Stingray Office, Chorlton-cum-Hardy, Manchester

Printed in Great Britain by
CPI Antony Rowe, Chippenham and Eastbourne

For my daughters Eve, Alyra and Leila,
who have shared me with Zemlinsky all of their lives

Ah, give me back those years when I
Myself was still developing,
When songs poured forth unceasingly
And thick and fast as from a spring!
Then still my world was misty-veiled,
Then promised wonders were in bud;
I picked the myriad flowers that filled
Those valleys in such plenitude.
My poverty was rich profusion;
I longed for truth and loved illusion.
Give unchecked passion back to me,
Those deep delights I suffered then,
Love's power, and hatred's energy —
Give back my youth to me again!

Goethe, *Faust*, Part I

Contents

List of Plates

The plates are placed between p. 140 and p. 141.

frontispiece: Alexander Zemlinsky in his study, 1930. Imagebank SVT, Sweden.

1   Zemlinsky, age 2. Courtesy of Peter Dannenberg.
2   Taborstrasse (Leopoldstadt), 1890. By permission of the Hotel Stefanie, Wien.
3   With his sister Mathilde. Arnold Schoenberg Center, Wien.
4   Vienna Musikverein, 1898. Photo by Josef Löwy, *Unsere Monarchie*. Georg Szelinski k.k. Universitäts-Buchhandlung, Wien 1898. Public domain.
5   Zemlinsky at the turn of the century, as Alma knew him. Arnold Schoenberg Center, Wien.
6   The photo of Alma that stood on Zemlinsky's writing table. Alma Mahler-Werfel Papers, Rare Book and Manuscript Library, University of Pennsylvania.
7   Ida Guttmann, 1904. Courtesy of Anne Skandara.
8   Ida and Johanna ("Hansi"). Courtesy of Anne Skandara.
9   Apartment in Vienna (Liechtensteinstrasse 68). Photo by the author.
10 Volksoper, Vienna. Österreichische Nationalbibliothek Bildarchiv.
11 Relaxing in St. Peter, Spindelmühle. Courtesy of Peter Dannenberg.
12 The composer in Spindelmühle. Courtesy of Peter Dannenberg.
13 The conductor in Prague. Courtesy of Peter Dannenberg.
14 Apartment in Prague (Havlíčkova 9). Photo by Marjorie Bagley.
15 Neues Deutsches Oper, Prague. By permission of the Prague State Opera Documentation Centre.
16 Zemlinsky at the helm of the Neues Deutsches Theater ensemble, Prague. Arnold Schoenberg Center, Wien.
17 Zemlinsky seated at his prized Bösendorfer piano, with Arnold Schoenberg (Prague, 1917). Arnold Schoenberg Center, Wien.

The epigraph on p. vi above is taken from Johann Wolfgang von Goethe, *Faust, Part One*, trans. David Luke (Oxford: Oxford University Press, 1987), 7–8 (Prelude on the Stage, ll. 184–97).

Acknowledgments

WHEN I SET OUT to write a book about Zemlinsky, I had no concept of how many days (and nights) of my life this project would consume. I began as a married but childless faculty member on sabbatical at an Ohio university. Eight years later I am living in North Carolina, the father of three girls. The number of people enlisted for help with this project is humbling. From my first days in Vienna, Prague and Berlin, amassing documents from Zemlinsky's life; to tying up loose ends with the help of librarians, archivists and scholars from Toledo, Ohio, and Washington, D.C.; from Basel to Brno; at every step I have benefitted from an army of support. Nearly every request I sent out, whether via post or email, was answered promptly and with genuine interest in my project. While it is impossible to thank everyone who worked on my behalf, I remain indebted to them all.

The following were particularly generous with their time and deserve special note. In Vienna: Silvia Kargl and the board of the Zemlinsky Fonds who helped underwrite this book; Otto Biba and his staff at the Gesellschaft der Musikfreunde; Therese Muxeneder of the Arnold Schönberg Center; staff members of the Israelitische Kultusgemeinde, the Österreichisches Theatermuseum, the Nationalbibliothek, the Music Division of the Stadt- und Landesarchiv, and Universal Edition. Dr. Mirko Herzog, of the Technisches Museum Wien, answered every question about life in Vienna at the turn of the century, providing details, for example, about Vienna's sophisticated postal system. The late Dr. Rosina Raffeiner supplied valuable information about the Theater in der Josefstadt, and Birgit Radspieler tracked down Zemlinsky's conversion records at Vienna's Lutherische Stadtkirche. In Prague I received invaluable help and materials from scholars Dr. Jitka Ludvová and Helena Turková, and from Dr. Tomá Vrbka of the Prague State Opera. I also received timely and much-needed information from each of the following: Dr. Dietmar Schenk and Frau Krukovski of the Hochschularchiv of the Hochschule der Künste Berlin; Peter Borchardt of the

Berlin Zentral-und Landesbibliothek; Beatrix Klein of the Köln Historisches Archiv; Edith Schipper of the Bayerische Staatsbibliothek; Henrike Hoffmann of the Paul Sacher Stiftung in Basel; and Dr. Thomas Siedhoff of the Bayerische Theaterakademie.

I am indebted to my splendid European hosts Gudrun Mayer-Dolliner (Vienna) and Helga Tümmler (Berlin); I hope to one day be able to return the favor. In the States I would like to offer special thanks to Nancy Shawcross of the University of Pennsylvania, Susan Clermont and the staff of the Library of Congress, the staff of the Houghton Library at Harvard University, and Ina Rubin Cohen of the Jewish Theological Seminary in New York. Karl Schleunes was consulted about the Nuremberg Laws, Marsha Rozenblit verified facts about Zemlinsky's conversion, and Burley Channer, Joachim Baer, and Rupert Buchner aided with some of the more intractable translations.

The late Professor Emeritus Bernhard Heiden, of Indiana University, and mezzo-soprano Risë Stevens welcomed me into their living rooms, where they spoke at length about their personal memories of Zemlinsky. Walter Levin graciously took time out of a hectic schedule to be interviewed, as did Michael Haas, who also read the final draft of my manuscript and provided invaluable feedback. Maestro James Conlon deserves my heartfelt thanks — an international conducting schedule never prevented him finding time when I asked for his help or advice. Cary Moskovitz, my brother and the closest thing to a renaissance man I know, laid the groundwork for the photographic plates and helped me rethink issues of organization, particularly with respect to the opening chapters and the epilogue. Jeffrey Dean, my project manager, exquisitely prepared the text and the printed book, with an eagle eye for detail. And if not for the enthusiasm and support of Michael Middeke, Senior Commissioning Editor at Boydell and Brewer, this manuscript might never have left my desk.

Lastly, three people were tireless in their support and found unlimited time for editing, advice and encouragement: Kristina Nilsson, my generous Boston proofreader; my dear friend Ron Samuels, who spent countless hours reading through my manuscript not once but twice and whose erudite suggestions were incorporated almost without exception; and finally Barb Carter, my wife and general counsel. Beyond the countless hours she spent editing my manuscript, from the first draft to the last, she was there time and again, whenever the words or the determination to see this project through failed me.

The insightful criticism and unending support of them all has improved every page of this book.

MDM
January, 2010

Preface

> It has to be said once and for all, that here, living inconspicuously, is one
> of the few masters, worth more than all the officially accredited "mas-
> ters" Pfitzner, Schreker, and the whole German and Nordic lot.
>
> Alban Berg on Zemlinsky[1]

I<small>T WAS</small> A<small>LEXANDER</small> Z<small>EMLINSKY'S</small> continued inconspicuousness that inspired this book. My interest in the late composer-conductor began in 1995,
when I taught an honors seminar focusing on *fin-de-siècle* Vienna. In the
course of my preparations, Zemlinsky's name occasionally turned up, but always in the context of more famous contemporary figures. Perusals of music
histories and biographies rarely included more than the most basic facts about
his life: Viennese born and trained; a conductor in Vienna, Prague and Berlin;
lover of Alma Schindler; brother-in-law to Schoenberg. More often, Zemlinsky's name was simply absent from the general English-language musical
literature. Also around this time I performed a concert of works by Viennese
composers, among them Zemlinsky. My reaction was similar to many who encounter his music for the first time — how has a composer this gifted remained
so obscure?

Minimal research made it clear that Zemlinsky's life and art embodied
a number of subjects that were becoming increasingly important to me: musical
post-romanticism, turn-of-the-century Vienna, and the role of Jews in both. The
more I learned, the more intriguing Zemlinsky became. Here was an approach-
able figure, a musician of ambition and humility, someone who struggled for
recognition and sought an environment where his talents could thrive.

Although Zemlinsky was associated with some of the most influential and

---

[1] Brand, Hailey and Harris (1987), 281.

talented musicians and artists of his generation, he kept no diary, left no memoirs and remained nonchalant about correcting biographical errors that appeared in print while he was alive. Alban Berg, a composer strongly drawn to
Zemlinsky and his music and who recognized the value of Zemlinsky's contributions, once considered undertaking a biography about him, but sadly he died
and the work never materialized. Had Berg's plan come to fruition, it might well
have bolstered Zemlinsky's reputation, particularly toward the end of his life
and in the immediate years that followed. At the very least, Berg's efforts would
have provided valuable information for future scholars. As it is, there are gaps
in Zemlinsky's life that are unlikely ever to be filled.

Fortunately, much of Zemlinsky's early, unpublished musical manuscripts
have survived, along with his later published compositions, and the music often
provides answers and insights into his life when words or hard facts are absent.
Certainly the most significant details about Zemlinsky's life are found in his
letters, two collections in particular which must be mentioned. The first is Horst
Weber's superb edition of Zemlinsky's letters to and from Schoenberg, Webern,
Berg and Schreker (*Zemlinskys Briefwechsel mit Schönberg, Webern, Berg und
Schreker*), published in 1995, which remains the definitive source of information
concerning Zemlinsky's whereabouts and activities at various times between the
years 1901 and 1923. Second are the letters Zemlinsky sent to Alma Schindler
during their courtship in the first years of the twentieth century. These letters
reveal an intimate portrait of Zemlinsky and provide insight into nearly every
aspect of his life at the time, including familial relations, his manner of dress,
and his personal attitudes toward art and love, all the while capturing his frail-
ties, sensitivity and humor. To read them is to appreciate the core of Zemlinsky's
nature, for they unveil the passion in everything he did and reflect the roller-
coaster of emotions he endured at Alma's hands. Only the most dispassionate
reader could not fail to be moved by the frustrations, disappointments, and endless longing to which Zemlinsky here gives voice. Although Zemlinsky confided
that he had great difficulty expressing all he felt, at times it seems that to read
more would be unbearable, a breach of privacy.

In 2000, during the early stages of this project, Antony Beaumont published
his scholarly tome *Zemlinsky*, and two years later Lorraine Gorrell's detailed
study of Zemlinsky's songs, *Discordant Melody*, appeared. But the work that
welcomed the non-academic into Zemlinsky's world had yet to be written, and
this is the gap I hope to fill. Trying to create as complete a picture of Zemlinsky
as possible, I pored through letters, scores, and all the biographical data I could
unearth. In addition to the previously discussed sources, I relied upon reviews
and criticism published during Zemlinsky's lifetime, as well as contemporary

scholarship, all of which are found in the bibliography. My research also turned up some previously unknown documentation.

Writing this book was also my way of trying to understand how one of the great musicians of the early twentieth century faded so quickly from European musical life and was passed over by music historians. Zemlinsky's talent alone should have ensured him a place in posterity. As one of the last in a long line of Viennese "complete musicians", Zemlinsky excelled as a pianist, was a conductor of the first rank, and wrote significant compositions in all genres: lieder, chamber and choral music, symphonies and opera. Few of his peers could make such claims. But then neither did Zemlinsky, and his modesty, though arguably a personal virtue, proved detrimental to his career and legacy. He never developed the skills necessary for self-promotion, and he rarely programmed his own music. Zemlinsky was fully conscious of his abilities, which he believed should have secured his reputation, and his seeming inability to promote his own cause: "I most certainly lack that special something that one must have — and today more than ever — in order to come out on top. Amidst such a crowd it does little good to have elbows — one must also know how to use them."[1] Years later, the theorist Theodor Adorno took up Zemlinsky's cause: "a man may be cheated of his desserts by nothing more than a lack of ruthlessness. It is possible to be too refined for one's own genius and in the last analysis the greatest talents require a fund of barbarism, however deeply buried. This was denied to Zemlinsky".[2]

But barbarism wasn't part of Zemlinsky's persona. Although he had a pronounced influence on a number of other Viennese composers, including the young Arnold Schoenberg, Zemlinsky possessed neither a dominant nor controlling personality. As a conductor he lacked the powerful ego and ruthlessness required to obtain and maintain a world-class position, such as that held by Gustav Mahler or Otto Klemperer. And while he demanded the highest level of artistic competency in every theater he worked, he did so through inspiration, conviction and intelligence, not through intimidation. Zemlinsky was "a conductor for the ears and not the eyes",[3] and an artist who gave himself tirelessly to his craft. His actions, almost without exception, were diplomatic.

Of course, the issues surrounding Zemlinsky's struggles and subsequent descent into obscurity extend well beyond his personality, although had he been eccentric, flamboyant or megalomaniacal — all fashionable characteristics of the artist that so often captivate the public and lead to posthumous celebrity — his

[1] *AZ/AMW.*

[2] Adorno (1992), 127.

[3] *Die Theater und Kino Woche*, 1. Jg., Wien, 1919, Nr. 5, in Biba (1992), 76.

reputation may actually have fared better. For one, there was the issue of poor timing, bad luck, or both, which dogged Zemlinsky throughout his life. There was also Zemlinsky's complicated relationship to Vienna, the city of his birth, a city that held seemingly unlimited possibilities but which often failed to support the talent in its midst. And finally, in the opening years of the twentieth century, a time that often welcomed — almost demanded — innovation and modernism, Zemlinsky was unable to forge a new musical path, unable to embark fully on his own *Weg ins Freie* or "road into the open", to borrow a phrase from the Viennese author Arthur Schnitzler. All of these themes worked in concert. They shaped the fabric of Zemlinsky's life, affected his reputation both during and following his lifetime, and are essential to understanding his musical and historical persona.

I have attempted to describe Zemlinsky as he lived and worked, whether in the opera house or the coffee house, revealing him as a victim of musical politics and world wars, as a musician who championed modern music but remained unwilling to forsake his classical pedigree, and as an artist living among, yet always in the shadow of, musical giants. With an introduction to Zemlinsky's life and music as my goal, I have purposely sought to maintain my focus on Zemlinsky, and have fought the urge to stray when describing the work or lives of his contemporaries, save in those cases when their development affected Zemlinsky's own. I have also intentionally avoided the clinical, theoretical language often associated with musical analysis, aiming instead to provide an informed yet friendly starting point for the general reader, avid concertgoer and enthusiast of classical and modern music. Finally, in spite of my unapologetic affection for Zemlinsky, I have tried to be fair and unbiased in my portrayal of his professional and musical successes and failures. My desire was to create a readable and broad picture of his life and art, which blossomed as Habsburg rule disintegrated, and faded with the unforeseen rise of an art-student-turned-*Führer* named Adolf Hitler. Among the most gifted musicians of his age, Zemlinsky was both a product and a victim of his time, and his story is a compelling tale and a window into that world.

MDM

January, 2010

Chronology

1896   Dec. 22: Clarinet Trio in D minor awarded third prize, Tonkünstlerverein Com-
       position Competition

1897   prepares *Sarema* for Munich premiere and composes Symphony in B-flat
       Oct. 10: premiere of *Sarema*
       Clarinet Trio in D minor, op. 3 published by Simrock
       Symphony in B-flat awarded Beethoven Prize by Tonkünstlerverein
       begins opera *Es war Einmal*

1898   publication of Gesänge, op. 5
       begins Walzer-Gesänge, op. 6, *Irmelin Rose und andere Gesänge*, op. 7, *Turm-
       wächterlied und andere Gesänge*, op. 8, and the Fantasies on Poetry of Deh-
       mel, op. 9

1899   Mar. 5: premiere of Symphony in B-flat
       Mar. 30: withdraws name from Vienna's Jewish community
       elected Vice-president of Tonkünstlerverein

1900   Jan. 22: premiere of *Es war einmal*, Vienna
       Feb. 11: premiere of *Frühlingsbegräbnis* cantata
       Feb.: begins courtship of Alma Schindler
       June 29: death of father, Adolf
       Sept.: appointed conductor with Carltheater

1901   composes ballet *Der Triumph der Zeit*
       Oct. 18: Arnold Schoenberg weds Mathilde Zemlinsky
       Nov: courtship with Alma Schindler terminated

1902   Feb.: begins *Die Seejungfrau*
       composes Drei Balletstücke (from *Der Triumph der Zeit*)

1903   Feb. 18: premiere of *Drei Balletstücke*
       May: Carltheater contract terminated
       renounces association with the Tonkünstlerverein
       joins newly formed Ansorge-Verein
       Sept.: appointed conductor with Theater an der Wien

1904   Apr. 23: together with Schoenberg founds Vereinigung schaffender Tonkünstler
       Sept.: appointed principal conductor, Wiener Volksoper
       Oct. 15: begins teaching duties at Schwarzwald School

1905   Jan. 25: premiere of *Die Seejungfrau*
       courtship of Ida Guttmann

1906   Oct.: completes *Der Traumgörge*

1907   May: appointed conductor with Vienna Hofoper at Mahler's invitation
       June 11: converts to Protestantism
       June 21: weds Ida Gutmann

1908   Feb. 15: Hofoper contract terminated, returns to Volksoper in spring
       May 8: birth of daughter, Johanna ("Hansi")
       Nov. 4: suicide of Richard Gerstl

1909   Aug: completes work on *Kleider machen Leute*

1910   begins composing Maeterlinck songs

Dec. 2: premiere of *Kleider machen Leute* under Zemlinsky's baton at Volksoper

Dec. 10: premiere of Psalm 23

1911   Apr. 29: final Volksoper performance (*Tannhäuser*)

Sept: begins duties as musical director of Neues Deutsches Theater, Prague

1912   June 12: death of mother, Clara

works on (incomplete) opera *Malwa*

1913   Mar. 31: Scandal concert, Vienna, featuring Zemlinsky's Maeterlinck songs

begins Second String Quartet

1914   Jan. 1: conducts first performance of Wagner's *Parsifal* outside of Bayreuth

Jan. 29: conducts premiere of Schoenberg's 3 Orchestral Songs, op. 8

1915   begins *Eine florentinische Tragödie*

1917   Jan. 30: premiere of *Eine florentinische Tragödie*, Stuttgart

1919   begins work on *Der Zwerg*

1920   begins duties at Prague's Academy for Music and Applied Arts

1922   Apr.: begins work on *Lyrische Symphonie*

Apr. 21: leads Czech Philharmonic for first time

helps found Prag Verein für musikalische Privataufführungen; first concert May 25

May 28: premiere of *Der Zwerg*, Cologne

1923   Oct. 18: death of sister, Mathilde

1924   June 4: conducts premiere of *Lyrische Symphonie*, Prague

June 6: conducts premiere of Schoenberg's *Erwartung*, Prague

Aug: begins composing String Quartet no. 3, op. 19 (premiered Oct. 27)

1927   appointed conductor of Kroll Oper, Berlin

1928   Nov.: begins teaching at Berlin Hochschule für Musik

1929   Jan. 29: death of Ida

1930   Jan. 4: weds Louise Sachsel

1931   July: closing of the Kroll

Dec. 21: conducts Weill's *Mahagonny*, Berlin

1933   Apr.: returns to Vienna

Oct. 14: premiere of *Der Kreidekreis*, Zurich

Oct. 22: first concert as conductor of Wiener Konzertorchester

1934   moves to Viennese suburb of Grinzing

Der Kreidekreis banned in Germany

1936   begins work on opera *Der König Kandaules*

1938   Sept. 10: emigrates to Prague

Dec. 14: sails to America

Dec. 23: arrives in New York

1939   begins work on *Circe*, sets texts by Irma Stein-Firner and composes school pieces

1940   moves to New Rochelle, N.Y.

        Dec. 29: Dimitri Mitropoulos conducts *Sinfonietta*, op. 23, New York

1942   Mar. 15: death in Larchmont, N.Y.

We who were born in Vienna, and grew up there, had no idea, during the city's brilliant period before the first world war that this epic was to be the end of the greatest development of history of music known to the world . . . We enjoyed the splendid city which was so elegantly beautiful, and never thought that the light which shone over it could ever be that of a colorful sunset.

Max Graf, *Legend of a Musical City*

PART I
Vienna: City of Dreams

Prologue

Zemlinsky's Vienna

IN 1867 THE CORNERSTONE of the Musikverein was laid on a wide tract of land just south of old Vienna, on ground generously donated by the Austrian Emperor. The new Society of Music was being built to replace a 700-seat hall in the city center that Vienna's concert-going middle class had outgrown. The project had been entrusted to Theophil Hansen, a Dane who harbored a predilection for the architecture of ancient Greece. Hansen's classically inspired design featured a three-tiered façade with arched porticos, flanked on both sides by two-story wings, all adorned with classical columns. When finished, the edifice stood stately, elegant and serene. Hansen had purposely reserved nineteenth-century opulence for the Musikverein's interior, a reflection of the high regard he, like the Viennese who would occupy its seats, held for the music itself.

Although the Verein houses five concert halls today, only two were part of Hansen's original structure: a small, intimate chamber music hall — the *Kleiner Saal* or Little Hall — decorated with a temple roof, Ionic columns and caryatids, and renamed for Johannes Brahms in 1937; and the Great Hall — the *Grosser Musikvereinssaal* — a room capable of accommodating an audience in excess of 2000. The Great Hall, known also as the Golden Hall, was Hansen's true gift to Vienna. The rectangular room blankets the listener with visual spectacle, from the caryatids in the stalls and elegant female sculptures molded atop the balcony doors, to the richly decorated golden balcony and ceiling, framed by rows of arched windows that flood the entire room in sunlight. Above it all, ceiling paintings of Apollo and the nine Muses keep watch on the music making below. But it is the room's rich golden sound that continues to make the Musikverein an inspiring musical experience. A century and a half later, the Great Hall's sumptuous acoustics remain among the best in the world.

As a city steeped in music and musical tradition, Vienna was home to a variety of concert halls, opera houses and theaters, venues for both the nobility and an ever-growing, music-demanding middle class. But when the Musikverein opened its doors three years after construction began, it soon took its place among the world's premiere cultural institutions, a result of the society's mission to "promote music in all its facets". In addition to its concert halls, the Verein was also home to an historic collection of musical documents as well as the Conservatory of the Society of the Friends of Music, the Konservatorium der Gesellschaft der Musikfreunde. The school's prestigious faculty began attracting students from Vienna and beyond, a list that would include Gustav Mahler, Alexander Zemlinsky, Leos Janáček, George Enescu and Jan Sibelius. Along with the Verein's vital concert life, the school's blossoming reputation ensured Vienna's prominent role in European musical life for years to come.

Vienna was, at the same time, in a state of monumental aesthetic transition. In 1858 the Emperor ordered the city's thirteenth-century city walls to be razed and replaced with a wide boulevard lined with majestic new buildings, a showcase of Habsburg grandeur. The Ringstrasse was the result, a horseshoe-shaped avenue that skirted the inner city. No longer walled, Vienna began its slow push outwards, evident in the construction of the nearby Musikverein, although in the decades immediately following Franz Joseph's decree, the most radical changes took place along the Ringstrasse itself. As ground was broken for one building after another, the Ringstrasse became framed in a potpourri of grand architectural styles — the Classical Greek Parliament, the French-Renaissance-inspired Hofoper, the City Hall in the Gothic style, museums inspired by the Italian Renaissance and the Baroque-influenced Burgtheater. Palatial apartments added to the Ring's allure, as did the beautiful parks, where the city's inhabitants or visitors could stroll, sip coffee, or waltz to the music of a live orchestra. Soon, trolleys were running the length of the boulevard, crisscrossing an open field that many of Vienna's residents could remember having been used for military exercises. In the course of a few decades, Vienna was transformed from a medieval walled community into a modern city.

Despite the activity at its edges, much of the old city looked as it had for centuries. For hundreds of years, the Viennese had walked its serpentine cobbled streets, or *Gassen*, and visited the plaza known as the Graben, the city square established to mark the cessation of the devastating Black Death. Three outdoor markets traced their origins back to the thirteenth century: the *Hoher Markt* or High Market, the city's first fish and bread market; the New Market or *Neuer Markt*, the medieval center for meat and greens; and *Am Hof*, or At the Court, the sea-fish and crustacean market, which dated back to about 1280. Two of

Vienna's most ancient and significant structures are still standing: the imposing St. Stephan's Cathedral, seat of the Roman Catholic Archbishop of Vienna, and the nearby Hofburg, the royal palace and seat of Habsburg government.[1]

Unfortunately, despite the appearance of prosperity and stability, anti-Semitism was again on the rise in Vienna. A phenomenon that had long been associated with Vienna, anti-Semitism surfaced in many guises over the centuries, some brutal, others subtle. In one of the more extreme cases, over two hundred of Vienna's Jews were publicly burned in 1421, and those who remained were herded into boats and shipped down the Danube to Hungary. But by 1867, Jews had been streaming into Vienna from the East for more than a century. In search of a better life and a modern education, Jews had been drawn to the Austrian capital ever since Joseph II passed the 1782 *Toleranzpatent* (Edict of Tolerance), granting Vienna's mercantile Jews citizenship and numerous other rights and freedoms.[2] Indeed, the year 1867 also brought the *Dezemberverfassung*, the December Constitution that accorded *all* Austrian citizens full emancipation. For the first time in Austria's existence, all Jews could live where they wanted, attend public schools and universities, engage in civil service, and pursue most public professions.

By the 1880s, Jews accounted for thirty-three per cent of Vienna's high school and university students, and "at least half of all Viennese journalists, physicians, and lawyers were Jews".[3] By 1910, nearly half of Vienna's teaching faculty were Jewish as well.[4] Jews became prominent members of the bourgeoisie, establishing themselves in every segment of Viennese life, from philosophy, politics, medicine and science to journalism, music, education and finance. But despite Jewish success, or maybe partly because of it, anti-Semitism thrived, and Vienna's Jews remained a target in times of crisis, such as the crash of Vienna's stock market in 1873. Following a wave of frenzied speculation, the bourse collapsed within days of the opening of the Vienna World's Fair. In the weeks and months that followed, as the economy stagnated and unemployment rose, fingers were pointed at Vienna's liberals and their Jewish allies. Widespread anti-Semitism

[1] Habsburg Austrian rule began in 1279, but it was not until 1483 that Vienna became the official residence.

[2] Joseph's reforms marked the beginnings of Jewish assimilation, particularly in Vienna; while the Jewish community witnessed a level of freedom and security previously unknown, Jews were simultaneously encouraged to adopt German surnames and attend German schools, and were ultimately pressured to undergo Christian baptism.

[3] Gay (1988), 19.

[4] Davies (1998), 851.

ensued, paving the way for future politicians with an anti-Semitic platform —
men such as Georg Ritter von Schönerer and Karl Lueger.

In a city so steeped in the past, struggling with Nationalism and anti-Semitism, it is all the more remarkable that Vienna developed into a cradle of modernism at the turn of the century. In only a matter of years, Vienna's cultural,
intellectual and political strains converged and fashioned an entirely new city,
one whose richness continues to inspire contemporary scholarship and debate
even today. In light of this, a brief overview, by its very nature, cannot hope to
do justice to such complex and nuanced subject matter. Nevertheless, a review
of some of the period's major trends and icons may be of value, as it was precisely during this period that Zemlinsky emerged as a composer and conductor.

Within the span of just a few years Vienna witnessed the birth of a number of
critical cultural institutions that came to symbolize the age of Viennese modernism. The Secession, for example, was formed in 1897 when the painters Gustav
Klimt and Carl Moll broke from the Association of Austrian Artists. The group's
literary organ, *Ver Sacrum*, appeared one year later. In 1899 the journalist Karl
Kraus founded *Die Fackel* (The Torch), arguably the most influential Viennese
periodical of the day. Two years later the Vienna-based music publisher Universal Edition was born and within a decade was recognized as one of the most
important publishers of modern music. And in 1903 the *Wiener Werkstätte*, the
Vienna Workshop, brought together a community of designers with the intent
of creating functional art accessible to the masses.

Not surprisingly, much of this activity sprung forth as a reaction to the
status quo. Universal Edition, for example, was created as an alternative to the
Leipzig-dominated music publishing industry. And in contrast to Ringstrasse
bombast and artificiality, the architects Otto Wagner and Joseph Maria Olbrich
designed pragmatic, streamlined buildings devoid of excess. Among Vienna's
most iconic structures, Olbrich's Vienna Secession Building of 1897, constructed
as exposition space for the progressive Secessionist group, and Wagner's Majo-
likahaus apartments of 1899 and his Postal Savings Bank of several years later
proved the perfect combination of functionality, striking originality and beauty.

A student of the revered but conservative painter Hans Makart, the artist Gustav Klimt and his fellow Secessionists regarded the romantic and lofty
subject matter of the earlier generation as out of date. Klimt's engagement with
issues of anxiety and death, elements associated with the inner psyche, paralleled the studies that Sigmund Freud, another of Vienna's residents, was then
pursuing. The erotic nature of Klimt's canvases at once confronted conservative
taste and opened doors for the next generation of artists, including Oskar Kokoschka and Egon Schiele. Richard Gerstl, who became caught up in Zemlinsky's

circle, was among the first artists in Vienna to absorb the important advances of Vincent Van Gogh and Edvard Munch, but because he was only tangentially associated with Vienna's modernist camp, Gerstl attracted no followers. Nevertheless, his aggressive and often tormented style, particularly evident in his self-portraits, points strikingly toward the future of Viennese Expressionism.

Crucial pioneering efforts were likewise underway in the disciplines of music and literature, as composers and writers searched for language that moved away from — and in some cases violently broke with — the comfort and romanticism of the nineteenth century. Alexander Zemlinsky, Franz Schreker and Arnold Schoenberg each sought the means to replace the ubiquitous Wagnerian aesthetic with a more personal language that reflected the expressionistic anxiety of a new age. Their solutions are presented to varying degrees in the pages that follow. In literature, Arthur Schnitzler was but one Viennese writer who abandoned the comforts (or denials) of the previous generation. Schnitzler sought a more honest portrayal of the "cruelly repressive aspect of conventional culture",[1] and his theater works in particular explored the harsh realities of life — self-destruction brought about by gratification; sexual aggression; murder. Taken as a whole, the very function of art, as practiced by Vienna's most progressive figures at the turn of the century, was rapidly changing. No longer created simply for decorative purposes, art had become a means to illuminate the dark reality of the human condition.

None of this is to suggest that progressive movements or ideas were welcomed or even encouraged on all fronts. Indeed, Viennese conservative taste constantly challenged and checked the innovations that were erupting within every discipline, whether science, education or design. Perhaps nowhere were the divisions more distinctly delineated than in the field of music, and Zemlinsky had to navigate his way through it all: the Conservatory faculty's disdain of music's newest currents (particularly those practiced by Wagner and his followers); the agendas of Vienna's various music societies, such as the conventional Tonkünstlerverein versus the Ansorge-Verein, which sought to draw together Vienna's progressive artistic circles; the programming undertaken by the city's two major opera houses, the Hofoper — whose repertoire was censored and reflected the conventional tastes of its audience — and the Volksoper, whose status as a private enterprise allowed its staff to pursue more adventurous offerings.

The opinions expressed by Vienna's music critics, like the papers that published them, ran the gamut — from conservative to progressive. There was the arch-conservative *Deutsche Zeitung*, for example, a rag that proudly advertised

---

[1] Schorske (1981), 11.

itself as "the only anti-Semitic German nationalist daily paper published twice daily in Vienna".[1] On a more moderate front, the *Neue Freie Press* represented Viennese journalism at its most sophisticated, a fact reflected in its circulation figures[2] and the quality of its editorial staff, which included Theodor Herzl. Among the *Neue Freie Press*'s music critics, Eduard Hanslick and his successor Julius Korngold, father of the celebrated composer, were the most eminent. Fiercely intelligent men with marked conservative tastes, both wielded journalistic influence and their views helped shape Viennese musical life. Although Korngold championed the music of Gustav Mahler and would one day sing the praises of Zemlinsky's opera *Kleider machen Leute*, he nevertheless held fast to the ideals of Vienna's glorious past, thus making life uncomfortable for many of Zemlinsky's circle, including Arnold Schoenberg and Franz Schreker. Fortunately, Vienna was also home to forward-thinking critics such as Rudolf Stephan Hoffmann and Paul Stefan, and later Theodor Adorno and Paul Pisk, men who demonstrated greater appreciation for and sensitivity toward the progressive tendencies of the younger generation.

One feature that made turn-of-the-century Vienna so unique was the regular contact between many of the city's artistic and intellectual icons. As the Viennese historian Carl Schorske and others have pointed out, in cities such as London, Paris or Berlin the intellectuals, artists and academics had little to do with one another, while Vienna's cultural élite kept common company.[3] They mingled, exchanged ideas and experienced unprecedented interaction and collaboration, and Vienna's cafés and salons figured prominently in this association. The coffee-house in particular, which thrived toward the close of the century, provided a relaxed atmosphere and proved the perfect breeding ground for revolutionary thoughts and the exchange of information. Around coffee-stained tablecloths, the air thick with smoke, one had access to dozens of local, national and international newspapers. Within any of Vienna's myriad cafés, artists met and stayed abreast of contemporary culture, businessmen gained insight into world events, finance and trade, and everyone fed on gossip and news of city happenings. In the words of Stefan Zweig, "The coffee house was still the best place to keep up with everything new."[4] Here, Lev Davidovich Bronstein (better known as Leon Trotsky), the philosopher Ludwig Wittgenstein and the Expressionist poet Richard Dehmel found sympathetic minds hungry for new ideas.

[1] McColl (1996), 22.

[2] The press' readership ranged from approximately 45,000 copies in 1896/97 to a circulation of 78,000 in 1930. See McColl (1996), 16.

[3] Schorske (1981), xxvii.

[4] Zweig (1964), 39.

To locate a particular intellectual, one simply needed to know which café he frequented. Freud could be found at the Café Landtmann, the author Robert Musil at the Café Central, Mahler at the Imperial. The Central was also the *de facto* home of the writer Peter Altenberg, who slept at the nearby Hotel Graben but spent his waking hours at the café, where he wrote, read, ate, conversed and received his mail. Café Griensteidl was the favorite of Zemlinsky and his circle. Here, Max Graf, a personal friend of Zemlinsky, remembered the twenty-eight-year-old composer as having exerted "a visible superiority over the rest of the musicians."[1] The Griensteidl was likewise home to the literary group *Jung Wien*, a circle of avant-garde writers and poets, including the journalist Hermann Bahr and the sixteen-year-old Hugo von Hofmannsthal, who were exploring new literary trends. One of the group's members, Leo Feld, who later furnished Zemlinsky with librettos for his operas *Der Traumgörge* and *Kleider machen Leute*, even depicted the Griensteidl and its patrons in his humorous play, *Die Lumpen* (The Scoundrels).[2] But it was the journalist Karl Kraus who had the last word about the Griensteidl and the artistic institutions it fostered. Kraus recalled that, before its demolition in 1897,

> professional life, work with its manifold nervous crises and upsets, took place in that coffeehouse, which like no other appeared suited to represent the true center of literary activity. More than mere preference assured the old establishment its place of honor in literary history. Who does not remember the almost crushing profusion of newspapers and journals that made the visit to our coffeehouse a virtual necessity for those writers who had no craving for coffee?[3]

This, then, was the atmosphere in which Zemlinsky came of age and where his career blossomed. It was a world of vibrant café life and intense politics, of traditional operetta and avant-garde art, literature and music. It was in Vienna where Zemlinsky first experienced musical triumphs, but also where he suffered heartbreak, personal loss and the machinations of musical politics. When Vienna ultimately failed to offer Zemlinsky the opportunities he needed to thrive, he sought new challenges elsewhere — first in Prague, then in Berlin and finally in America. But Vienna stayed with Zemlinsky forever and, at least as an ideal, it remained the world to which he longed to return.

[1] Graf (1969), 218.

[2] *Die Lumpen* premiered at the Carltheater during Zemlinsky's tenure there.

[3] Segel (1993), 65.

Chapter 1

Finding Brahms

J UST BEYOND THE NORTHERN EDGE of central Vienna lies Leopoldstadt, the birthplace of Alexander Zemlinsky. Among the various districts spreading out from the old city, Leopoldstadt is unique, both a result of its geography — it is actually an island situated in the heart of greater Vienna, bordered by the Danube to its north and the Danube Canal that runs along its southwestern bank — and its history of Jewish life. It is a history dating back to the early seventeenth century, when Vienna's Jews were transferred from elsewhere in the city to a ghetto established on the island. Here the Jews remained, separated from Vienna proper by a series of footbridges spanning the Danube Canal, until 1670, when Emperor Leopold I drove the Jews from the city altogether, destroyed their synagogues and appropriated whatever was left. In appreciation of what their emperor had done, Vienna's grateful citizens named the suburb Leopoldstadt.

For the next two and a half centuries, the island witnessed a gradual renewal of Jewish life. The Jews came back slowly at first at the invitation of Leopold, who hoped their return would reverse the economic crisis that ensued after their absence. More followed, some fleeing persecution, others arriving in the wake of specific events such as the 1848 revolution, or the December Constitution of 1867, both of which promised greater liberalization and tolerance.[1] By the 1870s — the decade of Zemlinsky's birth — the Jewish population of greater Vienna had climbed to well over 40,000. By the century's end, that figure had more than

---

[1] Just as often, policies promising freedom and tolerance were quickly rescinded or were not applicable to all Jews. The *Toleranzpatent* of 1782, for instance, pertained only to Vienna's wealthier Jews, whose resources were beneficial to the greater population.

tripled.[1] During this period, Jews populated neighborhoods throughout the city, including the Alsergrund, the ninth district that Zemlinsky would also one day call home, but the majority still preferred Leopoldstadt,[2] now nicknamed *Mazzesinsel* or Mazzoh Island on account of its sizable Jewish population. Many of those flocking to Vienna arrived in Leopoldstadt by rail, at the terminus of the Northern Railway, disembarked and initially settled nearby. Those lacking the resources or the desire to assimilate remained there. Others regarded Leopoldstadt as a temporary stop and moved across the canal as soon as the opportunity arose. The Strauss family, Sigmund Freud, Gustav Mahler, Arthur Schnitzler, Theodor Herzl — all called Leopoldstadt home at one time.

Leopoldstadt was diverse and atmospheric, a place where the poor and the wealthy often lived in close proximity. On its streets one encountered smartly clad businessmen, Orthodox Jews in their traditional black garb, shoppers and pushcart vendors. Leopoldstadt's coffee houses were numerous and Jews, the predominant patrons, came for the newspapers and fellowship as much as for the beverage. At the nearby Prater — a 2,000-acre pleasure garden conceived in 1891 to honor the centenary of Mozart's death — one could stroll, hunt, bowl, dance, visit the racetrack or the circus, or take an excursion on the Danube. A visitor to the great rotunda "was shown the history of Music and the Theater of all nations and periods through an enormous richness of musical instruments, manuscripts, prints, illustrations and portraits . . . and national operas and comedies were played by French, Italians, Poles, Hungarians and Czechs".[3] Brahms was a frequent visitor of the park, and in the summer of 1902 Richard Strauss and Zemlinsky both conducted concerts here. Leopoldstadt's larger thoroughfares, which included Taborstrasse and Praterstrasse, were home to businesses, hotels and fashionable apartments, while the neighborhood's poorer residents lived in the cramped housing that lined the district's small lanes and alleys. One such street was Odeongasse, tucked neatly between the Taborstrasse and Praterstrasse, just off Zirkusgasse. It was here, in a small apartment located at Odeongasse 3, where Alexander Zemlinszky was born and where the earliest years of his life were spent.

On January 8, 1871 Clara Semo, half Jewish and half Muslim, and a member of the Viennese Sephardic community, married Adolf von Semlinsky, son of Anton Semlinsky and Cäcilia Pulletz. Adolf, Catholic by birth, had undergone conversion to Judaism two months earlier, in order to gain the consent of Clara's

---

[1] By 1890 there were in excess of 118,000 Jews in Vienna. See Beller (1989), 44.

[2] See Goldhammer (1927), 10.

[3] Hanslick in Stuckenschmidt (1977), 29.

father, Shem Tov Semo.[1] Following his marriage to Clara, Adolf also changed
the spelling of his name — Semlinsky became Zemlinszky, a more Semitic spelling that he hoped would afford him better footing in the Sephardic community.
On October 14, 1871, the couple's first child, Alexander, was born and circum-
cised eight days later, in accordance with Jewish law. Alexander was given the
Jewish name Shem Tov, after his maternal grandfather, Shem Tov Semo. Within
a few years of Alexander's birth, Adolf and Clara gave birth to two more children. Bianca, born in 1874, died a short time later. Mathilde, their second daughter, was born in 1875. The Zemlinszkys remained tenants in the Odeongasse for
three years after Alexander's birth, then changed apartments three times within
the district of Leopoldstadt — first to Springergasse 6, then Pillersdorfgasse 3,
where the family was living at the time of Alexander's matriculation to the Conservatory, and finally, in 1896, to Pazmanitengasse 2.

During this time, Adolf was in the employ of the Danube Insurance firm and
in 1871 or 1872 was also appointed secretary to Vienna's Turkish-Israelite community. Adolf's passion, however, was literature, and he authored a number of
paperback short stories and novels, such as *The Count from Montfort*. In 1888
he fortuitously documented the history of the local Sephardic community in *Geschichte der türkisch-israelitischen Gemeinde zu Wien* (History of the Turkish-
Israelite Community of Vienna), in the process unwittingly creating a work of
great cultural and historical importance that was destined to live on far beyond
his death in 1900. Following the destruction of the Sephardic synagogue by the
Nazis during *Kristallnacht* in 1938, Adolf's volume became the sole surviving
document of that community's history, providing invaluable insights and information to scholars of Austrian Jewry and European Jewish life in general.[2]

Adolf also served as editor of *Wiener Punsch*, a small publication in the style
of the popular Viennese *feuilleton*, consisting of poems, aphorisms, announce-
ments and small stories, with plenty of illustrations and humorous caricatures.
Such journals combined "the melancholy of the synagogue and the alcoholic
mood of Grinzing"[3] and served as the city's best-known form of communication. Dozens of such journals were already in circulation during Adolf's lifetime,
although Karl Kraus's *Die Fackel* stood out both for its intellectual bent and its
widespread readership. Adolf's association with the genre nevertheless anchored
him securely to Vienna's intellectual community and helped expose Alexander

[1] The Semo family emigrated from Bosnia (then under Turkish rule) to Austria, probably
on account of the Russo-Turkish War and the ensuing Alliance of Vienna, established in 1873 to
aid the influx of Rumanian and Serbian Jews.

[2] See Fraenkel (1967), 327.

[3] Alfred Polgar in Beller (1989), 179-80. Grinzing is the famous wine district of Vienna.

to the city's rich literary tradition. Moreover, Alexander's maternal grandfather Shem Tov Semo served as editor of the Sephardic newspaper *El Correo di Vienna*. Thus, Alexander could trace his love of literature to both his father and his maternal grandfather.

Alexander's musical abilities can be loosely traced to his paternal great-grandfather, Wenzel Pulletz, a professional theater musician who may have worked at the Theater an der Wien, where Alexander later conducted. Otherwise, there is little to suggest a musical heritage. Alexander's paternal grandfather, Anton, held a number of jobs, from secretary for the city water works and foreman for the Schönbrunn railway line to tobacconist. Anton's father served as postmaster, and married Anna Roissal, the daughter of a cavalry captain. For generations, neither side of the family showed any proclivity for music.

Two aspects of Alexander's family name should be mentioned here, since he altered both over time. The first concerns the spelling of Zemlinszky, which Alexander continued to use at least as late as 1892, the year of his first publication, the *Ländliche Tänze*, op. 1. Sometime thereafter he simplified matters by dropping the second 'z', and it is this spelling — Zemlinsky — that appeared on the title page of his op. 2 collection of 1897.[1] Alexander also eventually eliminated the "von", a prefix implying nobility, found on a number of Adolf's formal documents but not on extant records of Adolf's forebears. Nonetheless, others, including Anton von Webern, continued to address Alexander as "von" as late as 1924, and Alexander was billed as "von Zemlinsky" on a concert poster in 1931.[2] That Alexander omitted the preposition from even his earliest publications suggests he harbored doubts about its authenticity early on and evidently preferred no such pretentious noble associations, a fact entirely consistent with his modest personality.

Aside from his name, faith, and a penchant for culture, Alexander, or Alex, as his friends called him, also inherited distinct personality traits from his parents. He described his mother Clara as "a shy, reserved woman, who lives a more introverted life than I. I have much of her in myself — the mischief, the frivolousness . . ."[3] He also attributed his sharp tongue and reckless character to Clara, although the latter trait was certainly tempered, if not altogether alleviated, with maturity. From his father Alexander claimed to have "inherited good things". He shared his father's passion for the theater, for example, and for arts

[1] Curiously, the older spelling is again found on the publication of the op. 5 lieder of 1898, although it is not known if this was due to a publishing error or Alexander's own indecision.

[2] Advertisement for *Aufstieg und Fall der Stadt Mahagonny*. See Schebera (1995), 164.

[3] AZ/AMW.

and letters, and it was largely because of Adolf's encouragement and support that Alexander was afforded the opportunity to study at the Conservatory.

As was common to the majority of families in their vicinity, the Zemlinszkys had little money to spare, but despite constant financial worries the family remained very close and, according to Alexander, they were always willing to make sacrifices for the comfort of one another. Such close-knit ties, however, did not extend beyond the immediate family:

> My father lived only for his family. My mother, an introverted woman, knew only her children. I love her as much as I possibly can — her smallest moments of ill temper become my greatest worry . . . We have hardly any social intercourse with relatives from my mother's or my father's side. Anyway, I hate relatives and it was because of me that everybody was offended. I was simply not able to find the understanding and warmth there that I needed to develop . . .[1]

Despite Adolf's secretarial work for the Sephardic community, a position that likely brought him more respect than financial reward, there is nothing to indicate that the family gravitated toward synagogue life or observed religious ritual. In fact, a glance at Alexander's early schooling provides a window into the family's attitude toward traditional religion and education. At the age of six Zemlinsky entered a Sephardic school, where he learned the *Aleph-Bet*, some preliminary prayers and rituals, and whatever biblical history a six-year-old is capable of grasping; however, within two years his parents had him transferred to a *Volksschule*, a public elementary school. If his religious education continued at all we have no record of it, nor is there any indication that he maintained any enduring association with the Jewish community, aside from his playing for synagogue services once he had gained sufficient skill. What is certain is that once Alexander discovered music, it became his religion.

Information about Alexander's earliest keyboard experiences is nearly nonexistent, save for accounts of a boarder whom the Zemlinszkys took in — most likely to bring in extra income[2] — when Alexander was approximately four years of age. Nothing about the boarder is known except that he studied piano and that Alexander was either allowed to listen in on the young man's lessons or allowed to study alongside him.[3] In either case, Alexander's abilities soon made it obvious that he would benefit from a teacher of his own, and he later recalled

---

[1] AZ/AMW.

[2] More than thirty years later, between 1900 and 1910, one out of every ten people in Vienna was still a *Bettgeher* (boarder). See Hoffman (1988), 47.

[3] Beaumont and Rode-Breymann (1999), 371, and NLZ (Ac 22a).

taking the initiative to memorize Mozart sonatas, precisely because music of such caliber was felt to be beyond his youthful ability. Far less to his liking was the music his parents occasionally asked him to perform for guests, student pieces such as *The Cloister Bells* or *The Maiden's Prayer*.[1] Having to perform such trivial music, however, was but a minor annoyance when weighed against receiving Adolf's support for musical education, and, despite the limits of his resources, Adolf saw to it that Alexander received the proper training.

Alexander's schooling continued at the *Gymnasium*, an institution that provided a classical education for its students and set them on a path to the university. But at the age of thirteen, Alexander's musical abilities came to the attention of one of his teachers, who suggested that Alexander continue his studies at the Conservatory. Following the advice, in September of 1884 Adolf submitted an application on his son's behalf to the Conservatory, and shortly thereafter an audition was arranged. That fall, Alexander was formally accepted into the Conservatory's preparatory program (*Vorbildungsschule*) as student number seven of pianist Wilhelm Rausch. Setting out from the Leopoldstadt to the Conservatory, a routine was quickly established that would be repeated countless times over the next eight years. As Alexander left behind the old-world atmosphere of Leopoldstadt for modern Vienna, the walk came to symbolize the larger journey upon which he was embarking. The Musikverein soon became Alexander's second home, a world of music and new ideas, a place where the public would hear his own music for the first time and the site of his first major successes.

In hopes of lessening the financial burden on his family, Adolf applied to the Conservatory for a tuition waiver for his son:

> For 12 years I have served as secretary of the Turkish-Israelite community of Vienna, assigned a yearly income of 600 fl[orins];[2] born in Vienna, married and in possession of Austrian citizenship. My son, as is clearly seen in the accompanying birth certificate, has reached 13 years of age and has benefited from 4 years of piano lessons. He thus appears to be especially musically gifted; however, as necessary means for his further development are lacking due to my above mentioned limited income,

---

[1] Beaumont and Rode-Breymann (1999), 371.

[2] Approximately $290 at the time; see www.cyberussr.com/hcunn/gold-std.html (accessed 10 March 2010), based on Chester L. Krause and Clifford Mishler, *1994 Standard Catalog of World Coins* (Iola, Wisc.: Krause Publications, 1993). The value in 2010 terms would be about $7,000; see http://www.minneapolisfed.org/community_education/teacher/calc/hist1800.cfm (accessed 10 March 2010).

I faithfully make my request to the honorable director, in hopes of receiving a favorable decision based on the results of the entrance exams.[1]

Adolf's request, however, was denied, and Alexander's family received no financial help during his first years at the Conservatory, nor was any money
forthcoming until the 1888-1889 school year, when Alexander was awarded
half-tuition. Judging from Alexander's obvious abilities, any financial decisions
on behalf of the Conservatory were probably less a reflection of his talent than
a result of the institution's limited resources.

In his first three years at the Conservatory, Alexander Zemlinsky's musical
education was limited to piano studies and classes in rudimentary theory. Zemlinsky's abilities were quickly recognized and his records from 1886–87 show
he was awarded the highest marks possible in both his primary and secondary
studies.[2] In 1887 Alexander was accepted into the Conservatory's secondary
program (*Ausbildungsschule*). Now began regular contact with the institution's
eminent faculty, pedagogues who could provide a first-rate musical education
and perhaps eventually help him establish a professional footing in Vienna's
competitive musical environment.

As a pianist Zemlinsky was enrolled with the eminent Anton Door, a former
pupil of Carl Czerny, a friend of Brahms and a founding member of the Conservatory. But of even greater significance to Zemlinsky's future, he now began
the training that would prove critical to his career as a composer. His harmony
studies commenced with the thorough but pedantic Franz Krenn and with Robert Fuchs, who by the end of his career would also count Mahler, Wolf, Sibelius,
Schreker and Korngold among his students. Fuchs's gifts were widely recognized, and Brahms in particular found Fuchs's music "so skillful, so charmingly
invented that one always has pleasure in it".[3]

Under Fuchs's watchful eye Zemlinsky was drilled in traditional counterpoint and analyzed works of the classical canon. Fuchs's time-honored
pedagogical approach left an indelible impression on the young Zemlinsky, who
eagerly absorbed those qualities associated with Viennese classicism: balance,

---

[1] Biba (1995), 207. This document contrasts with information Adolf provided on Alexander's formal application to the Conservatory. On that application, Adolf listed his profession as
"Beamter" (civil servant), a reference to his employment with the Danube Insurance Company,
although there is no evidence that his work there continued beyond 1871. On neither application did he indicate any secondary employment or income he received as an author.

[2] Biba (1992), 14.

[3] Heuberger in Pascall (1977), 115.

polish, first-rate craftsmanship and, above all, the dominion of melody. As some of Zemlinsky's compositions would soon reveal, the significance his teacher placed on motivic development — the technique of spinning out material from a small melodic cell or idea — had an equally profound effect on the younger composer. Still, Fuchs's music remained rooted in the nineteenth century. Despite living until 1927, he demonstrated no interest in breaking new ground and tolerated none of the progressive musical tendencies practiced by Wagner or any of his followers — the so-called "New German school" — in the work of his students. Thus, while Zemlinsky was provided with a strong musical foundation, there is nothing to suggest he was encouraged to cultivate a more modern means of expression. Given Vienna's flourishing atmosphere of progressive intellectual and artistic thought in the final decades of the century, one wonders how Zemlinsky's own approach to harmony, timbre or form might have developed had the Conservatory faculty encouraged experimentation.

Zemlinsky continued to excel as a pianist. Compositions of the Conservatory faculty constituted a good part of his repertoire during his final year, a reflection of the insular nature of the institution. Thus, on September 1, 1889, Zemlinsky performed Robert Fuchs's Piano Concerto in B-flat minor, and for his diploma concert the following July he played Joseph Labor's *Scherzo in the form of a Canon* for two pianos, in addition to the first movement of Schumann's A minor Piano Concerto. One month earlier he had been recognized as "Best Pianist of the Conservatory" at the annual Conservatory piano competition, where his performance of Brahms's Handel Variations earned him both a gold medal and a Bösendorfer piano.

Zemlinsky continued to impress critics, friends and colleagues for years with his pianistic ability, but, while he possessed a formidable technique and was inherently musical, he lacked the flamboyance and temperament necessary to launch a career as a soloist. For Zemlinsky, the piano was a means, not an end. Thus, evident though Zemlinsky's keyboard abilities were, he decided to devote himself to the study of composition and upon graduation was immediately accepted into the class of Johann Nepomuk Fuchs (Robert's brother), the Conservatory's director. J. N. Fuchs proved a devoted and highly competent teacher of form and analysis, composition, orchestration and score reading. Under Fuchs's tutelage Zemlinsky became equipped with the basic tools needed to pursue work as a composer. The two-year course of study capped Zemlinsky's Conservatory training, ensuring that the elements that had governed the rules of classical composition since Bach's day would shape Zemlinsky's approach to musical composition.

In June of 1891 Zemlinsky revealed just how much he had learned when he entered the Conservatory's annual competition for composition students with *Des Mädchens Klage*, a song set to a text by Vincenz Zusner, the Austrian poet who sponsored the competition. Zusner's text, which Zemlinsky cast in C-sharp minor, tells the passionate story of a woman's loss of marital hope, which is likened to a withered garden. Zemlinsky retained the poem's four-stanza design and juxtaposed stormy and peaceful characters within a modified ABAB structure. If the passionate outburst heard at the outset and the unexpected tonal shifts that follow bring to mind Franz Schubert, Zemlinsky can hardly be faulted for succumbing to the influence of a master of the Viennese lied. The inspiration proved judicious — Zemlinsky's submission earned him first prize and twenty gold kronen. It also revealed that Zemlinsky possessed a natural affinity for song.

Additional accolades followed. In 1892, Zemlinsky's final year at the Conservatory, he took second prize for the same competition during a year when no first prize was awarded. Zemlinsky had again chosen a text by Zusner, this one entitled *Der Morgenstern*, and his setting earned its composer ten gold kronen and the jury's compliment that the song exhibited "beautiful sounds".[1] That same year the prestigious publishing house of Breitkopf & Härtel issued Zemlinsky's *Ländliche Tänze* for solo piano. Published as his Opus 1, the dances were charming, naïve, eminently playable and certain to find a place in the parlors of the middle class. And, while hardly the sort of work that would rocket Zemlinsky to fame, it was an auspicious debut nonetheless. It also presented Zemlinsky with a unique opportunity to thank his teacher publicly. Before sending his dances to press, the composer added a note on the title page that read, "To the highly honorable professor and music director J. N. Fuchs, from his thankful student, Alexander Zemlinsky."[2]

Despite his attention to his studies, music was not Zemlinsky's sole preoccupation at the time. A watchmaker's daughter, one year his junior, had caught Zemlinsky's eye. She was a singer and fellow Conservatory student, and her name was Melanie Guttmann. Little is known about their relationship except that Zemlinsky dedicated three songs to "meiner lieben Mela" — *Der Tag wird kühl*, *Unter blühenden Bäumen*, and *Klopfet, so wird euch aufgethan* — and, following their courtship, the two appear to have become engaged, albeit briefly. Zemlinsky's subsequent infatuation with Alma Schindler probably contributed to the cooling of relations with Melanie, although Melanie remained a close

---

[1] Biba (1992), 21.
[2] Ibid., 16.

family friend until her departure for America in 1901.[1] Though not destined to become Zemlinsky's wife, Melanie did become family when Zemlinsky married her sister Ida in 1907. Years later, Melanie reappeared when she attempted to sponsor Zemlinsky's immigration to the United States during World War II.

Moreover, in 1892 Zemlinsky was required to appear before the military board to be judged fit for service. He stood just over five feet tall, with pointed features and thick dark hair swept back from a stately forehead. By his own accounts, he was very thin. Matters of physique aside, Zemlinsky was also non-aggressive and politically dispassionate. In sum, he didn't cut an impressive figure, at least as far as the military was concerned, and not surprisingly was deemed insufficient for duty. Because Zemlinsky remained eligible to serve for two more years, he was required to undergo the humiliating assessment two more times, but the initial verdict was never overturned — he would never be allowed to enlist.[2] The Austrian novelist Robert Musil once described his country's military as "the second weakest among the great powers", despite the ruinous sums devoted to its existence,[3] yet even an army with so feeble a reputation had standards to maintain. Spared military duty, Zemlinsky was able to devote all his time and energy to making music.

On July 11, four months to the day after his first military inspection, Zemlinsky stepped to the podium of the Great Hall of the Musikverein and led the first movement of his First Symphony in D minor. The concert, which celebrated the outstanding members of the Conservatory's graduating class, marks the first documented performance we have of Zemlinsky in the role of conductor. The musicians who responded to his quirky gestures, fellow students of the Conservatory, were no doubt well acquainted with the twenty-one-year-old's skills as a pianist and composer, but in the summer of 1892 Zemlinsky was still a novice on the podium. Most of what he knew about the art he had learned by watching others, since conducting had not yet been integrated into the Conservatory curriculum.[4] J. N. Fuchs, who had held a string of European conducting posts including a position at the Vienna Hofoper, had certainly tutored Zemlinsky in the fundamentals of baton technique, but a deeper understanding of the craft

[1] Melanie married the painter William Clarke Rice and lived in New York until her death in 1961.

[2] Information provided by the Vienna War Archives.

[3] Musil (1995), 29.

[4] It was only in 1909, with the appointment of Franz Schalk as head of the first conducting class at the newly renamed k.k. Akademie für Musik und darstellende Kunst, that conducting would become part of the Conservatory curriculum. *Ministerium für Kultus und Unterricht, Jahresbericht* (1909–1910), 19.

could only be acquired by observing professionals in rehearsal and performance. Zemlinsky left no written accounts of his early conducting experiences
but it is likely that Hans Richter also had a hand in helping shape Zemlinsky's
understanding of the art.

Richter held court both at the Hofoper and in the Great Hall of the Musikverein, literally steps from the Conservatory classrooms, so those students wishing to observe one of the great conductors of the day need not even leave the
building. As conductor of the Vienna Philharmonic for over two decades, Richter brought the ensemble into its so-called *Goldene Ära*, its Golden Age, and led
the premieres of Brahms's second and third symphonies and Bruckner's first,
third and fourth, and in 1892 conducted the first performance of Bruckner's
Symphony No. 8, an event which Zemlinsky most certainly attended. Richter's
monumental interpretations of Beethoven and Wagner — with whom Richter
had worked closely — must have made a deep impression on the young Zemlinsky. So too would Richter's dedication to the Czech repertoire, which Zemlinsky
would conduct to great acclaim in Prague years later. In rehearsal, Richter's
stick technique and rapport with his players could be witnessed first-hand, and
Zemlinsky had ample opportunities for such observations. Given that Richter
exuded the very qualities later associated with Zemlinsky's mature work on the
podium — a fine attention to detail and phrasing, an instinctive grasp of the
right tempo, the ability to make clear the most elaborate contrapuntal passages
and the avoidance of false sentimentality, gymnastics and affect[1] — it is evident
that Richter played a significant role in shaping Zemlinsky's conducting style.

Among those listening to Zemlinsky's music in the Great Hall of the Musikverein on July 11, 1892, was Johannes Brahms. J. N. Fuchs had no doubt spoken to Brahms about his gifted student and had perhaps inquired if his more
famous colleague might consider taking Zemlinsky under his wing, now that
his formal studies were through. But the master was not yet ready to make any
formal overtures, evidently preferring to quietly chart Zemlinsky's progress for
the time being. He did, however, make the young man's acquaintance before
leaving the hall, a meeting that marked the start of one of the most critical relationships of Zemlinsky's life. It was a moment Zemlinsky never forgot:

> I recall the period when I had the personal fortune to meet Brahms — it
> was during the last two years of his life. I recall precisely how fascinated
> and inescapably influenced I was by it, the bewilderment that his music

---

[1] An account of Richter's contributions and conducting qualities, originally printed in the
London Times, was reprinted for American readers in the *New York Times*. See "Critic Lauds
Richter; His Skill as a Director", *New York Times* (April 16, 1911).

worked on me and all of us at that time . . . I was still a student at the Vienna Conservatory, was thoroughly familiar with most of the works of Brahms and I was possessed by this music. Adoption and mastery of this wonderful, unique technique became my goal.[1]

Meanwhile, Fuchs, in an effort to promote the music of his prize-winning pupil, led the premiere of Zemlinsky's D minor Symphony in its entirety the following February. As the opening strains of the *Allegro ma non troppo* reverberated in the Musikverein for the second time, Zemlinsky's lyrical gifts and fine sense for orchestration were immediately apparent, but his lack of technical command quickly got the better of him. Already in the exposition Zemlinsky began to break down small motives, a skill acquired under Robert Fuchs's eye. But by concentrating so extensively on this material before the development proper, where the true potential of his ideas should have been revealed, Zemlinsky undercut the drama of what followed. Still, the symphony as a whole contained many fine passages, even if it revealed a pastiche of inspiration from established masters: powerful Bruckneresque build-ups in the *Allegro*'s brief development; the rustic Dvořák-inspired *Scherzo* with its shifting stresses; and the pastoral lines of the Brahmsian *Trio*. If the score revealed little that was stunningly original, it nevertheless displayed the competent hand of a young composer coming to terms with traditional symphonic composition and, as the critics acknowledged, held promise of more impressive work to come.[2]

As Zemlinsky launched himself as a composer in the Austrian capital, he was surrounded by talented contemporaries. Julius Bittner, for example, studied for a period with Josef Labor, a blind organist and highly respected teacher in Vienna, but Bittner was largely self-taught and composed on the side while pursuing a career as a lawyer. The gifted Walter Rabl, who left the city to study at the Mozarteum in Salzburg, returned to Vienna just as Zemlinsky was embarking upon his career. Zemlinsky and Rabl squared off in 1896 during a competition sponsored by the Tonkünstlerverein, but Rabl eventually devoted himself to teaching and conducting. Another impressive newcomer, Franz Schreker, secured a reputation as a choral conductor while still in his teens and in 1908 founded the Philharmonic Choir, an organization Zemlinsky came to know very well. Seven years Zemlinsky's junior, Schreker did not develop a relationship with Zemlinsky until the second decade of the new century, but their paths

---

[1] Zemlinsky (1922), 69. Brahms would live another five years, not two as Zemlinsky stated.

[2] See, for example, the *Neue Freie Presse* (February 13, 1893).

crossed repeatedly over the years, in Vienna, Prague and in Berlin, and their friendship was enduring.[1]

Of the previous generation, the great song composer Hugo Wolf was quickly slipping from Viennese musical life — succumbing to insanity, he attempted to drown himself in 1899 and then spent his remaining years institutionalized — and Brahms and Bruckner were nearing the end of their lives. Neither Brahms nor Bruckner were native to Vienna, but both had been fixtures of Viennese life for so long they had been claimed by the city. Bruckner's struggle for acceptance had been particularly agonizing. Ostracized as a Wagnerian within the Brahms-dominated environment of the Conservatory, Bruckner's first five symphonies were dismissed as "unplayable", "wild", "nonsense", and "a fiasco". The critics struck down his Seventh for its "interminable stretches of darkness, leaden boredom, and feverish over-excitement".[2] With time, Bruckner's music won over the Viennese, but the journey was tortuous. For Zemlinsky, however, neither the struggle for recognition nor the abundant talent in his midst deterred him. Bent on pursuing life as a composer, he adhered to his course with unwavering determination.

On November 1, 1893 the music journal *Neue Zeitschrift für Musik* published an announcement for a competition, sponsored by Prince Luitpold of Bavaria, for the best new German opera written by any Austrian or German composer. Victory came with an award of 6,000 Marks and a Munich premiere. The initial submission date was set for November 1, 1894, but the date was soon pushed back a year to provide the contestants and the judges with a more realistic timetable.[3] To accept the challenge, an undertaking beyond the scope of anything Zemlinsky had yet contemplated, he would need all the time available. He considered setting Salomon Mosenthal's tale *Die Folkunger*, a saga about the medieval Swedish and Norwegian king Magnus Ericsson, but that plan never progressed beyond some initial sketches. Zemlinsky turned instead to Rudolf von Gottschall's *Die Rose vom Kaukasus* (The Rose of the Caucasus), a story of mortal enemies and a woman torn between her people and the man she loves. Zemlinsky had found his subject.

Gottschall's fictional tale was inspired by a series of actual battles fought between the Russian and Circassian armies in the 1850s. As the drama opens,

---

[1] In February of 1907, for example, Schreker received an appointment to the Vienna Volksoper, probably at Zemlinsky's recommendation. Years later Schreker returned the favor, securing an appointment for Zemlinsky at Berlin's Hochschule für Musik.

[2] Hanslick in Cooke (1980), 358.

[3] Weber (1971), 82. Weber suggests that the request, submitted by an anonymous member of the Vienna Tonkünstlerverein, may have been made specifically on Zemlinsky's behalf.

Gottschall's Circassian heroine, Sarema, sits in a Russian prison, guarded by Count Tcherikov, the Russian colonel who saved her from the Cossack army when it overran her people. Sarema has since fallen in love with her captor, despite her betrothal to Asslan, a Circassian prince. Asslan soon attempts to rescue her but is caught and imprisoned, though Sarema manages to stay his execution long enough for her to return home. Back among her people, Sarema's father demands that she contemplate the moral implications of her treasonous acts: she has betrayed her people and fallen in love with the enemy, and her actions have placed one of their own in harm's way. Sarema now convinces the Circassians of the need to attack at once, and with her father's blessing she leads their army into battle. This time it is the Russians who are overrun and Tcherikov who is imprisoned. Despite knowing Tcherikov 'will never shed a tear' for her, Sarema secures his release. Then, seeing no other means of atoning for her sins, Sarema plunges a dagger into her breast.

During the months of December and January Zemlinsky gave himself over to fashioning the opera's libretto, and at some point he may have engaged the help of his father, whose literary background would have made him a valuable — and affordable — resource.[1] By February of 1894, Zemlinsky was ready to commence work on the piano score. For much of the writing he relied on intuition and his own melodic gifts, traits that had so far served him well. Otherwise, there were established masterworks for help with effective styles of accompaniment, or for insight into connecting fabric and motifs, technical issues with which he had no personal experience. Now that he was beyond the walls of the Conservatory, Zemlinsky was at liberty to try his hand at previously *verboten* stimuli, ideas he had been absorbing for some time. Richard Wagner provided the single greatest attraction, and here, Zemlinsky was not alone. The late Bayreuth master's novel approach to harmony and operatic structure proved an unshakable force to nearly all of Zemlinsky's generation. *Sarema* offered Zemlinsky the perfect vehicle for passionate Wagnerian expression — individual introspection and large choral numbers, blood and thunder and unattainable love — and he made the most of the opportunity. If hints of *Der fliegende Holländer*, *Lohengrin*, *Tannhäuser* and *Tristan* echoed throughout his score, the critics didn't seem to mind.

From a technical standpoint, there is little to suggest that Zemlinsky was confronting the challenges of opera for the first time. He handles the dramatic action with confidence; displays a consistent command of his forces, whether writing for solo voice, chorus or orchestra; spins out phrases of considerable

---

[1] For more on the preparation of *Sarema*, see Hilmar (1976), 58.

harmonic subtlety and moves smoothly and effectively between arioso phrasing and recitative, striking an ideal balance between the singers and the orchestra. Zemlinsky also explores a wide range of textures, whether supporting his vocalists with a static orchestral carpet or punctuating the drama on stage with driving, syncopated rhythms in the pit. The more reflective passages are handled with likeminded finesse. In Act I, scene iii, for example, Sarema is left alone to contemplate her betrayal of family and homeland. As she prays for the mercy of Allah — "Oh holy land of my birth, we are cut off from one another. Let me cry my final tears. May Allah have mercy upon us both" — Zemlinsky contrasts her inspired melody with a series of false resolutions, subtly mirroring her betrayals. In another superbly executed moment, the words "Oh heiliges" (Oh holy) are set to a dramatic octave leap that resolves deceptively on the word "Land", as Sarema acknowledges her infidelity to her homeland. And as the act draws to a close, delicate harp arpeggios and ethereal strings evoke a mood of perfect solemnity that brings relief, however temporary, to the anguish of reality.

Zemlinsky worked quickly, and by mid-June 1894 had completed the short score. He could now turn his attention to *Sarema*'s orchestration. *Sarema*, however, was not the only work presently on Zemlinsky's plate. At the start of the 1893/94 season he had been inducted into the *Wiener Tonkünstlerverein*, the Viennese Composers Society, a self-governing organization founded in 1884 by the Conservatory faculty professors Anton Door and Julius Epstein. The society met in the Musikverein, where it held a regular series of chamber-music and lieder recitals and sponsored a number of competitions for promising young composers. Since Zemlinsky could also be counted on to serve as a collaborative pianist, it was only natural that his name be added to the Verein's roster, a list that included Brahms, who served as honorary president, and Zemlinsky's teacher J. N. Fuchs. Zemlinsky had made his Tonkünstlerverein debut in November 1893 as pianist in his own D major Piano Quartet, a work that survives only in part. Shortly afterwards, Zemlinsky was offered another performance date, this one scheduled for April 1894.

Thus, on New Year's Day Zemlinsky began mapping out the opening to a Cello Sonata in A minor, his first large-scale work for that combination and his first composition written under the auspices of the Tonkünstlerverein. As had been the case with three short pieces written in 1891,[1] he composed with the cellist Friedrich Buxbaum in mind, a friend from his Conservatory days and another newcomer to the Tonkünstlerverein. The momentum that had accompanied the opera's composition now spilled over to the sonata; fueled by the fire of

---

[1] *Humoreske, Lied*, and *Tarantell*.

inner creativity and an external deadline, Zemlinsky worked at a feverish pace. He needed little more than a week to complete the opening movement, with the slow movement requiring approximately three weeks more, partly owing to a false start — he had initially entertained ideas of a brooding, chromatically charged opening before finding his way with a more transparent approach. On March 7, just nine weeks after the initial sketches, Zemlinsky penciled in the double bar of his completed finale, followed by the date. Enough time remained to work through the sonata with his collaborator, rehearse, and still make any needed adjustments.

Zemlinsky had constructed his sonata's opening bars by expanding on the cello's two-note, whole-step motive, proving undeniably that he continued to place great stock in the technique of motivic variation. He was, however, not about to fall victim to his own inventiveness again, as he had done with his D minor Symphony a year earlier. Before allowing the sonata's exposition to collapse under its own weight, Zemlinsky introduced two additional ideas, a jaunty dotted rhythm and an expansive E major *dolce* theme in the cello's middle register. Both serve as sufficient foils to the opening two-note cell, whose exploration he now reserves for the development proper. The sonata pivots around its lush F major *Andante*, a movement cast in ABA form whose outer portions explore the decorative *Jugendstil* flourish of the opening bar and encase a stormy and impassioned middle section (*Bewegter*). As with the first movement, Zemlinsky based the concluding *Allegretto* on a series of distinct ideas, including a lilting opening line that gives way later to playful counterpoint and a stately, chordal secondary theme. He also saved one of the sonata's most inspired moments for its final bars, a nostalgic conclusion that finally tapers off in a wisp of Viennese tenderness.

On April 23 Zemlinsky and Buxbaum, the sonata's dedicatee, gave the work its premiere. Nothing more is known about it, aside from the fact that neither ever played the work again. The score was laid aside and forgotten, which is how it remained for over a century.

Zemlinsky's ongoing involvement with the Tonkünstlerverein continued to bring him prestige and visibility in Vienna's musical community, and his value to the Verein grew quickly in the years that followed — he was elected to its board of directors in 1897 and served as its vice-president two years later. But because others determined the extent of his involvement, Zemlinsky also craved opportunities where he could play a more substantive role. He thus began entertaining thoughts of founding his own ensemble, and in 1895 the Musikalische Verein Polyhymnia was born. Zemlinsky would later recall Polyhymnia — a rag-tag band of musicians, the majority of whom were actually medical students — with humor and his own personal brand of sarcasm, but his efforts and intentions at the time of the group's inception were anything but frivolous:

> The orchestra was not too large. A pair of violins, a viola, a cello and a double bass — in reality only half an orchestra. Despite our lack of knowledge, we were actually quite satisfied with our efforts. We were all musically hungry and young, playing well and poorly once a week without fail. Now, such societies have always existed, that was nothing out of the ordinary. However, as the only cellist sat a young man who, with equal amounts of passion and bad intonation, abused his instrument (which hardly deserved better treatment — it had been sold by its player for a hard-earned three gulden in Vienna's so-called Tandelmarkt), and this cello player was none other than Arnold Schoenberg.[1]

Polyhymnia not only provided Zemlinsky valuable organizational and conducting experience, it brought him together with Arnold Schoenberg, a man who would become Zemlinsky's colleague, brother-in-law and life-long friend, and a composer whose reputation eventually eclipsed all others of Zemlinsky's generation.

Schoenberg's parents had come to Vienna's Leopoldstadt from Bratislava, and like most of their new neighbors, they struggled financially (Schoenberg's father kept a shoe shop). Music had been part of Schoenberg's life from the beginning, both parents having passed their passion for music down to their children. By the age of eight, Arnold was playing violin and composing pieces for the instrument. Viola studies followed — he taught himself on a viola fitted with zither strings — and then cello. With the death of his father, the young man was forced to drop out of school, lay his passion for music aside and earn a living. He gained employment as a clerk in a small private bank, a job he retained for about five years, most of them unhappy. David Bach, a musician, linguist, philosopher and friend to Schoenberg, remembered the day Schoenberg proudly proclaimed, "I am so happy, I have just lost my post."[2] The bank was becoming insolvent, and so Schoenberg was let go. Nothing could have pleased him more, for he could now dedicate himself to his musical passions. Although his greatest struggles still lay ahead, if Schoenberg had learned anything as a young man it was how to survive with little or no money. The knowledge would serve him well in the years to come.

---

[1] Zemlinsky (1934), 33–34.

[2] Bach (1924), 319. Bach was indebted to Schoenberg, who "greatly influenced the development of my character by furnishing it with the ethical and moral power needed to withstand vulgarity and commonplace popularity". Schoenberg (1984), 80.

Zemlinsky first encountered Schoenberg, three years his junior, in the days after the would-be musical revolutionary lost his job, although the exact circumstances surrounding their initial introduction are sketchy. Schoenberg, who until then had received only minimal formal musical instruction, likely sought out Zemlinsky to further his musical training, perhaps on the advice of Josef Labor.[1] On the other hand, Schoenberg's sister, Ottilie, maintained that Zemlinsky and Schoenberg first met at a worker's choral society that Schoenberg was then conducting and, along with some others, decided to form an organization devoted to the performance of their own compositions.[2] Regardless, it was with Polyhymnia that the mutually nurturing relationship between Zemlinsky and Schoenberg was begun in earnest.

Since leaving the Conservatory Zemlinsky had been composing prodigiously, trying his hand at an array of musical genres. It was only logical that as a gifted pianist he would focus attention on the keyboard, but composing strictly for the piano seems to have interested him the least. After completing four piano ballades in 1893, Zemlinsky wrote little for piano solo for the next few years other than his *Albumblatt*, a brief solo work he dedicated to his "dear pupil, Catharina Maleschewski". Song composition, on the other hand, proved an endless source of interest, and although it is difficult to assign dates to many of Zemlinsky's early songs, by the end of the decade he had composed more than sixty, setting a wide array of poetry to a wealth of styles. Work on *Sarema* continued, but the closer the opera came to completion, the more frequently Zemlinsky interrupted its orchestration to turn to newer compositions.

Zemlinsky's interest in chamber music flourished between the years 1893 and 1896, beginning with the Piano Quartet in D major and an early String Quartet in E minor. His Cello Sonata and a D minor String Quintet were completed in 1894, and between 1895 and 1896 Zemlinsky composed a Serenade for violin and piano, the *Waldgespräch* for soprano, two horns, harp and strings, a new finale to his Quintet, a Trio for clarinet, cello and piano, and a String Quartet in A major. By March of 1895, Zemlinsky had also completed two orchestral works, his *Lustspielouvertüre* and a three-movement Suite for orchestra.

The orchestral Suite was premiered in its entirety in March of 1895, on

---

[1] From whom Schoenberg learned the rudiments of cello playing is another matter. Stuckenschmidt suggests that Friedrich Buxbaum, Zemlinsky's schoolmate, taught the cello fingerings to Schoenberg's boyhood friend Oskar Adler, who in turn passed them on to Schoenberg. See Stuckenschmidt (1977), 31.

[2] Ibid.

a jubilee concert at the Musikverein that also featured works of other former students of the Conservatory, among them Hugo Wolf and Felix Mottl.[1] The concert provided Zemlinsky with another opportunity to rub shoulders with Brahms, who concluded the program by conducting his own *Academic Festival Overture*.[2] Still, with the sole exception of *Sarema* and the String Quintet, these compositions never received more than a single performance during his lifetime. As with the greater bulk of his youthful work, Zemlinsky probably regarded them as learning tools. Having served their function, they were subsequently placed on the shelves and forgotten.

From March until the close of August 1895, *Sarema* occupied most of Zemlinsky's attention. Then, three days before the competition's deadline, he packed up the score and sent it to Munich. While awaiting the results of the competition, Zemlinsky received news that he had been awarded a stipendium by the Imperial-Royal Ministry for Culture and Education. He had come to the ministry's attention through the recommendation of Brahms and Eduard Hanslick, members of the ministry committee who attested to Zemlinsky's "beautiful talent, serious bearing and already respectable artistic accomplishment".[3] As private lessons were Zemlinsky's primary source of income at this time, the ministry's recognition and financial support were timely. The notification, which arrived on October 10, 1895, was further indication that Zemlinsky had what was required to succeed in Vienna — talent, ambition and musical connections.

Meanwhile, Zemlinsky continued to devote time to the Polyhymnia ensemble. Rehearsals took place at the National Hotel in the Taborstrasse of Leopoldstadt and at the more centrally located Zur grossen Tabakspfeife, a restaurant located at 29 Graben, a stone's throw from St. Stephan's Cathedral. In November of 1895 Polyhymnia gave its first performance, at the Hotel Zur goldenen Ente. Afterward, sensing the need for stronger leadership, the orchestra elected as its president Alois Botstiber, father of Hugo Botstiber, a mutual friend of Zemlinsky and Schoenberg.[4] On March 2, 1896, the ensemble gave the highly successful premieres of Schoenberg's *Notturno* for solo violin, harp and strings and Zemlinsky's *Waldgespräch*.

Several years earlier Zemlinsky had set Eichendorff's dramatic text for voice and piano, perhaps sensing dramatic possibilities left untapped by Schumann, who had drawn on Eichendorff's poem for his *Liederkreis*, op. 39. In January

---

[1] Mottl was never to gain a reputation as a composer but as a conductor emerged as one of Wagner's greatest interpreters.

[2] Biba (1992), 24.

[3] Based on papers of the Ministerium für Kultus und Unterricht, in Clayton (1983a), 86.

[4] Biba (1992), 26.

of 1896, Zemlinsky revisited the poem and tailored it specifically to the Polyhymnia ensemble, scoring it for voice, two horns, harp and strings. The singer
at the premiere was none other than Melanie Guttmann, whom Zemlinsky had
dated as a Conservatory student. Zemlinsky now spun Eichendorff's poetry into
an inspired extended scene, brilliantly capturing the mysteries of the forest and
the heartache of lost love. With a host of songs, instrumental music and even
substantial portions of an opera behind him, Zemlinsky approached *Waldgespräch* as an admixture of them all, deftly combining the intimacy of song and
chamber music with exquisite orchestration and operatic drama, all within
a flexible formal framework. Zemlinsky's command, evident throughout, stands
most fully revealed in the part writing, particularly the evocative horn scoring
and sensuous contrapuntal string solos that wind around the vocal lines like
Jugendstil tendrils.

In the week following the concert a review appeared in the *Neues Wiener
Tagblatt*, noting the high level of artistry Zemlinsky brought to an ensemble
composed largely of amateurs:

> Zemlinsky's *Waldgespräch* is a successful illustration of the beautiful
> Eichendorff text and accomplished in both invention and orchestration
> . . . The first-rate, highly trained orchestra under the direction of Herr
> Zemlinsky executed it as well as the other orchestral numbers (Grieg's
> *Herzwunden* and Boccherini's *Menuett*) with great exactness and a re-
> fined understanding for the intentions of the composers.[1]

Zemlinsky's life was now poised to take a significant turn. Three days following the Polyhymnia concert, Zemlinsky's String Quintet in D minor received its
premiere by the Hellmesberger Quartet, an ensemble that had been a dominant
force in Vienna's musical life ever since its founding in 1849. The quartet, named
for its founder violinist Joseph Hellmesberger,[2] had premiered music of Schubert and collaborated with Brahms at his inaugural concert in Vienna in 1862,
with a performance of Brahms's own G minor Piano Quartet. Hellmesberger's
ensemble had a reputation for championing new music — it had given the first
performance of Bruckner's String Quintet in 1875, for example — and now lent
its support to Zemlinsky. Another review in the *Neues Wiener Tagblatt* suggests
that Zemlinsky could not have asked for a more committed interpretation:

> It is a work of a deeply sensitive, well-trained musical talent, and offers
> a fine exchange of ideas, from polished serenity to passionate seriousness.

[1] *Neues Wiener Tagblatt* (March 9, 1896).
[2] Evidon (1980), 463.

It offers up an audible portrait of the conditions of an impressionable, easily excitable artistic soul.[1]

Positive reviews were always welcome, but the concert yielded an event of far greater significance. Johannes Brahms was again on hand to hear Zemlinsky's music and now admitted the young man was "bursting with talent."[2] Few people had followed Zemlinsky's development over the past few years as carefully. Whether Brahms sensed that time was running out — later that year he would be diagnosed with liver cancer — or simply felt Zemlinsky had reached a plateau and would benefit from personal advice, he chose this moment to offer his services. He requested a copy of the score and invited Zemlinsky to pay him a visit. Then, in his customary sarcastic manner, Brahms casually added, "Naturally, if it would be of interest to you to speak with me about it."[3]

The opportunity of a lifetime had arrived, and with it came a mixture of anticipation, thrill and dread. In his *Jugend-Erinnerungen* (Youthful Experiences) Zemlinsky recalled how the offer caused him anxiety. Brahms had approached *him*, but the actual prospect of personally discussing his music with one of the greatest composers alive "only heightened my already tremendous respect to the point of fear".[4] Not so long ago Adolf had first approached his son about auditioning for the Vienna Conservatory, and now Alexander had been summoned by one the greatest composers ever associated with the city.

And so with excitement mixed with trepidation, Zemlinsky made his way to Brahms's third-floor Karlsgasse apartment, less than five minutes by foot from the Musikverein, and directly across from the majestic Baroque Karlskirche, the Karls Church. Inside the apartment was Brahms's magnificent library, filled with books and rare manuscripts, and the *gemütlich* music room, where some of the most profound music of the nineteenth century had been created. Next to the window that overlooked the Karlskirche stood the Streicher piano, lid closed. Within easy reach was the Kaffe machine, and on the ceiling a curious electric light hung from a track, allowing it to be positioned over the piano or the coffee table next to it. On the walls were sources of inspiration, Brahms's personal pantheon of the gods of music: a bust of Haydn, an engraving of Cherubini — a composer Beethoven had held in high regard but who was now quietly slipping into obscurity — and a bronze-colored bust of Beethoven that looked over Brahms's shoulder when he sat at his piano. Years earlier, Robert

[1] *Neues Wiener Tagblatt* (March 14, 1896).
[2] Heuberger in Clayton (1983a), 86.
[3] Zemlinsky (1922), 69.
[4] Ibid.

Schumann had proclaimed Brahms heir to Beethoven's legacy, and Brahms had since grown old with the giant's shadow looming above him. Zemlinsky must have taken it all in.[1]

Brahms sat at the Streicher's keyboard and played through Zemlinsky's Quintet manuscript, noting those passages that interested him, either because he found them good or because he found them wanting. Zemlinsky not only received valuable advice but was also subjected to Brahms's notoriously curt manner during the coaching: "Questions and answers were short, gruff, seemingly cold and often very ironic."[2] On the other hand, Brahms was thorough and played through Zemlinsky's entire quintet, an indication of his genuine interest in Zemlinsky's edification. Zemlinsky also noted Brahms's penchant for consulting past masters when facing a musical problem. For Brahms, that most often meant looking to the music of Bach and Beethoven, whose scores he kept near his writing table. As Brahms proceeded to make considerable corrections to Zemlinsky's manuscript, Zemlinsky recalled receiving no words of praise or encouragement, but he nevertheless understood the master's intentions: "As I tried shyly to defend the development section, which to me seemed rather Brahmsian, he threw open a Mozart string quintet and explained to me the achievement of its 'yet to be excelled' construction. It therefore sounded entirely justified and understandable when he added, 'Thus does one go about getting from Bach to me!'"[3]

Zemlinsky etched the experience in his memory and two decades later he could still recall all of it clearly, a testament to the significance of the event and what it meant for his future. Association with the master was critical both to Zemlinsky's musical development and early professional status, and getting to Brahms would prove one of the defining moments of Zemlinsky's life. Getting beyond him would be another matter entirely.

[1] For a discussion of Brahms' apartment, see Swafford (1999), 545.

[2] Zemlinsky (1922), 69.

[3] Ibid., 69–70.

Chapter 2

Conflicting Allegiances

T HE YEAR 1896 was shaping up to be a very busy year. In addition to preparations for Polyhymnia's March 2 concert, which proved to be the ensemble's last, and the premiere of Zemlinsky's String Quintet, Zemlinsky was also at work on a new trio, a response to the Tonkünstlerverein's latest challenge. In January, the Verein had announced a competition, open to all Austrian and Hungarian composers, for a new chamber work involving at least one wind instrument. Submissions were due the final day of July. Brahms, the Verein's president and one of the competition's judges, was also personally underwriting the prize money for the top three works selected — 400, 300 and 200 kronen, respectively. The inclusion of a wind instrument was probably also the elder statesman's choice, the result of his own relatively recent interest in the clarinet.[1]

Zemlinsky responded to the Verein's call with a clarinet trio, unquestionably a nod to Brahms's recent work. In all probability, Zemlinsky began drafting his ideas for a D minor trio after digesting Brahms's comments about his String Quintet. Although no detailed record exists about what transpired, Brahms would certainly have remarked on the Quintet's lack of cohesion and unorthodox presentation of ideas, problems evident today in the extant score to the composition's first movement. Studying the score, it is clear now, as it must have

---

[1] Before 1891, Brahms had never incorporated a wind instrument into a work of chamber music, save the Horn Trio of 1865. Then, in March 1891, he encountered the artistry of clarinetist Richard Mühlfeld in the town of Mannheim. Stirred by Mühlfeld's abilities and range of expression, Brahms composed both his Clarinet Trio in A minor and the B minor Clarinet Quintet the same summer. Three years later came the last works of chamber music Brahms would ever write, the two Clarinet Sonatas, op. 120.

been clear to Brahms then, that Zemlinsky was not yet in command of his material. Zemlinsky was determined to improve, and, if writing a clarinet trio for the competition opened him up to criticism for its overt Brahmsian influences, Zemlinsky seemed unconcerned; to the contrary, he eagerly embraced Brahms wherever possible:

> From that point on my work, more than ever, stood entirely under the influence of Brahms. I remember that even with my colleagues it was considered praiseworthy to compose in as "Brahmsian" a manner as possible. We also soon became tagged as notorious "Brahmins" in Vienna.
>
> Naturally there followed a reaction. In the effort to find one's individuality, there was an energetic turning away from Brahms, until such a time when calm, critical re-evaluation gave way to a lasting love of Brahms's music. And today when I conduct a symphony or play one of his gorgeous works of chamber music, I again come completely under the spell of that time and every measure becomes an experience.[1]

The Clarinet Trio revealed to what extent Zemlinsky had become a confirmed Brahmin. Like the older composer, Zemlinsky sought to exploit the unique traits and timbres of both the cello and the clarinet, and to maximize the dark, haunting qualities of the ensemble by gravitating to minor keys, although it is the middle-movement *Andante* where Zemlinsky unfurls the full extent of his devotion. Here, like Brahms, Zemlinsky set his slow movement in D major, opening with a soaring clarinet melody in the instrument's upper clarion register before eventually giving way to a gypsy-inspired rhapsody, exactly the sort embraced so passionately by Brahms. It is only in the Trio's outer movements where Zemlinsky stakes his claim to individuality.

Brahms's Trio is lean, terse, and free of excess, as if he consciously sought to avoid former indulgences; Zemlinsky's Trio shows the depth of his potential, for the first time fusing his impressive understated lyrical gift with his mastery of the art of developing variation.[2] The stunning economy found in the Trio's opening bars are a microcosm of what's to come. Nearly every aspect of the theme's eight bars is pulled from the first three notes (D–E–F), yet the ear is drawn to the larger gesture, a sweeping *espressivo* theme that begins in unison

---

[1] Zemlinsky (1922), 70.

[2] The term is Schoenberg's, who used it to define Brahms's principle of varying a motif or derivation of subsequent material from an initial source. Zemlinsky's own successful adoption of this technique had a profound impact on Schoenberg, perhaps first revealed in the latter's String Quartet in D major, which has been the source of some study. For more about Zemlinsky's Trio and his relationship to Brahms, see Clayton (1983a).

and concludes with the cello winding itself around the clarinet's plaintive melody, even as the cello continues to vary the opening motive. Zemlinsky's efficient handling of material elsewhere in the Trio is no less striking. At the outset of the finale, for example, he simultaneously looks backward and forward, recalling the theme of the first movement while forecasting the clarinet theme to follow. And at the Trio's conclusion, Zemlinsky reintroduces the opening motive by superimposing it with fragments from the finale. Such unbridled virtuosity exemplifies how far Zemlinsky had traveled in so short a time; it could not have escaped Brahms's critical eye.

Work on the Trio occupied Zemlinsky until the second week of July, at which time he turned his attention to another chamber work, a String Quartet in A major. Three years earlier Zemlinsky had completed a draft of a String Quartet in E minor, but, dissatisfied with the results of his first foray into the medium, he set it aside. By mid-1896, however, everything had changed. Zemlinsky was now a composer with abundant technique and a mountain of confidence, and he saw his A Major Quartet through to the end.[1] Once again, unabashed, Zemlinsky reveals his indebtedness to Brahms, from the sunny, passionate melodies recalling Brahms at his most joyous, to the juxtaposition of duple and triple rhythms and grouping of themes in pairs, traits synonymous with Brahmsian technique. Not surprisingly, Zemlinsky's first quartet is also conceptually conservative, modeled on the quartet literature dating back at least to Haydn. It retains the traditional four-movement architecture of its predecessors and relies on the schemes of the movements so thoroughly reinforced in the Conservatory's curriculum: a sonata-form Allegro, an ABA scherzo, a lyrically expansive slow movement marked *Breit und kräftig*, and a closing *Vivace*, again in sonata form.

In Zemlinsky's subsequent quartets, things would play out differently. Each of the three that followed, over the course of four decades, reflect a composer bent on pursuing a strikingly individual and progressive path, but in 1896 Zemlinsky relied on his Conservatory pedigree, Brahmsian models, and Viennese classicism to shape his music. Still, even within this framework, one catches glimpses of a distinctive musical voice in the first quartet, whether in the folksy interlude of the second movement (*Allegretto*) or in the violent interruption heard in the slow movement (*Breit und kräftig*), a quality Horst Weber rightly suggests had not found its way into quartet writing since late Beethoven.[2]

---

[1] Zemlinsky dedicated the work to Eusebius Mandiczewsky, director of the Archives of the Gesellschaft der Musikfreunde and a close personal friend of Brahms.

[2] Weber (1982), 15.

Brahms provided Zemlinsky nearly everything he needed to gain a foothold in Vienna. He offered him musical counsel, welcomed him into the Tonkünstlerverein, recommended him for financial assistance and even contacted his publisher on Zemlinsky's behalf. As well, Brahms's music itself was a powerful source of inspiration. However, one genre was missing from Brahms's catalogue — opera. The medium had eluded him entirely. Brahms had contemplated various subjects and librettos over the years but he eventually realized that his musical language was unsuited to the dramatic stage. If Zemlinsky wanted to write opera, he would have to seek guidance elsewhere. In the closing years of the nineteenth century, Zemlinsky's search for operatic inspiration ended with Richard Wagner.

Wagner was Brahms's antithesis in nearly every respect. Brahms never married and lived simply. Although he was eminently aware of his reputation as one of the greatest of living composers, he remained humble and was generous with his wealth, his time and his energy, and professed solidarity with Jews. Wagner, on the other hand, carried on affairs with the wives of friends and married twice. He was self absorbed, lived in luxury well beyond his means — believing it his divine right to do so — and was a known anti-Semite. When the scope of Wagner's larger-than-life music dramas exceeded the capabilities of the ordinary opera house, Wagner persuaded King Ludwig II of Bavaria to fund construction of a new theater in Bayreuth, dedicated exclusively to the performance of Wagner's music.

Brahms and Wagner were likewise on opposite ends of the musical divide. Brahms, heir to Beethoven and the Viennese Classical tradition, held fast to traditional practices and forms, principles that continued to resonate within the Tonkünstlerverein and the Conservatory. For Brahms and his camp, which included the prominent violinist Joseph Joachim, the pianist and composer Clara Schumann, and the critic Eduard Hanslick,[1] music existed for its sake alone

---

[1] Hanslick, prior to becoming a champion of Brahms, had himself been an ardent Wagnerian. He had come to Vienna in the autumn of 1846 and almost immediately fashioned himself a local, assuming the Viennese custom of taking a leisurely breakfast at a café near the university and reading the papers while seated on a red velvet sofa. He was active as a critic for the *Wiener Musikzeitung* and the *Neue Freie Presse*, which he helped to found, and for forty years he lectured about music at the Old University, always with a piano at his side for demonstration purposes. In those lectures Hanslick frequently discussed his views about Brahms and Wagner, specifically how the former had come to represent all that was pure, honest and beautiful in music. Hanslick, like Brahms himself, acknowledged Wagner's genius, but lamented the results: "I know very well that Wagner is the greatest living opera composer, and the only

and was predicated on the Classical ideals of clean formal outlines, balance and moderation. Wagner came to regard music as but one component of a larger ideal, the *Gesamtkunstwerk*, an amalgamation of the various arts, including music, dance, architecture and sculpture, the synthesis of which would result in a universal work of art, or in Wagner's words, "The Artwork of the Future". For his followers, who included first and foremost Franz Liszt, but also Anton Bruckner, Hugo Wolf,[1] Engelbert Humperdink and the conductor Hans von Bülow, among others, music's future rested with rich chromaticism, free forms and programmatic compositions — in short, the converse of nearly everything Brahms stood for.

Although his early stage works were deeply indebted to French and Italian grand opera, Wagner soon regarded the style as artificial, due in large part to its emphasis on the formalized aria, which brought the plot to a halt and served only as a vehicle for the singer. Wagner's solution was unending melody, lines that were sung but not cast in predictable phrase lengths. For building blocks, Wagner relied on leitmotifs, small but memorable individual musical gestures used to represent everything from objects to emotional states. These motives could be developed, altered, and used in combination with other motives, and because they were often consigned to the orchestral fabric, they worked on almost a psychological plane; the listener could perceive what the singers were feeling or thinking without the need for words. For Wagner, this was how art was fashioned, not by composing antiquated arias or working with outmoded sonata-form structures.

Having freed himself of the limitations of classical structure and harmony, Wagner spoke to those who fashioned themselves avant-garde. In the words of the historian Peter Gay, "To be in the camp of Liszt and Wagner was to be origi-

one in Germany worth talking about in a historical sense. He is the only German composer since Weber and Meyerbeer whom one cannot disregard in the history of dramatic music. Even Mendelssohn and Schumann — not to speak of Rubenstein and the newer ones — can be ignored without leaving a gap in the history of opera. But between this admission and the repulsive idolatry which has grown up in connection with Wagner, and which he has encouraged, there is an infinite chasm." See Pleasants (1950), 206.

[1] Wolf, whose genius for song composition was countered by his increasingly unstable personality, had taken a path opposite to that of Hanslick: once a devoted admirer of Brahms, Wolf had since switched allegiances. As music critic of the *Wiener Salonblatt*, Wolf clung to every opportunity to assail the Viennese master whom he accused of having once insulted his own abilities: "He has, to be sure, never been able to raise himself above the level of mediocrity, but such nullity, emptiness and hypocrisy as prevail in the E Minor Symphony have come to light in no other of his works. The art of composing without ideas has decidedly found its most worthy representative in Brahms." See Swafford (1999), 506.

nal, to be youthful; to be opposed to the *Zukunftsmusiker*, the musicians of the future, was to be uninventive and hide bound."[1] Not since Beethoven had any one composer exercised such influence on the world around him. Despite his controversial persona, the power of Wagner's genius and the allure of his ideas attracted a growing army of devotees in the years following his death in 1883. The Germanic values and qualities in his music resonated with those caught up in the politics of nationalism and pan-Germanicism, while his ability to unite Norse myth with mystical tales of Christianity gained him more followers still. Remarkably, Wagner even appealed to a number of prominent Jewish musicians, in spite of his well-known anti-Semitic ideas. The composer Karl Goldmark, the conductors Hermann Levi and Felix Mottl and the theater director Max Reinhardt, with whom Zemlinsky would later collaborate, were but four of a long list of Jewish artists and intellectuals whose ardent love of Wagner's music helped fuel their own talents.[2]

The effects of Wagnerianism, extending far beyond musical circles, reverberated throughout the wider artistic community, particularly in Vienna. In his book *Der Weg ins Freie* (The Road into the Open), the Viennese novelist Arthur Schnitzler describes how the "aural veil" woven by Wagner's *Tristan* enveloped the lovers Georg and Anna and "isolated them from all the other listeners,"[3] while Ulrich, the protagonist of Robert Musil's magnum opus, *Der Mann ohne Eigenschaften* (The Man Without Qualities), becomes as addicted to Wagner's music, "as to a thickly brewed, hot, benumbing drug."[4] The architect Camillo Sitte, one of Vienna's most prominent designers, decorated Vienna's State Trade School with scenes from Wagner's four-part music drama, *Der Ring des Nibelungen* (Ring of the Nibelungen), and named his first son Siegfried after Wagner's hero.[5] And decades later, the Bauhaus architect Walter Gropius still dreamt of art and artists working together to produce a single, unified work of art, clearly resonating with Wagner's philosophy of the *Gesamtkunstwerk*: "the new building of the future . . . will be everything together: architectural and sculptural and painting, the product of the hands of millions of craftsmen which, in a single shape, will rise to heaven as a crystal symbol of a new emerging faith."[6]

[1] Peter Gay (1978), 267.

[2] Nor were Jews free from the ill effects of Wagnerianism. The infamous anti-Semitic views of the Jewish psychologist Otto Weininger, for example, are directly attributable to Wagnerian influence.

[3] Schnitzler (1992), 145.

[4] Robert Musil (1995), 50.

[5] Schorske (1981), 68–69.

[6] Quoted in Wingler (1962), 39.

Although the battle lines separating the camps of Wagner and Brahms were drawn decades prior to Zemlinsky's birth, these divisions remained acute during Zemlinsky's life.[1] This was particularly true in the Vienna of Zemlinsky's youth, where Brahms remained a driving musical force but where performances of Wagner's music, such as those by Hans Richter, held audiences in rapt attention; where the Vienna Philharmonic made it a point to program the music of both composers; and where distinct music societies grew up around both men — the Brahms-dominated Tonkünstlerverein and the Viennese Academic Wagner Club. For now, Zemlinsky had no intention to limit himself to either camp. Rather, he looked to both Brahms and Wagner to provide whatever style or technique best suited his needs while his own personal language emerged. With time, these influences were replaced by others, from Richard Strauss to Kurt Weill, but the conflict that pitted tradition against progression would never be fully resolved in Zemlinsky's mind. He would forever attempt to navigate waters banked on one side by the traditional strictures imposed by Brahms and his followers and on the other by the *avant-garde* philosophy embraced by many of his colleagues.

In October 1896 Zemlinsky learned that his first opera, *Sarema*, had been chosen among one hundred entries as a finalist for the Luitpold Prize in Munich. Unable to select an outright winner, the judges awarded prizes of equal value to Ludwig Thuille's *Theuerdank*, Arthur Könnemann's *Der tolle Eberstein* and Zemlinsky's *Sarema*. All three operas would be premiered in Munich the following season. Meanwhile, closer to home, Zemlinsky's Trio for clarinet, cello and piano was faring well with the Tonkünstlerverein judges, having been short-listed along with eleven other chamber works. All twelve were to be performed throughout the months of November and December, after which three winners would be chosen. Zemlinsky's Trio was slated for the fourth concert of the series, to take place on December 11. The date followed a flurry of musical activity. On November 20, in the first of the competition concerts, Zemlinsky performed as the pianist in an another finalist's horn trio. The following day Zemlinsky received a rousing ovation in an unrelated concert in the Bösendorfer Hall following a performance of two of his *Ländliche Tänze*, op. 1, by pianist Hedwig Ulmann. And at a concert on December 2, the Fitzner Quartet

[1] In 1860 the *Neue Zeitschrift für Musik* published a manifesto denouncing the practices of the New Germans. The intended document was to have been published with as many notable signatures as possible, yet it contained only four when it first appeared in print: Brahms, Brahms's collaborative partner and confidant, the violinist Joseph Joachim, the composer and conductor Julius Otto Grimm, and the conductor Bernard Scholz. Brahms's career was in no way affected by the debacle, but the affair was an embarrassment nonetheless.

premiered Zemlinsky's A major Quartet along with a performance of the String Quintet by Anton Bruckner.

Zemlinsky's Quartet pleased the public, but the critics had widely differing views as to the work's success. Max Kalbeck of the *Neues Wiener Tagblatt* expressed confidence in the young man's future but found parts of the quartet "unbeautiful and eccentric,"[1] while the critic of the *Neue Freie Presse* reported that "each of the four movements of this new quartet reflects personal characteristics, skillful technique and a wealth of ingeniousness . . . Herr Zemlinsky's Quartet received a thunderous reception."[2] There were no such accolades from the critic of the *Österreichische Musik und Theaterzeitung*, whose critique scathingly and unapologetically took the composer to task:

> Much of it sounds poor, the contrapuntal work has little significance, one would almost say it was awkward, and many seemingly endless passages were produced in this manner, producing a yet more boring product . . . The composer, Herr Alexander Zemlinsky, should have listened to Bruckner's Quintet — that would have granted him a great learning experience! Doing so would have taught him more than has his teacher Fuchs.[3]

The severity of the review must have left Zemlinsky wondering if the critic harbored some prejudice toward the Society, the Conservatory and its students, or Fuchs. But it was also a warning: if Zemlinsky were to succeed in Vienna he would have to win over the harsh and often unforgiving Viennese press.

Nine days later Zemlinsky's prize-winning Clarinet Trio received its premiere, but the competition was stiff. The gifted young composer Walter Rabl had submitted a Quartet for clarinet and strings, and a Septet by Czech-born Josef Miroslaw Weber was scheduled for the final concert on December 22. Both works ultimately edged out Zemlinsky's Trio, which placed third, netting Zemlinsky 200 kronen, equivalent to about $40.50 at the time and about $875 in 2010.[4] Soon after, the work attained far greater visibility than came from being awarded third prize by the Tonkünstlerverein. At the end of the month Brahms passed Zemlinsky's score on to his publisher, Simrock, adding, "I can recommend the man as well as his talent."[5] Simrock subsequently took Brahms's advice and published the trio as Zemlinsky's op. 3 the following year.

---

[1] Kalbeck in McColl (1996), 222.

[2] *Neue Freie Presse* (December 12, 1896).

[3] *Österreichische Musik und Theaterzeitung* (December 15, 1896).

[4] See the sources cited at p. 15 n. 2 above.

[5] Weber (1977), 12.

Five months before *Sarema's* premiere, Johannes Brahms was laid to rest. He died wondering how history would judge his music, but the pageantry of his funeral left no doubt that he would not soon be forgotten. Brahms's funeral procession took place on April 6, 1897, and stretched for miles, with mourners lining every street along the way.[1] Those paying their respects included a stream of public officials, many of Brahms's friends and Conservatory colleagues, various local musicians, the wife of Johann Strauss jr., Antonín Dvořák, and emissaries from orchestras from Budapest to Berlin. There were also the thousands who Brahms never knew but who understood the magnitude of the event and came to pay their respects. Led by a standard-bearer on horseback, the lengthy procession followed seven funeral cars that had departed that morning from Brahms's apartment in the Karlsgasse. Stops were made for a performance at the Musikverein and an invocation at a Protestant church, before arriving late that afternoon at the Zentralfriedhof, the Central Cemetery. Eulogies were delivered and Brahms was fittingly laid to rest among the graves of Johann Strauss jr., Schubert and Beethoven.

With Brahms's passing, the floodgates of a new age swung open. Musically, Brahms's death eased the way for composers like Zemlinsky to embrace fully the progressive tendencies so long suppressed by Brahms's overwhelming presence. But Viennese artistic and political life was also experiencing radical change at the time, so Brahms's death served as an apt metaphor for the end of one era and the start of another. Seemingly overnight nearly every aspect of Viennese life was dramatically altered. The actual start of the twentieth century was still more two years away, but Vienna was already severing its ties to the 1800s.

On April 3, the very day of Brahms's death, the fashionable painter Gustav Klimt and a diverse group of young artists broke from Vienna's conservatively governed Künstlergenossenschaft, the Association of Austrian Artists. With the motto "Der Zeit ihre Kunst, der Kunst ihre Freiheit" (To the era its art, to art its freedom), the act distanced them from the mentality of their predecessors and immediately placed them among Vienna's *avant garde*. Driven by a collective desire to explore their artistic instincts and satisfy personal individuality, Klimt and his fellow Secessionists — among them the artist and graphic designer Koloman Moser, the architect Joseph Maria Olbrich and the designer Josef Hoffmann — symbolized the progressive stance of their generation. While at first absorbed with the highly stylized, flowing, and sensuous style known as *Jugendstil* — the German equivalent of *Art Nouveau* — the painters in par-

---

[1] Brahms's funeral is described in detail in Swafford (1999), 620–21.

ticular slowly moved toward a less ornamental and more honest expression of the human condition, a style that became known as Expressionism. Backed by the young generation of writers called *Jung Wien*, as well as by Vienna's most prominent architect, Otto Wagner, the Secessionists quickly gained a strong following and amassed financial support from a number of Viennese intellectuals, including the industrialist Karl Wittgenstein, father of the brilliant philosopher Ludwig Wittgenstein and the pianist Paul Wittgenstein. Soon a new building known as the Secession was erected. Designed by Joseph-Maria Olbrich, a disciple of Otto Wagner, its express purpose was to house exhibits by the group. Topped by a huge, gold-leaf globe, the Secession's interior walls were no more than simple adjustable partitions that could be moved to fit the requirements of any exhibition. The windowless Egyptian-influenced structure immediately became synonymous with the most radical of modern art.

Two days after Brahms's death, it was announced that Gustav Mahler would succeed Hans Richter as Kapellmeister of the Hofoper. Mahler had been a student at the Vienna Conservatory a decade before Zemlinsky and had since gone on to conducting appointments in Kassel, Leipzig, Prague, Budapest and Hamburg, encountering or creating problems with his staff in nearly every theater he worked. In Vienna, Mahler would experience glorious music making, frustration, and relentless anti-Semitism. His return to Vienna also had vital implications for Zemlinsky, whose work and life benefited greatly from Mahler's personal involvement.

While Zemlinsky anxiously watched for Mahler's presence around the Hofoper that April, Vienna was also experiencing dramatic political change. Not only had an ordinance been passed by Parliament that recognized Czech as an official government language — a concession that was to have increasing significance as nationalistic fervor continued to grow throughout the empire — but Karl Lueger was officially proclaimed Vienna's new mayor. In reality, Lueger had already been elected mayor several times, largely a result of having gained popular support among the working class by consistently playing to Vienna's latent anti-Semitism — particularly as it related to capitalist corruption — and inherent mistrust of the wealthy, but with each victory the emperor refused to sanction the parliamentary vote, fearing the impact Lueger's anti-Semitic policies would have on an empire growing less stable every day. But by 1897, Emperor Franz Joseph could no longer ignore Lueger's popularity and was forced to officially recognize the election results.

To his credit, Lueger embarked upon a great many projects that vastly improved Vienna's physical conditions and helped bring about the city's modernization. He municipalized the gas and electric plants, developed the city's transportation network, implemented much needed changes in labor rules, and built more than one hundred new schools. In addition to the city's basic postal services, which included hand delivery of letters or notes twice daily, by 1900 Vienna (like other major cities in Europe and America) also possessed pneumatic dispatch (*Rohrpost*), a sophisticated system whereby messages traveled at one kilometer per hour through an intricate subterranean network of pressurized tubing that extended fifty-nine kilometers underneath the city. Lueger also improved the city's water supply and had the foresight to implement a program of afforestation to preserve the nearby Vienna Woods.[1]

But Lueger's anti-Semitic platform kept him and his supporters rooted in Vienna's dark past. Regarded by Hitler as "the greatest German mayor of all time",[2] Lueger is remembered for the words "Wer ein Jud ist, bestimme ich" (I decide who is a Jew). Complex and politically astute, Lueger once remarked, "I'll only be happy after the last Jew has disappeared from Vienna",[3] and although he saw to it that the financially strained Arnold Schoenberg received a pension of 1,000 crowns, by consistently fanning Vienna's anti-Semitic flames Lueger ultimately paved the way for Hitler and his troops eventually to march into the city.[4]

With *Sarema*'s premiere scheduled for October 10, 1897, Zemlinsky spent the bulk of the summer overseeing the production of a vocal score so that the Munich singers could adequately study the opera. Zemlinsky entrusted much of this project to his friend Arnold Schoenberg. Both men spent the summer holidays of 1897 together in Payerbach, a resort town in lower Austria where, far from the distractions of Vienna, they could devote much of their collective energy to the score's preparation. Reducing the full score for piano proved a valuable pedagogical vehicle for Schoenberg, to whom Zemlinsky previously had taught the rudiments of counterpoint and provided some musical guidance but who otherwise lacked formal musical training. Zemlinsky completed a number of sections within the first act of the vocal score himself — including portions up through the fourth scene, portions of the fifth scene, and the act's final bar — before turning the project over to Schoenberg. From there, Schoenberg relied

[1] Hoffmann (1988), 143–44.

[2] Hitler (1971), 55.

[3] Geehr (1990), 15.

[4] Whether Lueger was a true anti-Semite or spewed anti-Semetic rhetoric to draw mass political support continues to be debated today. For more on the subject see, for instance, Hamann (1999), 286–91.

on Zemlinsky's own hand as an example of how to carry on. Thus, not only
did their friendship deepen during these summer months, but this was also the
period in which Zemlinsky exerted the greatest influence on Schoenberg, who
later acknowledged Zemlinsky as "the one to whom I owe most of my knowledge of the technique and the problems of composing".[1] It was the first of many
summers the two would share together.

Schoenberg's involvement with *Sarema* allowed Zemlinsky time to tend the
completion of his Second Symphony, another competition piece with which he
hoped to win the Tonkünstlerverein's coveted Beethoven Prize. Begun around
the time of Brahms's death, the Symphony in B-flat was brought to a close on
September 9, 1897. Zemlinsky's latest opus was steeped in nineteenth-century
symphonic tradition: four-movement structure, reliance on sonata-allegro form,
rich romantic orchestration and a strong display of thematic development. The
work opens with a three-note signal call, followed by a broad *Sostenuto* introduction that derives equal inspiration from the chorale writing of Anton Bruckner, who had died one year earlier, and the Austrian countryside. At the outset
of the Allegro proper Zemlinsky seizes on the opening signal call, from which
he spins out an expansive, driving theme with further echoes of Bruckner. The
secondary material, laced with Viennese nostalgia, is tailed by a sprightly dance
with the unmistakable flavor of Dvořák. Zemlinsky resolves ideas from both
the introduction and the exposition in a well-crafted development, which grows
steadily in intensity before cadencing with the signal call. The equally satisfying
recapitulation abridges and re-examines prior ideas. The air of Dvořák returns
in the quirky, syncopated and Slavonically-inspired *Scherzando* and again
in the lush *Adagio*, a tripartite movement that at times suggests the *Largo* of
Dvořák's Ninth Symphony.

The *Moderato* fourth movement springs directly from the *passacaglia* finale of Brahms's Fourth Symphony. Zemlinsky opens with a martial eight-bar

---

[1] Schoenberg (1984), 80. Zemlinsky's musical influence on Schoenberg did not end with
Sarema. Indeed, Schoenberg's early String Quartet in D major, which was subsequently submitted to Zemlinsky for criticism, was also a product of that summer. Although Schoenberg's
original quartet version no longer exists, it is known that a number of significant changes
were made under Zemlinsky's supervision, including the complete revision of one of the
movements. An overriding spirit of Brahms pervades the work, most likely also a result of
Zemlinsky's influence. In March of 1898 Schoenberg's Quartet was privately performed at the
Tonkünstlerverein, which Schoenberg had recently joined, no doubt a result of Zemlinsky's
recommendation, and in December of that year the work received a public performance by
the Fitzner Quartet, a contact also borne of Zemlinsky's association with the group's cellist,
Friedrich Buxbaum. For more on Zemlinsky's involvement with Schoenberg's D major String
Quartet, see Weber (1971), 84–85.

progression, a *cantus firmus* that gives way to twenty-six variations that run the gamut from lush orchestral writing to skeletal fragmentation retaining but the merest hint of the original subject. As a crowning Brahmsian touch, a new fugato subject — fashioned from the movement's opening chords — does double-duty as a counter-subject, over which themes from earlier movements return. The triumphant final bars bring to a close Zemlinsky's strict reliance on traditional models — it would be the last such work the devoted Brahmin would ever compose along such pure, classical lines.

Around this time Zemlinsky also returned to a cantata composed during the summer of 1896, the *Frühlingsbegräbnis*, a work similarly imbued with a Brahmsian flavor. Set to a text by Paul Heyse, a poet also embraced by Brahms, Zemlinsky had gone so far as to incorporate a theme reminiscent of the March from Brahms's *Ein deutsches Requiem*. Perhaps hoping to be included on a memorial concert for the late Viennese master, Zemlinsky now completely overhauled the cantata's orchestration and then inscribed it "to the memory of Johannes Brahms", but any hopes for its inclusion on a program honoring Brahms's memory went unfulfilled. In the end, Zemlinsky's dedication proved purely cathartic. Despite at least one additional revision, the cantata received but a single performance during Zemlinsky's lifetime, and then only by the Vienna Philharmonic Orchestra under Zemlinsky's direction, in February 1900.

In early October 1897, Zemlinsky left for Munich — after years of working and waiting he was finally going to experience the production of his first opera. On October 10, four days before the composer's twenty-sixth birthday, the curtain of the Munich Court and National Theater went up and *Sarema*, some four years in the making, got underway. By all accounts the production was a triumph and proved a worthy birthday gift. Zemlinsky was repeatedly called to the stage at the conclusion of both acts II and III, where he gracefully acknowledged his audience and his singers,[1] and critical acclaim followed over the next few days. The critics were astounded that the opera was the product of someone so young about whom virtually nothing was known. Although some expressed concern about the work's overall evenness, which was felt to falter in its latter half, and criticized its occasional lapses into conventionality, Zemlinsky's theatrical sensibilities, inherent feel for melody, and sensitive balance of forces were indisputable. In the case of at least one reviewer, not even Wagnerian impulses were objectionable:

> The splendid premiere of this first operatic work is all the more praiseworthy for the overwhelming ovation it received. The 23-year-old

[1] *Münchener Neuste Nachrichten* (October 12, 1897).

[*sic*] composer is unknown even within professional circles and neither his picture nor his score is to be found in the windows of our music stores. Nothing more is known about him save that he was awarded the *Luitpold* prize . . . Why was this opera, which was not previously campaigned before the public, so successful? What was it that thrilled the unprejudiced public, whose enthusiasm mounted from act to act? It was the experience of being in the presence of a talent who has something to say, whose musical sensitivity has not been sickled o'er with the pale cast of thought[1] . . . I do not mean to imply that the young Polish [*sic*] composer took refuge in sensually appealing melody and rhythm. On the contrary, his musical language is permeated by a different kind of pathos, which is accompanied by an inclination toward the sentimental. And as nobody can evade Wagner's influence, so do the numerous recitative-like passages in Zemlinsky's music demonstrate the attempt to make an artful use of the modern recitative [*Sprechgesang*]. However, the old operatic forms have been used in many effective and beautiful scenes. Thus, Sarema is an opera in which the old forms are reconciled with the dramatic-musical laws founded by Wagner. An example! What role does the so-called leitmotif play with Wagner's followers who use it to hound a few poor thoughts and the poor listener to death? Even Zemlinsky uses repetition to characterize his dramatis personae and the action, yet in a much more moderate and effective manner . . .[2]

Sarema's success established Zemlinsky's reputation nationally and demonstrated to both the public and the critics that, in spite of his youth and operatic inexperience, and despite the extraordinary artistry required for operatic composition, he already possessed impressive aptitude for the genre.[3] In 1896, it appeared nothing lay beyond Zemlinsky's grasp.

Songs had long been Zemlinsky's musical passion. As a young musician in Vienna he was surrounded by lieder, particularly those of Schubert, Schumann, Wolf and Brahms, masters past and present. Zemlinsky was certainly drawn to the genre's intimate nature — the personal connection to a text and the musical

---

[1] The critic here is quoting from Shakespeare's *Hamlet*, Act III, scene i.

[2] *Münchener Post-und Augsburger Volkzeitung* (October 13, 1897).

[3] Despite its success, *Sarema* was to receive only one additional production during Zemlinsky's lifetime, in Leipzig on November 16, 1899. Thereafter the work fell into obscurity until its revival in Trier, Germany, in March of 1996.

dialogue between singer and pianist, particularly when Zemlinsky was the one
at the keyboard — but song composition was also far less onerous than symphonic or operatic composition, genres that required long-term pacing, scoring
for a battery of instruments and other skills. And although a song was rarely
polished in a day, it could certainly be sketched in one, with the fleeting emotion that sprung from a text or an event quickly captured and notated before it
got away.

Zemlinsky's predilection for lieder blossomed during his Conservatory years,
and in those that followed, songs continued to flow from his pen. By 1897 Zemlinsky had composed some fifty songs, but, as with his other early work, song
composition was as much a part of the learning process as a vehicle for personal
expression. While naturally he would have thrilled to hear his compositions
sung in public, it is unlikely Zemlinsky had great designs for them at the outset,
beyond the lessons gained from their writing. This changed with Zemlinsky's
Lieder op. 2, the first published collection of his songs. In 1897, a pivotal year for
both Zemlinsky and Vienna, Wilhelm Hansen (Copenhagen, Leipzig) published
thirteen of his songs in two volumes. Zemlinsky dedicated these songs to the
great lieder singer Anton Sistermans, the man who one year earlier had premiered Brahms's *Four Serious Songs*, op. 121. Believed to have been composed
over a period of two years, between 1894 and 1896, op. 2 was conceived neither
as a cycle nor as a collection, and thus the individual songs reflect varying influences and styles rather than homogeneity of language. Hansen chose to publish
them as a group anyway, since doing so allowed the publisher to sign one of Vienna's most promising musical talents while simultaneously feeding the public's
appetite for *Hausmusik*, music to be performed at home.

The collection tells us much about Zemlinsky's diverse literary tastes. Various songs predictably bring to mind the Romantics, especially Goethe and
Eichendorff, but others surprisingly harken to the moderns — von Leixner,
Heyse, Storm, and even Paul Wertheimer, who Zemlinsky knew personally
from his visits to the Café Grienstiedl. And although folk music never played
much of a role in Zemlinsky's musical development, he nevertheless found early
inspiration in the folk texts of this collection, a Turkish love song and a *Minnelied*, a song common to the traveling minstrels of the early Renaissance. Not
unexpectedly, influences of prior masters of the lied dominate the settings, such
as the Schumannesque lilt of the vocal line at the outset of *Um Mitternacht*,
or the darker Brahmsian hues of *Heilige Nacht*. Nevertheless, the collection
also hints at Zemlinsky's growing interest in unusual keys (E-flat minor, G-flat
major) and unpredictable harmonies, even if such moments, like those found in
Frühlingstag's brief twenty-one bars, remain more the exception than the rule.

A worthy successor to Vienna's great song tradition, Zemlinsky was proclaimed a "talent of unusual power" by the critic of the Leipzig newspaper *Signale für die musikalische Welt*.[1] Secure in the knowledge that his songs were now highly sought after, more followed quickly, as did more attention abroad. When the Stuttgart *Neue Musikzeitung* introduced Zemlinsky to its readership, it included a song from the Gesänge, op. 5, Zemlinsky's latest publication:

> Recently a highly talented lieder composer appeared with his first musical efforts, which created quite a stir in the concert hall. It was Alexander Zemlinsky, whose op. 5 collection of songs has just been brought out by Wilhelm Hansen. We have chosen for today's supplement a short, modest, delicate song entitled *Tiefe Sehnsucht*. The tone of longing could not have been brought about with greater loveliness and tenderness than it has in this piece.[2]

The choice to reprint *Tiefe Sehnsucht* was made on account of its brevity — it requires just over a half minute to perform. But the collection did contain more substantial music — *Im Korn* for instance, whose breathless piano writing evocatively portrays sexual passion, and *O Blätter, dürre Blätter*, a poem about withered love whose emotional highs and lows Zemlinsky captured through the masterful juxtaposition of D major and D minor. The latter song was unquestionably one of Zemlinsky's most inspired to date, but it is what the songs reveal about Zemlinsky that lends the op. 5 particular interest.

Aside from Zemlinsky's youthful romance with Melanie Guttmann and his intense involvement (still to come) with Alma Schindler, virtually nothing is known about any other intimate relationships with women he may have had during the closing years of the century. Zemlinsky would, however, confess to Alma, "If you ever thought of me as an innocent young man, I must set you straight. To the contrary, my last years have been wild indeed and I've been disgustingly lucky in this regard!"[3] There is little reason to believe these were idle boasts, particularly as he also confessed to not understanding his good luck "in this regard!" Zemlinsky would never have been described as handsome — a photograph from this period reveals a high forehead, a prominent nose, thin lips, close-set eyes and a soft chin. Nevertheless, his eyes radiate intelligence, and he projects an air of confidence. More important, he was a young and celebrated musician living in an age when people looked to artists to stir their

---

[1] *Signal für die Musikalische Welt*, 56 (1898), 177.
[2] *Neue Musik-Zeitung*, 20 (1899), 23.
[3] AZ/AMW.

emotions. Zemlinsky was not inclined to catalogue his conquests, yet his youthful ardor, however it played out, is captured in his music. The op. 5, published by Hansen in 1898, conveys everything Zemlinsky associated with love — longing, fulfillment, disillusion — concepts that place him squarely amidst the prevailing *Zeitgeist*, a time when love of a woman still meant a quest for the ideal womanhood: *das Ewig-Weibliche*, in Goethe's words.

Like its predecessor, the op. 5 ensemble comprises songs most likely written with no thought of them being grouped together, yet the overall tone of this collection is considerably more melancholy than what came before. Half of the songs are set in minor keys, the poetry providing a window into Zemlinsky's romantic yearnings. Taken as a whole, the group suggests that by his midtwenties, Zemlinsky had developed a mature artistic sensibility toward love, bliss, pain and vulnerability. Soon, Zemlinsky would meet Alma Schindler and succumb to them all.

Zemlinsky was now working more confidently than ever. The Walzer-Gesänge, op. 6, of 1898, published by Simrock the following year, comprises the first of his songs intentionally composed as a group, and they demonstrate a composer beginning to find a personal voice and a command of the medium's potential. For this collection Zemlinsky turned to six Tuscan poems by Ferdinand Gregorovius (1821–1891), a German who spent years exploring the sunny south, whose interest in Italian history stretched from Lucrezia Borgia to the Jews of Rome, and whose eight-volume history of medieval Rome remains a classic. Zemlinsky, who gravitated toward texts of lost love and false lovers, had yet to set foot on Italian soil, but Gregorovius' poetry inspired the composer to capture in sound the joy and passion often associated with Italy. The group harbored one exception, *Ich gehe des Nachts* — not wholly unexpected, since for Zemlinsky unbridled joy was but a temporary state. The poem concerns a woman whose nocturnal search for her lover brings her face to face with death. Zemlinsky successfully tapped into the poem's dramatic potential, portraying the woman's desperate, anguished state of mind with wide vocal leaps, a technique that would soon become a favorite expressionistic idiom. Nevertheless, the song is brief, and the overall tone of the collection remains distinctly joyous. The collection concludes with one of the most rapturous songs Zemlinsky would ever compose, *Briefschen schrieb ich*, a soaring work that reflects the sweet taste of victory won through passionate struggle.

Zemlinsky's interest in Ferdinand Gregorovius was a short-lived experiment and came to an abrupt end with his discovery of Richard Dehmel, Jens Peter Jacobsen, Christian Morgenstern and Detlev von Liliencron. Each was individual and a master. In Morgenstern's work, life tended toward the absurd, while the poetry of Dehmel, a fellow Expressionist, was passionate and often oriented toward the erotic. And though Liliencron and Jacobsen were both linked to Naturalism, a movement that sought to portray life as it really was, the work of each was distinct. Liliencron, a Prussian, sought vividness and accuracy of detail in his poetry, while Jacobsen, a Dane who had died in 1885 but whose work remained very influential, gravitated toward melancholy and wistful themes. These poets were forging a strikingly modern language, something direct, immediate, honest and capable of portraying ordinary man as a product of an everyday environment, or as someone susceptible to human passion and physical drives. Indeed, sexuality was treated with unprecedented frankness, as if it too were a subject for scientific examination.

The language was fresh and exhilarating, beautiful and powerful, and paralleled the experimentation and search for new forms of expression then taking place in Vienna. In 1898, just as Zemlinsky was discovering these new poetic sources of inspiration, Sigmund Freud was working on his monumental study, *The Interpretation of Dreams*, having already spent years in Vienna examining human neuroses and hysteria. And the same year also witnessed the first exhibit of Vienna's Secessionists, whose artwork reflected the group's collective intent to create a "sacred spring" of artistic renewal. As Josef Hoffmann's Ver Sacrum room demonstrated, the Secessionists were not bound by any singular artistic style but instead sought to eliminate the pre-existing distinction separating "high art" from "handicraft."[1] For Zemlinsky, it was similarly a time for exploration, and the modernist poets offered keys to doors previously locked.

Two sharply defined collections, both composed during the years 1898–99, were the immediate result of this exploration: *Irmelin Rose und andere Gesänge*, op. 7, and *Turmwächterlied und andere Gesänge*, op. 8. The latter collection, three of whose songs depict the passing of time, was by far the more moderate. Fittingly scored for baritone or deep voice,[2] these settings of Jacobsen and Liliencron ware characterized by relaxed vocal lines and extended piano introductions, interludes and codas, making them the longest songs he had yet composed.[3] The five songs of *Irmelin Rose und andere Gesänge*, on the other hand, stood apart from anything Zemlinsky had written, primarily on account of their harmonic daring.

[1] Brandstätter (2003), 7.

[2] Zemlinsky dedicated the set to Johannes Messchaert, one of the great baritones of the day.

[3] The songs' slow and stately tempos contribute to their expansiveness, as do the extended piano solos. As Oncley points out, nearly half of *Turmwächterlied's* ninety-two bars are scored for piano alone. See Oncley (1975), 144.

Until now, Zemlinsky's development as a song composer had been steady, albeit gradual, but the modern poetry of Morgenstern, Jacobsen and Dehmel triggered the need for a radically new musical approach, one that could capture the intense, direct expression found, for example, in Morgenstern's *Da waren zwei Kinder*, a poem that speaks about the death of two children with scientific objectivity ("There were two children, young and good, but their blood flowed much too fast"),[1] or Dehmel's erotically charged *Meeraugen* ("Your hair is black, your hair is wild, it crackles under my glow"). Zemlinsky answered the challenge with bold chromaticism that often borders on the atonal and unpredictable chord progressions and modulations, evident at the very outset of both of these op. 7 songs. Although Zemlinsky continued to be guided by the dominion of melody, the poetry inspired — or perhaps demanded — a more adventurous harmonic vocabulary. Chords rich in sevenths and ninths are no longer determined by "rules" but rather chosen for color, intensity or mood. Intense chromatic passages, such as one found at the very opening of *Meeraugen*, which draws on eleven of the twelve possible semitones, were crafted to relate the poetry's message as faithfully as possible. The result was a collection of songs as progressive as anything written at the time.

At the close of the century both Zemlinsky and Schoenberg found themselves increasingly drawn to the work of Richard Dehmel, whose poetry fired their imagination and inspired a variety of compositions. Dehmel had sprung to public attention in 1897 when he was brought before a Berlin court to defend his recently published collection of autobiographical poems, entitled *Weib und Welt* (Woman and World), on charges of immorality. Dehmel responded with the following words:

> First, I must disagree that to an unprejudiced mind the overall content of the book can appear immoral — whether blasphemous or lewd. To be sure, the book shows how a human being, contrary to his holiest principles, abandons himself to a sensual passion, and is thereby driven by the most painful emotional turmoil, finally to a disgraceful death. Clearly it cannot be the artist's task to disguise or conceal the seductive charms that lie naturally within every passion. But I believe that anyone who helps the human soul open its eyes to its bestial urges serves true morality better than many a moralistic accuser.[2]

[1] There is no indication that Zemlinsky was aware that Mahler had begun work on his own *Kindertotenlieder* the very same year.

[2] Dehmel in Frisch (1993), 81.

It is easy to understand Schoenberg and Zemlinsky's mutual fascination with a writer willing to explore the human condition so unapologetically. Speaking for both composers, Schoenberg wrote Dehmel, "You, far more than any musical impression, were the one who opened up the way for our programmatic faction's experimentation. From you we learned the ability to listen within ourselves and therefore to become people of OUR time."[1]

Although Schoenberg's 1897 setting of Dehmel's poem *Mädchenfrühling* suggests he was the first of the two to draw on the poet's texts, Zemlinsky was the first to find inspiration in Dehmel's work for something more substantial. In addition to his *Irmelin Rose und andere Gesänge*, Zemlinsky set Dehmel's *Aurikelchen* for four-part women's chorus in 1898, and probably around the same time based a set of solo piano pieces on four of Dehmel poems, *Stimme des Abends, Waldseligkeit, Liebe* and *Käferlied*, published as the *Fantasien über Gedichte von Richard Dehmel* (Fantasies on Poetry of Dehmel), op. 9.

As a pianist, it was logical that Zemlinsky chose to convey intimate musical thoughts through this instrument — he had done so about a dozen times before, stretching back ten years to his earliest piano sonata — but considering that the Fantasies were among the last works Zemlinsky composed for solo piano, the experiment evidently proved less than satisfying. Zemlinsky turned instead to greater forces, including the human voice, to fully communicate the power of the written word. To this end, Zemlinsky began a setting of Dehmel's *Die Magd* (The Maid), a story of a maiden whose lover perishes in the summer heat. Scored for soprano and string sextet, Zemlinsky's composition marked one of the earliest settings for voice and small chamber ensemble. It might well have become a significant chamber work had it been completed. Yet, inexplicably, Zemlinsky broke off work after setting only two stanzas of Dehmel's poem. Perhaps he was unsure how to adequately convey the tragedy of a young girl, alone and pregnant, who is driven away and later kills her newborn child, like Gretchen in Goethe's *Faust*. Perhaps he was made impotent by Schoenberg's string sextet, *Verklärte Nacht* (Transfigured Night), another Dehmel-inspired work that flew from Schoenberg's pen in just three weeks. In any case, the 200-plus bars that remain of Zemlinsky's score, published posthumously as *Maiblumen blühten überall*, evidences an inspired and motivically tight composition and suggests the new ground he might have broken had he seen the work through to the end.

Schoenberg, meanwhile, did break new ground. In the summer of 1899, which he spent with Zemlinsky in their favorite summer retreat of Payerbach, Schoenberg set at least one Dehmel poem, *Erwartung*, before embarking on

---

[1] Dehmel in Andraschke (1995), 146.

Verklärte Nacht, the string sextet that transformed Dehmel's novel *Zwei Men-schen* (Two People) into an explicit programmatic setting. Three weeks after it was begun, Schoenberg's tone poem for chamber ensemble was complete. Its progressive musical language — what might be described as hyper-Wagnerian — and its free, single-movement formal scheme reflected Schoenberg's desire to pursue the most crucial elements associated with the "New German" school of Wagner and Liszt. The work made clear just how rapidly Schoenberg — un-encumbered by the restraints imposed by formal Conservatory training — was developing as a composer. If *Verklärte Nacht*'s instrumentation invites specula-tion as to whether it or Zemlinsky's unfinished sextet was the first conceived, the two Dehmel-inspired sextets also offer clear proof of the rich exchange of ideas between Zemlinsky and Schoenberg that occurred at the close of the century.

In addition to Dehmel's lyrics, Zemlinsky's sister Mathilde was also fueling Schoenberg's emotions. Mathilde, who accompanied her brother and Schoen-berg to Payerbach during the summer of 1899, was no doubt at least partially responsible for the impassioned echoes of Wagner's *Tristan* that can be heard in *Verklärte Nacht*. Mathilde was Schoenberg's ideal mate in many ways. Like her brother, she possessed a clever wit and was a highly educated musician. She was also clear and direct and could resolve complicated situations with just a few words, qualities Schoenberg came to appreciate over time.[1] The three continued to summer together over the next few years. In October of 1901, Schoenberg married Mathilde. Thus, Zemlinsky and Schoenberg became more than friends and colleagues — they became family.

In the final year of the nineteenth century Zemlinsky was elected vice-presi-dent of the Tonkünstlerverein and witnessed the premiere of his Second Sym-phony, which a year and a half earlier had earned him the Tonkünstlerverein's Beethoven Prize, Vienna's most prestigious musical award. Neither event sug-gested Zemlinsky was a musical radical. To the contrary, the Tonkünstlerverein remained one of Vienna's most conservative musical bastions, and the Second Symphony was tangible evidence of Zemlinsky's attachment to conventional musical principles. His op. 7 songs did signal that he was moving in new direc-tions, but it would be years before his other music began to reflect similar pro-gressive tendencies. Time and again Zemlinsky proved his willingness to move ahead musically or make significant changes in his personal and professional

---

[1] Weber (1995), 256.

life, but he did so only gradually, and after much deliberation. He was not a risk taker, nor did he throw caution to the wind.

The length of time Zemlinsky took to convert from Judaism to Christianity exemplifies his cautious nature, or at the very least shows his unwillingness to act impulsively. On March 29, 1899, he visited the courthouse and registered with the city magistrate as *Konfessionslos*, or undenominational. One day later he entered the Vienna synagogue, which housed the headquarters of Vienna's Jewish community, the Israelitische Kultusgemeinde, and withdrew his name from its records.[1] It was a decision entirely consistent with his character, a result of months — perhaps years — of consideration about both his past and his future. In truth, Zemlinsky's connection to his Jewish heritage had actually been terminated years before — he simply had never taken steps to make it official.

Zemlinsky's Jewish roots undoubtedly shaped his mentality, but Judaism itself had ceased to play a role in his life since early childhood.[2] Although he had been commissioned to compose a Jewish wedding song, *Baruch haba; mi adir*, in 1896 (published posthumously as *Hochzeitsgesang*), and over time set three biblical psalms to music, his larger body of work did not stem from Jewish inspiration. Since his early teens, music was the dominant force in Zemlinsky's life, and by 1899 he evidently found less reason than ever to maintain a Jewish identity. For Zemlinsky, as for any other Jew in Vienna, anti-Semitism was a way of life, even if it was not confronted every day and he had grown up with the understanding that a clear but unspoken gulf separated Jews from Vienna's fully assimilated gentile citizens — Vienna was, after all, the only capital in Europe that had elected an anti-Semitic municipal government.[3] For some, conversion eased the way into a social class where Jews were otherwise unwelcome; for others, forsaking their Jewish heritage cleared the way for their ascendance to positions in the higher bureaucracy where Jews were otherwise essentially barred. It also often meant the difference between receiving a promotion or not within legal and military professions, or receiving a position at all in academia and the arts.[4] It was no secret that Mahler had converted to Catholicism solely

[1] Based on information provided by the Magistrat der Stadt Wien and the Israelitische Kultusgemeinde Wien, respectively.

[2] Zemlinsky never exhibited a religious bent of any kind, so it is not surprising that he did not return to his Jewish roots later in life as did, for example, Schoenberg. Lorraine Gorrell has noted that the majority of Zemlinsky's friends and students were Jewish, as were both his wives, but Zemlinsky was drawn to them all — or they to him — first and foremost because of talent and musical inclination. See Gorrell (2002), 19.

[3] Beller (1989), 188.

[4] Ibid., 189–90.

to attain the directorship of the Hofoper.[1] Schoenberg too had converted, as had record numbers of Vienna's Jews by the turn of the century.[2] Zemlinsky's visit to the Vienna Synagogue at the end of March 1899 therefore probably came as little surprise to the synagogue officials. But slow to change as ever, Zemlinsky's formal conversion did not occur until years later.

At the dawning of the twentieth century, Zemlinsky found himself in an enviable position. He was considered one of Vienna's most promising musical talents, his music was sought after by some of Europe's leading publishers, he had support from the Ministry for Culture, and he was in demand as a private teacher. His contributions to his father's income also made it possible for his family to finally leave the Leopoldstadt, which they did in 1899. But Zemlinsky's life was about to change dramatically. The luxury of composing hours a day would abruptly come to an end when conditions at home necessitated the need for more substantial income. He would also soon be introduced to Alma Schindler, one of Vienna's most alluring women. Well accustomed to male attentions, at the start of the century Alma found herself captivated by Zemlinsky's passion, talent, celebrity and tutelage. Their affair, which ranged from tantalizing to tumultuous, was among the most significant experiences of Zemlinsky's life.

---

[1] Years later Alma would write, "He was afraid [to remain Jewish] lest otherwise he might find it difficult as a Jew to get an engagement in Vienna." Mahler-Werfel (1969), 44.

[2] Since 1868, the conversion of Jews to Christianity in Vienna had more than doubled with each successive decade, from 2 in 1868 to 22 by 1870, 61 by 1880, 169 by 1890 and finally 559 between the years 1890 and 1900. See Rozenblit (1983).

Chapter 3

Once Upon a Time

A T THE START of the twentieth century Zemlinsky experienced one of the greatest triumphs he would ever receive at the hands of his fellow Viennese. When Gustav Mahler led the premiere of Zemlinsky's newest opera, *Es war einmal* (Once Upon a Time) on January 22, 1900, Zemlinsky was forced to acknowledge the ovation — including the war-whoops from the younger members of the audience — at the conclusion of each act. Both thrilled and embarrassed, Zemlinsky bowed awkwardly from the Hofoper stage.[1] Such accolades had been commonly accorded to composers like Johann Strauss jr. or Franz Lehár, darlings of Vienna's operetta world, or even occasionally to Johannes Brahms, particularly toward the end of his life, but ovations of this nature were something Zemlinsky had only experienced once before, at the premiere of *Sarema*. Coming off that opera's success, it appeared Zemlinsky had found his calling.

Brahms's death three years earlier had left Zemlinsky without vital support in the musical establishment, but Mahler quickly moved to fill the vacuum. Following the successful Munich debut of *Sarema*, Mahler, who was looking at a Hofoper diet comprising Mozart and Wagner, along with occasional productions of Tchaikovsky's *Eugene Onegin*, Thomas's *Mignon* and Smetana's *The Bartered Bride*, approached Zemlinsky about bringing *Sarema* back to Vienna.[2] While doubtless flattered at the prospects of having a work premiered under such auspicious circumstances, it appears that Zemlinsky sought to convince Mahler that he was capable of much better. Keenly aware of the success

---

[1] *Österreichische Volks-Presse* (Jan. 28, 1900), 9.
[2] Letter to E. Berté, *Sarema*'s publisher, in Weber (1971); cf. 89.

Engelbert Humperdink, Karl Goldmark and Hans Pfitzner had had with fairy tale operas, Zemlinsky too wished to try his hand at the genre and indeed had already sketched out some ideas. Mahler gave his consent, and in August of 1897 Zemlinsky set to work in earnest.

Zemlinsky turned to Holger Drachmann's *Der var engang*, a grand five-act national drama that had been played in Vienna in 1894. Drachmann's fairy tale pivots around a Princess for whom no courtier is good enough and a Prince who is determined to win her love. Tricked into marrying a gypsy (the Prince in disguise), the once haughty Princess is reduced to living in a forest hut and selling pots in the marketplace. Though initially contemptuousness of her new life, she gradually re-evaluates her world and her desires and develops a genuine affection for her husband and their simple life together. The fidelity of the former Princess is soon put to the test, but her love for the gypsy remains steadfast, even in the most tempting of circumstances. By the story's close, the Princess confesses to having found a love greater than even a Prince could provide. Her transformation complete, the gypsy-prince finally unveils his true, aristocratic identity.

At the end of June of 1898, Zemlinsky submitted an early draft of *Es war einmal*'s piano score to Mahler, but Mahler's initial impression was far from encouraging. There was no question that the younger man possessed a formidable talent and technique. Zemlinsky's characters possessed distinct musical profiles, and his language was efficient and refined, with rhythmic and melodic vitality that never overpowered the voice. It was the work's overly derivative nature that troubled Mahler. Some degree of outside influence could be expected, since building on the ideas of others was a natural part of the learning process and Zemlinsky had not yet turned thirty. Nevertheless, the manuscript Zemlinsky presented to Mahler was "so full of resemblances and plagiarisms" that its composer "must have a very bad memory to have failed to avoid them".[1] Mahler had put his finger on a critical issue: Zemlinsky had learned all that can be taught and had a complete grasp of the elements associated with orchestral and vocal writing. What he had yet to find was the one thing nobody could give him: a distinctive sound, a sonic fingerprint, the unexpected turn of a phrase that says "Schubert", or the unique orchestration that renders Mendelssohn or Shostakovich or Copland immediately recognizable. Zemlinsky would, of course, find his personal idiom, a voice distinctly his own, but that ownership was still years away. In the meantime he continued to rely heavily — far too

---

[1] La Grange (1996), 550.

heavily, Mahler thought—on the music of others to help lead the way. The critics would concur.

To his credit, Mahler was willing to have his misgivings allayed. Zemlinsky took Mahler up on his offer and played the opera through for him at the piano. Whether because of the conviction of Zemlinsky's own interpretation, the realization that the work did indeed have potential, or the reaffirmation of Zemlinsky's undeniable talent, the music director agreed to accept *Es war einmal* for performance. But the offer came with a caveat: the score would have to undergo significant modifications. For Zemlinsky, Mahler's proposal held two benefits: first, Mahler's experience with the demands of the theater would help transform Zemlinsky's efforts into an opera worthy of being offered up to Hofoper audiences and critics who had come to expect productions of the highest caliber; second, the project would again place Zemlinsky directly under the wing of one of Vienna's most influential and powerful musicians. Zemlinsky didn't have to think twice about the offer.

Mahler's own knowledge of the theater stemmed more from his dedication to the operas of others than to his own stage works. His only personal operatic attempts had occurred much earlier, and he had long since given up on the idea of composing opera. Years in the theater had taught him what was needed to bring a story—even a fairy tale—to life, and this was precisely the information and experience for which Zemlinsky thirsted. Under Mahler's direction, the entire opera—music and text—was overhauled, resulting in significant cuts, modifications and rewrites. Mahler's understanding of stagecraft—the complexities of which Zemlinsky was only beginning to learn—also resulted in a number of practical suggestions and revisions, such as lengthening the Interlude to Act I, which allowed greater time for a costume and scene change. In December of 1899, the full score was complete and the following month the curtain rose on *Es war einmal* for the first time.

The press was largely united in its approbation of the work. Albert Kauders of the *Neues Wiener Journal* was astonished by Zemlinsky's command of both the technical and practical elements of the production, and by his having attained such refined artistic ability so early in his career.[1] The *Neue Freie Presse*, the *Neues Wiener Tagblatt*, the *Deutsche Zeitung*, the *Reichswehr*, and the *Arbeiterzeitung* also carried favorable reviews.[2] Other critics, including the highly respected and highly feared Eduard Hanslick, were unanimous in their praise of Zemlinsky's talent but expressed concerns about what they perceived

[1] *Neues Wiener Journal* (Jan. 23, 1900).
[2] See Pass (1976), 86.

as an overt Wagnerian influence. Having spoken highly of Zemlinsky's brilliant technique, for example, Hanslick went on to write that because the "public and the critics have greeted the excellence of this novelty with such favorable approval, it could not harm anything at this stage to also make mention of one of its drawbacks . . . Must everything be so Wagnerian?"[1] The critic of the *Neue Musik-Zeitung*, also lamenting Wagner's influence, seconded Hanslick's view:

> This beginner appears to possess the experience of one at the close of his career and has learned a frightening amount. Because his dramatic sense is evident in every measure of the score . . . we believe in his future and await — not that he adds to his understanding but rather that he forgets some of it — thereby enriching German opera with his valuable and lasting gifts.[2]

The critic and composer Richard Heuberger, whose music Zemlinsky would soon know intimately, commented on Zemlinsky's natural "theatrical talent" and paid tribute to his virtuosic orchestral writing, his feel for the dramatic and his instinct for "illustration," yet he also drew attention to the overt Wagnerian influence.[3] And not unexpectedly, the anti-Semitic *Volks-Presse* confirmed Zemlinsky as a first-rate composer but stated that whatever music had not been influenced directly by *Meistersinger* was trite and uninteresting, and that the evening's real kudos had been earned by the Heldentenor Erik Schmedes. Criticism of this nature sparked Max Graf to attack his fellow writers, whom he believed were overly critical toward their fellow Viennese. Graf, who knew Zemlinsky from the Café Griensteidl, blasted his journalist-colleagues: "When I ask myself what astounds me most about my highly critical colleagues, it is this: the astonishingly certain judgment toward a new presence, which is always accompanied by doubts and scruples . . . The appearance of a young artist in the artistic history of a city and an era should instead be a day of celebration for the critic."[4]

Among the reviews of *Es war einmal*, one proved particularly prescient: the critic of the *Österreichische Volks-Presse* predicted that after five or six performances, *Es war einmal* would fall from the repertory. Zemlinsky may initially have shrugged the prediction off, since his opera went on to experience eleven

[1] Hanslick (1900), 44–46.

[2] Friedmann in Stephan (1978), 14.

[3] La Grange (1995), 222. By "illustration" Heuberger meant that Zemlinsky's music was too overt and that it would have been more convincing if the music had captured the characters' feelings and emotions rather than simply the dramatic action.

[4] Quoted in Ottner (1995), 226.

more Hofoper performances in the weeks that followed. It was an honorable run, especially for a new work by such a young composer, but the Hofoper performances were the last for many years. *Es war einmal* was not heard again until Arthur Bodanzky conducted it in Mannheim over a decade later, and then again when Zemlinsky conducted it in Prague on October 20, 1912. Thereafter, for seventy-five years, nothing more was heard of it.[1]

As one of Vienna's most celebrated musical talents, Zemlinsky now found himself a frequent guest of Vienna's cultural elite. His wit and charm invariably scored high marks with his hosts and fellow guests, and he could converse at length about literature, theater and, of course, music. Zemlinsky's literary interests ranged from Casanova to Edgar Allan Poe, but also included the recent German philosophers Schopenhauer and Nietzsche. He valued the classics but was equally drawn to modern literature; hence his familiarity with the works of Strindberg, Ibsen, Gorky and Zola.[2] Frequent attendance at the theater had also introduced him to the dramas of Tolstoy and Gerhart Hauptmann.

On February 26, 1900, Zemlinsky was invited to the home of Dr. Friedrich Spitzer, a chemist whose father had left him a wealthy man by way of a successful sugar factory. Alma Schindler was invited to the Spitzer residence as well, and it was here that Zemlinsky and Alma formally met for the first time. It seems unlikely the two had never previously crossed paths. Alma's artistic pedigree and reputed musical talent most certainly would have brought her into Zemlinsky's sphere, where at the very least her beauty would have caught Zemlinsky's eye. And we know from her diaries that Alma had attended the successful premiere of Zemlinsky's *Frühlingsbegräbnis*, the Brahms-inspired cantata he had conducted in the Great Hall of the Musikverein a few weeks earlier.[3] At the concert, Alma thought Zemlinsky's gestures on the podium comical and exaggerated.[4] In person, Alma found Zemlinsky much more to her liking.

[1] *Es war einmal* was first recorded in 1987 (Danish Radio) and revived for a 1991 production in Kiel.

[2] AZ/AMW. It was to the German writers that Zemlinsky most frequently looked to for librettos. Among those who Zemlinsky discussed in letters to Alma were Scheerbart, Keller and Bierbaum, the latter whose work Zemlinsky humorously wrote tasted "unmistakably like a [Bavarian] Spätbräu."

[3] The concert, which involved the Vienna Singverein and the Vienna Philharmonic, took place on February 11, 1900.

[4] Beaumont and Rode-Breymann (1999), 245. Alma's observations are interesting, particularly since on the podium Zemlinsky was afterwards known for avoiding theatrics. However, at such an early date his style was not yet honed.

For her part, Fraülein Schindler cut a striking figure. She was both beautiful and talented, and at the start of the century was among Vienna's most desirable women. The daughter of the well-known painter Emil Schindler, Alma's artistic bearing came naturally, but it was through her mother Anna's subsequent marriage to Carl Moll (Schindler's former assistant), a founding member of the Secession, that Alma gained entrance to Vienna's progressive artistic and cultural *milieu*. Gustav Klimt had already succumbed to her charms, but as Alma's interest in music grew, she increasingly sought the company of musicians. As one of Vienna's fastest rising stars, Zemlinsky was therefore a natural candidate for her attention.

Alma and Zemlinsky's conversation at the Spitzer home centered around Mahler, whom Alma longed to meet and to whom Zemlinsky was indebted. They raised a toast to the famous conductor who was to play an increasingly crucial role in each of their lives. When Alma then confessed *Tristan* to be her favorite among Wagner's operas, Zemlinsky "became entirely transformed" in Alma's eyes; "He grew truly handsome." Writing in her diary that night, Alma continued, "Now we understood each other. I find him quite wonderful."[1] So began Alma's infatuation with and repulsion to Zemlinsky, who from the beginning triggered an emotional tug-of-war within Alma, candidly laid out in her diary. And while Zemlinsky's charm and wit may have captivated her, it was undoubtedly his blossoming reputation in Vienna that sparked her initial attraction toward him.

Successive encounters came sparingly at first. Zemlinsky didn't rush matters, and the pair didn't meet up again until March 10, this time at the home of Hugo Conrat, honorary treasurer of the Tonkünstlerverein. Accustomed to being pursued more aggressively, Alma inquired why he appeared to take so little interest in her. Zemlinsky responded that he found her insufferably flirtatious, and indeed that very evening she also shared her affections with Fernand Khnopff, the Belgian painter in whose honor the party was given, along with several others. On the other hand, Zemlinsky confessed that a song she had submitted to him earlier for his examination had pleased him greatly and revealed she had obvious talent, and that he wished to dedicate a collection of his songs to her.[2] Whatever designs Zemlinsky may have had for distancing himself from Alma physically, she clearly had not escaped his thoughts.

Still, Alma's coquettishness was a quality Zemlinsky could not suffer, and

---

[1] Beaumont and Rode-Breymann (1999), 254.

[2] The collection *Irmelin Rose und andere Gesänge* appeared in print the following year with Alma as dedicatee.

he described their distinct temperaments in operatic terms — his of the more tragic sort, hers revolving around balls and brilliant parties.[1] The depiction was intentionally melodramatic — his life had, up until then, been anything but tragic. And though he may not have shared her love of social gatherings, he was no recluse; he could be found in upscale society one night, in the company of friends at cafés and taverns the next, and his strong affinity for the opposite sex had evidently led to a number of escapades. Vying for Alma's affections, however, particularly in settings where she invariably became the center of attention, held little attraction for him. On the contrary, it was a source of frustration that plagued Zemlinsky throughout their courtship but which he was powerless to change.

For Alma, Zemlinsky's physical appearance was a major stumbling block in their relationship, though such sentiments were fortunately confined to her diary. Following their March 10 rendezvous, for instance, Alma admitted that his candidness and generosity had made a strong impression, as had his looks: "He's a dear fellow, and I do like him so. — He's as ugly as sin!"[2] Zemlinsky was fully cognizant of the physical gulf that separated them, but to his credit was willing to acknowledge it to her: "I am terribly ugly, I have no money, perhaps also no talent, and on top of that I am horribly dumb." Later, again in reference to himself, he wrote, "You are ugly, too small."[3] But he wasn't always so dour. Alma's beauty may have cast Zemlinsky's physical imperfections in high relief, but to his credit he could also treat the matter with good humor. In a letter to Alma, Zemlinsky wrote mockingly, "You must have received my unattractive photograph", and elsewhere related having been to the theater where he saw an actor even more ugly than himself. Zemlinsky also discussed his personal habits with similar candor. He was a confirmed smoker and excused himself for not laundering his clothes more regularly, owing to not having "as much money as Wagner". Nowhere was his wit and humor more apparent than when he, tongue in cheek, graded his own imperfections for her:

> Until recently I believed that it was because of my BEAUTY that I created such an impression! But you people have destroyed my illusion! Now I look at myself more exactly: small, lean (already completely insufficient): 7. Face, nose: everything on my face is impossible: same grade. Hair too long, but that can be helped. To be prudent I took an even closer look at myself in the bath (pardon!!). No protuberances nor deformities,

[1] AZ/AMW.

[2] Beaumont and Rode-Breymann (1999), 258–59.

[3] Ibid.

muscles not too weak . . . surprisingly well developed! Otherwise, everything else has been accounted for. In summary: abominable!!

Inner form: spirited, mischievous, incalculable, moody, with a penchant for roguishness; also perhaps too perverse to be a soldier but too
little to be Wagner, Goethe or, say, Dr. Muhr.[1] Therefore, insufficient: 5 . . .[2]

Zemlinsky's personal charisma and energy made an equally strong impression on Alma and others of his circle. Egon Wellesz, Schoenberg's first
biographer, later recalled that Zemlinsky "radiated an air of great fascination.
His speech was highly animated, if also cynical",[3] which Wellesz humorously
attributed to Zemlinsky's years of having conducted operetta. And Hans Heinsheimer, an employee of Universal Edition, not only remembered Zemlinsky's
"ill-fitting tuxedo, the severe glasses on his nose, his tousled hair," but also the
"deep intensity one could read in his eyes and his gestures".[4] It is precisely such
qualities that stand fully revealed in various photographs for which he posed.
His seriousness and intelligence are already evident in photos of him as a young
man. If not particularly handsome, his boyish face nevertheless projects an alluring air of confidence. Over the years, his photographs reveal how age, work
and frequent disappointment took their toll, but his intensity remains vividly
apparent. To Alma, Zemlinsky stated that he preferred not to be photographed,
believing such things "were for beautiful people",[5] but the wealth of photographs for which he posed during his lifetime suggests otherwise; whatever
misgivings Zemlinsky may have had about his appearance, he seemed able to
overlook them. In vain he desired Alma to do the same.

Throughout their courtship, which continued through December of the
following year, Alma's feelings toward Zemlinsky fluctuated wildly. Even her
physical descriptions of him were extreme. One moment she saw Zemlinsky as
"a caricature — chinless, small, with bulging eyes . . ."[6] and the next found "him
neither hideous nor grotesque, for his eyes sparkle with intelligence — and such

[1] Felix Muhr, an architect whom Zemlinsky knew was vying for Alma's affections.

[2] AZ/AMW.

[3] Wellesz and Wellesz (1981), 36.

[4] Heinsheimer (1987), 9.

[5] AZ/AMW.

[6] Beaumont and Rode-Breymann (1999), 245. Many years later, just before the Zemlinskys' emigration to America, the writer Elias Canetti was still obsessing with Zemlinsky's chin:
"black birdlike head, jutting triangular nose, no chin . . . Every time I saw him I looked for his
chin. When he appeared in the doorway, I gave a little start and began to search. Will he have
one this time? He never did, but even without a chin he led a full life." Canetti (1999), 796.

a person is never ugly."[1] Years later her recollections remained very mixed: "He was a hideous gnome. Short, chinless, toothless, always with the coffee-house smell on him, unwashed — and yet the keenness and strength of his mind made him tremendously attractive to me."[2] The physical disparity of their appearances created great tension for her, which was further exacerbated by the opinions and influence of those around her. Alma's mother, in particular, exerted an especially strong influence on her impressionable daughter, and saw no reason for Alma to settle for someone of Zemlinsky's looks and station.

Regardless of Alma's reservations, by the end of March 1900 she was regularly exchanging letters with Zemlinsky and meeting him frequently. And despite having been a composition pupil of Joseph Labor since the age of 14, Alma was by then also submitting her work to Zemlinsky, the lessons providing ample opportunity to further their relationship. Friction then arose following an April 19 concert, at which Zemlinsky led a performance of Joseph Suk's Serenade for String Orchestra. Zemlinsky had sent Alma tickets for the concert, and there she recognized Melanie Guttmann, his girlfriend from his Conservatory years, sitting behind her. Following the concert, a jealous Alma confronted Zemlinsky about his relationship with Miss Guttmann, believing the two to be engaged, which Zemlinsky promptly denied. He then promised to visit Alma the following Monday. Zemlinsky kept his word, and on Monday morning the two even discussed some of her songs, but the events of the previous week were not smoothed over for some time.

At the start of May, Alma and Zemlinsky were both present at a number of concerts, but Zemlinsky remained distant. No effort was made to remedy the situation until they met again at the Conrats' home on May 12, where Karl Kraus, the eminent journalist and founder of Die Fackel, was a guest. As the evening progressed, Alma inquired of Zemlinsky why matters had become so strained. Zemlinsky expressed annoyance with her half-hearted musical endeavors and her lack of passion toward him. The episode concerning Melanie Guttmann was not expressly discussed, but when asked what she wanted from their relationship, Alma replied "a nice, innocent relationship, as it used to be". The conversation ended abruptly when Zemlinsky retorted that such a "friendship as between a brother and sister — that's not always possible".[3] Following the meal, Zemlinsky and Kraus escorted Alma home together.

Of one thing Alma was sure — she wanted Zemlinsky as her teacher, certain

---

[1] Beaumont and Rode-Breymann (1999), 332.
[2] Mahler-Werfel (1958), 13.
[3] Beaumont and Rode-Breymann (1999), 284.

that his guidance would prove invaluable. Curiously, she had reservations about his music. Having finally attended a performance of *Es war einmal*, she enjoyed much of it, but sided with the critics in finding the Wagnerian influence too overt. Significantly, her reserved feelings toward Zemlinsky, at least in the early stages of their relationship, were intricately bound up with her opinion of his music. In response, he angrily accused her of not trusting him as an artist or a man,[1] and although she eventually came to appreciate both, she was never completely won over by either. As her amorous feelings continued to waver over the next year and a half, her vacillating emotions brought Zemlinsky to the edge of despair. She envied Zemlinsky his talent, present success, and total commitment to his art, yet she remained plagued by doubts about whether he could satisfy her completely.

Zemlinsky's feelings toward Alma gradually intensified, as did the irritation brought about by Alma's flirtatious nature. He watched in exasperation as a steady stream of suitors called upon her almost daily. In the months that followed, Zemlinsky constantly begged Alma to look beyond his physical appearance and recognize his love and devotion. His letters display a mixture of frustration, desire and need, particularly when Alma pulled back, and he wrote that he would do anything for her. On a number of occasions he found himself waiting endlessly to hear from her and though he could not bear the thought of a future without her, at times he was sure matters would never work out. In his most insecure hours Zemlinsky responded angrily, confused as to why she did not write him more frequently. Over the course of time, however, he gained control and perspective. He temporarily mastered his jealousy and was able to look beyond her beauty into her innermost soul, an ability she was never able to return. His fantasies ranged from physical desire to the two building a life together. Years later Zemlinsky would recall his time with Alma as "the best, most beautiful hours of my existence."[2] Yet, many of his letters from the time reveal his frustration, both emotionally and sexually, and they are filled with the pain, doubt and disappointment he suffered at her hands. On the whole, Alma's role in Zemlinsky's life was something akin to idol worship; while she served to inspire him, she nevertheless consistently eluded him physically and emotionally.

Zemlinsky and his family were by now living at Obere Weissgerberstrasse 12, in Vienna's third district just beyond the Danube canal, but still an easy walk to the Leopoldstadt of his youth. Zemlinsky's study was adorned with a bust of Brahms and pictures of Brahms and Wagner, the latter a gift from Alma;

[1] AZ/AMW.
[2] Ibid.

a portrait of Alma, another gift, stood on his writing table. On June 29, 1900, Alma called upon him at the Weissgerberstrasse address, having come to deliver some music after visiting her father's grave at the Central Cemetery. Melanie Guttmann, who had remained a close friend of Zemlinsky's family, met Alma at the door. Melanie informed Alma that Zemlinsky's father, ill with kidney stones, had died early that morning after an agonizing, all-night struggle.

Zemlinsky's mother Clara was now a 52-year-old widow. Adolf's death immediately and forever altered the course of Zemlinsky's professional life. Before his father's death, Zemlinsky had taken whatever work came his way, be it as a teacher or an accompanist, while still having ample time for composition. Afterwards, he was compelled to support his family and seek immediate employment that would provide a steady and substantial income. Finding time for composing became a luxury he could scarcely afford.

A dutiful son, cognizant of his mother's hardships, Zemlinsky remained close to his mother until her death twelve years later. In the years following his father's death, he assiduously avoided sending her news about his struggles whenever he felt such information would upset her. But struggle he did.

Zemlinsky's circumstances soon brought him to the doors of the Carltheater. Situated in Leopoldstadt's Praterstrasse, the theater stood a short distance from the apartment of Zemlinsky's birth and conveniently close to his family's apartment in the Weissgerberstrasse. Originally named the Leopoldstädter Theater, the Carltheater claimed a rich history. Its tenants had once included Beethoven, who lived in the building from 1803 to 1805 while composing his opera *Fidelio*, and the grandparents of the writer Arthur Schnitzler. Constructed on the site of a Baroque theater that in the early 1800s "enjoyed the reputation of being a meeting-place for whores",[1] the theater was leveled and rebuilt in 1847 by Eduard van der Null, one of the Hofoper's chief architects.[2] The famed Austrian playwright Johann Nepomuk Nestroy served as the theater's director from 1854 to 1860, and in 1883 Gustav Mahler was employed as conductor for two months before moving on to the opera house in Kassel, Germany. Some six years after Mahler left, the Carltheater experienced a renaissance, touched off by a performance of *Wiener Blut*, written by Johann Strauss, who had died just months earlier.

[1] Stuckenschmidt (1977), 50.

[2] Although it became one of the city's most beloved structures, the initial designs for the Hofoper drew such harsh criticism that Van der Null hanged himself before the Hofoper was even completed.

Tragedy struck the theater in February of 1900, when its director, Franz von Jauner, committed suicide. Jauner had overseen a successful string of performances but had mismanaged the books and, with the coffer literally bare, took his own life. On March 11, 1900, the Carltheater shut down with the 100th, farewell performance of Sidney Jones's *The Geisha*. But the theater reopened in September with a new director, a new administration and a new series of performances.

It was under these circumstances that Zemlinsky paid a visit to Leopold Müller, the theater's recently appointed administrative director. Keenly aware of Zemlinsky's reputation, Müller was unconcerned with Zemlinsky's lack of practical experience as a conductor — he knew that natural talent was Zemlinsky's most precious commodity and believed that time would take care of the rest. Müller also had the gift of persuasion and characterized the theater and its productions in such glowing terms that young musicians at the start of their career were soon tantalized by the prospects of conducting there. According to the critic Ernst Rychnovsky, the up-and-coming musicians were subjected to Müller's hard sell approach and pressure "until they no longer knew *what* they should be conducting but rather *that* they should be conducting, and after an hour [with Müller] the ominous contracts with the opera conductors were signed".[1] Müller's tactics were no different with Zemlinsky. Müller persisted and Zemlinsky, despite his initial hesitation, consented.

As Chief Conductor of the Carltheater, Zemlinsky inherited responsibilities that required him to abandon life as a free-lance composer. Whatever concerns he may have had about doing so proved well founded — the Carltheater position marked the first of a long line of conducting engagements that significantly reduced his time for composition. But the reality was that Zemlinsky now had his family to support. As he explained to Mahler, he accepted the offer not simply because he felt he had a talent for theater work but because doing so would "also enable me to rely on an income far more secure than that which can be had from giving lessons".[2]

Conducting operetta was neither the career Zemlinsky had envisioned for himself nor one that would long satisfy his serious aspirations as a musician. But, while work at the Carltheater ultimately failed to deliver true musical gratification, it was an excellent training ground and provided the young Zemlinsky with an invaluable opportunity to hone his conducting skills and refine his rehearsal technique. It also helped him develop relationships with a large number of musicians and singers. Additionally, the education he acquired of

[1] Rychnovsky in Curjel (1975), 208.
[2] Letter to Mahler (March 8, 1902), Austrian State Archives, in Clayton (1982), 120.

stagecraft and direction helped round out his overall knowledge on the podium, bolstering his growing reputation as a music director to be reckoned with. Increased visibility and a comfortable income also allowed Zemlinsky the luxury to be discriminating in whom he accepted as students, including Karl Weigl, Arthur Bodanzky — and of course Alma Schindler. Despite this, the obligation Zemlinsky felt toward teaching the next generation was honored for the next thirty-three years, until the Nazi threat forced him to resign from his last formal teaching post. During this time, Zemlinsky also continued to teach and practice piano, which also cut into his increasingly limited personal time. Years later Schoenberg recalled how Zemlinsky had, through necessity, become a model of efficiency:

> He had a peculiar method of using his time rationally, since he was forced to give many piano lessons in order to earn a living. He would alternately compose and practice the piano. Writing in ink one page of music, he had to wait for the page to dry. This interval of time only could he spare for practice. A busy life![1]

In the summer of 1900, having secured work for the coming season, Zemlinsky left Vienna for Seeboden in Carinthia and Rodaun near the Vienna Woods, where nearby lakes and woods satisfied his passions for swimming and hiking. Aware that in September, when he would start conducting at the Carltheater, his lifestyle would be radically altered, Zemlinsky understood that these precious weeks could well be the last he would experience without the burden of professional concerns. Whether Alma was in Zemlinsky's thoughts during those summer months is not known, but his father's death surely weighed on his mind. And so, as had been the case with Brahms's death several years earlier, Zemlinsky turned to music for chorus and orchestra as a means of grieving.

After considering various biblical texts Zemlinsky settled on the tempestuous Psalm 83, *A Prayer for Help against Enemies of the People*, whereby the people of Israel beg God to strike down their enemy:

> O God, do not be silent; do not hold aloof; do not be quiet, Oh God!
> For Your enemies rage, Your foes assert themselves.
> They plot craftily against Your people,
> take counsel against Your treasured ones . . .
> Pursue them with Your tempest, terrify them with Your storm . . .
> May they be frustrated and terrified, disgraced and doomed forever.[2]

---

[1] Schoenberg (1984), 55.
[2] Tanakh (1985), 1207–8.

No letters survive attesting to what the loss of Zemlinsky's father meant to him, but his choice of text reflects the pain and anger he experienced. Throughout the years, Adolf had steadfastly supported Zemlinsky in his musical ambitions. Then, just months before his son ascended the podium for the first time as a professional conductor, he died. Adolf's death was agonizing and tortuous. Appropriately, the text and character of Zemlinsky's requiem was equally anguished.

The music begins peacefully enough, the contrapuntal writing recalling the rich polyphony of Brahms and an earlier era. In the Psalm's opening bars, the principal motive, whose importance Zemlinsky establishes over time, is presented as a brief but poignant fugato in the strings, and immediately juxtaposed with a choral passage in the winds, ushering in an air of joyousness. With two distinct characters now established, the violins begin rocking plaintively between major and minor, foreshadowing the struggle to come. God's awesome power is then reflected in a canonic passage set atop tremolo strings, bringing to a close the orchestral introduction.

The soprano soloist and chorus now enter, imploring God to come to their aid, and in a bit of word play, Zemlinsky sets the text "They plot craftily against Your people . . ." to a brief fugato. An orchestral storm is now unleashed, whirling sand and fire, marked *schnell und stürmisch im Ausdruck* (fast and stormy in expression). An aggressive ostinato figure in the lower strings pierces the choral fabric, as outbursts of fragmented motives are shot through with violins, flutes, piccolos and trumpets, each entering and receding with the suddenness of lightning. Then, abruptly, the chaos of the tempest is cut short and replaced by a grand fugue, uniting the entire orchestra and chorus in a glorious conclusion set to the words, "May they know that Your name, Yours alone, is the Lord supreme over all the earth."

Zemlinsky finished work on Psalm 83 on September 10, 1900. The summer had been emotional but also productive. His time away had provided Zemlinsky with the solace, diversion, reflection and time to come to terms with his loss. A critical chapter of his life was now behind him and he readied himself for what lay ahead at the Carltheater — a prelude to what was to come.

In September 1900 Zemlinsky stepped in front of the Carltheater orchestra for the first time to begin rehearsals for the theater's reopening performance, the premiere of Edmond Audran's *Le Grand Mogol*, scheduled for September 29. Performances of Audran's operetta occupied Zemlinsky until the middle of October, when rehearsals began for the house's next production, Sidney Jones's *San Toy, oder Des Kaisers Garde*. Riding the wave of success of *The Geisha*, Jones had crafted another "oriental" operetta that proved nearly as successful.

It would experience a Carltheater run of sixty performances, fifty-eight of which Zemlinsky would himself conduct.

Zemlinsky could hardly have experienced a more exhausting introduction to theater life. Alma, whose diary entries and letters reveal she was receiving lessons from both Labor and Zemlinsky, felt the consequences of Zemlinsky's demanding schedule, for he was frequently unable to keep his appointments with her. Their relationship had picked up precisely where it left off. On October 22 Alma noted in her diary, "Zemlinsky didn't come. I'm absolutely furious with him. What kind of behavior is that? I shan't write to him any more."[1] Nine days later Zemlinsky again failed to show for her lesson. Work at the theater had kept him tied up at the theater from nine until six, and Alma found herself "waiting for Zemlinsky, in vain of course!"[2] By the first week of November she had become so vexed by Zemlinsky's lack of consideration and interest in her and her studies that she considered saying goodbye for good. However, a week later he arrived as scheduled and, despite having found little respite from his theater duties, officially proclaimed himself her teacher.

As Alma's tutor, Zemlinsky was critical of her technique and musical knowledge — her counterpoint exercises revealed to him how little she had learned from Labor in her six years of studies[3] — although he was complimentary about her talent. Zemlinsky schooled Alma in basic harmony, motivic development and the construction of formal procedures, exactly those elements that had been drilled into him as a student of the Conservatory. His own training was also reflected in his criticism of her themes, which he felt needed to project stronger contrast, not simply to produce a clearer delineation but also to provide adequate material for subsequent development. Suggesting that she use Beethoven as a role model, Zemlinsky demanded greater energy and power from her melodies, condemning her penchant for socializing for the effect it had on her music-making: "Don't always whisper; it's always like chocolate, dried fruit, and white dresses at soup time, society queen!"[4] He was also adamant that she not ignore her piano studies and strongly advocated practicing scales and etudes, stressing that "playing the piano well has its merits".[5] Still, Zemlinsky remained highly critical of Alma's lax work ethic and her social superficiality, and as late as

---

[1] Beaumont and Rode-Breymann (1999), 333.

[2] Ibid., 337.

[3] Alma's lessons with Labor nonetheless continued until October of 1901, at which time Labor demanded she choose between the two. See Beaumont and Rode-Breymann (1999), 436–37.

[4] AZ/AMW.

[5] Ibid.

March of 1901 bitingly demanded she make a choice: "Either compose or socialize — one or the other. If I were you, I'd stick to what you do best — socialize."[1]

By November's end, Zemlinsky had led twenty-one performances of Jones's operetta, and in December he tacked on twenty-eight more. After a New Year's Day repose, he returned to the Carltheater podium for eight additional performances, and on January 4, 1901, Zemlinsky ushered in the premiere of Eduard Gärtner's *Die verwunschene Prinzessin*, which he had also orchestrated. The time and energy devoted to the Carltheater was bearing fruit, evidenced by the laurel wreaths strewn about his apartment, gifts of an appreciative Viennese public. And though much of Zemlinsky's time was usurped by theater demands, he could occasionally be found having dinner with friends at the Hotel Sacher or enjoying a game of cards or Tarock, and the opportunity to play four-hand piano music was known to keep him up until three or four o'clock in the morning.

Although Alma felt Zemlinsky was frustrating and confrontational, she was becoming comfortable in his presence and increasingly found him sensible and entertaining. The pair shared a passion for Wagner and on March 12 attended a performance of Wagner's *Tristan* together. At some point that evening Zemlinsky casually remarked that he was planning a visit to Breslau, where a post was expected to become open in the coming year. Zemlinsky may have shared the news with Alma to hear her thoughts, though in truth he feared that an extended absence from Vienna could prove detrimental to his career there. In a letter to Gustav Mahler, he confessed it "difficult for me to leave Vienna, where I have after all acquired a certain reputation, particularly through your kind interest in my opera [*Es war einmal*]. Three years would obliterate me completely from the memories of influential people."[2] Zemlinsky may have also wanted to see Alma's reaction because he feared that she too would forget him. Although work in Breslau never materialized, the mere possibility of Zemlinsky's leaving spiked Alma's interest. Like many beautiful women, Alma shamelessly demanded that her suitors come to her, and with Zemlinsky it was no different. Whether for a lesson or a rendezvous, it was Zemlinsky who was made to feel guilty if he failed to keep an appointment, not Alma. Her diary entries portray her careless take-him-or-leave-him attitude, as the moment dictated. But now Zemlinsky was threatening to leave when she most wanted his attention and guidance. Alma had once confessed to having moral reservations about becoming emotionally involved with her teacher, but such ethical concerns were now

[1] Beaumont and Rode-Breymann (1999), 380.
[2] Letter to Mahler (March 8, 1902), Austrian State Archives, in Clayton (1982), p. 120 a.

hastily abandoned. Zemlinsky was not immune to the lure of Alma's newfound ardor, which quickly rekindled Zemlinsky's doomed hopes for a future together.

During one of his visits to Alma's home that March, Zemlinsky excitedly shared with her news about *Der Triumph der Zeit* (The Triumph of Time), a mime-drama by Hugo von Hofmannsthal that currently absorbed him. Having conceived of the work as a ballet to celebrate the new century, Hofmannsthal offered the work to Zemlinsky after Richard Strauss respectfully declined, on the grounds that he already had a ballet subject in mind that he planned to take up "as soon as a small opera [*Feuersnot*] is finished."[1] Strauss, with a wealth of experience behind him, may also have glimpsed the difficulties, if not impossibilities, of bringing Hofmannsthal's drama to fruition. But unlike Strauss, Zemlinsky was in no position to pass up an offer of collaboration with a writer of Hofmannsthal's stature, and if Zemlinsky perceived the dramatic problems that lay ahead — Hofmannsthal wanted the ballet completed by autumn — he nevertheless believed that somehow he could find a way to make it work.

Zemlinsky remained consumed with other theater activities, teaching, and a number of additional orchestration projects beyond those required of the theater. Any remaining time was spent on his compositions. At the request of the newly founded Universal Edition (UE), which would become one of Europe's most prestigious publishing houses and the exclusive publisher of Zemlinsky's music during his lifetime, he prepared many piano reductions to help satisfy the growing demand for accessible versions of operas, symphonies and the like for amateur performances at home. His reductions included four-hand arrangements of operas such as Beethoven's *Fidelio*, Mozart's *Die Zauberflöte*, Lehár's *Die lustige Witwe*, choral works including Haydn's *Die Schöpfung* and Mendelssohn's *Elijah*, and two-hand versions of Lortzing's operettas *Zar und Zimmermann* and *Der Waffenschmied*. Among Zemlinsky's most significant and successful projects during this period was his orchestration of Richard Heuberger's *Der Opernball*, which Zemlinsky premiered at the Carltheater in 1901. Heuberger's work, described by one critic as "no ordinary sparkling wine, rather, a fiery, bubbly champagne",[2] took Vienna by storm, but it was Zemlinsky's

---

[1] Strauss and Strauss (1952), 15.

[2] Traubner (1983), 147. Heuberger's *Opernball* became so strongly associated with the Viennese consciousness that the double agent Colonel Alfred Redl used it before the First World War as a code name through which he received information from Russian informants. Redl's involvement in a homosexual affair was discovered by the Russian secret service, and he was blackmailed into confessing names of Austrian spies located within Russia. Austrian officers subsequently observed him collecting payments for his betrayal, and after a full confession Redl killed himself with a loaded revolver with which the officers had presented him. An

exceptional orchestration that contributed to much of the operetta's brilliance. As the journalist Karl Kraus pointed out, "it was not the composer who gave the 'Opernball' its intriguing orchestral hue but A. v. Zemlinsky, who has orchestrated the largest part of the operetta".[1]

Still, busy though he was, Zemlinsky made time for Alma. On April 10, 1901, following a lesson during the height of the Viennese spring, Zemlinsky and Alma abandoned the teacher-student pretense:

> He kissed my hands, bent his head over them. I laid my head on his. We kissed each other on the cheek, held each other for an eternity. I took his head in my hands, and we kissed each other on the mouth, so hard that our teeth ached . . .[2]

Scenes of a similar nature continued over the next few weeks, yet conflicts continued to arise. Zemlinsky's perception of Alma's coquettishness was not helped by the two marriage proposals she received the last week of March. And Alma's conflicted feelings toward Zemlinsky, evident from the start of their relationship, never subsided, reflecting the immaturity of her professed love. On April 18 she admitted in her diary that she loved him fervently and no longer found him unattractive, yet acknowledged that his feelings were stronger than her own.[3] The following day she wrote that the ecstasy of the previous week had already dissipated, and within two more days her emotions had turned colder than ever. Her description of the two of them standing at the altar hardly seems penned by the same person who just days earlier felt so in love:

> I pictured to myself: if I were to stand at the altar with Z. — how ridiculous it would look . . . he so ugly, so small — me so beautiful, so tall. I can summon up no feelings of love for him, no matter how hard I try. I want to love him, but I believe, as far as I'm concerned, it's already over. Should I go on deceiving him or — tell him the truth?[4]

But their relationship was far from over. By the month's end Alma was fantasizing about marriage. As before, her passion was fueled by the thought of separation, although this time it was not Zemlinsky's leaving that sparked her desire but her own. On May 18, Alma's family would leave for St. Gilgen for the

attempt to hush up the incident failed, setting off an international scandal. See Hoffman (1988), 154–55.

[1] Kraus (1901), 27.
[2] Beaumont and Rode-Breymann (1999), 395
[3] Ibid., 397–98.
[4] Ibid., 399.

summer holiday. Zemlinsky, too, felt anxious about their separation, and shortly before Alma's departure he described how he waited endlessly for a few words from her, nervously pacing and kissing her photograph. All attempts to compose were in vain; he was too distracted by the thought of her impending absence, believing she would soon forget him for other men. As feared, separation provided the physical distance Alma needed to reflect objectively on the situation. Despite her vacillating emotions, she remained painfully aware of the gulf that prevented her from losing herself in Zemlinsky completely. Her strong sense of devotion toward her musical mentor remained, but she simply could not reconcile herself to his looks or her own fickleness. "I have only half a soul — he has only half a body. One of us should have been born complete",[1] she wrote, and shortly thereafter summed up the situation completely: "my body is ten times too beautiful for his . . . his soul is one hundred times too beautiful for mine".[2]

In St. Gilgen, Alma's family also began to work on her, offering up advice and warning of the realities of the situation. Those around her were well aware that Alma's relationship with Zemlinsky had progressed far beyond that of teacher and student. The overriding sentiment, of course, was that Zemlinsky was not a suitable fit, and what he did have to offer needed to be carefully weighed. Her family regarded Zemlinsky's Jewish heritage as further reason to terminate the relationship, which only exacerbated Alma's hidden repulsion for Jews. Alma's anti-Semitism had already surfaced in her diary the previous March. At the conclusion of a lieder recital at which Zemlinsky had played piano,[3] and where both Alma and Melanie Guttmann had been present, Alma had left annoyed that Zemlinsky had not greeted her afterwards. Back within the walls of her family home she opened her diary and noted, "Jewish sneak, keep your hook-nosed Jew-girl. She's just right for you."[4] Now, during the summer of 1901, she regarded having children with him as giving birth to "little, degenerate Jew-kids".[5] Learning of Zemlinsky's intentions to convert merely

---

[1] Ibid., 400–401.

[2] Ibid., 404.

[3] The concert included a performance of *Irmelin Rose*, which Zemlinsky had dedicated to Alma.

[4] Beaumont and Rode-Breymann (1999), 381.

[5] Ibid., 421. According to Jewish law, lineage is passed on maternally, and thus any children the two may have had would not have been Jewish by birth. This aside, Alma's anti-Semitism was by no means directed solely toward Zemlinsky but rather at any number of individuals with whom she had contact, be they suitors or dinner hosts. Considering her views, her subsequent marriages to Gustav Mahler and Franz Werfel, both of Jewish birth, seem all the more remarkable.

convinced her that he was "one of those little half-Jews who never succeed in freeing themselves from their roots".[1]

Zemlinsky, of course, remained ignorant of Alma's anti-Semitism, her cruel attitudes about his repulsive (to her) physical shortcomings, and anything else she found intolerable. Yet many of his letters during this period reflect his growing passion and his growing frustration with her endless doubts and constant changes of heart. In his darkest moments he questioned the depth of her love, unable to fathom how her feelings could swing from hot to cold so quickly. Aware of Alma's desire to marry a man with money or of noble birth, he was forced to accept that his love would never be enough. In an effort better to express his state of mind, Zemlinsky sent her a poem by Theodor Storm:

A Beggar's Love

Oh let me remain at a distance,
standing silently in your gaze;
You are so young, you are so beautiful,
your eyes laughingly radiate joy.

And I so poor, have grown so tired,
I have nothing to win your heart;
Oh, if I were only a king's son,
and you a poor, lost child![2]

Not all of Zemlinsky's letters to Alma that summer projected such a somber tone. At times he joyfully fantasized about spending his life with her; at other moments he provoked her with stories of time spent boating on the Danube, bicycling, and playing tennis with other women. He had, for example, enjoyed the companionship of Sofie Rakanow, a singer at the Carltheater. Sophie may have provided Zemlinsky with sexual fulfillment, serving as an outlet for his frustrated physical relationship with Alma that had yet to progress beyond a series of passionate kisses.

With the Carltheater dedicated to spoken theater during the summer months, Zemlinsky turned to his own music, while evenings were spent free of his baton and concert attire. His routine, which he sketched out for Alma, typically started with a leisurely breakfast at 8:30, followed by work and correspondence until 11:30. Noontime meant a walk in the Prater and then rest until 2:30 or 3:00, after which Zemlinsky practiced and composed until 6 pm.

[1] Ibid., 402–3.
[2] *Bettlerliebe*, in Storm (1889), 240.

In the evening he either attended the "unrivaled" theatrical performances at the Carltheater or, when the theater offered little appeal, returned to the Prater for dinner. Zemlinsky was particularly fond of areas of the Prater, which, by virtue of their country-like ambience, nearly made him forget he was still in the city.

Zemlinsky continued work on his ballet *Der Triumph der Zeit* during the first half of the summer of 1901 and kept Alma up to date on his progress. He even inserted a motif composed for Alma, recognizable only by the two of them. But in May Zemlinsky turned his attention to a mime-drama with piano accompaniment, a work entitled *Ein Lichtstrahl* (A Ray of Light). The music had been commissioned by Ernst von Wolzogen, impresario of the Überbrettl cabaret,[1] a Berlin theater troupe then in residence at the Carltheater. Considering the complicated nature of Hofmannsthal's ballet, *Ein Lichtstrahl*'s uncomplicated vaudevillian subject matter — a man, a woman and a seducing tailor — was easily brought to life by Zemlinsky. Indeed, the music, though hardly representative of Zemlinsky's impressive caliber, took but eight days to compose. Around the same time, Zemlinsky was apparently composing another theater piece for the cabaret, entitled *Die Juli-Hexen* (July Spells), based on a text by Otto Bierbaum, but unfortunately, it has not survived.[2]

In July, work on *Der Triumph der Zeit* ground to a halt. Not so long before, Zemlinsky's prestigious collaboration with one of Austria's foremost writers had seemed so promising, but just as with Alma, Zemlinsky was either blind to the insurmountable difficulties or believed they could be overcome with sufficient skill, effort and persistence. The ballet's primary difficulty lay in its complex plot, which involved a significant use of allegory and metaphor. Influenced by the symbolist poetry of Maurice Maeterlinck, Hofmannsthal called for Cupid, fauns and allegorical Hours and Minutes to preside over Humanity when not slumbering and dreaming in the fields of Parnassus — indeed, it may have been *Der Triumph der Zeit*'s overburdened complexity and unwieldy storyline that initially convinced Richard Strauss to pass on the project. Completed portions of the score reveal passionate melodies and a virtuosic handling of the

[1] The name Überbrettl reflected Wolzogen's hope of creating an institution that would rise above or beyond (*über*) what he regarded as the rather dubious quality of the Parisian-style caberets, known colloquially in Germany as boards (*Brettl*). The cabaret also went by the name of Buntes Theater.

[2] Zemlinsky mentions *Die Juli-Hexen* in a letter to Schoenberg. See Weber (1995), 4. Two songs, *In der Sonnengasse* and *Herr Bombardil*, may also have been composed for Wolzogen, though they date from the previous January. In a letter that summer to Alma, Zemlinsky also alludes to another song, *Eine ganz neu Schelmweys*, perhaps again written for Wolzogen. The song, however, is also lost.

orchestra, and provide a glimpse of Zemlinsky's elated mood as he composed, at least partly explainable by his feelings for Alma when their relationship was most promising. As a ballet, however, it simply did not work.

Years later Zemlinsky would write to Alma that his recollection of the ballet's opening bars continued to evoke "the sunny mood of those days! Other than that it contains no more worth for me."[1] Nevertheless, having invested far too much time, energy and emotion into the project to simply abandon it wholesale, Zemlinsky salvaged what he deemed the strongest portions of the work. The result, a virtuosic and shimmering orchestral suite entitled Drei Balletstücke, rose from the ashes of *Der Triumph der Zeit* at the start of 1902. *Reigen* (Round Dance), with its ground bass pedal, rippling flute lines, and delicate violin murmurs, captures the grandeur of Parnassus; the *Fauntanz* (Dance of the Fauns) displays Zemlinsky's ability to fully capture both the fantastic and the ancient; and, in a humorous syncopated $\frac{6}{8}$ dance marked *Sehr schnell*, the Hours are juxtaposed with a grandiose brass motive depicting Humanity's lofty gates. Zemlinsky's transformed score dances effortlessly between moods both wistful and frenetic, with a Strauss-inspired coda bringing the work to a brilliant conclusion. The Balletstücke received a successful premiere in February 1903,[2] with Zemlinsky on the podium and Gustav Mahler and Alma in attendance, but subsequent hopes that Strauss might perform the work went unfulfilled. Zemlinsky then reworked portions of the second act and attached the title *Ein Tanzpoem* (A Dance Poem), but Mahler, perhaps considering it old wine newly bottled, likewise declined to program it. *Ein Tanzpoem* was never heard in Zemlinsky's lifetime.

At the start of August of 1901, a restless Zemlinsky, accompanied by his friend Hugo Botstiber, left Vienna to experience Wagner's Bayreuth. After attending a disappointing performance of *Parsifal*, Zemlinsky did some additional sightseeing, visiting Nuremberg, Munich and Salzburg. He sent Alma details of his travels, describing both his whereabouts and addresses where he could be reached along the way. In Munich, Zemlinsky visited exhibitions at the Glass Palace, the Old and New Pinakothek museums and the Schack-Gallerie, and attended a "glorious" performance of *Figaro* at the Resident Theater, the likes of which "one rarely encounters in Vienna".[3] Whether or not a rendezvous with Alma was initially part of his itinerary, he now tried repeatedly to orches-

---

[1] AZ/AMW.

[2] The performance took place on February 18, 1903, given by the Wiener Konzertverein, predecessor of the Wiener Symphoniker. Ferdinand Löwe, the orchestra's musical director and conductor, allowed Zemlinsky to conduct his own work.

[3] AZ/AMW.

trate a tryst. A crescendo of excitement builds through a series of letters, as Zemlinsky pleads with Alma not to fail him and attempts to pin down a time and a location for their meeting. But in the town of Ischl, where he hoped to be reunited with her after months apart, Zemlinsky waited in vain. "That I find it deplorable that we didn't meet, I need not tell you", Zemlinsky wrote her on August 12. A little over a week earlier Alma had written of her unbounded love for Zemlinsky, that she would surely already have married him by now if not for those "conventional" people around her persuading her to do otherwise. But one day before Zemlinsky's hoped-for encounter, Alma's passions, inconstant as ever, cooled yet again. "I feel absolutely nothing" for him, she confessed to her diary, fearing only losing him as her teacher.[1] Her cold capriciousness was soon laid bare: "[I am] relieved at the outcome . . . I have absolutely no regrets."[2]

By the time Alma returned to Vienna toward the end of September, Zemlinsky was already caught up in his Carltheater obligations, and it was some time before they met face to face. By the time they did, Alma had convinced herself yet again of her love for Zemlinsky. Their reunion was filled with passionate embraces. Alma's fervor reached its zenith in the days that followed, as her diary entries bear witness:

> October 5. We stared into each other's eyes, held hands . . . At parting we kissed so hard that I had the feeling I was melting! My body became unbelievably pliant & clung to his. My longing for him — for his embrace — knows no bounds.[3]

> October 7. I love him. My whole being breathes for him. I wish to be his for eternity. To be his wife, his beloved . . . When he kissed me, although he twisted my spine and pressed his body against mine, I had the sensation of something holy. A powerful, searing rite — like something God-given . . . I would gladly be pregnant for him, gladly bear his children. His blood and mine, commingled: my beauty with his intellect . . . He is dearer to me than everything, everything in the world.[4]

As October dissolved into November, their passion reached its climax:

> November 2. I found his lips — & he responded like one possessed. Later — he clasped my hips, I slid between his legs, he pressed me with them, and we kissed to the accompaniment of soft exclamations . . . he forced

---

[1] Beaumont and Rode-Breymann (1999), 425.

[2] Ibid.

[3] Ibid., 435.

[4] Beaumont and Rode-Breymann (1999), 436.

me roughly into a chair, leaned over me, kissed my eyes and my forehead
— and then on the mouth. Afterwards I felt completely shattered — I could
scarcely come to my senses.[1]

But within one week's time everything had changed again, and this time forever. Alma had met Gustav Mahler. By November 12 Alma, who just days earlier
could think of nothing save giving herself entirely to Zemlinsky, felt nothing
for him. She now set her sights on Mahler and was determined to conquer the
greatest musical prize Vienna had to offer.

Alma was introduced to Mahler at the home of Emil and Berta Zuckerkandl,
on the first Thursday in November. Mahler arrived late, after attending a performance at the Musikverein that Zemlinsky conducted. Ironically, whereas
Zemlinsky and Alma had discussed Mahler so enthusiastically at their first encounter nearly two years earlier, now Alma and Mahler's conversation revolved
almost exclusively around Zemlinsky. As Berta Zuckerkandl herself dramatically recollected,

> After dinner, the guests split into groups and Mahler contrived to remain
> near the girl [Alma], who was now discussing physical beauty and its
> many criteria. Mahler said that Socrates' head was beautiful. The girl
> said that she thought Alexander Zemlinsky was handsome too, because
> of the intelligence that shone in his eyes, even though he was reputed
> to be one of the ugliest men in Vienna. Mahler shrugged his shoulders,
> and said he thought that was going a bit too far. A few moments later,
> Frau Zuckerkandl heard voices raised in anger and came over to the
> group. Alma Schindler, flushed with anger, eyes blazing, was confront-
> ing Mahler, who, equally furious, was hopping madly about, sometimes
> halting abruptly, like a wading bird, one leg raised. They were quarreling
> about a ballet by Zemlinsky entitled Das goldene Herz [sic].[2]
>
> "You have no right to keep a score that's been submitted to you lying
> around for a whole year", Alma was saying, "especially when it comes
> from a real musician like Zemlinsky. You should have given him an an-
> swer, even if it was only 'no'." "But the ballet is quite worthless", Mahler
> complained. "No one will be able to make sense of it. How can you, who
> are interested in music and who are, I believe, studying it, possibly de-

[1] Ibid., 441.

[2] *Das gläserne Herz* (The Crystal Heart). Located in the Library of Congress is a holo-
graph short score titled *Das gläserne Herz* and a typescript synopsis in which the title *Der
Triumph der Zeit* has been crossed out and replaced with *Das gläserne Herz*. It is not known
which title Zemlinsky preferred for the ballet.

fend such trash?" "In the first place, it's not trash and you've probably not even taken the trouble to have a good look at it. And secondly, even if it is bad music, that's no excuse for not being polite!"

Mahler bit his lip, but then held out his hand saying, "Let's make peace! I don't promise to put on the ballet, of course, but I like the way you support your music teacher so courageously and express your opinion so frankly. I do promise therefore to send for Zemlinsky not later than tomorrow."[1]

Despite Alma's defense of Zemlinsky that evening, Mahler had left his mark and Alma's on-again-off-again feelings for Zemlinsky, which had vacillated wildly for well over a year, waned quickly. On December 12, she delivered the deathblow:

> Alex,
>
> You have not called because you know everything. You know all that has happened. You can even read my most secret thoughts. For me, these last weeks have been torture.
>
> You know how very much I loved you. You fulfilled me completely. Just as suddenly as this love came, it has vanished — been cast aside . . .
>
> Some things are beyond our powers. Maybe you have an explanation for that. You — you know me better than I know myself. I shall never forget the joyful hours you have given me — don't you forget them either. One thing though: don't desert me! If you are the man I think you are, you will come here on Monday, give me your hand — and our first kiss of friendship. Be a dear fellow, Alex. If you so wish, our friendship could be really meaningful. We could stick together always, as old comrades. Above all, answer me at once without reserve — Mama will not read the letter.
>
> Once again: forgive me — I no longer know myself.
>
> Your Alma[2]

Accepting her invitation, Zemlinsky visited Alma the following Monday, visibly shaken but rational. Alma found him "sarcastic, as ever, but otherwise kind, touchingly kind".[3] And despite the pain the termination of their relationship caused him, he too desired that their friendship continue.

---

[1] Zuckerkandl in La Grange (1995), 419.

[2] Beaumont and Rode-Breymann (1999), 458.

[3] Ibid., 460.

December brought yet another disruption to Zemlinsky's personal life when Arnold Schoenberg left Vienna for Berlin. Two months earlier, Schoenberg had wed Zemlinsky's sister Mathilde, now pregnant with the couple's first child, and, with the need for a steady income, Schoenberg had accepted an offer to join Ernst Wolzogen's Überbrettl cabaret in Berlin. That December the Schoenbergs packed their belongings and headed north. But the correspondence that commenced with Schoenberg's departure marked the start of an exchange that was to continue for the better part of the next forty years. On December 28 Zemlinsky wrote,

> Dear Friend, herewith I begin the first volume of the Zemlinszky [sic]–Schoenberg letters. It is not because of my name that the title doesn't have a better ring to it ... I say that I begin [the correspondence] because your two [previous] letters aren't good enough: in our letters to one another we should speak more and more positively about ourselves, no? After all, others don't do it, do they? We should, however, do our best to overshadow the crowd at the Café Megalomania.[1]

Zemlinsky then brought his brother-in-law up to date on Alma's engagement to Mahler, announced in the press one day earlier and which Zemlinsky shrugged off as "Neuigkeit", a piece of recent news. Zemlinsky's words are followed by an enigmatic series of dashes, perhaps masking pain or an attempt to put the affair with Alma behind him, an indication that he simply had no more to say about that chapter of his life.[2]

Professionally, Zemlinsky's responsibilities remained with the Carltheater. October ushered in Heuberger's *Opernball*, in addition to operettas by Carl Millöcker and Alfred Zamara, and a pattern was now established whereby Zemlinsky rehearsed and conducted the opening productions of each new work before turning over a number of subsequent performances to his assistant, Arthur Bodanzky, a former private student of Zemlinsky's who went on to hold a variety of posts in Vienna, Prague, Mannheim and finally America.[3] Thus

---

[1] Weber (1995), 2–4. Although the Café Griensteidl had by now been demolished, Zemlinsky nevertheless continued to poke fun at the egos once associated with it, hence its nickname, Café Megalomania. Note also that Zemlinsky had still not altered the spelling of his name.

[2] Zemlinsky would return to the subject of Alma in a subsequent letter to Schoenberg in October 1902. See Weber (1995), 33.

[3] Bodanzky left the Carltheater in 1903 to become Mahler's assistant at the Hofoper and was subsequently appointed Music Director of the Theater an der Wien. He went on to work in Prague and Mannheim (where he conducted *Es war einmal* during the 1912 season) prior to

freed up from Heuberger. Zemlinsky turned to the next work on the roster, Heinrich Reinhardt's *Das süsse Mädel*.

New Year's Day 1902 found Zemlinsky again in the pit with Heuberger's *Opernball*, while the months that followed ushered in more performances of Reinhardt's popular operetta, in addition to rehearsals and performances of music by Carl Weinberger (*Das gewisse Etwas*) and Jeno Fejér (*Der kleine Günstling*). Meanwhile, Zemlinsky's musical activities elsewhere continued unabated. On January 31 he conducted a concert at the Tonkünstlerverein featuring the violinist Stefi Geyer[1] performing Beethoven's Concerto and Hubay's *Carmen*-Fantasy, and in the third week of February he was back to accompany several of his own songs. Still, Alma was never far from his mind. He eventually confessed to Schoenberg that he shared the plight of Tristan and Werther, heroes of myth and German literature who preferred death to life without their beloved, and that he "simply had nothing else to hope for".[2]

For Zemlinsky, the solution was a symbolic death expressed in music: *Vom Tode*, a Symphony of Death. There exists, however, no evidence that Zemlinsky had the vaguest notion where such a dark source of inspiration might lead. Perhaps he envisioned a full-blown programmatic symphony, something akin to Berlioz's *Symphonie fantastique*, or a tone poem along the lines of Strauss's *Tod und Verklärung*, but all that is known is that the concept was hatched during one of the most turbulent periods of Zemlinsky's life, a period overflowing with romantic and professional frustration. In the end, the idea remained just that — an idea — but the music written as a study for his Symphony of Death — *Die Seejungfrau*, based on Hans Christian Andersen's *The Little Mermaid* — provided Zemlinsky the means to channel his feelings constructively and creatively. A century hence, *Die Seejungfrau* remains one of Zemlinsky's most recognized compositions.

The Carltheater demands, meanwhile, continued to take precedence over all else, week in and week out. Zemlinsky was not opposed to hard work, but he loathed inferior work. At the Carltheater there was too much of both. Over time, Zemlinsky's attitude toward much of the substandard fare he was forced to conduct became increasingly sarcastic, his mood ever more bitter. In a letter to Schoenberg Zemlinsky predicted that with his luck Reinhardt's *Das süsse Mädel* would play one hundred times. The prediction was a gross

emigrating to the U.S. In 1915 Bodanzky went to work for the Metropolitan Opera as its German opera specialist.

[1] The composers Béla Bartók and Othmar Schoeck both fell in love with Geyer and wrote violin concertos for her.

[2] Weber (1995), 33.

understatement — it ran in excess of two hundred performances! The following May Zemlinsky wrote to his mother from Dresden, where the Carltheater troupe were then in residence, summing up his attitude about the unfortunate success of Reinhardt's music: "Das süsse Mädel has unfortunately played here with great success. I am sick and tired of it . . . the world would be such a beautiful place if only there were no operetta! [Alles wär schön auf der Welt — wenn's keine Operette gäbe!]."[1] What little of his time the theater did not consume was usurped by Zemlinsky's furious attempts to meet a Universal Edition deadline for the completed arrangements of *Die Zauberflöte* and *Die lustige Witwe*. Having shielded his mother from the realities of his life, Zemlinsky was more forthright with Schoenberg. In June, two days before the arrangements were due, he revealed his dire straits:

> The only thing that presently brings me any joy is my own work, for which I have absolutely no time here in Dresden. My engagement [at the theater], and everything that's associated with it, is dreadful. I cannot describe it, nor can anyone feel it save me alone. Don't tell my mother any of this. She has no idea how horrible this is for me. You understand, moreover, my pessimism — perhaps that is also part of it.[2]

Back in Vienna Zemlinsky was engaged to conduct a number of performances at the Prater in June for an exhibition called *Venedig in Wien* (Venice in Vienna), which featured a gigantic re-creation of Venice and its canals. But by July his frustrations with the Carltheater escalated, and he contemplated resignation. He was immediately offered a position at the Theater an der Wien, where Beethoven had once conducted his *Eroica* Symphony and where his sole opera *Fidelio* had received its 1805 premiere. The rival theater promised better pay, better singers, more appealing repertoire, and Zemlinsky would gain a measure of control over the repertoire he was expected to conduct. But Müller, the Carltheater's administrative director, would not allow Zemlinsky simply to walk away. Determined to retain Zemlinsky for at least another season, Müller took him to court for attempting to nullify their contract. The trial, whose records were later destroyed by fire, took place on July 18, but a settlement was reached and Zemlinsky was forced to return to the Carltheater for a final season. The events only exacerbated Zemlinsky's dislike of Müller, whom he said "lied like a swine" during the course of the trial.[3] Though he lost the case, Zemlinsky

[1] Weber (1995), 15.
[2] Ibid.
[3] Ibid., 20.

regarded news of the ordeal a boon to his reputation, since the papers reported that two theaters had fought over him.

In early August 1902 Zemlinsky left for Altmünster, a town whose beautiful lake and mountainous backdrop offered a welcome relief from the proceedings of the previous month and the prior season's laborious work schedule. Friends and family joined him, including his mother — who was recovering from an illness — and Bodanzky, all of whom helped establish a joyful atmosphere. The time away from Vienna and his professional responsibilities granted Zemlinsky much needed time for composition. When he returned to Vienna later that summer, he brought with him a good portion of his new symphonic work.

Die Seejungfrau was Zemlinsky's first foray into the world of the symphonic tone poem, a genre that provided Richard Strauss with much success. The work is constructed of three parts, each of approximately equal length, and scored for strings, winds (including four flutes and three bassoons), brass (six horns, four trombones and bass trombone), two harps, and a full arsenal of percussion including glockenspiel, suspended cymbals, timpani and tubular bells.[1] Part I is organized on a modified sonata-form structure, depicting the undersea world and the Mermaid's mid-storm rescue of the Prince. For Part II, wherein the Mermaid renounces her aquatic existence and her voice in order to dwell with the Prince among humankind, Zemlinsky opted for an ABA scheme. In Part III, having learned that the Prince is betrothed to another, the Mermaid sets out to murder the Prince but spares him instead, in so doing sacrificing her chance to return to her ocean home. As an acknowledgement of her kind deed, she is allowed to join the Daughters of the Air. Zemlinsky regarded this last part as the most "innerlichste" or introspective of the three,[2] and its formal outlines — perhaps best thought of as an apotheosis, transfiguration and recollection — are consequently the most abstract.

In Straussian fashion, Zemlinsky constructed his score around a series of motifs, each representing the different elements of the story (the Mermaid, the Sea, the Prince and so forth). His first task was to create a list of representative musical figures. Some, like the accumulation of ostinato fragments at the work's opening — an ascending A minor scale, the descending pattern heard in muted violins, and the gently alternating fourths and fifths played by the winds and harp — evoke the mysterious world of the sea. Other ideas are more truly thematic, such as the sentimental violin solo that depicts the Mermaid's joy; or the

---

[1] Before his revision, the composer had also planned to include an off-stage wind band.

[2] Weber (1995), 41.

Prince's theme, a joyous waltz symbolizing both his nobility and a world wholly foreign to a heroine without legs.[1]

Two ideas found in Part II represent the Mermaid's transformation into human form: a chorale-style descending fourth motive, described by Zemlinsky as "der unsterblichen Seele des Menschen" (Man's immortal soul),[2] and a lush, expansive theme in the cello's tenor register. In Part III, Zemlinsky refashions prior ideas, some so substantially as to render them almost anew. For example, upon throwing herself into the Sea, the Mermaid feels her body dissolving into foam, evident in the return of the original ostinato passages. With the appearance of the diaphanous Daughters of the Air, the harmony shifts suddenly from A minor to E-flat major, as orchestral strings whisper an ethereal and nearly inaudible chorus (marked *pppp* in the score). The music draws peacefully to a close with the return of the "Immortal Soul" theme, as the Mermaid undergoes her final transformation and ascends to life in the clouds.

Zemlinsky's choice to contrast A minor with E-flat major, a tritone relationship that also frames the work as a whole, was deeply significant and rests with the letter names of the pitches themselves, A and E-flat, the latter pronounced *Es* in German — A.S. — the initials of Alma Schindler.[3] The message was vintage Zemlinsky, not a heart-on-the-sleeve gesture but rather a code so beautifully subtle as to have gone almost entirely unnoticed — a musical tale of love and loss imbedded with personal meaning.[4]

By September of 1902, Zemlinsky was once more at the Carltheater and lamenting that the circus had begun all over again. The big operetta successes that season included Heuberger's *Das Baby*, Reinhardt's *Der liebe Schatz* — which Zemlinsky deemed "dreadful! abominable! ghastly!!"[5] — and Lehár's *Der Rastelbinder*, which ran repeatedly throughout the following season as well. To

---

[1] Zemlinsky had also depicted mankind by means of a waltz theme in his ballet *Der Triumph der Zeit* and in that work's subsequent orchestral adaptations. Considering the plight of *The Mermaid*, the waltz nevertheless seems especially poignant here.

[2] Weber (1995), 33.

[3] The conductor James Conlon has suggested the initials A.S. may refer to Arnold Schoenberg, with whom Zemlinsky was also becoming very close at this time. Considering the romantic nature of the composition, Alma seems a more compelling dedicatee.

[4] Completed at the close of March of 1903, *Die Seejungfrau* went unpublished following its unimpressive premiere on Jan 25, 1905. When Zemlinsky immigrated to the United States in 1938, he brought just two of the work's three parts with him. The composition remained in an incomplete state until the early 1980s, when the three movements were once again reunited.

[5] Weber (1995), 30.

his credit, Zemlinsky's work on the podium gave no indication of his abhorrence for the works or his dissatisfaction with his job. To the contrary, his conducting continued to draw accolades from the press. Reviewing the Carltheater's 1902 performance of *Der Rastelbinder*, for example, The *Wiener Allgemeiner Zeitung* attributed much of the operetta's success to "the orchestra under the prudent and assured direction of its director Alexander von Zemlinsky, who understands precisely how to draw forth the beauty of the charmingly instrumented score".[1]

Of course, not all the music that Zemlinsky conducted was as skillfully crafted as that of Lehár or (naturally) Zemlinsky's own orchestration of Heuberger's *Der Opernball*, and by the middle of September he was complaining that "Because of this damned theater I once again have little time [to compose]."[2] Nor was time spent at his writing table any guarantee of success. In 1903, for example, Zemlinsky began preliminary work on an opera based on Maxim Gorky's *Malva*, but when Mahler was consulted for his opinion, he concluded that Gorky's text was unfit to be dramatized in music and that Zemlinsky was unlikely to demonstrate otherwise. In a letter to Ernst Hutschenreiter, whom Zemlinsky had engaged to construct the opera's libretto, Zemlinsky admitted that Mahler's opinion served only to confirm his and Hutschenreiter's previously held misgivings:

> Dear Herr Hutschenreiter,
>
> You have not heard from me for some time firstly because I have really been very busy and secondly because I have been awaiting Mahler's answer. It arrived only two days ago: he is totally against it. He believes that it contains neither the stuff to dramatize nor that I would be the one to do it. So!? I no longer have any interest in it — not that his criticism cost me my courage, but ultimately it suggests to me a confirmation of our doubt.[3]

Fall turned to winter and then to spring with more work at the theater and more forgettable music. Finally, on May 29, 1903, as the final strains of *Der Rastelbinder* faded from the hall, Zemlinsky acknowledged his ensemble and stepped down from the Carltheater podium for the last time, his contract now legally fulfilled. Whatever his feelings toward the Carltheater and its director, Zemlinsky could look back at the last three seasons with pride; his

[1] *Wiener Allgemeinene Zeitung* (December 22, 1902), in Rode (1992), 187.

[2] Weber (1995), 29.

[3] In a letter from Zemlinsky to Ernst Hutschenreiter, April 21, 1903. See Biba (1992), 53. Zemlinsky's interest in the naturalistic dramas of Tolstoy and Ibsen among others was likely a result of his exposure to their work at the Carltheater in May and June of 1902. For more on the subject, see Rode (1992), 185–89.

accomplishments were indisputable. He had given the theater his all, he had
conducted innumerable performances of thirteen operettas including six premieres, he had molded the orchestra into a first-class ensemble, and he had
raised the level of the theater's productions to unprecedented heights. Upon
hearing the Carltheater doors swing shut behind him for the last time, of one
thing Zemlinsky was certain: he had no interest making a career out of conducting operetta. Drained after three exhausting seasons, Zemlinsky confessed
to Schoenberg, "I am lacking your optimism, your patience, your humor, your
love of life. I have become very different than I was. You would hardly recognize me . . ."[1] The positive, self-assured attitude of just a few years earlier had
vanished, replaced by disillusionment with theater work, disillusionment with
Alma, and a growing disillusionment with Vienna.

[1] Weber (1995), 41

Chapter 4

Auf Wiedersehen

Z EMLINSKY'S CONDUCTING PROSPECTS were slow to improve. In September 1903 he officially joined the staff of the Theater an der Wien, but aside from being out from under the yoke of Leopold Müller, life was only marginally better across town. Zemlinsky did have the advantage of being released from work for weeks at a time, but when on duty he remained chained to uninspiring repertoire such as Béla von Ujj's *Der Herr Professor*, with Offenbach's *Contes d'Hoffmann* being the sole exception.

Zemlinsky was afforded a welcome diversion, however upon Arnold and Mathilde's return to Vienna. Schoenberg's work at Wolzogen's Überbrettl had dried up a year earlier when the theater closed, and though he had gone on to teach composition at the Stern Conservatory, that too had ended in the spring. In May Schoenberg had written to Zemlinsky, informing him about their possible move. Zemlinsky welcomed the thought of having the Schoenbergs back in the Austrian capital, where Mathilde would be reunited with her family and Zemlinsky could resume his friendship and musical discussions with his brother-in-law in person. But Zemlinsky warned Schoenberg about making any hasty decisions:

> Come first to Vienna for a couple of weeks in the summer, try to establish some contacts, to renew matters, take a look at your Vienna and its famous concert conditions very closely, and then should you decide to build here from a small base, return alone to B[erlin], wrap everything up and come back. Don't get yourself in a bind, especially when there is so little available as now, even when you get "it" (which I doubt will happen, for "it" is always to be had by someone else). Here there are

but few prospects, particularly for a beginning. I advise you to consider patiently, you with such longing for Vienna. *I* know all of the conditions precisely; you may think it's all an exaggeration — everything is, however, an understatement![1]

Despite Zemlinsky's counsel, Schoenberg and his family, which now included the Schoenbergs' one-year-old daughter, Gertrud, resettled there in July. Zemlinsky and the Schoenbergs took adjoining apartments at Liechtensteinstrasse 68–70, located in Vienna's ninth district and near the Volksoper, where Zemlinsky would one day conduct. Zemlinsky's gloomy warnings to Schoenberg were unfortunately borne out in the years of financial, professional and personal misfortune that followed.

Schoenberg and Zemlinsky had never lived in such close proximity, so now it was a pleasure, and inspiring, to be able to freely discuss their work and exchange ideas.[2] As quickly became evident, however, Schoenberg's music was moving swiftly in a radical direction, causing Zemlinsky a certain degree of consternation. Two works from this period illustrate the widening gulf forming between them: Zemlinsky's *Die Seejungfrau*, with its clean, clear textures and melodies that occasionally tend toward sentimentality, and Schoenberg's *Pelleas und Melisande*, a somber, formally complex composition constructed of an intricate web of Wagnerian-style leitmotifs and densely layered fabric of counterpoint, a work that also introduces polychords and whole-tone scales. In a letter to Schoenberg, Zemlinsky himself acknowledged the artistry but also the overwhelming complexity reflected in Schoenberg's score:

> I am astounded that you could be angry with me for not yet having given you a detailed impression of your work. Believe me, I have given much of myself and my entire "intellectual energy" to its study; but *you do not understand*: it is the most monstrously difficult of all that that I have yet undertaken. R. Strauss's *Heldenleben* is but child's play when compared to it. I am only able to progress with great effort. I need only blink and I lose the melodic or harmonic thread and must begin again, and finally my head and eyes hurt so much that I have to stop. One thing I know already today: it is the most artistic work produced in our time. I believe that R. Str.[auss] will not remain your friend for long!!! . . . But for the moment the main point to consider is what orchestra, or even

---

[1] Weber (1995), 45.

[2] They now lived so close to each other that Schoenberg had to contend with Zemlinsky's piano playing: "Zemlinsky was pounding away at it all the time, till the noise practically drove Uncle Arnold crazy." Newlin (1980), 196.

more, what conductor save myself (and that is no claptrap) would devote such an absurd amount of effort to it! It would require 4 weeks for one to simply learn the piano reduction, and again as much for rehearsals! I do not think I exaggerate about that. I implore you, just once compose a "peaceful work"! Something practical, more abridged, *if also entirely Schoenberg!*[1]

If Zemlinsky believed that Schoenberg was tempting fate by storming onto the Viennese scene with compositions too complex for performer and public alike, he remained devoted to his friend's musical development. Indeed, his loyalty was one reason Zemlinsky's association with Vienna's Tonkünstlerverein came to an end. Until recently, the institution's concerts, competitions and support had provided Zemlinsky with valuable Viennese musical and professional opportunities. But Zemlinsky had become increasingly critical of the society's conservative agenda, in particular its unwillingness to take seriously the music of his friend and brother-in-law Arnold Schoenberg,[2] and in 1903 Zemlinsky departed.

During the period from 1903 to 1904, Zemlinsky became involved with two new artistic and music societies as he strove to promote new music. The first was the Ansorge-Verein für Kunst und Kultur (Ansorge Society for Art and Culture), Vienna's newest artistic organization. Recently founded by the music critic Paul Stefan and the writer/director Wilhelm von Wymetal, the society had been named for Berlin pianist and composer Conrad Ansorge (1862–1930), a pupil of Franz Liszt and a great proponent of modern music and literature. It was not the intention of the Ansorge-Verein, however, solely to promote new music. Rather, the organization sought to encourage an equality of both old and new, to bind together various artistic genres, as proclaimed by its Secessionist-style motto, "Jede grosse Kunst alter und neue Zeit zu pflegen" (To nurture all great art, both old and new). The poet Detlev von Liliencron, the Burgtheater actor Ferdinand Gregori and the singer Moriz Frauschner were all founding members, a reflection of the society's diverse nature. The Ansorge-Verein sponsored poetry readings by Liliencron, Stefan George and Richard Dehmel. Performances of music by Zemlinsky and Schoenberg, set to these texts, were also offered, as were art exhibitions organized by Heinrich Lefler.[3]

[1] Weber (1995), 42–43.

[2] In one instance, one member of the Verein criticized Schoenberg's *Verklärte Nacht* for sounding "as though someone had smeared the still-wet score of Tristan!" Zemlinsky (1934), 34.

[3] Lefler, along with Klimt, would break from the Secession two years later.

As a charter member of the Ansorge-Verein, Zemlinsky was recruited to
serve as the organization's pianist. Paul Stefan later recalled that

> in my eagerness [to interest Zemlinsky] I brought along my violin in
> order to realize the vocal line. Naturally with Zemlinsky it was not nec-
> essary. Much more than the mere difficulties of the songs rang out from
> his piano, such that we decided at once that only he would be allowed to
> accompany the concerts.[1]

Stefan went on to write that at one of the first concerts, Zemlinsky's song *Tod
in Aehren* made a particularly strong impression. But it was Zemlinsky's accompanying at these concerts that most caught the attention of the press. In
a review from the Ansorge-Verein's inaugural concert, the critic Max Vancsa
was highly dismissive of most of the program but praised the performances of
Frauschner and Zemlinsky, whom Vancsa felt were responsible for "saving the
honor of their art":

> The first Ansorge Evening of the Society, on 29 November, ostensibly
> should have been "for invited guests" only, but despite its taking place
> on a Sunday, and at an unusually late hour, it actually attracted a mas-
> sive and curious crowd, who packed the otherwise roomy hall of the
> Engineering and Architectural Society to such a capacity that many were
> turned away . . . It was only the Hofoper singer Frauschner and Music
> Director Zemlinsky, the excellent vocal accompanist, who did justice to
> the poets . . .[2]

In spite of Zemlinsky's initial dedication to the organization, his involvement
was short-lived, largely a result of the increasing weight the society placed on
literature. As the balance began to swing in favor of the spoken and written
word, even the press became sensitive to the inequality, claiming that it was only
amidst the pauses of the literary evenings that any music was to be heard at all.[3]
Thus, despite promising expectations, the Ansorge-Verein ultimately provided
Zemlinsky with little satisfaction, and he again turned his attention elsewhere.

Zemlinsky's determination to find a suitable place and an appreciative
audience for new music resulted in formation of another new society, the Vereinigung schaffender Tonkünstler, or Society for Creative Musicians. Founded

---

[1] Stefan (1921), 227.

[2] *Neue musikalische Presse*, 13 Jg. (1904), Nr. 2, 29–30.

[3] Rathgeber (1992), 201.

by Zemlinsky, Schoenberg and several others,[1] the society was the first Viennese institution devoted exclusively to modern music. Taking their cue from the well-established Tonkünstlerverein, which had thrived under Brahms's leadership, Zemlinsky and Schoenberg approached Mahler, in the hopes that such a figurehead would lend their young organization valuable credibility and critical visibility. In a letter to Zemlinsky, Mahler graciously consented to becoming the Vereinigung's honorary president:

> It was with pleasure that I openly declared my association with your undertaking and lent my strongest support of your goal. Since you feel it would be beneficial or useful to publicly make known my belief in the [Society's] future by my accepting such a title, then call me what you will.[2]

A brochure published by the Vereinigung proclaimed its mission to promote contemporary music and the strategies it would undertake to achieve that goal. The Vereinigung members were cognizant that the complex nature of new music produced barriers that could be overcome only through repeated performances. To insure that the composers' wishes would be faithfully realized, painstaking and sufficient preparation was regarded as essential. And, understanding that success required a public that would meet it halfway, the Vereinigung pledged "to give modern music a permanent home in Vienna, where it will be fostered; and to keep the public constantly informed about the current state of musical composition".[3]

On April 1, 1904, the musicologist Guido Adler introduced the organization to the public in a long article published in the *Neue Freie Presse*, in which he brazenly criticized the Viennese and the "unshakeable respect of the Austrians for their classic tradition, and thus for their past".[4] Adler may have seized the moment to rail against his perception of Vienna's habitual conservatism, but in truth, Zemlinsky and Schoenberg's intention was to provide a venue for their

---

[1] Additional founding members included Franz Schmidt, Oskar Posa, Karl Weigl and Rudolf Stephan Hoffmann.

[2] Archiv der Gesellschaft der Musikfreunde in Wien (Briefe Gustav Mahler 42).

[3] Reich (1971), 19. The society also declared that "no 'movement' or stylistic genre will be specially preferred . . . there will be performances of works from the classicist school and from the new-German, and works with Apollonian and Dionysian tendencies, insofar as they manifest a powerful artistic personality, expressing itself in a manner that is formally above reproach."

[4] Quoted in La Grange (1995), 688.

music and that of their contemporaries. This new generation of musicians, with their ears tuned to music's newest currents, had lofty goals. They aimed to

> set up a permanent institution for the encouragement of contemporary music in the capital, and create direct contact between its musicians and the public; keep the latter informed of current developments in musical creation; cultivate and promote contemporary musical works and the development of artistic personality by arranging public performances of important new compositions which have not yet been adequately appreciated; support the professional interests of its members.[1]

On May 5 came the invitation to composers, also published in the *Neue Freie Presse*:

> The Society of Creative Musicians in Vienna held its constitutive General Assembly on the 23rd of last month. Hofoper Director Gustav Mahler was unanimously elected Honorary President; he had already declared himself willing to be elected. Then the Committee was elected and the decision was taken to organize three orchestral and three chamber and Lieder concerts next season with programs consisting exclusively of new works, to establish contact with the Vienna Concert Society over the provision of an orchestra and to engage soloists for the chamber music and Lieder recitals. An invitation is now being sent to all Austrian and German composers, as well as all foreign composers living in Austria and Germany. Those who would like to be heard at these concerts should send in works (manuscripts in fair copy) to the archivist . . . until 31 May this year. Works received after this date can be given only secondary consideration.[2]

The Vereinigung's first concert took place at the Musikverein on November 23, 1904, with Zemlinsky conducting music of Siegmund von Hausegger, an ardent Wagnerian, and Hermann Bischoff, a follower of Strauss. After the intermission, Mahler led a performance of Strauss's *Sinfonia domestica*, the first time the work had been heard in Vienna. Then the problems began. For the second concert, slated for the Great Hall of the Musikverein on January 25, 1905, Zemlinsky chose to conduct the premiere of his *Die Seejungfrau*,[3] Schoenberg would lead the premiere of *Pelleas und Melisande*, and Oskar Posa, secretary of

---

[1] La Grange (1995), 688.

[2] Quoted in Blaukopf (1976), 236.

[3] Zemlinsky's work appeared as *Die Seejungfrau, Phantasie für Orchester*.

the society, would conduct five of his orchestral songs based on texts by Detlev von Liliencron. Preparations did not go well. The orchestra proved especially unruly toward Schoenberg and his *Pelleas*, and Mahler was finally brought in to establish some order. Matters did not improve at the concert. The reception was cool, and some of the audience members simply walked out. In the days that followed, the critics took their turn. The *Neue musikalische Presse* stated that Zemlinsky's music contained little that was original and that its eclecticism was "derived from the proven modern masters such as Wagner and Liszt to Mahler and Strauss".[1] Another critic remarked, "The three leaders of the Vereinigung schaffender Tonkünstler, Arnold Schoenberg, Alexander von Zemlinsky and Oscar Posa, have devoted an entire evening to their cause. The most talented of them — Schoenberg — was the most unpalatable."[2] This last critique made a lasting impression on Zemlinsky. The society had not been established to benefit its members in particular, yet Zemlinsky and his two colleagues had monopolized the Vereinigung's second program. For years after, Zemlinsky programmed and conducted his own music only as a last resort. Distancing himself from his own music, however, proved devastating to his reputation. Since few conductors championed his music, his decision contributed significantly to his eventual slide into musical obscurity.

Meanwhile, the Vereinigung's plans continued unabated. Four days later Mahler conducted his songs from *Des Knaben Wunderhorn* and the *Kindertotenlieder*.[3] Subsequent concerts that season included a chamber music and lieder evening on February 20, featuring the D minor String Quartet of Max Reger, a set of songs by Theodor Streicher and Bruno Walter's Piano Quintet in F-sharp minor, and an orchestral concert on March 11, with works by Hans Pfitzner and Richard Strauss among others. But the Vereinigung failed to prosper. Despite a highly organized society that promised to deliver a product unlike any other within the city, it survived but a single season,[4] and although both Zemlinsky and Schoenberg remained active promoters of new music, neither organized another institution dedicated to its cause for more than a decade. Still, Zemlinsky had publicly proclaimed his dedication to the cause of contemporary music, a stance that defined his artistic ideals for the rest of his life.

[1] Quoted in Gülke (1995), 58.

[2] Quoted in Slonimsky (1949), 49.

[3] A repeat performance took place on February 3. See Biba (1992), 54.

[4] Ernst Hilmar suggests that this may have been owing to a miscalculation of costs required to maintain a qualified orchestra. See Hilmar (1976), 66.

Zemlinsky's tenure at the Theater an der Wien lasted for one blissfully brief season and ended with an offer to join the Kaiser-Jubiläums-Stadttheater. Located
in the Währinger Gürtel northwest of the Ring, just blocks from Zemlinsky's
Liechtensteinstrasse apartment, the Kaiser-Jubiläums-Stadttheater of 1904 was
a markedly different place from what it had been at the time of its inception.
Built in 1898 to celebrate the fiftieth anniversary of Franz Joseph's reign, the
theater was the brainchild of Adam Müller-Guttenbrunn, a theatrical director
who felt there was a need for theater in the outlying areas of Vienna. But Müller-
Guttenbrunn also believed that a predominance of Jewish literature was poisoning Austro-German culture and wished to build a cultural institution free of any
Jewish influence. The so-called "Aryan Theater" was his answer — a house built
beyond the inner city that excluded Jewish authors and actors. During its brief
lifespan, Müller-Guttenbrunn's institution was home to virulently anti-Semitic
plays, including a mangled production of Shakespeare's *The Merchant of Venice*. Mayor Karl Lueger was one of the Aryan Theater's strongest supporters,
particularly during its early years, and once told a Christian Social Workers'
assembly that it was only to such a theater that Christian men could safely
"take their families, without fearing that the ears of their poor children will be
dirtied by smut".[1]

As a house of Aryan culture, the Stadttheater stood on shaky financial
ground, and bankruptcy was declared in the autumn prior to Zemlinsky's engagement.[2] In 1904 the theater ushered in a new administration. Rainer Simons,
the theater's newly appointed intendant, sought a music director and believed
Zemlinsky to be the perfect choice. True, Zemlinsky had established his reputation on the podium largely with light opera, but his consistently high level of
integrity and impressive musicianship were by now well known. For Zemlinsky,
the chance to build an ensemble with sophisticated repertoire was a golden
opportunity. He eagerly accepted Simons's offer and wasted little time proving that Simons had made the right decision. In his capacity as music director,
Zemlinsky soon developed a reputation for precision and consistency with his
new company, gained a strong following, and proved himself one of Vienna's
most capable conductors. Under his musical guidance, the Stadttheater, soon
known as the Volksoper, provided Vienna with an alternative to the city's long-

---

[1] Quoted in Geehr (1990), 193. Jewish actors were occasionally but infrequently employed
by the theater, and still more rarely were Jewish works even performed. At such times Müller-
Guttenbrunn invariably drew harsh criticism from the anti-Semitic press for his blatant disregard of the so-called "Aryan clause". The clause was abandoned with Simons's administration.

[2] Plans for a new theater initially included a statute whereby Jewish children were to be
denied any of the 400 free tickets distributed for its performances. The theater was never built.

established Hofoper. Compared to the state-supported Hofoper, the privately run Volksoper operated with greater freedom, made evident when Strauss's *Salome*, barred from the Hofoper for its eroticism, was performed to critical acclaim at the Volksoper under Zemlinsky's baton.

Before the start of his first season at the Volksoper, Zemlinsky left Vienna for the town of Gmunden, located on the picturesque Lake Traunsee. Here he was again joined by Arthur Bodanzky, his colleague from the Carltheater, and the author Leo Feld (born Leo Hirschfeld), whom Zemlinsky knew from his days at the Café Griensteidl. Feld had crafted the libretto for Zemlinsky's new opera, *Der Traumgörge*, which he had been working on for well over a year. Feld was precisely the kind of librettist Zemlinsky needed — someone with talent, knowledge of the theater and a willingness to form a true collaboration. Miles from his duties in Vienna, Zemlinsky seized the uninterrupted stretches of time to work on his latest opera. But the summer of 1904 was not all work. Zemlinsky knew from experience the importance of beginning the season well rested and refreshed, so he spent time hiking in the warm, sunny air and taking daily swims in the cool water. In a letter from late July, Zemlinsky jokingly wrote that Schoenberg would be pleased to know that he had the appetite of two and that he had yet to put on one of his stiff white shirts![1]

By August Zemlinsky was back in his apartment in the Liechtensteinstrasse. And the following month the stiff shirts came out when Zemlinsky stepped in front of his Volksoper colleagues for the first time to begin rehearsals for Weber's *Der Freischütz*. From the first downbeat, Zemlinsky experienced a quality of opera far beyond anything he had previously known — in some cases he literally graduated from the ridiculous to the sublime. The repertoire for the Volksoper's opening season included a handful of favorites, including Auber's *Fra Diavolo*, Rossini's *Il barbiere di Siviglia*, Gounod's *Faust*, Bizet's *Carmen* and Verdi's *La traviata*,[2] and over the course of the next six seasons the theater would mount productions of much of the major operatic repertoire from Mozart to Wagner, along with quality lighter fare by Lortzing and Nicolai.

In addition to the duties required of him by the Volksoper and the Vereinigung schaffender Tonkünstler, it was during this period that Zemlinsky became involved with a teaching project organized by Eugenie Schwarzwald, wife of the financier and economist Dr. Hermann Schwarzwald.[3] Three years earlier,

---

[1] Weber (1995), 50.

[2] Zemlinsky apparently felt no affinity toward the Italian repertoire and, with the exception of *Tosca*, delegated that repertoire to his assistants Ferdinand Hellmesberger, Oscar von Posa and Josef Czerin.

[3] Eugenie was later depicted as the enterprising Diotima in Robert Musil's *Der Mann ohne*

Eugenie — whose literary efforts, charitable works and progressive views on pedagogy and women's rights would have made her an extraordinary woman in any age — had begun a private girl's school (*Mädchengymnasium*), an example of both her altruism and her pioneering efforts in the field of education. Frau Schwarzwald intended to educate a new feminist élite, enabling them to overcome many of the social barriers that women confronted. The school attracted a high percentage of Jewish girls[1] and ultimately came to be regarded as a school for the Jewish bourgeoisie. The weekly classes, which ran from October to May, were taught in the Wallnerstrasse, near the Hofburg palace in the heart of the city, in a house comprising several floors and a covered garden. As befitted such a modern undertaking, the house had been designed by one of the city's preeminent modern architects, Adolf Loos.

Through Loos, Eugenie Schwarzwald became acquainted with Schoenberg. Finding it disgraceful that a composer of Schoenberg's ability should have to wait for students to come to him, she placed the school at his disposal, allowing for the development of a conservatory-style institution that was free to students of both sexes. Classes were held on afternoons when her school for women did not convene. Schoenberg, in turn, asked Zemlinsky and the music critic Elsa Bienenfeld to work with him.[2] Zemlinsky was engaged to teach form and analysis and instrumentation, while Schoenberg taught harmony and counterpoint. Unfortunately, the student turnout for the music division's first year was disappointingly low, and it failed to improve in the year that followed. Nonetheless, the school attracted a number of high-caliber students, including Anton Webern, Alban Berg, Egon Wellesz and Heinrich Jalowetz, and provided Zemlinsky with his first formal teaching post.

Zemlinsky's activities at the Volksoper during the next few seasons were exhausting but he could no longer complain about what he was conducting: *Figaro*, *Zauberflöte*, *Tannhäuser*, *Tosca* and a single operetta, *Die Fledermaus*. The theater demanded nearly all of Zemlinsky's time and attention, and he gave himself tirelessly to the task. One of the few distractions he allowed during this period was his courtship of Ida Guttmann, the sister of Melanie, Zemlinsky's sweetheart from his student days. Following his affair with Alma, Ida appears to have been the first woman with whom Zemlinsky contemplated a future, but

---

Eigenschaften, and both she and her husband became characters in Karl Kraus's mammoth drama *Die letzten Tage des Menschheit*.

[1] In 1910, 113 out of 164 girls at the school were Jewish. See Beller (1989), 216.

[2] Bienenfeld was later murdered in an extermination camp during World War II.

because Ida's name never appears in any of Zemlinsky's letters before 1910, little is known about their time together.

With a concert season that allowed little time for personal music making, Zemlinsky devoted his summers to composing — his opera *Der Traumgörge* was nearly completed during the summer of 1906 — and socializing with family. The summers of 1906 and 1907 were spent in the town of Rottach-Egern on Bavaria's Tegernsee lake. Rooms were rented in a two-story apartment containing a garden and a balcony overlooking the water, providing Zemlinsky with an idyllic setting in which to compose, swim, walk and relax. Unfortunately, he experienced a setback in the summer of August 1906 when he developed a throat infection. After being bed-ridden for ten days with a fever and what he described as "terrible pain."[1] Zemlinsky was forced to return to Vienna to have an abscess lanced. But during his convalescence, he gradually returned to composing, and by the end of October *Der Traumgörge*'s orchestral score was complete.

It had been approximately two years since Mahler's performances of *Es war einmal*, and in *Der Traumgörge*, Zemlinsky had returned to the world of operatic fairy tale. In 1902 he had written to Schoenberg about a new idea for an opera, one based loosely on Heinrich Heine's *Der arme Peter* (Poor Peter) and Richard von Volkmann-Leander's *Vom unsichtbaren Königreich* (The Invisible Kingdom). Confident that he was creating something of significance — "ich glaube das wird was"[2] — Zemlinsky wrote briefly, though sensitively, of the opera's subject matter:

"Der arme Peter" is an idealistic young wanderer or dreamer (I do not know from what milieu) whose longing for love left him unloved during his brief life. He yearned not only for a woman's love but lived, misunderstood, in his own dreams, being so totally different from the rest of society. Friends, loved ones, everyone turns from him first with ridicule, then perhaps with anger and suspicion. Perhaps only his mother still believes in him. Though she hopes that he will master his life, she dies wondering whether he has the energy to do so. He feels the same himself.[3]

Zemlinsky and his librettist, Leo Feld, eventually pieced together the following plot: Görge, a misanthrope, lives in a world of books and dreams. In a dream, Görge is visited by a beautiful princess who beckons, so he leaves his community, his betrothed and the mill he has inherited to pursue his dream of

[1] AZ/AMW.
[2] Weber (1995), 30–31.
[3] Ibid., 31.

"making fairy tales come to life". In the years that follow, Görge moves from outcast to revolutionary hero — a command of language gained from his book-ish early years alone has made him a natural orator. But in all his years abroad Görge has established intimacy with only one other individual, a fellow sufferer named Gertraud, who Görge recognizes as his ideal mate and the embodiment of his former muse. Together they return to Görge's village, where they marry, build a school and have a child. His years abroad have helped bring about Görge's maturity and personal transformation — a recluse no more, he has gained a family and his deeds have garnered the admiration of the community. He has come to realize that the idyllic life he leads is the stuff of dreams and Gertraud is his princess come to life.

First Brahms, then Wagner, and now Strauss and Mahler — the string of influences on Zemlinsky's music is easily traceable. Mahler's spirit is audible almost at the start of *Der Traumgörge*. Dispensing with a formal overture, Zem-linsky opts for a brief but evocative musical backdrop to the rural scenery on stage, recalling the static harmony and atmospheric opening of Mahler's First Symphony.[1] Echoes of Mahler are quick to return in the start of Görge's solo — "In tiefer Nacht ganz sacht, ganz sacht . . ." (In the dead of night, very, very cautiously . . .) — where Mahleresque French horn stopping and clipped wind fragments evoke the mysterious air of the ghostly cat's chorus.

But there is ample evidence that Zemlinsky is also stretching himself, searching for ways to establish a personal voice and shake free from surround-ing influences. His orchestral and vocal lines are increasingly chromatic, more daring than in the earlier operas, enhancing the opera's dream-like atmosphere. *Der Traumgörge* also displays Zemlinsky's foray into advanced harmony, relied upon in the opera's darkest moments, such as when Görge portends experiences that lie ahead as he sings: "Glück und Verderben, Leben und Sterben!" (For-tune and ruin, life and death!). As noted by Horst Weber, Zemlinsky juxtaposes the distantly related but chromatic keys of C minor, B major, E major and E-flat major to depict "the richly wild, if also tempting and threatening, aspects of life".[2] At other moments the music attains an almost expressionistic air. In the fifth scene of Act II, for example, Görge asks Gertraud to look within him. A sin-uous orchestral web underscores dark and disjointed vocal lines, heightening an already loose tonal framework. Even Görge's language is expressionistic: "What have they done to me? Just look at me! . . . Doglike, stinking, a paunch, a drunk,

---

[1] The various wind motifs also sound curiously similar to those in Strauss's *Rosenkavalier*, although the latter opera was not composed for another five years.

[2] Weber (1991), 117.

that's what I am. A piece of spleen attached to a throat." The realization that "real" life is more sinister than that experienced in dreams is acutely embodied in the music's harmonic ambiguity. This scene directly follows Gertraud's lamentation of her own alienation,[1] and her lines, when at their most extreme, are similarly harmonically unstable. The message is clear: both characters, equally foreign to the world, have only one another. The overall atmosphere of such moments foreshadows Schoenberg's expressionistic *Erwartung* of 1909 and even Berg's *Wozzeck* from 1922.

When Zemlinsky is not looking forward or casting sideways glances at Mahler or Strauss, he remains connected to an earlier, more innocent time. Whether this is a result of the years Zemlinsky just spent directing operetta, or is simply another indication of the hold that his Viennese pedigree continued to exert, moments such as Gertraud's aria in Act II, scene iii, "Träume kommen und Träume Wandern" (Dreams come and dreams go), confirm that Zemlinsky could write in the best Viennese tradition. This pastiche of influences does not detract from the significance of the opera. On the contrary, the score unites progressive musical thought and lyrical warmth — "searing beauty and, at times, overpowering intensity", in the words of historian Antony Beaumont.[2] Furthermore, its fairy-tale characters struggle with issues of integrity, alienation and transformation, thematic concerns common to Zemlinsky's operatic *oeuvre*.

Zemlinsky did not wait long to find a venue for the opera's world premiere. Mahler, always ready to extend support, soon offered a Hofoper debut. *Der Traumgörge*'s future seemed secure.

By the start of the 1906/7 Volksoper season, Zemlinsky already knew to expect a rigorous schedule, but despite his lofty title of Musical Director he often felt more slave than master. Rumors circulated that Mahler was working behind the scenes to find Zemlinsky work at the Hofoper, but Zemlinsky knew only that Mahler had requested that he supervise the Hofoper's *Traumgörge* rehearsals for an October 4, 1907, debut. Then, in October of 1906, Zemlinsky received an official invitation to join the Hofoper conducting staff the following season. Overwhelmed by Mahler's offer, Zemlinsky dashed off the following note:

> Highly honorable Herr Director,
> Even at the risk of boring you once more, you must permit me to tell you how infinitely grateful I am to you. Not only because of the fact

[1] She has been branded as a witch by a local village.
[2] Beaumont (2000), 155.

that through you, dear Herr Director, I attain that position which it has always been my greatest wish to hold, [but also because] your interest in my abilities has bolstered my at times rather shaky self-confidence, and of all living musicians only you, dear Herr Director, only you were capable of doing this in so full a measure. Excuse me if I grow tiresome, but today I really had to get it off my chest at all costs. Be assured that I will ever be conscious of the enormous gratitude I owe you for the happiness you have bestowed on me today.

I remain in constant devotion and gratitude your most respectful,
Alexander Zemlinsky[1]

The letter is valuable not simply because it reveals the import Zemlinsky placed on a Hofoper position — "the highest goal of my wishes" — but because it so clearly demonstrates the rather extreme — almost obsequious — veneration Zemlinsky displayed toward Mahler. Nor is this the only example of such devout reverence. Zemlinsky had once confessed to Alma how he had often stood in Mahler's presence but found himself unable inquire about a conducting post. Zemlinsky also evidently preferred asking questions or favors of Mahler by way of Alma, doing so with the greatest trepidation, in order to avoid being considered a bother or a nuisance. Asking if Alma might put in a good word or lend a hand, Zemlinsky wrote, "Might you do so when the Herr Director is in a good mood? But don't tell him that I asked you. Agreed? That would be sweet of you. *But you do not have to do it*!" As for his personal impressions of Mahler's music, Zemlinsky was likewise incapable of addressing Mahler directly:

> I write to you and not to Herr Director Mahler because it is so horribly difficult for me to look at someone in the face or even to write to him directly in order to say what I absolutely must say today . . . It would give me such inner satisfaction to be able to say that [the Third Symphony] has revealed to me the complete illumination of his magnificent individuality and tremendous artistry . . . yesterday I said to my friends: *That is really something!* [Das ist Einer!] and we were so lucky to have been present yesterday in order to experience the future of music history. Perhaps that is what I wanted to tell you, improperly stated though it may be, but you will understand and know that I don't say such a thing lightly. If

---

[1] Zemlinsky in La Grange (1999), 482.

you think that this letter would be of some interest to Herr Mahler, then please—but if not, please simply relate to him my greatest esteem.[1]

Mahler had thus far remained largely Zemlinsky's mentor. He had provided Zemlinsky valuable counsel, willingly lent his support to the ill-fated Vereinigung schaffender Tonkünstler, and actively promoted Zemlinsky's music. In return, Zemlinsky had occasionally played the role of factotum, attending numerous rehearsals and, at Mahler's request, arranging the piano reduction of his Sixth Symphony. Mahler's offer for Zemlinsky to join his staff therefore represented a significant breakthrough for the younger conductor, who had worked his way up through Vienna's theaters to achieve just such a position. Years spent in the city's opera pits and concert halls had taught Zemlinsky invaluable insights into molding an ensemble, and Mahler clearly valued the prospect of a conductor of Zemlinsky's ability and seemingly inexhaustible energy working under him, especially one upon whom he had exerted so strong an influence. Though the offer represented a demotion from director to assistant, and one of several at that, it appears Zemlinsky never hesitated. For an opportunity to work with Mahler at the Hofoper, Zemlinsky was willing to become a slave once again.

In the late December of 1906, Mahler needed to replace Francesco Spetrino, an assistant conductor who had tendered his resignation.[2] Rather than fill the gap temporarily, Mahler had Zemlinsky's contract pushed up to May, before the close of the present season. Zemlinsky was scheduled to lead the premiere of a brand new production of Verdi's *Otello*, despite his never having conducted any Verdi at all. In February 1907, Zemlinsky led the Viennese premiere of Puccini's *Tosca* at the Volksoper; two months later, he took leave of his Volksoper colleagues in anticipation of his new position.

As a student walking to the Conservatory, Zemlinsky had passed the imposing Hofoper countless times; in the years since, Zemlinsky had attended numerous Hofoper rehearsals and performances, including those for his opera *Es war Einmal*. He was thus intimately familiar with the hall and well acquainted with its acoustics and had only to familiarize himself with conducting in the great hall. Rehearsals for the new *Otello* production likely began in the latter part of April, although Zemlinsky was formally contracted to begin work May 1. The performance, on May 3, went well enough—years later, the music critic and author Rudolf Stephan Hoffmann would still recall Zemlinsky's "beautiful" *Otello* debut.[3] But for the first time in his career, Zemlinsky harbored concerns about

[1] AZ/AMW.

[2] Spetrino nevertheless remained at the Hofoper until 1908.

[3] Hoffmann (1910), 193–97.

a perceived lack of respect from his orchestra musicians.[1] He nevertheless remained confident that with time he would win the ensemble over, and in June he appeared twice, conducting performances of *Carmen* and *Die Zauberflöte*. When the Hofoper closed its doors for the summer, Zemlinsky left on a solid footing.

The summer months provided Zemlinsky with time to reflect upon his new professional status and the upcoming season. Personally, there was also much to consider. Zemlinsky had been courting Ida Guttmann for two years, and the couple had decided to marry. Ida had been eleven years old when Zemlinsky courted her sister Melanie. Melanie had since moved to America and married the painter William Clarke Rice, but one can imagine Zemlinsky's interacting with Ida at the Guttmann household so many years ago, playfully teasing her, perhaps hoping to make a good impression on her older sister Melanie. Like Zemlinsky, Ida had been granted admission to the Vienna Conservatory's preparatory school because of her talent, and she later pursued piano studies with Wilhelm Rausch and then Franz Zottmann. Ida's passionate musical interests undoubtedly drew her to the young conductor and him to Ida, and their shared history must have been a part of their mutual attraction. And so, over course of their two-year romance, their relationship blossomed.

Zemlinsky had long ago drifted away from the Jewish community but had never converted to Christianity, a trend by now common among ambitious Jews eager to assimilate within Vienna's cultural and intellectual community. His choice to convert now, just as he was about to begin conducting under Mahler at the Hofoper, suggests the position may have hinged on his conversion. It was, after all, common knowledge that Mahler had converted prior to his own appointment as the institution's director. In any case, on June 11 1907, Zemlinsky and his bride-to-be entered the Lutherische Stadtkirche, the Lutheran City Church, and, with Schoenberg as witness, underwent conversion.[2] When all three returned to the Church ten days later, Zemlinsky and Ida were wed.

There exist few details about their life together, but Zemlinsky seems to have found the institution of marriage pleasant, at least early on. In a letter to Alma, Mahler wrote that "Zemlinsky has been to see me too; you will be surprised how

[1] AZ/AMW.

[2] The Lutherische Stadtkirche was a "second stop" to many of Vienna's Jews for whom Catholicism was too radical an alternative. Even the church itself, wedged neatly into the Dorotheergasse, a side street in the inner city, drew far less attention to itself than did the imposing St. Stephan's Cathedral, a gothic monument to centuries of European Catholicism that triumphantly occupied a city block on the nearby Kärntnerstrasse, one of the city's major pedestrian thoroughfares. The theological demands of the Protestant church were likewise minimal, and its officials had become accustomed to marrying converts, both Jewish and Catholic.

fat in the face he is now. Marriage appears to suit him."[1] One year later Ida gave birth to the couple's only child, Johanna ("Hansi").

But summer joys were cut short when rumors began circulating that Mahler was contemplating resigning from the Hofoper, leaving Zemlinsky to wonder about his future there. Considering Mahler's tumultuous history, the disturbing news must not have come as a complete surprise. For a decade, Mahler had flown in the face of Viennese convention. Remaining true to his credo, "Tradition ist Schlamperei" (Tradition is slovenliness), Mahler, together with the house's production chief Alfred Roller, had refashioned operatic masterworks according to Mahler's conceptions. This involved, among other things, uncut operatic performances, in contrast to the more common practice of exercising artistic license to shorten scores. To be sure, the theater had attained new heights under Mahler's leadership, but at great cost. By 1907, the 47-year-old music director had developed a heart condition, his singers and orchestra were worn down by his dictatorial methods, his radicalism fanned the flames of his opponents among the critics, and even his relations with Roller had seriously deteriorated. Mahler felt he could no longer remain.

Since the end of the previous season the Viennese press had been awash with speculation about Mahler's intentions and possible successors. Indeed, it appeared that Mahler was simply awaiting word about who was to be enlisted as his replacement before making the news public. Many in Vienna urged the maestro to stay on, among them a host of eminent authors including Hugo von Hofmannsthal, Stefan Zweig, Peter Altenberg and Hermann Bahr, but their entreaties were of no avail. Mahler refused to do battle any longer.

Zemlinsky's return to the Hofoper following the summer intermission should have been among the most joyful periods of his life. Newly married, he had left the theater in the spring on a positive note and was now returning at the start of August to begin preparations for *Der Traumgörge*, its October 4 premiere scheduled to coincide with the Austrian Emperor's name day. But Mahler's impending resignation cast a dark shadow over everything, and Zemlinsky shuddered at the thought of what it could mean to his own welfare. To Alma he penned a bleak message:

> Now *my* suffering is about to start. For the moment I can't imagine what is going to happen, especially in my situation. For me it is a disaster! I know exactly what I will be losing, whoever is named his successor. I am in a dreadful situation.[2]

[1] Mahler-Werfel (1969), 289.
[2] AZ/AMW.

Zemlinsky soon had his hands full with last minute modifications to *Der Traumgörge*'s score, which Mahler had required, in addition to a battery of meetings with directors and designers.[1] He was also scheduled to make his first Hofoper appearance of the season with Wagner's *Tannhäuser* on August 20. Then, earlier that day, Zemlinsky, along with the rest of Vienna, read the official announcement in the press: Felix Weingartner had been named Mahler's successor. Enmeshed in *Der Traumgörge* cuts and reeling from the latest news, it's impossible to imagine Zemlinsky's state of mind as he mounted the podium that evening to take the Hofoper ensemble through Wagner's *Tannhäuser*. The following evening brought *Carmen*. Then, with nothing on the docket until an August 31 performance of *Otello*, Zemlinsky at last was provided a respite to ponder what life would mean under Weingartner.

A conductor and composer whose formidable abilities were generally recognized by all who encountered him, Weingartner was Mahler's antithesis in almost every way. Weingartner's baton technique was clean, efficient, and unexaggerated, and his musical tastes gravitated toward the classics and comic opera. The two did share one character trait: a quarrelsome nature. Arguably Mahler was the greater autocrat, but Weingartner wasted little time amassing detractors. He had been appointed Kapellmeister of the Berlin Opera in 1891, but opposition led him to resign seven years later. As musical director of the Vienna Hofoper, Weingartner would survive only half as long.[2]

Weingartner was not scheduled to begin work at the Hofoper until the start of the New Year, but the direction the theater was to take now rested in his hands. He set to work immediately cleaning house. There would be less Wagner and more cuts, and in preparation for his January debut, Weingartner set about redesigning Mahler's entire production of Beethoven's *Fidelio*, regarded by many at the time as sacrosanct. At the start of Weingartner's tenure, Zemlinsky, a seasoned diplomat, remained cordial with the new musical director, even as he watched Weingartner break from everything Mahler represented. "As far as I am concerned," Zemlinsky declared in late August of 1907, "Weingartner is like everyone else, either favorable or detrimental! More than that I cannot tell."[3] He would know soon enough.

At the start of September, Zemlinsky took over rehearsals of *Die Zauberflöte* for Mahler, who was struggling with arm inflammation caused by a smallpox inoculation. Although Mahler still planned to lead the September 4 perfor-

[1] Weber (1995), 56.

[2] Weingartner nevertheless continued to conduct orchestral concerts in both cities long after he resigned his operatic posts.

[3] Weber (1995), 56.

mance, he cancelled at the last moment, fearing the pain would hinder his conducting, and Zemlinsky conducted instead.[1] Four days later an announcement
appeared in the *Fremden-Blatt* that Zemlinsky had decided to make further
changes to *Der Traumgörge*'s score, and its premiere was therefore being postponed.[2] According to Henry-Louis de la Grange, Weingartner had attended *Der
Traumgörge* rehearsals and demanded further changes, which Zemlinsky was
initially unwilling to accommodate.[3] Now, either Zemlinsky had had a change
of heart or, what seems more likely, the Weingartner administration had stepped
in and made an official announcement in order to place the opera's future on
indefinite hold. With Mahler on the way out, any promises to Zemlinsky about
the work's production now meant little. For Zemlinsky, the prospect of seeing
Der Traumgörge mounted at the Hofoper must have appeared bleak indeed.

Throughout the months of September and October Zemlinsky conducted at
the Hofoper just five times — twice in September, and thrice in the month that
followed. On October 5, the Emperor officially released Mahler from his contract. Ten days later Mahler stepped to the podium to lead a final performance
of Beethoven's *Fidelio*, bringing to a close a ten-year musical reign, by far the
longest tenure of any Hofoper conductor to date. Soon Mahler and Alma were
en route to America, where Mahler was already contracted to conduct at the
Metropolitan Opera in New York.

In their final days in Vienna, as they made preparations for their departure,
the Mahlers fit in formal farewells where they could:

> Dear Zemlinsky,
>
> We do want to say goodbye to you. — Couldn't you and Schoenberg
> drop in again for a while? I'm afraid we are engaged every evening, so
> it would have to be in the afternoon. — Preferably *at 4 o'clock*, when we
> are always in. — Please also bring my score (Seventh Symphony). You can
> have it back on my return.
>
> All good wishes. Yours,
>
> Mahler[4]

Zemlinsky's Hofoper position continued to deteriorate. In November he led
only four performances, in December only two and a half, the latter a shared
bill with Julius Lehnert, another assistant. It was clear Weingartner had little
use for him.

---

[1] La Grange (1999), 484.
[2] Cited in La Grange (1999), 484.
[3] Ibid.
[4] Archiv der Gesellschaft der Musikfreunde in Wien (Briefe Gustav Mahler 38).

The Paris express, with the Mahlers aboard, pulled out of Vienna on December 9. Zemlinsky was slated to conduct *Tannhäuser* again that evening, but he must have been among the two hundred well-wishers gathered at the West Railway Station to bid the Mahlers *auf Wiedersehen*. Gustav Klimt was there, and was heard to utter "Vorbei" (It's over) as the train left the station. The painter, like others on the platform, recognized Mahler's departure as the end of an era.

Elsewhere in the country a darker era was dawning. That same December, in the northern Austrian town of Werfenstein, Adolf Josef Lanz, founder of an Aryan religion known as the Order of the New Temple, raised a flag emblazoned with a striking, ancient symbol: the swastika.[1] And unbeknownst to Lanz, three months earlier a prospective art student had arrived in Vienna.[2] After twice being rejected from the Academy of Fine Arts, Adolf Hitler drifted aimlessly for several years, living in cheap accommodation and closely following the anti-Semitic policies of Mayor Karl Lueger. In the beginning, Hitler was unable to distinguish Vienna's 200,000 Jews from among its other inhabitants. But over time Vienna's Jews "became distinguished in my eyes from the rest of humanity. Particularly the Inner City and the districts north of the Danube Canal swarmed with a people which even outwardly had lost all resemblance to Germans."[3]

At the start of 1908, Weingartner, setting a new tone, severed all connections with his predecessor and cancelled the *Der Traumgörge* production. The score, which Weingartner may never have even bothered to read, was relegated to the theater's archives. Two years of work, revisions, planning, rehearsals and more revisions had come to nothing. Weingartner thus spurned the opportunity to introduce an important new work to the repertoire and to offer the public a much-anticipated follow-up to *Es war einmal*.

Eleven years later, in 1919, Schoenberg's protégé Anton Webern wrote to Zemlinsky,

> I have been occupied with your *Traumgörge* since the summer, and it pleases me more than I can say. I so long to hear this music. When will I finally, finally have the opportunity to do so? That this work has still not been performed is a sign of how low the music business has sunk![4]

[1] Hoffman (1988), 148.

[2] Hitler claimed to have attended performances led by Mahler of *Tristan und Isolde* at the Hofoper. See Hoffman (1988), 147.

[3] Hitler (1971), 56.

[4] Weber (1995), 291.

Zemlinsky never heard *Der Traumgörge* performed. Years later, he sat at the piano and played through the score, alone.[1]

On February 15, 1908, after a fifteen-week hiatus from the Hofoper, Zemlinsky's contract was terminated. He had lasted less than a single season.

What might have been, had Zemlinsky stayed, or Mahler never left? Two outcomes seem inevitable. Had Weingartner kept him on, Zemlinsky would have withered under the new regime. Despite being a seasoned professional, Zemlinsky was a devoted Mahlerian, and it is doubtful he could have tolerated the changed musical direction Weingartner decreed. Yet had Mahler remained, Zemlinsky would have conducted in the famous man's shadow, his brilliance stifled. Unbearable as it was to be forced from such a prestigious institution, Zemlinsky was saved from enduring a subordinate role that would have drained his creativity and confidence.

A short time later Mahler wrote from Philadelphia, expressing regrets about the entire matter:

> Dear Zemlinsky,
>
> A completely unexpected quarter of an hour of leisure and solitude during a "guest"-tour gives me a chance to send at least a cordial greeting in reply to your delightful and interesting letter.
>
> I'm afraid the news of your adventures with the new regime did not come as a surprise to me. Still, I should not have thought W.[eingartner] would so blatantly flout his *promise* to produce your opera before anything else.
>
> This is a serious blow to you, as I can see for myself. Altogether I feel I *too* am very *much to blame*, even though "not guilty". And I very often have a bad conscience. But — who could have foreseen all this?
>
> What I think now is that you must do everything possible to get your work produced at the Jubiläumstheater [Volksoper] . . .
>
> Yours sincerely,
> Mahler[2]

Mahler closed his letter with the reassurance that "there is a future to

---

[1] As late as 1921, the critic Rudolf Stephan Hoffmann lamented the opera's history: "The German stage must be overripe in order to be able to give up such a prize . . . Like *Traumgörge*, the 'World' is against him." Hoffmann (1921), 216. Although a piano reduction was prepared by Arthur Bodanzky, for which Zemlinsky retained the copyrights, a full orchestral score was never published. The opera itself lay dormant until October 11, 1980, at which time it finally received its long overdue premiere in Nuremberg.

[2] Letter dated March of 1908. Martner (1979), 353.

everything," but Zemlinsky could not envision anything positive on the horizon. His Hofoper future quashed, prospects for an operatic premiere of *Traumgörge* seemed doomed. Both blows were among the most crushing defeats Zemlinsky ever experienced, and his strongest ally was now an ocean away, powerless to lend a hand.

Believing that Vienna had little else to offer, Zemlinsky began contemplating leaving the country. Hearing of a conducting post at a new opera house opening in New York, he wrote Alma, asking if Mahler might put in a word for him with the theater's director. Mahler, after all, had found success on American shores and perhaps Zemlinsky could do likewise. Zemlinsky knew little about America or its musical life, and still less about the conducting post, but he considered his current predicament desperate and proclaimed to Alma, "I would gladly go over there!"[1] The inquiry led nowhere.

Disheartening as it was, Zemlinsky limped back to the Volksoper. But things at his old house had changed. The Czech conductor Oskar Nedbal now occupied Zemlinsky's former position, leaving Zemlinsky the role of first *Kapellmeister*, a subservient position that to Zemlinsky signified further defeat. Still, the Volksoper could offer Zemlinsky a number of significant projects that would have been difficult, if not impossible, at the highly bureaucratic, state-supported Hofoper. Almost immediately Zemlinsky conducted the first performance in a German-speaking land of Paul Dukas's opera *Ariane et Barbe-bleue*, which he premiered at the start of April 1908. Additional projects included a critically acclaimed production of Strauss's *Salome* and the premiere of Zemlinsky's next opera, *Kleider machen Leute*. He was also scheduled to lead a new series of six orchestral concerts per year at the theater. This got off to a strong start with a program featuring Weber's overture to *Oberon*, and the C major Piano Concerto and Fifth Symphony of Beethoven. But his success in the wake of the previous string of disappointments was little consolation, and as Zemlinsky's activities became routine, he struggled to find inspiration. Vienna became distasteful to him, and as his dissatisfaction grew, so too did his desire to leave, even if it meant accepting an inferior post elsewhere.

The year 1908 also brought to a close a tragic series of events involving Zemlinsky's circle and a twenty-three-year-old painter named Richard Gerstl. Difficult by nature, Gerstl was defiant and trying as a student, and his paintings convey why his teachers found him exasperating. His canvases reflect the garish and angry qualities associated with Expressionism, and his self-portraits in particular reveal a less-than-stable psyche. Gerstl's style was strongly influ-

[1] AZ/AMW.

enced by those whose work he encountered at various Viennese exhibitions, particularly Edvard Munch, Vincent van Gogh and Paul Gauguin. According to the art historian Kirk Varnedoe, Gerstl may have been the first Viennese painter to echo the impact of such artists,[1] but it was the nature of his work — a progressive style that ranged from mild and fluid to anti-naturalistic and violent — that troubled his teachers.

Just how Gerstl found his way into Zemlinsky and Schoenberg's circle is unknown, but their mutual friendship developed rapidly, aided in part by their common passion for Mahler and because Gerstl lived in the Nussdorferstrasse, just minutes by foot from the Liechtensteinstrasse apartment. Soon, Zemlinsky and the Schoenbergs were posing for the artist, and Schoenberg was inspired to take up painting.[2] On a small scale, the relationship between these men reflected the larger cultural interaction for which Vienna is remembered, but in the case of Gerstl, the results were disastrous. In 1907, Gerstl, at Schoenberg's invitation, joined the composer and his wife Mathilde during their summer holidays in Gmunden. Over the course of the next year, as Gerstl's contact with Mathilde grew increasingly intimate, Schoenberg became increasingly insular,[3] but by the summer of 1908 he believed the matter resolved. Gerstl again joined the family on vacation, where Schoenberg eventually confronted Mathilde about their affair. Her actions made it clear where things stood: she left her family and returned with Gerstl to Vienna, and it was only through the persistent pleas of Schoenberg's friends, particularly those of the young composer Anton Webern, that she was eventually persuaded to return to her husband and children.

While Mathilde had a family to return to, Gerstl had none. Not only had an intense romantic tie been severed, his camaraderie with the entire circle was subsequently jeopardized. The following autumn Gerstl withdrew into himself completely. On November 4, having recently completed two self-portraits, the 25-year-old painter retired to his atelier, set fire to a number of his works, and hanged himself. With the events too tragic for life to continue as before and their funds low, the Schoenbergs soon left Liechtensteinstrasse for the suburb of Hietzing. The Zemlinskys stayed on until 1910, when they left Liechtensteinstrasse 68 for Fuchsthallergasse 4, closer still to the front steps of the Volksoper.

---

[1] Varnedoe (1986), 165.

[2] Schoenberg's earliest experiments with painting bore fruit in 1911, the year he met the artist Wassily Kandinsky and showed four paintings in Munich's *Blaue Reiter* (The Blue Rider) exhibition.

[3] Stuckenschmidt considers this event and Mahler's departure for America as the two defining incidents that plunged Schoenberg into a state of inner turmoil at this time. Painting therefore served as a means to further isolate himself. See Stuckenschmidt (1977), 94.

To what extent communication between Schoenberg and Zemlinsky continued in the aftermath of Mathilde's affair is unknown — any correspondence between the families that may have existed from this time has not survived. In all likelihood, there was an extended period of silence, as Schoenberg and Mathilde attempted to put their lives back into some sort of working order. For Zemlinsky, whose compositional productivity had already slowed to a trickle, the awkward events only served to further dam up his creative output.

Zemlinsky had begun drafting a new opera, *Kleider machen Leute*, in the early summer of 1907, before marriage took precedence. Then came the disappointing string of events at the Hofoper and subsequent return to the Volksoper, all of which further ate into Zemlinsky's time and negatively affected his ability to concentrate. Schoenberg's work also probably adversely affected Zemlinsky's compositional proficiency. Living in such close proximity, Zemlinsky looked on as his one-time student advanced musical boundaries. In the weeks immediately following Zemlinsky's formal dismissal from the Hofoper, Schoenberg began composing his Second String Quartet; by the time it was finished a year later, Schoenberg no longer regarded dissonance as something to be resolved. His ties to Vienna's golden past severed, tonality no longer played a governing role, often any role at all, in his music.

And then, on May 8, 1908, while the events surrounding Mathilde, Gerstl and Schoenberg were being played out in Gmunden and in the Liechtensteinstrasse, Ida gave birth to a baby girl, Johanna. In the weeks that followed, familial joy turned to anguish, as little "Hansi" struggled with bouts of illness. But once her convalescence was assured, Zemlinsky managed to dash off a celebratory song in her honor — *Der chinesische Hund, oder Der englische Apfelstrudel* (The Chinese Dog, or The English Apple Strudel).

In the wake of such tumultuous events, composing music of any kind was immensely difficult, so it is no surprise that by the summer of 1908 Zemlinsky's work had all but stopped. Since 1907 Zemlinsky had written nothing except a few songs, among them five based on texts of Richard Dehmel, a fragment of a Quintet in D minor for strings, and preliminary work on *Kleider machen Leute*. Finally, in 1909, initial drafts of the opera were completed. But it would be another year before anything new flowed from Zemlinsky's pen.

Based on Gottfried Keller's 1874 novella of the same name, *Kleider machen Leute* (Clothes Make the Man) tells the story of Strapinski, a poor tailor who, lacking work in Keller's imaginary Swiss town of Seldwyla, sets out for the village of Goldach with nothing to his name save the finery he wears. When his carriage pulls into Goldach, Strapinski is announced as Count Strapinski of Poland. Stupefied by the warm reception he receives and too hungry to reject a delicious meal, Strapinski plays along with the charade, especially after meeting the beautiful Nettchen. Melchior Böhni, a local procurator who is also vying for Nettchen's affections, suspects something is amiss and begins to look into Strapinski's past. In an effort to expose and publicly humiliate his rival, Böhni stages a play-within-a-play (*Clothes Make the Man*), wherein Strapinski's deception is revealed to all. Strapinski now attempts to defend his masquerade, claiming that he only acted out the role that the townspeople themselves had created. His only guilt, he pleads, stems from having deceived Nettchen, but once the girl understands the tailor's heart, she is willing to remain his, even if it means life as a tailor's wife instead of a countess.

Among the most influential German writers of the nineteenth century, Keller frequently explored social themes and the injustices brought about by class strata, and *Kleider machen Leute* is no exception. Along with the story's wit and charm resides an unflattering depiction of society, a subject Keller subtly and bitingly portrays, and Zemlinsky brings to life in Strapinski's *Schneiderlein*, a song about a starving tailor and the well-dressed society he serves. While the librettist Leo Feld may have fretted over Keller's minute attention to detail, a challenge in the world of stagecraft, evidence suggests he encountered no such struggles with Keller's wit and sarcasm, but rather expanded on Keller's intent. To Keller's golden roofs (the town is indeed named Goldach) for example, which carried the self-righteous inscriptions "Internal Honesty", "External Honesty" and "Civic Virtue", Feld contributed the attributes "Divine Providence", "Valour" and "Justice". And when Pütschli-Nievergelt observes Strapinski sitting down to a meal later in Act I, Feld brings bourgeois society home to Vienna: "A distinguished gentleman! He must be from Vienna, he eats so much!"

With the libretto in hand, Zemlinsky faced the question of how to construct a musical score that, like Keller's tale, operated on two levels. For the thirty-eight-year-old composer, rich, full-blooded Romanticism would no longer suffice — only sharp musical teeth could keep pace with Keller's dark wit. He now understood that simplifying matters would produce a stronger effect. Zemlinsky's solution was a lean, direct tone that conveyed Keller's dry, sarcastic humor. In the words of critic and musicologist Theodor Adorno, Zemlinsky "came closer than anyone to the ideal of distilled comedy: subtle and not overloaded with meaning . . . ."[1]

Kleider machen Leute opens with overlapping wind entrances, a series of

[1] Adorno (1992), 119.

rising fifths (D–A / G–D / F–C / B♭–F / E♭–B♭) purposely crafted to avoid any declaration of major or minor tonality. The unstable atmosphere sets the stage — in Goldach nothing is as it appears. Zemlinsky then works with a rich, chromatic palette and chooses chords for the colors or timbres they evoke. Nevertheless, he continually supplies sufficient tonal reference to stabilize the harmony and the angular vocal writing, as when Strapinski sings that his coat and hat are as necessary as life itself ("Doch der Mantel und die Mütze sind mir wert wie Luft und Leben!"), found near the start of the Prologue.

Whether set to simple homophonic song or virtuosic counterpoint, each character and moment is vividly portrayed: the simplicity of village life depicted in the unison opening lines of Strapinski and his apprentices; Litumlei, whose dry and uninteresting lines reflect a man with nothing important to say; the stuttering Federspiel. Later, when Strapinski sips coffee and puffs on a cigar in the ceremonious company of men, Zemlinsky keeps pace with Keller's caricature by setting the tableau as a waltz — parodying comfortable Viennese life — and scoring the conversation of Strapinski and company in counterpoint, mocking their self-satisfied air. In Act II, Nettchen's naïveté is aptly revealed in song — "Lehn' deine Wang' an meine Wang'" (Place your cheek next to my cheek) — while her bourgeois audience, content in the Biedermeier salon, find themselves smitten by the song's overblown sentimentality.[1]

With the first draft of the score completed in 1909, Zemlinsky began the search for a performance venue. In July of 1910, the extant correspondence between Zemlinsky and Schoenberg resumes, and in the first surviving letter Zemlinsky laments over the dreadful work required to correct the parts for the Stuttgart Hofoper.[2] All the same, a premiere seemed imminent — Max von Schillings, the *Generalmusikdirektor* of the Stuttgart Hofoper, had secured rights to host the opera's first performance, making this premiere the first time a Zemlinsky opera would be heard outside of Vienna since the Munich performance of *Sarema* in 1897. During the course of the summer Zemlinsky feverishly set about preparing a readable and error-free version of the score, but disappointment soon set in. Owing to resistance by the Stuttgart company, Schillings's invitation was withdrawn. In Vienna, Rainer Simons was willing to produce it at the Volksoper and inquired if Zemlinsky would be willing to conduct it himself the following season. Zemlinsky remained wary of championing his own cause, so in an act just short of desperation, he suppressed his pride and

---

[1] In order to drive the point home, Zemlinsky instructs the song to be sung very sentimentally.

[2] Weber (1995), 57–58.

antipathy toward Felix Weingartner and offered him first performance rights to what Zemlinsky described as his "musical comedy in a prelude and three acts".[1] But true to form Weingartner's reply, while diplomatic, was disheartening — he would gladly familiarize himself with the opera, but was unable to commit further. Two options remained: Zemlinsky could either undertake the project himself at the Volksoper, or he could let another opera go unperformed. In a rare instance of self-promotion, Zemlinsky accepted Simons's offer. On December 2, Zemlinsky's *Kleider machen Leute* received its premiere.

Kleider machen Leute's musical wit and subtlety, virtuosic technique, and progressive yet accessible language seemed ideally suited to Keller's story-line, and, at the highly successful first night's performance, Zemlinsky and his company took innumerable curtain calls. Yet the days following the December premiere brought mixed reviews. Ludwig Karpath's critique in the *Neues Wiener Tagblatt* was an example. Although he acknowledged Zemlinsky as a genuine, honest and warm-blooded artist, Karpath was paradoxically of the opinion that Zemlinsky's "comic" opera suffered precisely on account of its subtlety:

> with virtuosity he can conceal the intricacies of the score, projecting the impression of simplicity . . . he delights with highly successful motivic work that carries us from voice to voice . . . but this method of composing carries a price: it appeals to the intellect at the expense of the soul. To the devil with intellectualism! We want more melody![2]

The composer and critic Robert Konta, espousing the opposite view, wrote that *Kleider machen Leute* achieved "an aristocratic smile" and "elegant cheerfulness throughout".[3] Konta was convinced that Zemlinsky's opera would "win for Zemlinsky new friends and convert numerous adversaries", suggesting that Zemlinsky already had his share of detractors, or possibly he was alluding to Schillings's unreceptive Stuttgart ensemble. Finally, the Viennese critic Rudolf Stephan Hoffmann seized the opportunity in *Der Merker* to recapitulate the various injustices to which Zemlinsky had been subjected — whether at the Hofoper or in the hands of an unappreciated press — and reflect upon Zemlinsky's unwavering integrity within a culture that, at least according to Hoffmann, placed far too little premium on such qualities:

> Clothes make the man! A cheap truism. Zemlinsky did not know it — or has rejected it. Never has he appeared in clothes other than his own.

[1] See Ottner (1995), 222.
[2] *Neues Wiener Tagblatt* (Dec. 3, 1910), 10.
[3] *Zeitschrift für Musik und Literatur* I, H. 2 (Jan. 1911), 14–16.

never has he been intent on seeming other than he is, never has he known how to make use of those people who make the clothes. Unfortunately, he is not at all cunning. He still thinks that an artist who achieves something will finally, step by step, and even with some patience, find recognition, even in — Seldwyla . . .

He debuted [at the Hofoper] with a beautiful *Otello* performance that I still recall well. And his new opera *Traumgörge* was taken on and its preparation nearly complete, but Mahler left and the new regime began with a huge house cleaning . . . *Traumgörge* was set aside, and Zemlinsky was ignored and urged to resign . . . he who has never concerned himself with politics or cliques, all of a sudden appeared compromised. *Der Traumgörge* remained unperformed, as did a Hofmannsthal tone poem,[1] and an unpleasant state of events surrounds the new comic opera that only now received its premiere. Will this ever stop?

People are too deeply rooted in Lortzing and Rossini, although they are merely modern in their subject but not in their substance. Zemlinsky is perhaps yet to fully attain the perfection that certainly resides in his unconscious, but he has come closer to it than anybody thus far. He has truly created a modern comic opera, and for doing so some may hold it against him . . .

In truth, this opera is clearly melodically constructed, from the vocal lines onward, which are given precedence at all times. The orchestra, with its virtuosic instrumentation, consists of only the necessary notes; there exists no padding, no excess. The opera is as chamber music. The sound is a thing in and of itself and as a result is out of the ordinary, always magical, always new . . . Despite the thick polyphonic texture, the line is never lost. One always knows where it is heading. The same is true for the harmonic structure. With utmost daring the chords and modulations remain totally faithful to the principles of tonality, which he is willing to display with the simplest of cadences, relying on the dominant seventh chord without hesitation, despite its being regarded as archaic . . .

Is all of this so insignificant in an opera that it can be dismissed with chilly reverence or a stupid joke, as some critics are accustomed to doing? Are we really so overly rich in productive talent that we can afford to make life difficult for each of them? Sadly, respect for the creators' artistic endeavors is at a low point indeed. It is the noblest and solely productive service of the critic to help heighten this respect, rather than

[1] Implied is the *Tanzpoem*, a reworking of a portion from the *Drei Balletstücke*.

undermine it. Each honest labor is entitled to encouragement; each con-
scientious criticism has the duty to do this. And if the critic contains even
a glimmer of artistry, as one would hope, then this duty should bring him
pleasure . . .[1]

Zemlinsky may have found Hoffmann's words consoling, but they nevertheless served to confirm that he had overstayed his welcome, if ever there was
a welcome, in the Austrian capital.

Eight days after the opening of *Kleider machen Leute*, Franz Schreker led his
Philharmonic Choir in the premiere of Zemlinsky's Psalm 23, *The Lord is my
Shepherd*. The composition of his second psalm setting had been a brief affair
— sketched at Bad Ischl in July of 1910, it was finished just a month later. The
result was effective, if curious. Set to the translation by Martin Luther, Zemlinsky's incorporation of celeste, glockenspiel, harps and tambourine lent the score
an exotic, biblical air, a quality he may have associated with his youthful years
spent among Vienna's Sephardic community. Constructed in two large sections,
the work opens with a pentatonic oboe solo (the Good Shepherd), whose pastoral lines set the tone for the entrance of the chorus. A two-note orchestral ostinato and a gently walking bass, both drawn from the work's early bars, underscore the simplicity of the opening unison choral. Zemlinsky reserved greater
depth for his Psalm's second stanza, where rich chromaticism, counterpoint and
layered chorale writing recall the spirit of Brahms.

Steely string tremolos and ominous descending brass herald the start of the
second major portion of the work, whose sinister text — "And, though I walk
through the valley of death . . ." — Zemlinsky effectively matches with descending vocal lines and increased orchestral agitation. Eventually Zemlinsky draws
the music back to the world of "goodness and mercy" with Wagnerian passion,
culminating in a dramatic climax for the entire ensemble. The gentle rocking
ostinato now returns and the peaceful spirit of the opening chorus is reaffirmed,
as the steady pulse of harp and celeste transports the Psalm to its final tranquil
bars.

Franz Schreker was in his fourth season as director of the Vienna Philharmonic Chorus when he premiered Psalm 23, along with Cyril Scott's Overture
to *Princess Maleine*[2] and Mahler's *Das klagende Lied* on December 10, 1910.

[1] *Der Merker*, 5 (1910), 193–97.
[2] Berg found Scott's overture "never-ending mush, no doubt modern, but it almost made
me nauseated". Brand, Hailey and Harris (1987), 87.

Schreker's commitment to performing the newest repertoire at the highest level possible was well known, but on this evening his interpretation of Zemlinsky's score failed to win over his audience. Berg was on hand for the concert and wrote, "Zemlinsky's magnificent work fell flat; most of the audience can't appreciate such chaste beauty, such slightly understated warmth."[1] Despite such a tight, picturesque and original choral work, it appeared that Zemlinsky's Viennese triumphs would be realized only with scores by other composers. He did not have long to wait.

On the eve of December 23, 1910, Zemlinsky conducted Richard Strauss's *Salome* at the Volksoper. Regarded as too radical to be performed at the Hofoper, Zemlinsky's production marked the first time *Salome* had been offered by a resident Viennese ensemble.[2] Since September, the house had already produced an eclectic array of major works including *Faust*, *Lohengrin*, *Mignon*, *La Juive* and *Carmen*, and with much of December devoted to Zemlinsky's own *Kleider machen Leute*, it hardly seemed a propitious time to schedule a work as demanding as *Salome*, which called for virtuosic performances both on the stage and in the pit. Nevertheless, Zemlinsky's forces rose to the occasion, and this time the press proved unanimous in its praise. The *Neues Wiener Tagblatt* proclaimed, "Music director Zemlinsky has produced a master work. How, with the joy of self-sacrifice, he and his musicians overcame the colossal difficulties of this work in such a relatively short time is admirable."[3] *Der Merker*, equally cognizant of the work's abbreviated rehearsal schedule, lauded Zemlinsky's command of orchestral balance, a trait for which he became increasingly well-known in the years that followed: "That all the voices were so clear and convincing is above all to Zemlinsky's credit, whose orchestra, despite relatively few rehearsals, brought forth all the magic of Strauss's tonal world."[4]

Salome saw a continued string of successful performances throughout the remainder of the season, but Zemlinsky's work at the Volksoper was nearing its end. By the time of his last appearance, a performance of *Tannhäuser* on April 29, 1911, Zemlinsky had not only secured summer employment in Munich but more important, had decided not to return to Vienna in the fall.

As April came to a close, the search for a new music director was underway 270 kilometers northwest of Vienna. Heinrich Teweles, playright, theater producer

[1] Brand, Hailey and Harris (1987), 87.

[2] *Salome* had been given its Viennese premiere in 1907 by a touring Breslau ensemble.

[3] *Neues Wiener Tagblatt* (Dec. 22, 1910), 13.

[4] *Der Merker*, Heft 7 (Jan. 1911), 315.

and critic of the *Prager Tagblatt*, had just been appointed head of Prague's Landestheater following the death of its illustrious long-time director, Angelo Neumann. The eminent institution, which counted Gustav Mahler, Karl Muck and Otto Klemperer among its former employees, had been without a music director since Klemperer's resignation the previous year. Thus, Teweles needed not only a first-rate conductor but also someone who possessed the understanding of general theatrical production and had the organizational skills to help run a major company. His search ended with Zemlinsky. His ticket out of Vienna would take him to Bohemia.

One week prior to Zemlinsky's final Volksoper performance, the journal *Bohemia* announced that Zemlinsky had been appointed the next music director of the Landestheater and carried with it Zemlinsky's own statement of acceptance:

> You have no idea how pleased I am to be at the head of the orchestra of the Prague Landestheater. It is a group of sound musicians, many of whom I know personally. I also know many of the soloists [i.e., singers] who work in Prague, whom I value and with whom I am pleased to be able to work hand in hand.[1]

Zemlinsky was finally leaving Vienna, yet he would still be within range of Vienna, both geographically, and artistically. By rail he could travel between Vienna and Prague comfortably in about six hours, and he would be kept abreast of the musical goings on in the city of his birth through constant contact with Schoenberg and their circle. But at the start of the new season Zemlinsky would no longer be the vital musical presence there that he had been for over a decade. Among those who regretted Zemlinsky's leaving Vienna was Erich Korngold, who Zemlinsky had tutored in harmony and instrumentation. Furthermore, Zemlinsky had also taken it upon himself to orchestrate the eleven-year-old wunderkind's ballet-pantomime *Der Schneemann*, which proved a sensation at its Hofoper premiere in October 1910.[2] Years later the Czech publication *Der Auftakt* devoted an entire issue to Zemlinsky's contributions, wherein Korngold expressed his regrets for what might have been for those of his generation had Zemlinsky remained in Vienna:

> I still lament today that my lessons with Zemlinsky were over so quickly when he was called to Prague. I had lost the ideal teacher, the most

---

[1] Quoted in Mahler (1972), 238.

[2] In 1914 Korngold set Teweles's comedy *Der Ring des Polykrates*, making for an interesting interconnection between Zemlinsky's student and his employer.

captivating musical inspiration of my early years, but Vienna also lost one of its strongest musicians. One must honestly consider if the next generation of Viennese talent might not have developed with greater consistency and surer direction had Zemlinsky remained in Vienna . . .[1]

In the second week of May, a dying Gustav Mahler returned to Vienna. He had fallen ill in New York following a string of concerts with the New York Philharmonic and been diagnosed with a bacterial infection and given little chance of recovery. Zemlinsky's contact with Mahler had been sporadic ever since Mahler's departure from Vienna on the heels of his Hofoper resignation; letters between the two men had been rare, and personal contact, limited to visits at the Mahlers' summer home in Maiernigg, rarer still. It is not even known if, after Mahler's death on May 18, 1911, Zemlinsky attended the funeral, although his absence from an event so significant and momentous is difficult to imagine. Surviving correspondence of Zemlinsky from the months that followed are also silent about the matter, but there can be little doubt that Mahler's death affected him deeply, and Zemlinsky's performance of Mahler's Eighth Symphony in Prague the following March was a profoundly moving experience. As with the death of Brahms years earlier, Zemlinsky had once again lost a close personal friend and important professional ally. Fortunately, the opportunity to move to Prague had come at the ideal moment, offering concrete proof that Zemlinsky could find success on his own. He would repay Mahler indirectly for his earlier support, by repeatedly championing his music in the Bohemian capital.

Instead of devoting the summer months of 1911 to composition and relaxation away from Vienna, as had become his custom, Zemlinsky accepted an engagement to conduct at the Munich Künstlertheater,[2] although he did take advantage of some time off between his Munich commitments to spend time on Lake Starnberg in southern Bavaria. In Munich Zemlinsky was warmly embraced, almost from his first downbeat, and enjoyed a concert-going public that he described as maintaining both "esteem and respect for those who have know-how".[3] His performances, which ran from July through September, included Offenbach's *La Belle Hélène* and *Orphée aux enfers*, and La Touche's

---

[1] Korngold (1921), 230.

[2] Munich's Künstlertheater was one of a number of German *avant-garde* theaters built at the start of the century. Known as "Reformtheaters", these were not traditional auditoriums with boxes but were smaller houses designed with ascending rows and no galleries. The Künstlertheater, destroyed during World War II and never rebuilt, was located on the premises of the Munich fair and exhibition grounds in the western part of the city and was home to lighter operatic fare during the summer months.

[3] Weber (1995), 60.

Thermidor. In a letter to Schoenberg that July, Zemlinsky proudly described the wondrous experience of being treated with proper dignity, a sensation all the more satisfying in the wake of the struggles he had consistently encountered in Vienna:

> Even with those of us at the Künstlertheater, a distinguished but never-theless private enterprise, the artist is everything. As it so happened, *Helena* was a tremendous success and from that point on I became every-thing to the people. They would like me to compose something for next season, which would then doubtlessly receive a first class production. They are also entertaining the idea of making me foremost artistic direc-tor (instead of Reinhard [*sic*])![1] For some changes I made to the score of *Thermidor* I am to be paid 500 Marks. I conduct when I want, sometimes only 2 acts! (To be sure the public won't know it — the orchestra plays in a pit). Moreover, exceptional people from everywhere are, without fail, to be found in the theater. Even Richard Strauss was at a performance and I heard that he warmly recommended me for the [Munich] Hofoper.[2]

Otto Klemperer, one of the "exceptional people" on hand that summer, heard Zemlinsky lead a performance of Offenbach and years later would invite Zemlinsky to work with him in Berlin.[3] Although once again at the mercy of operetta, Zemlinsky remained so impressed with the theater's quality and the generous reception he encountered that he immediately contacted Prague and cleared his calendar for the following summer, in order to return to Munich.[4] The critics were equally impressed with his work, evident in Edgar Istel's review of his performance of *La Belle Hélène*: "What a blessing to hear this valuable composition performed under a real conductor!"[5]

For Zemlinsky, Munich proved ideal in every way. His artistry was greatly admired, he had been asked to compose something for the following summer, and he was even being considered for the festival's directorship. When he pre-ferred not to conduct a complete performance, an assistant would cover. And in one case, when he refused to conduct one of the horrid "novelties" on the roster,

[1] Max Reinhardt, a theater director most known for his work in Berlin and his founding of the *Salzburger Festspiele*.

[2] Weber (1995), 60.

[3] Klemperer would later write that Zemlinsky "was an excellent musician . . . as a col-league he was extraordinarily sympathetic and considerate." Klemperer (1982), 88.

[4] Zemlinsky was to return to Munich's *Künstlertheater* for three successive summer sea-sons (1911–13).

[5] *Die Musik* (1910), 252.

a meeting of directors was immediately called and *Orphée* substituted in its place.[1] Although grateful for the status the Munich company afforded him, the experience offered Zemlinsky something far more vital: it imbued him with new life and reconfirmed his faith in his art.

Munich had been a pleasure. Now, with his summer obligations behind him, Zemlinsky returned to Vienna to prepare for the move to Prague. At the start of September 1911 Zemlinsky, with his wife and daughter, boarded the train for the Bohemian capital, where they took an apartment at Havlíčkova 9 in Prague's second district, the "New City". The flat, which Ida regarded as "huge",[2] was ideally located. Its centrality granted an easy walk to both the old town and the Deutsches Theater, while Prague's sophisticated trolley system provided easy access to the city's major neighborhoods and parks, such as the Kinsky'scher Gardens, located on the opposite bank of the Moldau (Vltava).

In Vienna, one bit of unfinished business remained — Zemlinsky had been contracted to lead a string of performances of *La Belle Hélène* with the touring Munich company at the Theater in der Josefstadt. While the production must have included some of the Munich core, a significant number of substitute singers and instrumentalists had been engaged for the Vienna run, many of whom Zemlinsky felt were not up to the task. Furthermore, the director Max Reinhardt was not on hand and Zemlinsky found Reinhardt's assistant, Berthold Held, intolerable. Although contracted to conduct performances throughout the entire month of October, Zemlinsky became so frustrated with the "impossible singers and a still more impossible orchestra"[3] that he refused to conduct any concerts. As a result, a huge row broke out between Zemlinsky and Held. Some feared a lawsuit imminent, yet by October 9 the matter was decided out of court. Fritz Behnfeldt was engaged to conduct, and Zemlinsky was absolved of any further responsibility.[4] Whether or not matters were as "impossible" as Zemlinsky depicted them, he was undoubtedly confronted with a group of musicians whose collective ability fell short of that to which he had grown ac-

---

[1] Weber (1995), 60. Neither the directorship nor a composition for the festival came to pass.

[2] From a letter dated May 8, 1920, generously made available by the Skandera family and translated from the Czech by Ľubica Malovecká. At the time of the letter, Ida lamented that they had but one servant! The Zemlinskys kept this apartment throughout their years in Prague.

[3] In a letter from Berg to Schoenberg, dated Oct. 7, 1911, quoted in Brand, Hailey and Harris (1987), 26.

[4] Indeed, whereas Zemlinsky was still quoted as the musical director in an announcement from October 4, no conductor was named on the playbills of October 7 and 8. The playbills are located in the Österreichisches Theatermuseum, but that from October 6 is lost.

customed in Munich. Rehearsing Offenbach from scratch, with new personnel, was a frustration he did not need.

Zemlinsky returned to Prague, where he rejoined his family and began preparing for the next stage of his life. And while Vienna would never be far from his thoughts, it was Bohemia where Zemlinsky now set his sights and pinned his hopes. Perhaps here he would finally attain the success and support for which he hungered but that eluded him at home.

The lamps are going out all over Europe;
we shall not see them lit again in our lifetime.

Sir Edward Grey (British Foreign Minister),
August 3, 1914

PART II
Prague and the Zemlinsky Era

Chapter 5

Scandals

BY THE TIME of Zemlinsky's arrival in Prague, Bohemia and Austria had struggled with an uneasy relationship for nearly four hundred years, beginning in 1526 when the kingdom of Bohemia was absorbed as a constituent state within the imperial Habsburg monarchy. In the centuries that followed, Bohemia fluctuated between periods of calm and struggle, as the Czech people sought to reassert their independence. The 1848 uprisings that swept across much of Europe, for example, were also played out on Bohemian soil and, although partially quashed, the events fueled the fires of Czech nationalism. Changes in suffrage laws eventually saw the German parliamentary majority give way, signaling a slow but steady shift in Bohemia's future. As Czechs gradually reclaimed their heritage, they began addressing issues ranging from language to religious freedom to state rights. As the nineteenth century came to a close, there were increasing indications that the Czechs were regaining control of their land. Some changes were subtle, such as a decision in 1892 to replace Prague's bilingual street signs with exclusively Czech signs. Other shifts, like population figures, were more dramatic. For example, estimates based on languages spoken show that in 1846 Prague harbored 66,046 Germans, compared with 36,687 Czechs, among the Christian population.[1] There were also 6,400 Jews in Prague's Josefov ghetto and portions of the Old Town at this time who largely preferred speaking German, but who also spoke Czech as well as Yiddish. By late in the second half of the century, the ethnic demographics began to swing dramatically in the other direction. The 1880 census of Prague and the

---

[1] Cohen (2006), 19.

inner suburbs counted just 39,000 Germans, as compared with 213,000 Czechs.[1] In the words of one professor at Prague's German university, "While previously the great capital was exclusively in the hands of the Germans . . . one will see in general a prodigious growth of the Czech nation, and the initiated will realize that it is not only prodigious but also powerful."[2]

As throngs of Czechs streamed from the countryside to the city in search of employment, the Czech middle class prospered and Czech intellectual life flourished. Czech-language newspapers, particularly those linked to various political parties, sprung up; the Czech language, so long subordinate to German, was officially recognized,[3] and in 1882 a Czech university opened its doors for the first time. Divisions separating the Czech and German population likewise became clearly defined: "Czechs and Germans frequented different cafés, listened to rival orchestras, attended different universities (using the same library on different days) and elected rival deputies."[4] And at the start of the twentieth century, census figures revealed a striking continuation of the demographic trend: by 1910, a year before Zemlinsky became a member of Prague's German community, the city's German population had shrunk to 33,000 (Catholics, Jews and Protestants), while the number of Czechs had soared to 405,000.[5]

Bohemia and Moravia provided *fin-de-siècle* Europe with an astounding array of artists and intellectuals — Sigmund Freud, Max Brod, Franz Kafka, Franz Werfel, Karl Kraus, Viktor Adler, Gustav Mahler and Adolf Loos, to name some of the best known — even if most of these talented people preferred life in Vienna. All had in common the quest for new modes of thought and practice. And Prague, the golden "City of a Hundred Spires", experienced rapid renewal in the last decades of the century. A massive modernization plan was set in motion, not unlike that begun in Vienna two decades earlier, transforming Prague from a medieval town into a modern city. The banks of the Moldau saw the preponderance of new growth between 1881 and 1884. Grand neo-Renaissance-style buildings were constructed, such as the Rudolfinum, where Zemlinsky occasionally performed, and the German Academy for Music and Applied Arts, where he later had an association. In 1894, electricity brought electric lights and electric tramcars to the central city, where four years earlier one-horse carriages were doubling as ambulances. The ghetto walls surrounding the neighborhood

---

[1] Cohen (2006), 65.

[2] Quoted ibid., 2.

[3] Consequently, bureaucrats were expected to be proficient in both Czech and German.

[4] Mansel (1995), 296.

[5] Cohen (2006), 65.

known as Judenstadt, renamed Josefstadt,[1] were razed, areas such as the Old City were sanitized to cure year-round epidemics and reduce high mortality rates, and the suburbs were expanded.

At the start of Zemlinsky's Prague tenure, the city was home to three opera houses. The oldest and the smallest was the Noztizsche Palais, the Estates Theater, a charming hall built in 1783 in the fruit market square. Here, Mozart had directed the premieres of *Don Giovanni* and *La clemenza di Tito* in 1787 and 1791 respectively. The two other houses epitomized the divisions separating Czechs and Germans: the Czech National Theater, built in the second half of the nineteenth century as a symbol of the rebirth of the Czech people; and the Deutsches Landestheater, renamed the Neues Deutsches Theater (New German Theater) after World War I. Additionally there was the Lucerna, a modern complex that housed arcades, restaurants, bars and the city's first cinema, along with a 3,500-seat concert hall where Zemlinsky was frequently engaged to conduct.[2]

Having outgrown the 650-seat Estates Theater, and not wanting to be outshone by the Czech theater that had been completed in 1883, Prague's German community began soliciting private funds for a new hall in 1884. Within a year, enough funds had been raised for construction to begin. Completed in 1888, the Neues Deutsches Theater stood south-east of the Old City on the site of the former New Town Theater. The structure was imposing and typical of the building style found throughout the city in the final decades of the nineteenth century: constructed along Classical lines, the facade was adorned with Corinthian columns and a pediment containing an ornate frieze, while the roof sported statues of mythological figures. Inside, the musicians' quarters were inadequate, and the backstage lacked sufficient height and depth. The public, unaware of these inconveniences, was treated to 1,900 seats, opulent ceilings cast of ornately gilded stucco, brilliant crystal chandeliers adorning a red plush lobby and most importantly, formidable acoustics, all of which endure today.

From its beginnings, however, the Deutsches Theater suffered from a lack of directorial stability. While the theater claimed an impressive list of music directors, all had lacked experience at the time of their appointment: Gustav Mahler

---

[1] Less than one-fifth of those still living in the quarter were Jewish.

[2] The Lucerna Palace, located just a few blocks from the Deutsches Theater in Wenceslas Square, was built in 1911 by Václav M. Havel, the paternal grandfather of the politician and poet Václav Havel. Havel was inspired by similar buildings in foreign cities and believed that Prague too would soon blossom into a European metropolis. In addition to being the city's first and largest entertainment complex, the Lucerna was Prague's first building constructed of reinforced concrete and contained the city's first theater equipped for talkies.

was active for only a single season (1885/86), Karl Muck for six (1886–92), and Franz Schalk for three (1895–98). Following a six-year conducting engagement, Leo Blech left for Berlin in 1906, and in his wake came Paul Ottenheimer and those of the next generation, including Arthur Bodanzky and Otto Klemperer. None remained long, however, before moving on to more promising engagements. Failure to secure long-term directorial stability had compromised the health of the relatively young theater, both with respect to the size of its audiences and the sense of tradition that can only be realized with an extended reign. At the time of Zemlinsky's appointment, theater attendance in general was also experiencing a decline, in part because of the overwhelming popularity of the cinema.[1] Furthermore, like all institutions, the theater was feeling the impact of growing nationalist tension throughout the Empire, and locally between the city's Czech and German inhabitants.

As an institution, the Deutsches Theater was, for all intents and purposes, a Viennese satellite. Constructed by a Viennese architectural firm, it recruited many Viennese singers, performers and conductors to be associated with the theater, many of whom maintained close ties with Vienna. Zemlinsky made it a point to promote the music of a number of his Viennese colleagues, in particular Mahler and Schoenberg; but also, for instance, Franz Schreker, who was struck by Zemlinsky's patience and good nature during rehearsals of Schreker's *Der ferne Klang*, as he encouraged the ensemble not to get bogged down with the score's more difficult passages.[2] Zemlinsky brought Schoenberg to Prague as a guest conductor and lecturer, providing Schoenberg with much-needed financial and professional support. And as will also be seen, Zemlinsky used his new position to help foster the career of the young Anton Webern, despite the latter's professional unpredictability.

From the start, Zemlinsky was the right man, both musically and politically, for the job. In addition to delivering exemplary performances, he also bridged the corrosive divisions existing between the German and Czech musical communities. He did this by establishing strong ties with the director of the Czech National Theater, directing concerts with the Czech Philharmonic, performing Czech repertoire at the Deutsches Theater, and combining personnel from both houses when repertoire demanded a larger body of musicians.

The Prague ensemble quickly came to understand and appreciate Zemlinsky's approach to conducting, qualities that Heinrich Jalowetz, a Zemlinsky

---

[1] Zischler (2003), 63.

[2] Schreker (1921), 232.

student and assistant at both the Vienna Volksoper and the Deutsches Theater, later summed up in an article for *Musikblätter des Anbruch*:

> The specific quality of Zemlinsky's conducting is purest objectivity. He never projects his personal will or personality on the production; his gestures demonstrate neither superiority nor false animation. His persona, completely dissolved in the music at hand, communicates the authoritative power of his will to the performers. He identifies completely with the work and through intuition and the keenest analytic comprehension derives the essential tempo, sound and phrasing. Despite the highest plasticity of detail and complete independence from pedantic time-keeping, he preserves a uniform tempo and achieves total symmetry of all architectural proportions, while still imbuing all the details with his personal interpretation. In addition, when he conducts an opera, his unusual innate sense for the demands of the stage allows him to shape the music entirely from the scenic element and, on the other hand, enables him to determine the style of staging on the grounds of the tonality. Thus, his performances derive an unusual liveliness from the constant interplay of staging and music.[1]

Not surprisingly, not everyone agreed with Jalowetz's description of Zemlinsky's "uniform tempo", but there seems to be no disagreement about the results:

> Whoever has sung under Zemlinsky's direction or followed a rehearsal with the score in hand, knows with what freedom he selects tempos, that when it appears necessary he will willingly take four different tempos in four consecutive measures in order to sculpt [*herauszumeisseln*] the appropriate character, in accordance with an optimal rendering. Consequently, every ritardando, every accelerando and every fermata is justified, either from a dramatic or musical standpoint and never fails to achieve its purpose . . .[2]

On the podium Zemlinsky had no need to dominate or intimidate his players or singers to heighten their collective ability. Rather, he communicated through the sheer will of his ideas and his conviction. His inherent sense for what was "right" resulted in interpretations that consistently won him accolades as one of the most versatile conductors of his generation. Thus, he could comfortably program music from Pergolesi to Weill. As a conductor he demonstrated a clean,

---

[1] Jalowetz (1922), 78.

[2] Zemlinsky-Schüler (1922), 122.

no-nonsense technique and made no attempt to "perform" for the audience; opposed to showy gestures, he preferred to let the music speak for itself. He steered clear of personal indulgence in an effort to faithfully serve the composer's wishes, whose desires Zemlinsky plumbed through meticulous score study.

Zemlinsky's energy as a conductor seemed inexhaustible. His rehearsals were exacting, although he never lost himself in the details, as he sought out every subtlety of shading, dynamic and color. He remained sensitive to the musical line and the overall form, and expected the same from his ensemble. If a piano stood nearby, he would use it to demonstrate a desired phrase. Even his facial gestures conveyed every nuance of his interpretation. Louis Laber, a tenor and producer at the theater who often had the advantage of observing Zemlinsky from the stage, recalled his being totally absorbed in the production at hand: "On the podium Zemlinsky's face mimes the entire opera, all the roles; he laughs, makes a fierce Alberich-face, assumes Wotan's dignified bearing, imitates the charming phrases of the duets between Papageno–Papagena, etc."[1] Zemlinsky could be charming one minute and brutally sarcastic the next, although he was no tyrant. Once, during a rehearsal of *Die Walküre*, Zemlinsky suddenly noticed one of the Valkyries missing and inquired as to her whereabouts. Upon learning that the singer's absence was due to inflamed vocal chords, Zemlinsky began to hit his head with his hands and in great desperation exclaimed, "Heaven forbid, only now does one even notice that she *has* vocal chords!"[2]

In time, Zemlinsky became especially beloved for his interpretations of Mozart, whose operas he treated as musical theater — as opposed to pure music — resulting in performances exuding a charm, humor and grace seldom experienced elsewhere. As Igor Stravinsky later recalled, Zemlinsky's instincts as a conductor were invariably true: "I think that of all those I have heard, I would nominate Alexander von Zemlinsky as the all-around conductor who achieved the most consistently high standards, and that is a mature judgment. I remember a performance of 'The Marriage of Figaro' by him in Prague as the most satisfying operatic experience of my life."[3] And as regarded the operas of Wagner and Richard Strauss, Zemlinsky's ability to elucidate even the thorniest textures rarely went unnoticed. With an unerring eye for the stage and an ear that placed the music's lyrical elements above all else, Zemlinsky strove to strike the perfect balance between the two:

[1] Laber (1921), 224.

[2] Excerpt from "Zemlinskyana", *Der Auftakt* (1921), 233.

[3] Stravinsky (1964), 28.

Within an operatic setting he sought to keep the orchestra as transparent as possible: He muffles with the hand. He puts his finger to his mouth. Hardly audible to the orchestra he says: "Up there, gentlemen, up there they are quite certainly singing. Please don't disturb this. Because up there they are singing very beautiful, soft, quiet, delicate things!" So speaks the sensible conductor Zemlinsky . . . and permits from his people no spoiling of the melody. Alexander von Zemlinsky with the face of a sibyl, guards the secrets. Quiet!![1]

Conducting opera brought its rewards, but it also provided Zemlinsky with an endless array of headaches. "Conducting concerts", he once confessed to Alma, "is one thousand times more beautiful than conducting in the theater. Above all, it's just good music making without having to be dependent on every half-witted [*vertrotteltem*] singer."[2] With only a single body of musicians to lead and no sets or directors, orchestral conducting allowed Zemlinsky to focus solely on the music. In Prague, Zemlinsky soon averaged four to six orchestral concerts a season, which not only introduced him to an entirely new repertoire — his work until now had been limited almost entirely to opera — but provided a diversion from his work in the pit.

Zemlinsky had only been in Prague a few days before securing a guest-conducting appearance for Schoenberg, clearly indicating that any prior tensions that may have existed between them had, at least for the time being, been resolved. Zemlinsky was keenly aware of his brother-in-law's dire straits. In addition to their financial struggles, the young son of the Schoenberg's Hietzing landlord had engaged the Schoenberg's 9-year-old daughter Trudi in sexual play, and when Schoenberg confronted the boy's father, the landlord spewed abusive and anti-Semitic insults. Though Schoenberg's first reaction was to file a lawsuit, in the end he and his family left the incident behind them and moved back to Berlin, where Schoenberg's job prospects appeared marginally better than what they had been in Vienna. Zemlinsky was now in a position to offer help, for which Schoenberg was extremely grateful. Zemlinsky proposed Schoenberg to direct the third orchestral concert of the season, a concert marked for February 29, 1912. With the cellist Pablo Casals as guest soloist, the concert was guaranteed to sell out, but program details had yet to be finalized.

---

[1] Diebold, in Curjel (1975), 266.
[2] AZ/AMW.

While Schoenberg waited to learn what had been decided, Zemlinsky immersed himself in another unrelenting schedule.

Zemlinsky's Prague debut came with Beethoven's *Fidelio* on September 24, 1911, before a sold-out house. Audience members had packed the hall to learn if their newly appointed conductor was the right choice to lead the theater into a new age. They were not disappointed. One critic wrote that the people came because of Zemlinsky but experienced a *Fidelio* of immeasurable intensity. Long before the performance was over the audience knew that the future of their house was secure:

> The success of the new conductor was already decided after the simul-taneously grandiose and refined overture. Following the closing bar, the small man with the striking profile had to appear on the stage. He was given an ovation which here is only granted to those greats who in May[1] come from elsewhere. And the people left knowing that the care for the work of our master [Beethoven] is now in good hands.[2]

Zemlinsky's discipline and work ethic was also immediately made apparent, as illustrated by Felix Adler's article in the Prague journal *Bohemia*: "In the six days since *Fidelio* everything was taken care of that needed to be taken care of: the purging of the great humdrum. And there was plenty to purge. One noticed the results of strict discipline".[3]

Fidelio was but the first of four productions slated within six weeks of Zemlinsky's arrival. Next came *Tannhäuser*, followed by *Der Freischütz* a mere six days later (October 15). The first evening of Wagner's *Ring* was staged on October 30. Zemlinsky also wasted little time bringing Mahler back to Prague —although he did so quietly at first—by beginning rehearsals in mid-October for Mahler's version of *Figaro*, with all of Mozart's traditionally removed recita-tives re-inserted. *Die Zauberflöte* was on the books for November; *Lohengrin* and *Rheingold* for January; *Tristan* and Wilhelm Kienzl's single-act opera *Der Kuhreigen* for February; *Die Meistersinger* and Mahler's Eighth Symphony for March. Then there were the first two orchestral concerts. On November 23, 1911, Zemlinsky led a highly successful performance of German staples — Schubert's Eighth ('Unfinished') Symphony, Beethoven's Fifth, and the First Piano Con-certo of Brahms. More adventurous programming followed in January of the New Year, with Strauss's nine-year-old *Sinfonia domestica* and Busoni's *Turan-*

[1] Prague was and remains home to a music festival each May.
[2] Adler, in Mahler (1971), 253–54.
[3] Adler, in Mahler (1971), 254.

dot Suite, op. 41, of 1904, which Zemlinsky regarded as possessing very little inherent musical value but believed would deliver an extraordinary sound.[1]

Deluged with administrative tasks, stacks of scores to learn, hundreds of hours of rehearsals and dozens of performances, Zemlinsky's correspondence with Schoenberg fell off. It was eventually decided that the February Philharmonic program would include a group of movements from Bach's B minor and D major Orchestral Suites, which Mahler had excerpted and arranged, and feature the Prague premiere of Schoenberg's Maeterlinck-inspired symphonic poem from 1902, *Pelleas und Melisande*. Casals would perform concertos by Haydn and Saint-Saëns.[2] But just what role Schoenberg was to play in the overall program was still to be ironed out. In November, Zemlinsky confirmed that he had received the *Pelleas* score but feared it would cause his orchestra tremendous difficulties. The following month, paraphrasing Strapinski's Schneiderlein song from *Kleider machen Leute*, Schoenberg wrote Zemlinsky wondering where matters stood:

> I really don't know what I am supposed to direct, as I feel no contact with you . . . Are you listening to me? Or have you just fallen asleep? Or do you have more pressing matters to deal with? I have no idea if you are still of this world or continue to exist?[3]

It was eventually decided that Schoenberg should conduct Bach and his own *Pelleas*, and leave Zemlinsky to handle the concertos, but in January he wrote asking if Schoenberg might come a week earlier than planned to prepare the entire concert. Then, as if to allay concerns, Zemlinsky later assured Schoenberg that the orchestra was "experienced" and that Schoenberg could expect the ensemble to be orderly and attentive.

Schoenberg's student Alban Berg came from Vienna to be on hand for his teacher's rehearsals and the concert, and although he relayed home that Zemlinsky was in good spirits,[4] Schoenberg noticed something eating away at his brother-in-law:

---

[1] Schoenberg was in agreement about the Busoni: "totally bad music, that is to say, entirely lacking!" Weber (1995), 69.

[2] Casals initially hoped to play the Dvořák Concerto, but because of strained relations between segments of the Czech and German populations, concertos by Haydn and Saint-Saëns were substituted.

[3] Weber (1995), 67.

[4] On February 25 Berg wrote to his wife back in Vienna, describing a reception at the Zemlinsky home. In a humorous attempt to put his wife at ease during his absence, Berg related that the party had included "mostly men — tenors, conductors and the like — and most of the

[Zemlinsky] seems to find that I am praised too much in my circle, and seems to want to stop me becoming a megalomaniac. Only he forgets how much I'm overlooked elsewhere. I do not believe he is jealous. But there's an element of anger and bitterness about the fact that so little notice is taken of him.[1]

Schoenberg believed that Zemlinsky was either troubled about Schoenberg's relationship with his students or wished to be similarly admired. And while it was true that Zemlinsky had never fostered a school of devoted followers, he may have harbored concerns that Schoenberg's students were blinded by their teacher's powerful persona, were swept up in Schoenberg's unswerving ambition to cut music loose from its past, or worse yet, considered their mentor a demigod.

Zemlinsky's brother-in-law was somehow eking out a living as a composer and teacher, despite his lack formal musical education and the financial stress he and his family were continually suffering as a result of his convictions. And his convictions were unrelenting. In 1908 there had been the songs from *Das Buch der hängenden Gärten*, with their emancipated dissonance and lack of structural harmony, and then that mysterious final movement from the Second String Quartet, with its text by Stefan George sung by a soprano— "I feel the air of another planet." The extraordinary op. 11 piano pieces followed in 1909, along with the brief but intense Five Orchestral Pieces, op. 16, and the expressionistic *Erwartung*, a half-hour long, dreamlike monodrama penned by Marie Pappenheim that Schoenberg had composed in a little over two weeks. In Schoenberg's hands, nothing was sacrosanct, neither the previously autonomous medium of chamber music nor tonality itself. Zemlinsky, on the other hand, had long ago forsaken composing full time for the security of a conducting post — with the death of his father it seemed the logical choice, perhaps the only choice. But the choice cost him irreplaceable time for composing. Despite the security conducting provided, had Zemlinsky become envious of his brother-in-law's devotion to the cause? Did he regret his own decision to forsake composition when he stepped onto the podium years ago? Would he still manage to break through with his own music? And would his efforts on the podium ever earn him greater distinction than he presently had, above all in Vienna?

Present jealousies and friction aside, Zemlinsky's commitment to Schoenberg and his music continued unabated. The friendship that had existed for so

women elderly and plain, wives and mothers of the other guests (Prague women seem to be on the plump side!)." Discussions about aesthetics and philosophy engaged many of the guests well into the night. See Grun (1971), 137.

[1] Schoenberg (1974), 30.

long between the men and the mutual esteem that marked their earliest history together so many years ago would always trump any tensions that arose. Indeed, in the days following his visit, Schoenberg wrote Zemlinsky, deeply thanking him for all he had done. Schoenberg's only regret was that Zemlinsky hadn't conducted *Pelleas* himself. If he had, perhaps Schoenberg's score would have fared better. The music had not gone down easily. To its credit, the audience remained attentive and in their seats until the performance was over, but the uproar that followed made it clear that to continue with his mission to program new music, Zemlinsky had his work cut out for him. One can only speculate that Zemlinsky would have produced more favorable results on the podium — by far the more experienced conductor of the two, he also commanded the trust and respect of the Deutsches Theater audiences. Zemlinsky would not make the same mistake twice.

On March 18, 1912, Schoenberg's monumental Second String Quartet, op. 10, a work representing the composer's first foray into atonality, was featured on a program by the Rosé Quartet with soprano Marie Gutheil-Schoder at the Rudolfinum. This time Schoenberg was not present. Despite the challenging nature of the music, and the hall's unflattering acoustics, the audience demonstrated greater enthusiasm than that displayed for Schoenberg when he had conducted *Pelleas* a month before. Zemlinsky informed his brother-in-law about the concert's success, humorously assuring him that very few people had been heard whispering in the quartet's first movement and that the audience called the musicians out a second time.[1] Schoenberg was back in Prague at the close of the following month to present a lecture in conjunction with the Prague premiere of Mahler's Eighth Symphony, on Zemlinsky's final Philharmonic concert of the season.

This time it was Webern who was present and who wrote to Berg, "It was marvelous yesterday at the Schoenberg lecture. Unheard-of."[2] For Zemlinsky, however, preparations for Mahler's "Symphony of a Thousand" were not going smoothly. Because of the size of the choir needed, the Deutsches Theater had pulled together singers from other parts of Prague, including a group of Czech participants, who, at the last moment, declined to sing. The reason remains cloudy. Most likely they were trying to make a statement, either anti-Semitic — the composer, the conductor and the theater's director, Heinrich Teweles, were all of Jewish origin — or nationalistic — Czech singers were refusing to sing with Germans or *in* German, the language of Mahler's text — in a misguided attempt

[1] Weber (1995), 80.
[2] Stuckenschmidt (1977), 173.

to turn what was arguably one of the most significant concerts Prague had experienced in years into some sort of protest. In the end, it was only through the
aid of Franz Schreker and his Philharmonic Chorus that the project avoided de-
railment. Having just given the work's Viennese premiere days earlier, Schreker's ensemble arrived in Prague by train for the final rehearsals. Meanwhile,
Zemlinsky had made good progress with the rest of his musicians, as was noted
by a local critic: "Already after the first rehearsal the orchestra and singers were
greatly inspired and followed him with exemplary discipline."[1]

The concert was a tremendous success and a particular triumph for Zemlinsky, whose personal and emotional association with Mahler and his music swept
the orchestra, singers and the audience up in more than ninety minutes of power
and emotion: "The conductor Zemlinsky, who was credited with the performance, produced great energy and inspired total respect."[2] The success paved
the way for more Mahler programming over the next three seasons — a second
performance of the dramatic Eighth Symphony, a production of the exquisite
Das Lied von der Erde and a performance of Mahler's rapturous Third Symphony. Of Zemlinsky's sixteen seasons in Prague, half included performances
of at least two Mahler compositions.[3] Although Zemlinsky considered *Das Lied*
his late mentor's most beautiful symphonic composition, the Eighth Symphony
carried the most meaning for him in Prague, as it established his opening season
in 1911 and then closed his career there in June of 1927. Zemlinsky's writings and
feelings about Mahler's music left little room for interpretation, and his belief in
the importance of Mahler's music, which had yet to gain a strong following in
the overall musical world, was borne out by history:

> I have an infinite, boundless respect for Mahler's work. He does not be-
> long to that for which one must fight; his towering personality and the
> breadth and depth of the pure humanity of his music already places him
> today above all party strife. I am of the opinion that Mahler will soon be
> counted among the sacrosanct.[4]

In his very first year in Prague Zemlinsky opened the door for another member
of his Viennese circle — Anton Webern, one of Schoenberg's most gifted compo-

[1] Quoted in Vysloužil (1995), 242.

[2] *Dalibor*, Jahrgang 34 (March 28, 1912), quoted in Mahler (1971), 254.

[3] During Zemlinsky's tenure, only two seasons lacked any Mahler at all and only Symphonies 5 and 6 went unplayed. See Ludvová (1983).

[4] Quoted in Weber (1977), 25.

sition students. Like Zemlinsky years earlier, Webern was in search of a conducting post to make ends meet. Their professional relationship, which lasted the better part of seven years, exemplifies Zemlinsky's commitment to mentoring and promoting young struggling composers of new music, and his patience. Webern exhibited idealism, patriotism during war, and unswerving dedication to his mentor, Schoenberg. But Webern was also a man of fragile health, whose indecision, confusion and capriciousness repeatedly tested the limits of Zemlinsky's generosity. The story of their association is not only a testament to Zemlinsky's belief in the younger man's abilities and his loyalty to his friend and colleague Schoenberg, it is a measure of Zemlinsky's unfailing professionalism. Despite Webern's repeated lack of commitment, last-minute cancellations, and failure to communicate with Zemlinsky directly, Zemlinsky's dedication to the talented young musician never wavered.

Zemlinsky's involvement with Webern began in September 1911, the same month that Zemlinsky began his own duties in Prague. Webern, then just 28, had been a student at the University of Vienna where he studied piano, cello and musicology. He had also been a chorus member of the Akademischer Wagner Verein (where he sang under Mahler, among others), and had been a private composition student of Schoenberg since 1904. Zemlinsky was interested in hiring Webern for his conducting staff at the Deutches Theater, and though Webern's actual experience was minimal, amounting to just over two years of on-the-job training conducting light music in towns like Bad Ischl, Teplitz and Danzig, Zemlinsky believed he would be an asset in Prague. If Zemlinsky was initially unsure what would be a suitable compensation, of one thing he was certain — the position would be of significant benefit to Webern's future.[1] Questions of finance made Webern uneasy, but in September of 1911 he accepted Zemlinsky's offer and traveled to Prague. He didn't stay long, preferring instead to join Schoenberg in Berlin the following month. Nevertheless, Zemlinsky magnanimously offered him a position two seasons later. In a letter to Schoenberg from 1913, Zemlinsky wrote that he looked forward to working with Webern the following season and hoped he remained healthy.[2]

Concerns about Webern's constitution were well founded. Plagued with doubts about his well being and despite Schoenberg's recommendation that he take a year off to build up his strength, Webern agreed to begin work with Zemlinsky's chorus at the start of August 1913, and so he traveled to Prague and secured a furnished apartment. This time, however, Zemlinsky exercised

[1] Weber (1995), 63.
[2] Ibid., 88.

foresight. Only after first arranging for a ready replacement should Webern again withdraw did Zemlinsky draft a letter to Webern, describing in no uncertain terms the work that lay ahead:

> Think the matter over carefully: that thus far described[1] is merely the activity of the first week!! There will be much more throughout the rest of the season. You will have 6–8 hours of work a day! I am writing to tell you that it is not insignificant; here one must give everything he has. Believe me, I am very healthy and by the end of the season I am completely finished!
>
> My opinion and well-meant suggestion is thus: before all else, get yourself totally healthy. Your nerves are more important than a year of musical business [*Kapellmeisterei*] in Prague.[2]

Webern took Zemlinsky's advice and canceled for the season. But he failed to notify Zemlinsky directly — Zemlinsky heard of Webern's last-minute decision only by way of Schoenberg. Considering that Webern cancelled a mere five days before the start of the new season, Zemlinsky displayed tremendous compassion toward the younger man. No appointment was forthcoming in the year that followed (1914/15), but in the autumn of 1915 Webern resumed correspondence with Zemlinsky in hopes of again securing a post. By then World War I was under way, and, believing it was his duty, Webern volunteered for military service, a decision no doubt influenced by Schoenberg's decision to do the same. Not unexpectedly, Webern quickly tired of military training and in September again turned to Zemlinsky, this time inquiring if the music director could intercede on his behalf. Fortunately for Webern, Zemlinsky had never lost hope that Webern would eventually commit to work at the theater, even if it took a world war to convince him of the position's merits. Coming through yet again, Zemlinsky drafted a petition to the military, stating the necessity of Webern's help at the theater. Although Zemlinsky's request was temporarily tied up in bureaucracy, the leave was eventually granted. With work to begin in January 1916, Zemlinsky's generosity elicited the following words from Webern: "Ah, I am insanely happy, Mr. von Zemlinsky . . . I am very happy that I shall see you so soon, and at last — in Prague. It will be beautiful. If only the war were over."[3]

Webern had not been in Prague a month when he suffered a change of heart

---

[1] Zemlinsky had listed the repertoire to be newly studied, rehearsed and performed and the requisite work required.

[2] Weber (1995), 283.

[3] K. Bailey (1998), 84.

—yet again—this time consumed with guilt for abandoning the war effort while his teacher was serving faithfully. On January 16, Webern wrote Schoenberg:

> I feel like a criminal. I would like to bury myself until April.[1] It is madness to play theater now. It is dreadful. And I assist in it. In the autumn when I wrote to Zemlinsky, I had such an overpowering longing to be able to occupy myself with music again. And I gave in to that longing. If only I had never done it![2]

True to form and without Zemlinsky's knowledge, Webern abandoned his theater post and returned to his prior military base in Leoben. Incredibly, that November Zemlinsky received a letter from Schoenberg stating, "I have just received word from Webern. What do you think he truly wants? You guessed it: to come to Prague. He is unfit for service on the front. Teweles has given him a promise. Is there any hope to this?"[3] Webern received his permanent discharge — owing to nearsightedness — on December 23, 1916, and the following season rejoined Zemlinsky's staff as choirmaster. He was put in charge of overseeing the chorus and soloists for *Lohengrin* and *Don Giovanni*, among others. Although Zemlinsky promised him an eventual conducting opportunity, Webern first had to endure several long months of work. Writing to Schoenberg, Webern related his routine:

> In the morning I have usually an hour or two of chorus rehearsal, followed by rehearsals with the soloists. I share these with the coach. Then I play for stage rehearsals. I also have stage service during the performances. All this is for operas only. I have nothing to do with operettas . . . My present subordinate role, however, is really difficult to bear. I feel this more and more.[4]

Finally, in mid-January of 1918, Webern was at last given the chance to lead four performances of Lortzing's *Zar und Zimmermann*. But the season would be Webern's first and final at the Deutsches Theater. He had made up his mind at last. Despite Webern's unpredictable nature, Zemlinsky was genuinely sorry to see him go. In a letter to Schoenberg, Zemlinsky wrote, "Webern will come to Vienna the week after next and sends you his heartfelt greetings. I terribly regret his leaving here. But I believe his decision to leave the theater once and for all is

---

[1] Webern's contract was due to terminate on April 5.

[2] Moldenhauer and Moldenhauer (1979), 215.

[3] Weber (1995), 157.

[4] Moldenhauer and Moldenhauer (1979), 220.

right!"[1] Schoenberg attempted to dissuade Webern from leaving Prague, as did
Webern's father: "The theater offers you, after all, the sole possibility of earning! From what else could you and your family live?"[2] Their entreaties were to
no avail — Webern's mind was made up. By the start of June he had moved to
the town of Mödling, outside of Vienna, only five minutes by foot from Schoenberg's home. In the immediate years that followed, Universal Edition began
publishing Webern's music, but in truth his income was earned from a variety
of conducting posts, including choral societies in Vienna.

Zemlinsky's role as Webern's employer and mentor had finally come to an
end. Through it all, Zemlinsky was a resource of incalculable worth, an unfailing ally whose offers, advice and employment allowed Webern to navigate his
way through wartime confusion and personal dilemmas.

The burdensome nature of the Zemlinsky–Webern association notwithstanding,
Zemlinsky's inaugural season of 1911/12 was deemed an unqualified success.
Zemlinsky lived up to the hopes Prague had pinned on him, and the press
lauded him for breathing new life into the Deutsches Theater. The composer
and conductor Jaroslav Křiča noted Zemlinsky's rigorous attention to detail and
the "effort made by the orchestra to perform above its normal level to which
those of us at the Deutsches Theater are accustomed".[3] Of Zemlinsky's work
ethic the press also took note:

> *A music director who really works.* In the local Deutsches Theater re-
> sides Alexander Zemlinsky, chief music director, who, despite lacking
> resources, is accomplishing truly joyous occasions for those with artistic
> sense enough to realize it. Of Wagner's music alone Zemlinsky, since
> autumn, has led entirely new productions of *Tannhäuser, Lohengrin,
> Meistersinger, Tristan* and *Walküre.* Then, add to that *Fidelio* and a to-
> tally charming production of *Le nozze di Figaro,* in addition to four (!)
> Philharmonic concerts, which included the [Prague] premiere of Mahler's
> Eighth Symphony. Such is the way of a theater where one *really works.*
> In our [Czech National] theater, instead of work one hears nothing but
> *complaints.*[4]

[1]   Weber (1995), 195.
[2]   Moldenhauer and Moldenhauer (1979), 222.
[3]   *Hudební Revue* IV (1911), 92.
[4]   Zdeněk Nejedlý, *Smetana,* 2 (1911), 293-94.

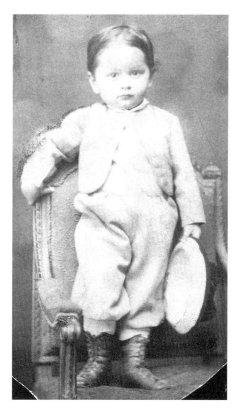

1   Zemlinsky, age 2

2   Taborstrasse (Leopoldstadt), 1890

3   With his sister Mathilde

4   Vienna Musikverein, 1898

5   Zemlinsky at the turn of the century,
    as Alma knew him

6   The photo of Alma that stood on Zemlinsky's writing table

7   Ida Guttmann, 1904

8   Ida and Johanna ("Hansi")

9   Apartment in Vienna (Liechtensteinstrasse 68)

11   Relaxing in St. Peter, Spindelmühle

13   The conductor in Prague

12   The composer in Spindelmühle

14   Apartment in Prague (Havlíčkova 9)

15 Neues Deutsches Oper, Prague

16 Zemlinsky at the helm of the Neues Deutsches Theater ensemble, Prague

17   Zemlinsky seated at his prized Bösendorfer piano, with Arnold Schoenberg
     (Prague, 1917)

18 Caricature with Schoenberg in
    preparation for the premiere of
    Erwartung

19 Caricature parodying the Egon Schiele poster prior to the June 25, 1912 concert of
    music by (clockwise from top) Webern, Schoenberg, Zemlinsky, Schreker, Novák
    and Suk (*Kikeriki*, June 20, 1912)

20 The only known photograph of Zemlinsky conducting — in rehearsal at the Prague Lucerna

21   The confirmed cigar smoker

22   Louise Sachsel and Zemlinsky, probably in Switzerland, c. 1934

23   Kroll Oper (Berlin)

24   Zemlinsky at the piano, with Kurt Weill (hand in air) and Bertolt Brecht, in rehearsal
      for the Berlin premiere of *Mahagonny*, 1931

25   House in Grinzing (Kaasgrabengasse 24)

26   Coffee at the Kaasgrabengasse house, *c.* 1936

27   House in New Rochelle (68 Kewanee Road)

28 Excerpt from the manuscript of *Circe*, Zemlinsky's final operatic project (with inset of libretto)

Zemlinsky's star was again ascending. He had firmly established himself as the head of a new regime, his work was beloved by Prague audiences and praised by its critics, and in May of 1912 his turn-of-the-century opera *Es war einmal* was staged in Mannheim under the baton of his old friend and colleague, Arthur Bodanzky. On May 21, Zemlinsky was on hand to conduct the work himself. At last there were indications that Zemlinsky's professional life was changing for the better.

The formal concert season ended on a sad personal note, however, when Zemlinsky's mother died on June 12. Zemlinsky had seen little of Clara in the years leading up to her death, and although she had visited her son in February, when Schoenberg came to conduct, little is known about their relationship during the previous decade. Zemlinsky never dedicated any compositions to her memory, as he had for his father and even for Brahms, so one can only speculate to what extent her passing affected him. All that is known is he sent Mathilde money for flowers to be placed on her grave and inquired about costs for its upkeep.[1]

At the end of June the Akademischer Verband für Literatur und Musik (Academic Union for Literature and Music), a four-year-old Viennese organization that sponsored lectures and concerts featuring eminent musicians and writers, hosted a pair of concerts of modern works by Josef Suk, Vítězslav Novák, Franz Schreker, Alban Berg, Arnold Schoenberg, Anton Webern and Alexander Zemlinsky. The artist Egon Schiele designed a striking poster for the event — subsequently lampooned in the anti-Semitic journal *Kikeriki* — and prominent writers such as Stefan Zweig contributed articles for the 32-page program guide. The first concert took place June 25, 1912, and included Zemlinsky's four songs on texts of Maurice Maeterlinck; four days later the Rosé Quartet performed his String Quartet in A Major, op. 4, of 1896.

Zemlinsky's youthful infatuation with song composition had tapered off significantly in the last decade. With professional obligations demanding more of his time, he devoted what was left to larger projects such as opera and orchestral works. The year 1907 had been an exception. That spring he and Schoenberg each set two dark ballads to music for a competition in Berlin — Victor Klemperer's *Der verlorene Haufen*, which tells the story of a lost troop of soldiers, and Heinrich Amann's *Jane Grey*, a grim depiction of the suicide of Lady Jane Grey. Zemlinsky used the opportunity to experiment with substantial piano introductions, dense textures and robust sonorities, all of which created great pianistic presence. In the end, the results mattered little. Neither

[1] Weber (1995), 83.

he nor Schoenberg even placed in the contest, and the accomplishments of the winners — Heinrich Eckl, Hans Hermann and Gustav Lazarus — like the winners themselves, were soon forgotten. The competition seems to have been but a passing challenge; it appears neither Zemlinsky nor Schoenberg gave any of it a second thought.

Then, in December of the same year, Zemlinsky set a series of five songs based on texts of Richard Dehmel, whose poetry had once pushed him to explore previously untapped expressive boundaries. In a year that produced no substantial work other than early drafts of *Kleider machen Leute*, and during which he suffered professional and compositional defeat at the Hofoper, it's difficult to understand why he now looked to Dehmel's stirring texts as source material. The answer may lie with his sister Mathilde's infatuation with painter Richard Gerstl. Their relationship, which by now would have been no secret to Zemlinsky, had been intensifying since the summer, and Dehmel's erotic subject matter, in particular its implications of unfulfilled desire, may have struck a sympathetic chord. Zemlinsky had also been charting Schoenberg's recent harmonic advances, in the light of his own work. The compact nature of Dehmel's poems thus provided Zemlinsky the opportunity to experiment stylistically on a small scale, while affording him a way to work through the crisis in meaningful musical terms.

The results, however, were extreme. Zemlinsky's search to conceive of a language capable of transmitting Dehmel's emotional states of desire and longing found articulation in intense expressionistic contours (*Vorspiel*), relentless syncopations (*Ansturm*) and liquid, Satie-esque piano writing (*Auf See*). Zemlinsky's music swirled in an atmosphere of directionless improvisation. True to Dehmel's poetry, the songs seemed neither to begin nor end, rather they simply existed, and then evaporated, before true fulfillment was attained. There is an excessiveness about the songs, suggesting Zemlinsky was struggling to find the right balance for personal expression, and the facts that he never pushed for the songs' performance, never saw to their publication, never revisited them, nor ever built on what he had started suggests he too was dissatisfied with the results. In *Vorspiel*, Dehmel had asked, "wie wird das enden . . ." (how will it end . . .), but Zemlinsky did not have an answer. Aside from *Der chinesische Hund*, the ditty written for his daughter, he did not compose another song for three years.

It was only in 1910 that Zemlinsky was again ready for song composition. That summer, when he left for vacation in the town of Bad Ischl, included among his belongings was the score to *Kleider machen Leute*, the first draft of which was nearly completed, and a copy of Maurice Maeterlinck's *Quinze*

Chansons in German translation.[1] When Zemlinsky needed diversion from his operatic work he turned to Maeterlinck's verses, and thus were born the four songs — *Die drei Schwestern, Die Mädchen mit den verbundenen Augen, Lied der Jungfrau,* and *Und kehrt er einst heim* — now being presented in June 1912.[2]

Typical of Maeterlinck's style, the poetry exudes an atmosphere of sensuality wrapped in a highly symbolic and mysterious air. As with much of Maeterlinck's work, true meaning, other than an impressionistic suggestion of death or life beyond, is left largely to personal interpretation. Consequently, Zemlinsky did not seek a literal retelling of the text; rather, he sought to imbue his scores with the poetry's spirit. Zemlinsky captured the impressionistic essence of Maeterlinck's verses with sliding chromaticism, unpredictability of motion and indefinable chords lacking any discernable harmonic direction. In *Die drei Schwestern,* for example, Zemlinsky evokes a dirge-like air by pitting a shrouded and unpredictable rising bass against a lifeless rocking figure, as the sisters head off in search of Death.[3]

The jump into such ambiguous territory comes only after the parameters of logic have been established, and with the knowledge that order will be restored by the close of each song. Melody, clearly definable phrase lengths, a steady rhythmic pulse — all are firmly in place at the outset, and none are absent for long. The phrase "Verirrt sich die Liebe" ("And if love should stray") in *Lied der Jungfrau,* for example, is made all the more stirring because of the majestic E-flat cadence that precedes it. Furthermore, the dominance of the vocal line, combined with moments of unapologetic warmth and beauty — born of Zemlinsky's unique phrasing, like the sensuous cadence on the word "Lächelte" ("smiled") that closes *Und kehrt er einst heim* — make it clear that in spite of Zemlinsky's search for a deeper, more intense means of expression, music, for Zemlinsky, still demanded a lyrical component. Zemlinsky had no intention of abandoning what he understood best.

Arguably the finest songs Zemlinsky ever composed, and one of the most significant vocal collections from the first quarter of the twentieth century, the

[1] Zemlinsky had first become intimately familiar with Maeterlinck's work while preparing a performance of Dukas's adaptation of Maeterlinck's *Ariane et Barbe-bleue* at Vienna's Volksoper in 1908.

[2] What initially drew Zemlinsky to these six seemingly unrelated texts, and ultimately inspired some of his greatest music, remains as mysterious as the poetry itself. Naturally, Zemlinsky may simply have found the poetry's inexplicable character and suggestion liberating.

[3] The overall effect was continued a few years later when Zemlinsky added two further Maeterlinck settings to the collection — *Als ihr Geliebter schied,* with its amorphous accompaniment, and the half-light of *Sie kam zum Schloss gegangen.*

‍‍‍ ‌‌‍‌‌

importance of the Maeterlinck songs was recognized immediately by Zemlinsky's contemporaries, and more recently by modern historians.[1] And while the songs illustrate the widening gulf developing between Zemlinsky and his more radically minded Viennese colleagues, they nonetheless made a strong impact on Schoenberg, Berg and Webern. In the months following their performance in Vienna, Berg relayed to Zemlinsky how much they meant to him and how he regretted having to part with the score.[2] Sixteen years later, Webern still felt their power, stating, "Dear God, it is all so beautiful. How beloved has this music become to me."[3]

At their Vienna performance in 1912, however, Zemlinsky's songs failed to impress at least one reviewer. The critic from *Der Merker* commented that Zemlinsky's music suffered from the same neurotic air found in the works of Suk, Novák and Schreker, described as a "pale and weary flirtation with illness and death".[4] No doubt the critic disliked the musical aesthetic common to much of the music composed on the eve of World War I, but in this case he also objected to Zemlinsky's style. Whereas in other works the critic regarded Zemlinsky's style as "full-blooded", here it came off as "atypical and restrained". A few nights later Zemlinsky's A Major String Quartet produced a markedly different impression. Now the same critic stated,

> How real and so much more himself [did Zemlinsky appear] in his Quartet in A, whose classic purity and fullness strike many today as outdated, but it was the only [work of the evening] that offered a content of restfulness and allowed for a gathering of strength amidst all the restlessness, discomfort, and anemic nerves . . .[5]

The Brahmsian Quartet stood in high relief against Webern's *Four Pieces for Violin and Piano*, which elicited laughter and ended with Arnold Rosé, the violinist, reprimanding the offensive audience members. At this point the architect Adolf Loos personally escorted the hecklers from the hall. But Zemlinsky's Brahms-inspired days were now a thing of the past. For him, the Maeterlinck songs were far more relevant, and he had requested their performance specifically to provide "a sense of his current compositional state".[6] Zemlinsky's music

[1] Rudolf Stephan Hoffmann recognized these songs as the first to truly display Zemlinsky's originality and extraordinary power of expression. See Stephan (1978), 18.

[2] Weber (1995), 304.

[3] Ibid. 290.

[4] *Der Merker* (August 1912) p. 596.

[5] Ibid.

[6] Weber (1995), 303.

had traveled vast distances since his youthful string quartet, even if some critics preferred otherwise.

There are periods in Zemlinsky's life about which we know nothing. Such is the case with the summer of 1912. With another season of concerts in the books, the Zemlinskys arranged to share a portion of the summer holidays with family, but in July or early August, Schoenberg and Zemlinsky had a falling out. Their letters offer no clues as to the cause of the quarrel, only the results: Schoenberg left without saying goodbye. By late August, Schoenberg was back in Berlin and Zemlinsky in Prague, where each reflected on what had transpired. However uncertain the source of the conflict, there is no second-guessing the consequences: deeply saddened and regretful for acting so immaturely, both acknowledged the depth of their friendship and expressed the desire to avoid such tensions in the future.

Life at the Deutsches Theater, meanwhile, forged ahead with a new season of productions that included nearly all of the major operas of Wagner, six Verdi operas,[1] four by Puccini,[2] plus works by Beethoven, Bizet, Blech, Goldmark, Gounod, Halévy, Humperdink, Kienzl, Kohout, Leoncavallo, Lortzing, Mascagni, Meyerbeer, Mozart, Offenbach, Rossini and Weber. All the energy Zemlinsky could muster went toward his job, and while he continued to delegate most of the Italian repertoire to his subordinates, his plate remained piled high with other works. That season Zemlinsky led new productions of Wagner's *Das Rheingold* and Strauss's *Salome* and *Ariadne auf Naxos*, conducting the latter less than two months after Strauss led the work's premiere in Stuttgart. Zemlinsky also led seven performances of his own opera, *Es war einmal*.

There was much satisfaction in a position with so much to offer and where his efforts and abilities were generously praised. Still, those very efforts renewed his frustration at having too little time to compose, and his musical development and quantity of work were affected. Matters did not improve in the years that followed. Zemlinsky's first decade in Prague saw the completion of only two one-act operas, his Second String Quartet, op. 15, several songs including two based on poems by Maeterlinck, and incidental music to Shakespeare's *Cymbeline*.[3] The paucity of work completed during this decade bears witness to the demands of his conducting responsibilities.

---

[1] *Un ballo in maschera, Otello, Falstaff, Rigoletto, La traviata* and *Il trovatore*.

[2] *La bohème, Madama Butterfly, La fanciulla del West* and *Tosca*.

[3] Several additional compositions were begun during this decade but never completed.

The 1912/13 season was only halfway through when "the greatest concert scandal that Prague has yet experienced"[1] unfolded directly in front of Zemlinsky's box seat. On February 24, 1913, a visiting ensemble performing Schoenberg's *Pierrot lunaire*, a song cycle for voice and five instrumentalists based on texts of Stefan George, struggled to be heard in Prague's Rudolfinum Hall. The work had already played to audiences in twelve Austrian and German cities, and now many of those present at the Prague premiere encountered atonality and *Sprechstimme* — vocal lines half-sung, half-spoken — for the first time. The sound was a perfect fit for George's nightmarish verses, and to its credit, the audience maintained a state of decorum long enough to get through the beginning without incident. But Schoenberg's score began grating on the audience, some of whom became increasingly agitated. Before the final song the musicians were met with coughing and hissing and suddenly, things exploded:

> When finally the last of the poems was nearly finished, one heard from a single individual a cry "Stop!" Now a storm began between the holders of different opinions, during which the last notes of the composition went unheard. Not only the excited young people, but also the musically educated part of the public was on the side of those who applauded after the last poems. The opposition was also prepared. They blew shrill whistles, and the door key came into its uncultivated rights as an instrument of criticism. Cries of *"Pfui"* tried to drown the loud Bravos, and the battle between the parties went on uninterruptedly until the lights were put out and the tumult gave way to silence.[2]

This backlash to new music in Prague was no isolated event. From Paris to Vienna, audiences were being challenged by radical concepts of art. In early 1912, Vaslav Nijinsky, choreographer and principle dancer of Diaghilev's *Ballets Russes*, unnerved a Parisian audience with a ballet set to Debussy's tone poem *Prélude à l'après-midi d'un faune*. And three months after *Pierrot's* Prague spectacle, Diaghilev tested the limits of Paris ballet-goers again — not once but twice. The first of these, *Jeux*, which revolved around a man, two girls and a game of tennis, might have fared better had Parisians been granted time to digest the ballet and Debussy's breathtaking music. But just over two weeks later came *Le Sacre du printemps*, a ballet about primitive fertility rites set to

---

including two operas, *Der heilige Vitalis* of 1915 and *Raphael (Das Chagrinleder)*. In 1913 Zemlinsky also broke off composition on his opera *Malva*, which he had begun in 1902.

[1] Stuckenschmidt (1977), 207.
[2] Adler in Stuckenschmidt (1977), 209.

Stravinsky's intensely driving score. Diaghilev had repeatedly challenged his audience's notions of western music and traditional ballet, but by now Paris had had enough. The performance, which has been well documented, erupted into riot. It was not that the French found eroticism offensive, they were simply not prepared for its association with high art. Stravinsky acknowledged that the sound coming from the orchestral pit would not be easily grasped, a fact that was underscored when every reviewer completely failed to reflect on its difficulty, preferring instead to compare it to noise and dismiss it as nonsense.[1]

A strikingly similar scene occurred two months earlier in Vienna. On March 31, 1913, the weather outside the Great Hall of the Musikverein was pleasantly cool and a gentle breeze was blowing. Inside, the atmosphere crackled with intensity, as the audience nervously anticipated another program presented by the Akademischer Verband. The evening was scheduled to include the music of Schoenberg, that of two of his most promising students, Webern and Berg, and works by his mentors Mahler and Zemlinsky, whose newly orchestrated Maeterlinck songs would receive their premiere. As indicated on the promotional poster, the Prelude to Wagner's opera *Tristan* would complete the program, but unfortunately, the evening's events precluded Wagner's music from ever being heard.

For Zemlinsky, the weeks leading up to the concert were, like the concert itself, fraught with difficulties. At the start of March he read in the Berlin papers that his Maeterlinck Songs had been struck from the program. Zemlinsky quickly dashed off a note to Schoenberg in Berlin, inquiring about the truth of the matter — if Schoenberg, who was organizing the concert, had truly eliminated the songs from the program, there was no need for Zemlinsky to rush their orchestration. The following day Schoenberg confirmed the songs were still on the program, yet Zemlinsky remained plagued by two issues. His first concern was that his music had been included out of a sense of obligation, in return for Zemlinsky having promoted Schoenberg so strongly in Prague. Schoenberg quickly put the matter to bed, writing on March 8, "On the contrary, this concert is a symbol for me. It is indeed rather obvious. You don't need to be so mistrustful of me!"[2] Zemlinsky's second worry, that his Maeterlinck songs would pale in comparison to Mahler's *Kindertotenlieder*, which was also to be performed, Schoenberg never addressed. And as it happened, the crowd in the hall ensured that this concern was never realized.

Zemlinsky continued to orchestrate his songs at unprecedented speed, but

---

[1] See Stravinsky and Kraft (1978), 614, cf. 173.

[2] Weber (1995), 89.

when Schoenberg, who was to conduct the program, confessed to working slowly and requested a copy of the music to study, Zemlinsky sent his brother-in-law the version for voice and piano. In a rare moment of humor amidst an otherwise tense period, Schoenberg inquired if Zemlinsky might at least be able to get him the actual parts a few minutes before the performance, thereby sparing him the embarrassment of passing out the music on stage!

In mid-March the fully orchestrated score arrived, and Schoenberg found the songs splendid: "They are glorious! They demonstrate an entirely original lyrical sound [*Lyrik-Ton*], perhaps only as Hugo Wolf had done. What purity! I never knew this side of you. I am colossally thrilled that I had the idea to perform them."[1] But problems soon followed. Schoenberg had scrambled to find a copyist, and when the parts came back they were riddled with errors. He informed Zemlinsky that the songs sounded fabulous but that valuable time had been lost correcting them.[2] Then there was the singer, Margarete Bum, whose inexperience and insecure intonation frustrated preparations and necessitated that Berg coach her intensely. Lastly, concert advertisement had yielded poor ticket sales, despite a recently successful performance of Schoenberg's *Gurre-Lieder*. It was rumored that Adolf Loos had purchased a block of tickets that he planned to give away to passersby on the Kärntnerstrasse, in hopes of bolstering the turnout, but it was anyone's guess how large or what sort of audience the concert would draw.

Owing to the threatening nature of the music by three of the featured composers, Webern, Berg and Schoenberg, Schoenberg was of the opinion that the concert should open with Webern: "It is best that they swallow the Webern first — the most bitter pill of the concert — since at the start the public would not yet be weary and impatient."[3] Schoenberg's intuition proved prescient. The premiere of Webern's Six Pieces for Orchestra, op. 6, was accompanied nearly from the start by catcalls and a spattering of laughter, the impromptu feedback resulting from an audience confronted by nightmarish sounds, clanking, grating dissonances and extremes that ran the gamut from silence to near deafening crescendos. Contained within the Six Pieces are a wealth of emotions and characters — catastrophe, fulfillment, remembrance and resignation — but the movements themselves rarely last more than a minute each. Sounds are fleeting, and ideas are often compressed into a single note or chord, the intensity allowing no time for thematic development. Webern's orchestral scoring is similarly

[1] Weber (1995), 90. The Maeterlinck songs concerned were nos. 1, 2, 3, and 5.
[2] Ibid., 92.
[3] Partsch (1989), 56.

untraditional. Despite calling for an orchestra of Mahlerian proportions, the entire ensemble is never employed at the same time — the fourth movement, *Marcia funebre*, for example, is scored only for winds and percussion — and Webern often requires solo instruments be played in extreme registers. Such were the manifold challenges Webern's music made on the audience, but most in the hall that night at least tolerated Webern's novel sounds, textures and colors. For some ten minutes Webern tested the limits of his listeners' endurance, yet his new work was heard through in its entirety. Berg, whose music was still to come, was not granted the same courtesy.

Singer Margarete Bum then took her place in front of the orchestra for Zemlinsky's Maeterlinck songs. The reception was markedly different than that of a year earlier, no doubt in part due to Zemlinsky's rich and colorful orchestration. Coming in the wake of Webern's atonal and athematic Six Orchestral Pieces, Zemlinsky's "beautiful songs . . . calmed the heated and belligerent spirits".[1] With total order now restored to the hall, Schoenberg then commenced to conduct his own single-movement Chamber Symphony, op. 9.

Schoenberg's Chamber Symphony had been premiered successfully six years earlier, but that mattered little now. In the span of twenty short minutes Schoenberg had packed an entire symphony, complete with an introduction and exposition, Scherzo, Adagio and Finale; but its angular themes, modern harmonies and strange doublings made the symphony difficult to grasp. Every one of the fifteen instrumentalists was caught up in demanding virtuosity, the rhythms were relentless and the whole piece — or what was heard of it — sounded frenetic. The audience quickly lost patience. Almost at once laughter broke out, accompanied by shouts and individual critiques, and the interruptions, no longer confined to the floor, began to emanate from the galleries as well.

The atmosphere deteriorated further with the start of the next work on the program, Berg's *Fünf Orchesterlieder nach Ansichtskartentexten von Peter Altenberg*, op. 4, as sung by the great Alfred Boruttau. From the work's opening *pianissimo*, the audience did not know what to make of the fog of sound emanating from the orchestra's complex web of overlapping and seemingly uncoordinated ostinato figures. The orchestral introduction was dense and atonal, and by the time Boruttau began to sing it became clear to everyone in the hall that this music, like that of Webern and Schoenberg, shared little connection with the past, or even to the present of Zemlinsky. Boruttau had not yet finished the first of Berg's songs before Schoenberg banged on the podium and shouted

[1] *Musikblätter des Anbruch*, 6 (Aug.–Sept. 1924), quoted in Moldenhauer and Moldenhauer (1979), 171.

for quiet, proclaiming that if necessary the police would be called in to maintain the peace. Boruttau managed to get through the second song with only minor incident until the very last line, which was met first with guffaws and then a full-blown uproar. Amidst the hooting, whistling and clapping, Webern yelled from the proscenium, "Ruhe, zum Teufel noch einmal! Hinaus mit der Baggage!" (Quiet, to the devil with you! Out with these rabble-rousers!), which did little to quell the tumult. There were those who were literally standing in favor of Schoenberg and the music of his disciples, but their shouting at the detractors served only to increase the overall din. By the time Marya Freund was ready to take the stage for Mahler's *Kindertotenlieder*, the hall had been reduced to total chaos. Some screamed that Mahler should not be a victim of such programming, but it quickly became apparent that Mahler would not be heard that evening.[1]

With the announcement that the Mahler songs were canceled, the hall lights came on and pandemonium broke out. Until now the disorder had existed only in the form of shouting. But one demonstrator who had been swearing repeatedly from the first row was suddenly smacked on the side of the head, his glasses flung from his face. Fearing for themselves and their instruments, the musicians quickly fled the stage. At this point everything went dark and the police cleared the hall. The screams and scuffles continued beyond the walls of the Musikverein as audience members pushed and shoved their way out into the Vienna night.

For days afterward, a flurry of criticism and editorials abounded. A lawsuit followed. According to Egon Wellesz, a medical doctor appeared in court as a witness and declared that some of the listeners had found the music nerve-racking and were already showing "obvious signs of severe attacks of neurosis".[2] By then Schoenberg had returned to Berlin, disgusted. Berg wrote to him that even Webern might be sued for his outburst, while Webern, convalescing on the Adriatic, reminisced about all of the pleasant memories he associated with the concert, other than the concert itself. Zemlinsky, who had remained in Prague, found himself frustrated with the press's portrayal of events and wrote to Schoenberg requesting to hear his side of the story.

In truth, what happened that evening was not totally unexpected. Schoenberg's music, and that of his students, had been stirring Vienna's musical pot for months, and audience and critics alike arrived knowing the evening promised to be a provocative one. Curiously, little information about the music itself could

---

[1] The following day David Bach of the *Arbeiter Zeitung* wrote, "It would have been the pinnacle of the scandal if, amidst this rowdy atmosphere, Mahler's Kindertotenlieder had been performed." *Arbeiter Zeitung* (April 1, 1913), 9.

[2] Egon Wellesz (1926), 35

be gleaned from reports of the concert in the days that followed. The problem was that with the exception of the Maeterlinck songs, all of the evening's performances were met with myriad interruptions — laughter, the jangling of keys, banging, screams, interruptions or all of these — so instead of intelligently critiquing the music, the reviewers concerned themselves with what was happening around them.[1] Because Zemlinsky's music had failed to set the audience's teeth on edge, his name had been left out of many of the reviews, and when it did appear, rarely was a passing word *about* his songs included.[2]

In spite of his insecurities about how his music might fare alongside Mahler's, and despite having dodged the abject scorn cast upon his comrades, Zemlinsky's songs all but disappeared in the outrage provoked by their revolutionary scores. Whether one embraced or rejected Schoenberg's, Berg's and Webern's innovations, a portentous storm was swirling: Vienna's musical past was under a state of siege and its future fraught with uncertainty. Zemlinsky had never considered that his songs might disappear in the mayhem that ensued that night. His name was not on anyone's lips when they left the Musikverein that evening because, inconceivably, his music had gotten lost in a sea of protests against a movement Zemlinsky himself never fully embraced.

Chapter 6

The Greatest Event of the Century

║ N THE SUMMER OF 1913, Europe's eyes were on the Balkans, where regional warfare was redrawing the map of European territories in the Ottoman Empire. Prior activity in the Balkan states of Serbia, Greece, Bulgaria and Montenegro had driven the Turks from most of European Turkey, but Serbia then desired more territory in order to gain access to the Adriatic Sea. Austria-Hungary, Italy and a now-independent Albania stood opposed to a "Greater Serbia", so Serbia turned its attention instead to Bulgarian-held lands in Macedonia. When Bulgaria attacked first, in June of 1913, the armies of Romania, Greece and Turkey quickly countered; by August the Second Balkan War was over. In the span of less than three months, Bulgaria had lost land to all of its enemies. Serbia, emboldened, now began looking to annex parts of Austria-Hungary. Austria desperately wanted to oust Serbia from its Bosnian territories, but Russia was ready to defend its Serbian ally and eager to protect its own interests in the region. France, with its eyes on the Levant, promised to back Russia, and Great Britain warned that if Germany attempted to upset the European balance of power by attacking either Russia or France, it would help defend either or both. While an apprehensive Europe waited for the first stone to be thrown, the German Field Marshal Helmuth von Moltke, appreciating the disastrous consequences of an all-out war, spoke out:

> If this war were to break out, no one could foresee how long it would last nor how it would end . . . Gentlemen, it could be a Seven Years' War; it could be a Thirty Years' War; and woe to the man who . . . first throws the match into the powder keg.[1]

[1] Quoted in Davies (1998), 875.

Such tensions seemed far removed from Kitzbühel, a medieval town nestled deep in the Tyrolean Alps, where the Zemlinskys chose to spend the summer holidays of 1913. Aside from a brief stint in Munich at the start of July, where he conducted a production of Gilbert and Sullivan's *The Mikado*, Zemlinsky remained in the Alps throughout the summer. Five weeks of rain kept him from the walks and swimming he loved,[1] but he put his time indoors to good use, completing two more Maeterlinck songs — *Als ihr Geliebter schied*, and *Sie kam zum Schloss gegangen* — and beginning work on his ambitious Second String Quartet, a project that would take two years to complete.

Aside from an enigmatic string-quintet fragment from 1907, Zemlinsky had shown little interest in composing chamber music since his Brahms-inspired A major Quartet of 1896, at which time his conception of string-quartet writing remained wed to its classical pedigree — an abstract composition constructed of four separate movements, bound by the logic of architecture and key relationships. But other than Zemlinsky's continued interest in compositional efficiency, there is little to connect Zemlinsky's Second String Quartet with what came before. Its organizational designs are elusive, rendering it nearly impossible to analyse according to traditional practices,[2] and many passages are devoid of any tonal gravity. And although Zemlinsky ascribed no specific program to the work, its sheer breadth and variety of moods, which range from contemplative and spirited to aggressive and violent, suggests a composition infused with the emotions born of personal experience. The single explicit influence on the quartet is Schoenberg, whose First Quartet from 1905 was similarly conceived as a single movement constructed from four distinct sections (whereas Zemlinsky's quartet comprises five sections).[3]

Among the most striking elements found in the quartet is its formal scheme. Years earlier Zemlinsky struggled to avoid indulging his expositions with too much developmental material. Now he "front loads" the quartet with its basic ideas, each of which flows directly into the next — an Impressionistic, quasi-modal opening figure based on a three-note group; a highly-charged secondary theme characterized by its clipped upbeat that quickly builds to a climax;

---

[1] Weber (1995), 97. Zemlinsky wrote Schoenberg about his desire to visit Venice, in hopes of catching a few days of sun before the summer vacation came to an end, but it's not known if the trip was ever made.

[2] See, for example, the contrasting analyses by Stephan, Weber and Loll, as laid out in Beaumont (2000), 236–37. The quartet's harmonic outlines, which revolve around D minor and, to a lesser extent, E-flat minor, are somewhat easier to follow.

[3] At the *mit Ausdruck* of the first movement, Zemlinsky also quotes Schoenberg's *Verklärte Nacht*.

and, following a brief caesura, a driving variant of the opening material, whose dreamy quality is replaced by contrapuntal vigor. Everything that follows the F-sharp minor opening is traceable back to one of these ideas, each unfolding like a stream of consciousness until the warm and relaxed character of the work's opening suddenly returns in the transposed key of D major.

A sustained cello pedal heralds the start of a series of variations based on the modal theme (*Andante mosso*). Each variation is distinctive, in character and pacing. The first begins with a reflective theme played by the solo violin, the second is characterized by running violin sixteenth notes, the third displays violent *pizzicato* accompaniment, but careful examination reveals that even the accompanimental material, however altered, has been heard before. An abbreviated return of the modal theme segues directly into the *Adagio*, whose opening recalls the work's primary material and its calm D major atmosphere. The explosive middle section, with its extreme registers, frenetic tremolo writing and dense contrapuntal activity, is almost programmatic in its expression and reveals a level of intensity that Zemlinsky never surpassed.

The Scherzo, marked *Schnell*, is a relentless tour de force that transforms the opening three-note motive into a jaunty theme, punctuated by *pizzicato* chords and wild *glissandos*. The lyrical gesture presented roughly two-thirds through the movement is vintage Zemlinsky, but it offers only transient relief from the breathless atmosphere surrounding it. An *Andante* briefly reprises the quartet's principal material before launching into the freely conceived *Allegro molto* finale. Here Zemlinsky inventively explores prior ideas with new textures and tempos, complete with a cello soliloquy. Likewise, the recapitulation, truncated to a fraction of the exposition's length, gives way to further development. The themes are recalled one final time in an extended passage (marked *Andante*) before the opening motive dissolves in a final ascent and the tonality of D major is calmly and unequivocally restored.

In August of 1913 Zemlinsky said goodbye to Ida and Hansi in Kitzbühel and returned to Prague alone to prepare for another year. The Philharmonic was slated to perform an all-Beethoven program in October, featuring the First and Fourth Symphonies and the G Major Piano Concerto,[1] Schubert's 'Great' C major Symphony in November and Mahler's Third Symphony in April. The

---

[1] In the years that followed, Zemlinsky programmed Beethoven with frequency and performed the complete Beethoven symphonic cycle twice, first during the 1914/15 season and again over the course of two seasons from 1917 to 1919. During Zemlinsky's entire Prague tenure, only the 1923/24 season was devoid of any Beethoven symphonies.

January program featuring Tchaikovsky's Fifth Symphony and Strauss's *Tod und Verklärung* was still to be finalized, but Zemlinsky hoped to round out the concert with Schoenberg. The theater's operatic spotlight, meanwhile, would be trained on Wagner.

From its inception, the Deutsches Theater was linked to the music of Richard Wagner. In efforts "to keep the great German dramatic tradition alive for the large German population of Prague",[1] the theater's commission had appointed Angelo Neumann the institution's first director in 1884. Neumann possessed energy, drive and experience, and his European tours of Wagner's *Ring* were legendary. Neumann's company had played from London to St. Petersburg, using original Bayreuth costumes and scenery purchased at Neumann's expense. So renowned were Neumann's Wagner tours that Wagner had personally tried to persuade Neumann to organize a Wagnerian Theater in Berlin, but Neumann declined, preferring a quieter existence in Bremen. As a condition for accepting the Prague position, Neumann insisted that the Deutsches Theater buy his Bayreuth wardrobe and props, allowing Neumann to recoup his investment from years earlier. After much deliberation, Neumann's demand was met, and the theater celebrated its inauguration with a performance of Wagner's *Die Meistersinger von Nürnberg*, the singers no doubt fitted in Bayreuth costumes. Thereafter, Wagner remained a staple of the theater's repertoire.

For thirty years, however, performances of Wagner's *Parsifal* were banned outside of Bayreuth, to ensure that Wagner's conception of the opera was scrupulously maintained, although unstaged concert versions were given in London (1884), New York (1886), Boston (1891), and Amsterdam (1896). The opera had even been staged "illegally" in New York in 1903 and Amsterdam in 1905, but on January 1, 1914, *Parsifal* became public domain. In preparation for that event, Zemlinsky scheduled eighteen rehearsals of *Parsifal*, arduous even by Zemlinsky's standards. To secure his staged performance of *Parsifal* as the first ever outside Bayreuth, Zemlinsky scheduled curtain time for 4:00 p.m., one hour ahead of the more conventional 5:00 time. The performance, which Zemlinsky half-jokingly referred to as "the greatest event of the season, the year, the century, etc. etc."[2] was a resounding success and earned accolades not only from Prague's German press but from Czech critics as well, even with a performance of the opera in Czech across town at the rival National Theater the same afternoon. O. Nebuška of the *Hudební Revue* deemed Zemlinsky's production "deserving of the highest honors", and went on to write, "We have formerly

[1] La Grange (1976), 131.
[2] Weber (1995), 110.

paid respects to Alexander Zemlinsky's excellent qualities. Here, in the overall production, he proved himself a student of Gustav Mahler. Zemlinsky is thus deserving of unlimited praise."[1] Having gained the unqualified endorsement of the Czech press, Zemlinsky's next step was unprecedented — to forge a musical alliance between the two theaters.

In an especially muddy and snowy January, Zemlinsky's attentions swung toward a new project, the world premiere of three songs from Schoenberg's Orchestral Songs, op. 8, planned for the end of the month. Preparations were hampered by the customary problems. Zemlinsky hoped that Emil Hertzka, director of Vienna's Universal Edition publishing house, would loan him the orchestra material without cost, a policy Zemlinsky believed was customary for premieres. In any case, because both Zemlinsky and Schoenberg had signed long-term contracts with the publisher, Zemlinsky felt that Hertzka earned enough money from their efforts to honor such a request outright. Hertzka was not of the same mind, and with the concert only weeks away and rehearsals already scheduled, the matter remained unresolved. Correspondence between Zemlinsky and Schoenberg reveals tenuous relations with Hertzka — Zemlinsky described him as a pig ("Hertzka ist ein Schwein!")[2] — but Schoenberg remained cautious and argued for moderation. "He is a dangerous man", Schoenberg warned, ". . . who can bring to bear colossal and in particular artistic injury!"[3] For Schoenberg, Hertzka may have been "the only person to whom I dare not speak my mind", and he was unwilling to jeopardize his relations with such a prestigious publishing house. Zemlinsky, too, understood the significance of remaining on diplomatic terms with Hertzka, but he confessed to Schoenberg that "doing so disgusts me".[4] In the end, the theater was probably required to pay for the orchestral parts.

In need of a vocal soloist but with time running out, Zemlinsky settled on Hans Winkelmann, a tenor he had previously worked with at the Vienna Volksoper who had followed him to Prague. Winkelmann proved up to the task, despite his apparent nervousness. Alban Berg, present for the rehearsals, described Winkelmann's voice as terrific, with the caveat that he had no breath control. Zemlinsky assured Berg that it was just stage fright, adding that Winkelmann would simply have to wear two pairs of pants for the performance.[5] The world premiere took place January 29, 1914. Sadly, the public reacted with disdain,

---

[1] Quoted in Mahler (1971), 255.

[2] Weber (1995), 97.

[3] Ibid., 98.

[4] Ibid., 118.

[5] Grun (1971), 151.

a reaction all too familiar to Schoenberg. Nevertheless, the performance had been impressive. In a letter, Berg wrote that Zemlinsky was even more inspiring on the podium than he remembered, and described the orchestra as "remarkably intelligent", a further tribute to Zemlinsky's leadership skills.[1] Schoenberg's recollections of Zemlinsky, which he extolled to Hertzka, were equally glowing:

> The orchestral songs in Prague were very beautiful . . . Zemlinsky conducted them with grandeur. Truly Zemlinsky is certainly the foremost living conductor. I heard a wonderful Parsifal performance by him and also saw him rehearse and perform Tchaikovsky [Fifth Symphony] and *Death and Transfiguration*. It is unbelievable what he wrings out of hardly first-class material. It is sad that one doesn't hear such things in the artistic capital [of Vienna].[2]

Difficult though Schoenberg's music was for Prague audiences, Zemlinsky remained convinced of its value and began contemplating a production of Schoenberg's *Gurre-Lieder*, a work requiring an immense orchestra and choir. Wisely, the project was put on hold until the following season. In the meantime, Zemlinsky dealt with a personal and professional matter involving Schoenberg's brother Heinrich, a member of the theater choir and an inadequate singer. Zemlinsky found himself in an awkward position — he wanted to be supportive, yet had the standards of his organization to consider. He had written to Schoenberg several months earlier pointing out Heinrich's weaknesses, despite his dedication and industriousness. As a gesture of good will, Zemlinsky had undertaken to work with Heinrich personally, but the effort proved futile — coaching only made Heinrich more nervous and as it was, his voice trembled dreadfully. Zemlinsky knew Heinrich could not remain, and had their relationship been solely professional, he would have acted immediately. As it was, Zemlinsky held out as long as possible, and asked Schoenberg not to mention the matter to Heinrich, "since doing so would only make him yet more insecure".[3] In the end, the Great War intervened, and within a matter of months Heinrich, like many of Prague's musicians, was called off to service.

On June 28, 1914, Field Marshal von Moltke's fears were realized — the match was thrown into the powder keg. Despite persistent warnings, Archduke Franz

---

[1] Ibid.
[2] Schoenberg (1964), 43.
[3] Weber (1995),109.

Ferdinand, heir to the Austro-Hungarian throne, and his Czech wife Sophie, duchess of Hohenberg, traveled to Sarajevo during the Serbian National Festival, where their presence outraged Serbians opposed to Habsburg rule. The archduke and duchess were slain at point-blank range, sending a continent on the brink of war spiraling into the abyss. Austria-Hungary responded by levying a series of hopelessly impossible demands on Russian-backed Serbia, and when Serbia failed to comply, Austria-Hungary declared war on July 28. In defense of Serbia and its Balkan interests, Russia began mobilizing the next day. Germany followed suit on July 30, as did France on August 1; that same day, the German Empire declared war on Russia.[1] In efforts to avoid fighting simultaneously on two fronts, Germany struck first to the west, expecting that a swift victory in France would allow it to turn its full energies eastward. England's initial hesitation to commit to its allies emboldened Germany to invade neutral Belgium, which left England with no moral ground but to join the fray. The War to End All Wars was under way.

In Prague, on the day following Austria's declaration of war on Serbia, Franz Kafka entered the name "Joseph K" into his journal. Several days later he began sketching out ideas for *The Trial*, his novel about a victim ensnared in a world whose machinations he did not understand and could not escape. But not everyone shared Kafka's pessimistic world view. Schoenberg, like many, believed the war would be over by the following Christmas, and author Thomas Mann believed, and hoped, that Germany would deliver a deathblow to the heinous police state of Russia. Even Sigmund Freud patriotically confessed, "Perhaps for the first time in thirty years I feel myself an Austrian, and would like just once more to give this rather unpromising empire a chance."[2] But the pacifists were notable and numerous, like the writers Karl Kraus, whose exposés in *Die Fackel* denouncing the stream of war propaganda were routinely censured; Arthur Schnitzler, who refused to write on the subject of war, knowing anything he submitted would be rejected; and Stephan Zweig, who resigned his position with the Austrian war archives after seeing the effects of the war in Galicia. When Zweig's anti-war play *Jeremiah* was produced in Switzerland, the author and his wife left Austria to attend the rehearsals and never returned. Fellow author Romain Rolland, already in Switzerland, summed up the feelings of those repulsed by war fever. Believing all was lost, he wrote:

> I'm devastated. I would like to be dead. It is horrible to live in the middle of this demented humanity, and to be present, but powerless, at the

[1] Willmott (2003), 29.
[2] From a letter to Karl Abraham of July 1914, quoted in Gay (1988), 346.

collapse of civilization. This European War is the greatest catastrophe in history, for centuries. [It's] the ruin of our holiest hopes for human brotherhood.[1]

Zemlinsky remained characteristically silent about politics. During the summer of 1914, which he and his family spent in Sellin, an island resort on the Baltic, they were also far enough removed from the theater of war not to be personally affected by world events. In contrast to the endless rain of the previous summer, this year they were blessed with gorgeous weather. Zemlinsky left Sellin refreshed and well rested, but the effects of the war soon became evident. With rail lines committed to the war effort, his family was unable to travel directly to Prague. A miserable eighteen-hour journey brought them only as far as Berlin. There, Zemlinsky finally awakened to the exigencies of the ongoing World War. Berlin, chaotic and frenzied in the midst of complete mobilization, was a jolt of reality compared to the relaxing and blissful Baltic Sea. Lamentably, there was no news from Austria, since no newspapers had arrived in days.[2]

Back in Prague, Zemlinsky initially found the atmosphere fairly optimistic, although the season commenced without opera since the theater lacked sufficient personnel, and Zemlinsky's wages were being paid day to day. By December, Zemlinsky's mood had darkened considerably, along with Prague's political climate. Zemlinsky wrote Schoenberg that the Czech population now celebrated any "bad" news from the front—bad, that is, from the Austrian point of view—while the city's Germans had become increasingly estranged in what Zemlinsky referred to as "enemy territory".[3] Zemlinsky soon became sensitive to distant events, particularly in Serbia and Russia, where winter brought severe casualties.

Zemlinsky's frame of mind was also bound up with life at the Deutsches Theater, which now faced formidable obstacles. The army's conscription of every eligible man had decimated the theater's work force, from the production staff to the chorus. With no choice but to scale back its number of stage productions, the theater increased orchestral concerts, although the orchestra personnel had likewise been culled of its men.[4] It was hardly the time for new undertakings; Zemlinsky stuck to standard fare. From November to May of 1915 he averaged approximately one orchestral concert per month and built his programs around the complete Beethoven symphonic cycle, rounded out

[1] Quoted in Davies (1998), 895.

[2] Weber (1995), 122–23.

[3] Ibid., 128.

[4] By September of 1915 the orchestra was operating with just under forty players.

with works of Haydn, Mozart, Schubert and Brahms. Operatic programming demanded more difficult choices, since manpower was in such short supply. There were highlights, among them the new production in February of Peter Cornelius' comic opera *Der Barbier von Bagdad*, which Zemlinsky conducted and produced. It marked the first time Zemlinsky was placed fully in charge of a Prague production, and he proudly regarded it as one of the theater's best.[1] But the season also had its share of disappointments, not the least of which was the cancellation of Zemlinsky's own opera *Der Traumgörge*. Heinrich Teweles had repeatedly proposed hosting the long-overdue premiere at the Deutsches Theater, which was finally planned for the 1914/15 season, but cutbacks forced Teweles to put the project on indefinite hold and wait for a more opportune time. It never came.

Through it all Zemlinsky somehow managed to find the time and energy to compose, and in March 1915 he finally brought his ambitious Second String Quartet to a close. He dedicated the work to Schoenberg, a gesture Universal Edition failed to note when it published the quartet as Zemlinsky's op. 15.[2] Within two days of the quartet's completion, he headed off in a completely different direction. The quartet was an intensely personal and progressive piece of writing, not likely to appeal to the greater public.[3] With that now behind him, Zemlinsky returned to the world he knew best — opera. Inspired by Oscar Wilde's *A Florentine Tragedy*, *Eine florentinische Tragödie* is pure entertainment, albeit with a serious vein, a private affair-turned-public where the tragic consequences of lust and power are played out on the stage.

The theater consumed Zemlinsky's time and energy, however, so the new opera had to wait until summer for any real attention. Meanwhile, other ventures and concerts came and went, including a commission from Bodanzky's Mannheim National Theater for incidental music to Shakespeare's *Cymbeline*. Zemlinsky masterfully set the action to music, faithfully retelling in sound the story of Britain's King Cymbeline, but the production became a victim of war-

[1] Weber (1995), 133.

[2] In a letter to Schoenberg from 1916, Zemlinsky wrote, "I have requested that Hertzka send you the quartet, which has recently appeared. Hopefully the copy will contain the dedication, which had been left out, despite its having been written in huge letters on the title page!!" See Weber (1995), 155.

[3] The Second Quartet received its premiere in April of 1918 but it was with a 1924 performance, given in Berlin by the Havermann Quartet, that its merits were fully realized. Declaring Zemlinsky's quartet "among the best efforts of modern music", the critic of the *Musikblätter des Anbruch* went on to stress the work's modernity, its thematic unification and Zemlinsky's ability to bring out the best qualities of each instrument. *Musikblätter des Anbruch* (1924), no. 4, 165.

time hardships and was subsequently shelved and forgotten. The concert season ended with music of Goldmark, Schubert, Wolf, Mozart, Brahms and Beethoven. Then the army called.

Zemlinsky received notification that he was to appear before the military board in September. Schoenberg doubted that his friend would ever see action, believing his constitution was too weak, but Zemlinsky was not so sure — he had heard that ninety percent of those registered had been called up and armed, and he was certain he would suffer the same fate.[1] He was not due to report for several months, so the family left town for Königswart (Lázně Kynžwart), in north-west Bohemia. There they rented a villa located in glorious wooded surroundings. Removed from the stress of the theater and world events, Zemlinsky reveled in the excellent air and seclusion, and although provisions were poor, the peaceful atmosphere lent itself well to composition. Zemlinsky threw all his energy into *Eine florentinische Tragödie*, energized by the belief that he was creating something of worth. The opera marks his first return to the tragic consequences of human passions since the halcyon days of *Sarema*. On July 22 he wrote Schoenberg that work on the piano-vocal score had gone quickly and easily — it had required only nine weeks — and predicted that the opera's orchestration would require just seven or eight weeks more to complete.[2]

Zemlinsky's decision to set Max Meyerfeld's translation of Oscar Wilde's *A Florentine Tragedy* was no doubt prompted by the success Richard Strauss had enjoyed with his one-act operas *Elektra* and *Salome*. But Strauss's influence went deeper, impressing itself on nearly every level of *Eine florentinische Tragödie* — from Zemlinsky's reliance on an Oscar Wilde tale of forbidden love, to the dynamic orchestration.[3] Set in sixteenth-century Florence, Wilde's tale pivots around the merchant Simone, who, having been away on business, returns home to find his wife Bianca in the company of Guido Bardi, heir to the duke of Florence. Although suspecting the true nature of Guido's visit, Simone remains gracious and initially treats the prince as an honored guest and a potential customer. Guido brazenly flaunts his attraction to Bianca, and

[1] Weber (1995), 139.

[2] Ibid., 141.

[3] Wilde, of course, knew a great deal about the consequences of forbidden love, in particular "the love that dares not speak its name". Celebrated well beyond his native Dublin for his wit and flamboyance, his life took a tragic turn in 1895 after he was accused of being a sodomite. When he sued for libel, he lost his case and was subsequently arrested for "gross indecency", and the trial that followed became an international sensation. This time he lost both the case and two years of his life when he was sentenced to hard labor. His last three years were spent penniless and in self-imposed exile.

as Simone becomes increasingly convinced of the prince's true motive and his wife's infidelity, his remarks become more barbed. When Guido finally decides to leave, Simone fetches his guest's cape and sword, whereupon he feigns awe with the steel's temper and delicacy. Simone then requests that Bianca bring him his sword, on the pretext of comparing the qualities of both. The two men now face one another, armed. Urged on by Bianca, Guido attempts to slay her husband, but Simone disarms the lover and kills him. Guido's death has an immediate cathartic effect on Bianca, who opens her arms to her husband and the two are reunited in a passionate kiss.

As a whole, *Eine florentinische Tragödie* is long on dialogue and short on action.[1] In the wrong literary hands the tale probably would have suffered a slow death, but Wilde deftly develops the personality of his characters. Simone's worldly knowledge of current events, economics and politics, for example, stands in sharp contrast to the young aristocrat's interest in nothing but Simone's wife. Wilde weaves allegory — Simone's reference to having killed a highway robber for attempting to take what belonged to him — and symbolic foreshadowing — Simone compares spilled wine with blood — into his text, and by allowing the merchant to carry on as if his wife and her lover are innocent, Wilde gradually develops tension. When Bianca desires to see Simone dead, the narrative is propelled forward to its violent conclusion.

Zemlinsky faced a number of obstacles with the preparation of the text, particularly the fragmentary survival of the original. Missing from Wilde's *A Florentine Tragedy*, for instance, was the opening love scene between Guido and Bianca. Zemlinsky circumvented the problem by substituting the missing scene with an orchestral overture, similar to what Strauss had done at the start of *Der Rosenkavalier*, whereby Guido and Bianca's illicit love is removed from the stage and is instead depicted in the orchestral score. In the abrupt closing scene, where Bianca unexpectedly transfers her passions back to her victorious husband, Zemlinsky faced a dramatic problem of a different nature. Until this moment, the drama has pivoted around Simone, the cuckolded husband who symbolizes the common man confronting the might and prestige of nobility. But with Guido's death the drama suddenly spins off in a wholly unexpected direction. Recognizing Simone as noble and true — a man willing to risk his life to save his marriage and honor — Bianca shrewdly professes a new-found love for her victorious husband, and Simone, in turn, looks beyond Bianca's infidelity to see a woman whose beauty inspires the passions of powerful men. Their rekin-

---

[1] The vocal style mixes a healthy dose of lyricism with recitative dialogue, and the only lines not sung are those of the dying Guido.

dled love is born of the tragedy — in Zemlinsky's words, "a human life had to be sacrificed in order to save two others"[1] — but Zemlinsky's challenge was how to execute this transformation in convincing musical terms.

The origins of Zemlinsky's solution lie in the piercing trumpet flourish at the outset of the overture, a motive that suggests the consummation of Guido and Bianca's adulterous affair. With Simone's entrance the motif is transformed into a shuddering, violent gesture, and although Simone's first words — "So langsam, Weib?" ("So slowly, wife?") — are distinctly set to the opening fanfare, it is the more sinister variation, with its chromatically-descending afterthought, that begins to thread its way through the orchestral fabric and repeatedly coincides with dramatic instances of recognition, conflict and resolution. This ill-boding version, for example, recurs with Simone's sudden realization that his wife is not alone, when Guido brashly suggests taking Bianca for himself, and again when Bianca softly implores Death to take Simone where he stands. Simone, having overheard his wife's plea, now sarcastically proclaims, "Let no one speak of death! What should death have to do with such a merry house . . . ?" Hollow descending octaves in the harp and winds underscore Simone's cold realization that he will kill the prince, while his words are temporarily reduced to emphatic recitative, but out of the sinister harp motif a new idea emerges: cloaked in the warmth of D major, Simone sings of the death required to cleanse the house of adulterous lust.

With Guido's death, Simone's prophecy is fulfilled, but the opera's denouement brings a shocking turn of events: out of the ashes of tragedy rises Simone and Bianca's love, reborn. Faced with Wilde's final lines — Bianca: "Why did you not tell me you were so strong?" Simone: "Why did you not tell me you were so beautiful?" — Zemlinsky reaches back to Simone's song of death and transforms it into one of reconciliation. In a single stroke, Zemlinsky provides a logical and musically satisfying resolution to the tragedy that has reunited the wedded pair. Over the haunting echoes of descending octaves, the orchestra now swells to a triumphant climax before fading gently away.

As was characteristic of Zemlinsky's mature work, *Eine florentinische Tragödie* reflected tendencies both modern and conservative. Much of the score lacks a key signature, chords are often freely constructed, and there is a strong, expressive use of dissonance that is frequently achieved by way of unresolved chords and clashes of passing tones over a static bass. Yet there is a prevailing lyrical nature to the work, from the overture's rich Straussian scoring to the lush strains accompanying Bianca and Simone's reunion at the opera's

---

[1] Weber (1995), 343.

conclusion. Into the mix Zemlinsky throws a healthy dose of counterpoint and programmatic musical effects, such as the bird calls suggesting sunrise near the overture's close, the ostinato depicting Bianca's spinning wheel, and the descending, stammering line that portrays Guido's dying breaths.

Only after completing the score did Zemlinsky realize there might be copyright issues associated with the Meyerfeld translation. The matter should have been settled before ink first met paper, but having worked one on one with librettist Leo Feld for his previous two operas, Zemlinsky apparently never gave the question of artistic permission a second thought — until now. Attempts to resolve the copyright matter were not helped by war and its restrictions on communication. Neither Wilde's London representative, Robert Ross, nor Max Meyerfeld were willing to grant consent. Meyerfeld's Berlin publisher Samuel Fischer could not, however, prohibit Zemlinsky from commissioning another translation. Zemlinsky hurriedly decided on another plan of action:

> I now intend to do two things. 1. Have a new translation made right away based on my music and perform it, even at the risk of being sued by Ross after the war. 2. My lawyer is seeking to contact Ross to obtain the authorization for a performance in accordance with the law. At any rate, I have to do *everything on my own*, because Hertzka has forsaken me completely, has put the problem aside and waits for — I don't know what. I am extremely upset with this fellow! Yesterday I emphatically impressed my plans on him and insisted that he take the work back up. After all, our contract covers this case! I accept the responsibility (morally and materially!), he the royalties.[1]

In the end, Universal was able to secure the rights, but negotiations cost the opera two years' time. Nevertheless, the curtain finally lifted on *Eine florentinische Tragödie*, and the opera went on to become one of Zemlinsky's most successful scores. Following the Stuttgart premiere in 1917, the opera played in Vienna, Prague, Graz, Leipzig, Aachen, Schwerin and Freiburg. Its final production during Zemlinsky's lifetime came in Brno in 1928, before it was all but forgotten until its revival in Kiel in 1977. Zemlinsky's score was greatly admired by Schoenberg, Berg and Emil Hertzka, who marveled at its beauty. Yet nobody was more enamored with the work than writer Franz Werfel. Impressed with Zemlinsky's powers of expression, Werfel wrote, "It is clear that this music was composed by a burning soul; it does not stem from calculation and dexterity but

[1] Weber (1995), 148.

is the product of music's innermost core. He has earned the highest title — he is a singer."[1]

Work on *Eine florentinische Tragödie* and a summer in the country provided Zemlinsky a temporary escape from the dark realities of the world. Meanwhile, the Austrian war machine, gaining ground in the Balkans, required manpower to fuel its efforts. In October it took control of Belgrade. One month earlier, a 44-year-old Zemlinsky had dutifully reported to the enlistment office to be examined for military service. The verdict: "unsuitable." Twenty-three years had done nothing to change the Austrian military board's decision regarding Zemlinsky's capacity to serve. Rather than express relief, Zemlinsky commented that one should feel ashamed at such results.[2]

Shamed or not, Zemlinsky was now free to leave all thoughts of military duty behind and focus on the future. He was once again considering adding Schoenberg's name to the 1915/16 season and in September suggested programming the Chamber Symphony, op. 9. But the composer, who had once demonstrated a remarkably cavalier attitude about how his music might affect the public, was now keenly aware that war was not the time to test the public's nerves, or his:

Dear Alex,

Much as I rejoice at your intention to perform my chamber symphony and however fervently look forward to hearing this work at long last (for it has never yet been sufficiently rehearsed and brought out in all its clarity), I do beg you to give up the idea until the war is over.

This request will surprise you, so I must give you my reasons in full.

You know that I have scarcely ever taken any account of whether my works were liked or not. I have become indifferent to public abuse and I have never had any inclination to do anything that wasn't dictated by the purely musical demands of my works. I can say this with a good conscience, and so I can also risk asking you to do something that people of ill will might interpret as making concessions: do, instead, perform one of my older works, either "Pelleas" or perhaps part of the "Gurre-Lieder", in a word, something that can by now count on being fairly well received by the public.

When I think of how badly my "Pelleas" was treated here and of the opposition with which even the Songs for Orchestra were received, but

[1] Werfel (1922), 76.

[2] Weber (1995),143.

above all when I remember the uproar about "Pierrot lunaire", after which my name was dragged through the mud of all the newspapers at home and abroad under the headline "Schoenberg Scenes in Prague", surely it isn't cowardly if I now try to avoid that sort of thing. In peacetime — which means war-time for me — I am quite prepared to go back to being everyone's whipping-boy, and everyone who is accounted indispensable today will be welcome to lash out at whatever bit of me he thinks most vulnerable. But for the present — more than ever — I should like to keep out of the limelight . . .

. . . Is it any wonder I should like to be left in peace just a little while longer (the only good thing the war has done for me is that I'm not being attacked by anyone), that I should like to enjoy this peace of mine just a little while longer, as long as the war lasts?

So don't be angry with me for asking something so odd and do, if you can, do as I ask.

Arnold Schoenberg[1]

Zemlinsky consented to his brother-in-law's wishes and performed the "Waldtaube" from the *Gurre-Lieder* rather than the Chamber Symphony in two highly successful concerts in February 1916, which also included Beethoven's *Eroica* and Strauss's *Alpine Symphony*, composed during the previous year.

Unwilling to yield to war-time hardships, Zemlinsky pushed ahead with demanding works such as Liszt's *A Faust Symphony* and Verdi's *Requiem*. He also programmed a considerable amount of music by fellow Austrians, most likely for patriotic reasons, among them Brahms, Bruckner, Robert Fuchs, Mahler, Mandl, Pfitzner, Reznicek, Rietsch, Schoenberg, Schreker and Wolf. The operatic repertoire performed during the war was no less impressive. In addition to the standard fare, Zemlinsky conducted Bizet's *Djamileh* and Goldmark's *Das Heimchen am Herd*, and premiered a handful of new works, including Max von Schilling's *Mona Lisa*, Erich Korngold's *Der Ring des Polykrates* and *Violanta*, Richard Strauss's monodrama *Enoch Arden*, and Felix Weingartner's *Kain und Abel* — this despite Weingartner's refusal to conduct Zemlinsky's *Der Traumgörge* in Vienna years earlier. But regardless of his Prague accomplishments, the thought of remaining in Czechoslovakia indefinitely had begun to gnaw away at him. For all the advantages of his present position, Zemlinsky felt trapped in a provincial city, isolated from the European musical mainstream and frustrated that despite all he had done for others, none were willing to return the favor:

[1] Schoenberg (1965), 52–53.

I am condemned to hopelessly waste all my talent (which, with even the best will in the world I cannot deny I possess) and ability in Prague . . . and yet I cannot find anyone — even if I am not looking for anyone — who still believes in me and is gladly willing to help me out, but rather I am forgotten, even by the best of friends . . .[1]

In a letter to Schoenberg from 1914, Zemlinsky mentioned his desire to leave Prague at any cost, even without an engagement elsewhere, but that was before the outbreak of war.[2] Now, in the midst of a world war, finding an attractive position outside Prague seemed impossible. Everywhere belts were being tightened and salaries and seasons were cut back. A year earlier an opportunity had presented itself when Arthur Bodanzky, Zemlinsky's former student and colleague, left his post at Mannheim's Nationaltheater for work in America. But despite the theater's initial interest in Zemlinsky, his request for a yearly salary of 14,000 marks proved beyond the theater's means.

In February of 1916 another position became vacant, this time in Frankfurt. Zemlinsky confirmed his interest in the job, but unbeknownst to him, Heinrich Jalowetz, another former student, had also applied. To complicate matters, Zemlinsky had recently presented Jalowetz with an offer to join the Deutsches Theater. Despite Jalowetz's appreciation and initial interest in coming to Prague, he wrote Zemlinsky later that month that such decisions would have to wait until he heard whether or not he was named Frankfurt's new director.[3] Stunned that Jalowetz was vying for the same position, Zemlinsky knew that if it came down to the two of them, the younger man would get the job since he could be hired for a third of what Zemlinsky would need to leave Prague. Zemlinsky was understandably frustrated. In Mannheim he had been asked to fill a post held by a former student, and now he was competing against one! He had always believed that his work ethic, talent and generosity would enable him to prevail, but he now realized that such qualities would take him only so far:

I make music and tirelessly work myself to the bone, always in the belief that talent, diligence, seriousness and idealism are better qualities than a big mouth, money and connections. Gradually I am taking on the role of "uncle", who brings with him something good for *everyone*, so that in the end he might be allowed to enjoy the bread of charity out of compassion. And *no one* thinks of me, *no one* helps me. And I would wager that

[1] AZ/AMW.
[2] Weber (1995), 118.
[3] Ibid.,152.

everyone would judge my fate as just and tolerable. Yet, today I have taken one final step in order to get away from here. It is my final effort. Following it — resignation. It is after all, nothing new, nothing out of the ordinary. "But to whom it actually happens, it does break his heart asunder." (I have already begun to embrace my destiny — that is always the last stage).[1]

In the end neither Jalowetz nor Zemlinsky was offered the position in Frankfurt. With Zemlinsky's Deutsches Theater offer still on the table, Jalowetz finally accepted and came to Prague, where he remained until 1923.

Productions of Zemlinsky's scores during the 1916/17 season temporarily provided some distraction from his rather dreary and melancholic existence. First came the world premiere of *Eine florentinische Tragödie*, staged in Stuttgart alongside Julius Bittner's Singspiel *Das höllisch Gold* on January 30, 1917. Zemlinsky, who arrived for the final dress rehearsal, found the performance mediocre but satisfying nonetheless.[2] His biggest complaint was with conductor Max von Schillings, whom he regarded as terribly incompetent. In a little more than a month, Zemlinsky would begin rehearsals for eight performances of the opera in Prague, more than enough time to improve on tempos, direction, clarity, expression and everything else he deemed substandard in the Stuttgart production.

If Zemlinsky was of the opinion that Schillings had not done justice to his opera, the critics saw it differently. The production was "ravishing, full blooded, inwardly stimulating and exhilarating"[3] according to the critic of the *Schwäbische Merkur*, and Wilhelm Maute of the *Münchner Zeitung* could not conceive of the inexorably gradual and horrifyingly tense build-up to catastrophe of Wilde's story being carried out in any other way.[4] In the *Neue Wiener Journal*, Felix Adler wrote:

> Zemlinsky lived up to the expectations aroused by the announcement of his new work. His Florentine Tragedy stood as a coherent whole, created in a single casting; Wilde's drama was created anew through its musical interpretation.[5]

[1] Weber (1995), 152–53. Quoted is Heinrich Heine's poem, "Ein Jüngling liebt ein Mädchen", from the *Buch der Lieder*. Schumann set this text in his *Dichterliebe* (no. 11).

[2] Weber (1995), 163.

[3] *Schwäbischer Merkur* (January 31, 1917), quoted in Hajek (1988), 101.

[4] *Münchner Zeitung* (February 1, 1917), quoted in Hajek (1988), 101.

[5] *Neues Wiener Jounal* (February 3, 1916), 14, quoted in Hajek (1988), 102.

Adler, like his colleagues, drew the inevitable comparisons with *Salome*, but stated plainly that Zemlinsky could in no way be regarded as a mere follower of Strauss. Furthermore, he recognized *Eine florentinische Tragödie* as a challenging work that forced listeners to meet it on its own terms rather than the other way around:

> One seeks in vain within the music of the Florentine Tragedy for the type of popular and pleasing melodic line, which, through a shift of mood willing to sink to any level of banality, seeks to soothe the audience following an orgiastic hail of dissonant tones. Where the drama leaves room for it, Zemlinsky's melodic treatment remains austere and chaste, arising from the soul, intent not on pleasing the ear, but demanding instead to be felt.[1]

Unfortunately, soon after the premiere, the war forced the closing of Stuttgart's Hoftheater, and Zemlinsky's opera, like other works on the theater's calendar, was put on indefinite hold. In Austria, meanwhile, Emil Hertzka wanted to introduce a new work at the Vienna Hofoper. Impressed with what he heard about Zemlinsky's opera from Stuttgart, he sent Hugo Reichenberger — Zemlinsky's successor at the Hofoper under Weingartner — to Prague to hear it performed under Zemlinsky's baton, along with Bittner's *Das höllisch Gold* conducted by Jalowetz. Under Zemlinsky's direction *Eine florentinische Tragödie* received an enthusiastic press, the *Prager Tagblatt* reporting the audience's fascination with the work and the subsequent celebration of its composer.[2] To Hertzka, Reichenberger reported that he found Zemlinsky's music "magnificently colorful and in places enchantingly beautiful".[3] It was now up to Hertzka to convince the Hofoper administration that Zemlinsky's newest opera was worthy of production.

In the second week of March, Hertzka began working on the Hofoper staff, assuring them that Zemlinsky's score would be relatively inexpensive to stage — it required but three singers and no scene changes — and that it could be performance-ready within three weeks' time. By March 21, the deal was concluded, and Zemlinsky received notice that everything was in order. *Eine florentinische Tragödie* was to share the bill with *Klein Idas Blumen*, a ballet featuring music by Paul von Klenau, works that would "hopefully make for a good and successful pair".[4] To ease Zemlinsky's concerns about the opera's production,

[1] Ibid.

[2] *Prager Tagblatt* (March 5, 1917), 3; cited in Hajek (1988), 103.

[3] Quoted in Ottner (1995), 227.

[4] Ibid., 230.

Hofoper director Hans Gregor sent a note informing him that Reichenberger would be conducting and that the artistic direction was in the hands of one of the theater's most successful producers, Wilhelm von Wymetal, an old colleague from the days of the Ansorge-Verein. Gregor also assured Zemlinsky that he would personally keep watch on matters. Zemlinsky's music was coming home.

For Vienna, Zemlinsky reworked the entire score, from notes to dynamic markings. On April 25 the dress rehearsal was staged, and the opera's Viennese premiere followed two days later. Astoundingly, the opera flopped: after only five performances, *Eine florentinische Tragödie* was dropped from the Hofoper repertoire. Klenau's ballet, however, charmed the public and was programmed by the house until well into the Second World War. Criticism of the opera was diverse, but unified in its dislike. There was little argument about Zemlinsky's masterful harmonic shading or rich orchestral color. But some found the text weighed down with exaggerated musical emotion, others considered Zemlinsky's overture an inadequate substitution for Wilde's missing text, and still others regarded the score as little more than a watered-down version of Strauss's *Salome*.

In a particularly scathing critique, Max Kalbeck, who years earlier had written disapprovingly of Zemlinsky's First String Quartet, wrote, "His opera is nothing more than the poet's drama submerged in music; both boatman and boat founder in the turbid flood of tones that swirl with fawning caresses about the abominations of the original, abandoning all responsibility."[1] Others agreed with Kalbeck that Wilde's original tale was unpalatable, dooming the project from the start. The stunning failure of *Eine florentinische Tragödie* may have been magnified by other issues beyond Zemlinsky's control — not only was the text penned by an Englishman, an unpopular notion in Germany and Austria during the war years, but it followed in the wake of Pfitzner's highly successful opera *Palestrina*. Less than a year later, *Eine florentinische Tragödie* was eclipsed by the triumph of Schreker's *Die Gezeichneten*, ending all hope of future performances.

Both Pfitzner and Schreker had achieved precisely what Zemlinsky had not — each had developed a language free of obvious external influences and consequently been launched to the forefront of the Austro-German music scene. The German-born Hans Pfitzner, two years Zemlinsky's senior, had always striven to find an individual sound despite the Wagner-inspired romanticism common to his earliest music. In 1912 he began work on *Palestrina*, an opera based on his own libretto about Giovanni Pierluigi da Palestrina's Pope Marcel-

[1] *Neue Wiener Tagblatt* (April 28, 1917), quoted in Hajek (1988), 107.

lus Mass, and though he made no attempt to re-create the harmonic language associated with the sixteenth-century polyphonic master, Pfitzner nevertheless imbued his music with an antiquated, polyphonic style, which, when balanced with a more austere modern sound, gave the listener a sense that the music pointed to a much earlier time. The opera's 1917 premiere propelled Pfitzner to international fame, and, although none of his other operas ever matched the significance of *Palestrina*, his status as one of Europe's leading composers was established.

As a long-time friend and colleague of Franz Schreker, Zemlinsky was well aware of Schreker's accomplishments. His ballet *Der Geburtstag der Infantin* and his opera *Der ferne Klang* had already played to great acclaim and led to his appointment at the Vienna Music Academy. It was the kind of success Zemlinsky could only dream about. For Schreker, things continued to improve. His opera *Die Gezeichneten*, whose libretto was initially conceived for Zemlinsky's use, played in twenty-two cities between 1918 and 1930 and, along with *Der Schatzgräber*, sealed Schreker's reputation as one of the best composers of his generation. *Der ferne Klang* was far more radical, a highly individual work rich in color and masterfully orchestrated. Schreker's score was an experiment in non-functional harmonies and tonal ambiguity, a progressive style that he drove still further with his opera *Irrelohe* of 1923. Schreker was ultimately unable to sustain the reputation he so deservedly established during the second decade of the twentieth century, but for the moment he epitomized the success to which Zemlinsky aspired. Schreker's ascendency represented what was possible if only one could escape from the gravity of the nineteenth century.

In the weeks following the Vienna production of *Eine florentinische Tragödie*, Zemlinsky's ego suffered a further blow. Alma had finally attended a performance of the opera and had sided resoundingly with the critics. Her disloyalty stung Zemlinsky deeply. Wounded and distressed, Zemlinsky expressed his disappointment in Alma's judgment and attempted to enlighten her misguided impressions of Wilde's text. Confronting Alma's opinions and reflecting on art and their relationship, he wrote:

> Dearest Friend,
>
> If I did not have complete trust in your whole being, your quality as a human being, your life experience, in everything that I have come to know of you, your letter would have — I beg your pardon — made me smile. However, as it is I cannot help but be shocked. Does a person of culture really speak like *that*? This pompous tone of voice, this pitiful criticism of "a few passages of music", this terrible misunderstanding of

Wilde's text!!! You, You! whom I know as an intelligent, sophisticated, circumspect woman, ahead of all others, surely never in the company of the others, must identify with the ridiculous viewpoint of Korngold, Bienenfeld,[1] etc., etc.!!! Pardon me — I must and must be permitted to write you as I feel the need. You misunderstand this text? You call it a perverted blunder? Do you know that it was only because of the newspapers that the best [people] conceived of the idea that it was written for the sake of a perverted punch line? Do you know how the drama goes? Two people, both with admirable qualities — beauty and vitality and enthusiasm for their profession — have become lost to each other because of the "power" of fate. He neglects beauty and the woman at his side because of his passion for work; she, waiting for a life at the side of her man, finds herself betrayed of youth and beauty, and becomes loveless and unhappy and seemingly full of hatred. Only a terrible catastrophe can wake the two up. In the face of death, two completely confused individuals are reawakened. A real tragedy, because a human life had to be sacrificed in order to save two others. And among all it was you who misunderstood — — ?!

... Nevertheless, I believe that you mean well with me. Therefore, I do not want to judge your blunder too harshly. However, I am sorry because I had to understand by it how little trust you took in me as an artist and a human being. Otherwise, you would have stood blindly by me and slowly convinced yourself of my art.

I hope and wish that these will not be the final words we exchange about this matter. Perhaps we will even grow closer because of this "catastrophe". "Why did you not tell me you were so — weak."!

Forever your trusted,
Zemlinsky[2]

Schoenberg attempted to assuage Zemlinsky by writing him that Alma's attitude was shaped as it was for two reasons. Her misconceptions about the text stemmed from failing to prepare herself adequately for the production; Schoenberg and Webern had been present at productions in both Prague and Vienna, and had strong knowledge of the score, yet Alma had come to the performance fully unprepared. And neither Zemlinsky nor Schoenberg had found time to visit her while in Vienna, an unforgivable insult that Schoenberg believed

---

[1] Elsa Bienenfeld, who had worked with Zemlinsky at the Schwarzwald School, was music critic for the *Neues Wiener Tagblatt* and for the *Neue musikalische Presse*.

[2] Weber (1995), 342–44.

contributed to her attitude.[1] What Schoenberg failed to acknowledge was that Alma probably read into the opera a personal connection to her life with Walter Gropius, with whom she had carried on a relationship during Mahler's final, health-plagued years. Like many, Zemlinsky may have felt that her affair with Gropius had hastened Mahler's death — it had, after all, driven Mahler to the couch of Sigmund Freud. Whatever the case, *Eine florentinische Tragödie* had touched a nerve, and Alma's criticism toward Zemlinsky, in turn, added insult to injury. Zemlinsky felt betrayed by both Vienna and Alma.

The continent remained awash in chaos and bloodshed. In October 1917 Russia collapsed in revolution, and, as its resistance declined, the Central Powers focused their resources westward. Meanwhile, Austrian and German armies fought together and broke through the Italian line at Caporetto, but despite the temporary victory — the surprise attack cost the Italians 300,000 men and great quantities of its artillery, while sending shockwaves throughout the Allied powers — it meant little in the end. British naval blockades were inflicting severe food shortages in Central Europe, even far from the fighting.

Zemlinsky could not complain — he had work and he wasn't in uniform. For Schoenberg, matters were far bleaker. Schoenberg's teaching opportunities had ground to a halt as his students were called off to serve, and in 1915 Schoenberg himself had enlisted. Though temporarily released the following year, he was called up again in September of 1917 before finally being permanently discharged that December on the grounds of being medically unfit to serve. During this time the Schoenberg family finances became desperate. With no paying position and no students, Schoenberg made a poor impression on prospective landlords, and his family was forced to live in a series of cheap boarding houses. In October 1917 Zemlinsky wrote an urgent letter to Emil Hertzka, imploring the publisher to come to Schoenberg's aid. "This is important, urgent: the Schoenberg catastrophe . . . He and his family are nearly without bread! Something must be done! There must be an easy way for you to come up with a thousand or so, either through your bank or through your relationship with

---

[1] Ibid., 170. Alban Berg had visited Alma the previous year, during which time she was married to Walter Gropius and pregnant with Manon. In a letter to his wife, Berg related that Alma had spoken about Zemlinsky with great enthusiasm. He went on to say that Alma was "slowly losing all her hair, she looked like a Red Indian squaw. Her stomach is like a bull, otherwise nothing exorbitant. Only, her feet — I couldn't believe my eyes — were sometimes sticking out under her dress: in straw sandals, with no stockings!" See Grun (1971), 198.

millionaires . . ."[1] Zemlinsky urged the publisher to act quickly and proposed putting up Schoenberg's *Gurre-Lieder* as collateral.

By now, milk and flour were among the countless items difficult to locate, and some went so far as to mix birch tree bark with beets and *ersatz* chocolate as a substitute for meat. Sugar was scarce, bread was being made from corn-meal, and all supplies, when available, were rationed. Finding or affording coal for heat also became critical. The Schoenbergs went for long stretches of time with none, which played havoc with Mathilde's health. Salka Viertel, sister of the pianist Eduard Steuermann and a frequent guest at the Schoenberg's home at this time, remembered how Mathilde, "always wrapped in a shawl, sat in the corner of the sofa freezing . . . there was such a scarcity of food, and we were always so cold and hungry that, when we visited each other, one talked about nothing else except where can one get some potatoes . . ."[2]

It is not known if Hertzka ever came through for Schoenberg, but Zemlinsky did. By the end of 1917 he had managed to secure his brother-in-law 1,500 kro-nen from a bank director; 1,500 more came the following February.[3]

In contrast to the Schoenbergs, the Zemlinskys were fairing significantly bet-ter. Despite Zemlinsky's persistent complaints of life in Prague — friction at the theater the previous April had again tempted Zemlinsky to go elsewhere — the city and his continued position provided him and his family with undeniable advantages. They stayed fed, warm and free of disease, and Prague had escaped bombardment, Europe's only major city to do so (Mannheim and Frankfurt, cit-ies to which Zemlinsky had applied for positions, were not so fortunate). Thus, while sympathetic to Zemlinsky's frustrations, Schoenberg understandably felt that Zemlinsky underestimated the worth of his position and reminded him that theater work would be equally exhausting regardless where he went. More-over, as Schoenberg could personally attest, this was no time to be unemployed.

Zemlinsky and his family spent the summer of 1918 in the "gloriously beau-tiful" town of Spindelmühle (Špindlerův Mlýn). Finding milk momentarily plentiful, they drank it by the liter and devoured cakes of butter. But by now it was clear that the war had changed things forever. To Schoenberg, Zemlin-sky confessed his belief that "this war will *never* end, at least as long as we are alive. I don't mean the war in its actual present sense. But in peaceful, ordered circumstances, neither of us will ever walk again."[4]

That fall, the tide of war began to turn. The Allies, which now included

---

[1] Letter of 1917, quoted in Weber (1971), 8.

[2] Smith (1986), 140.

[3] Weber (1995), 179, 182.

[4] Ibid., 195.

American troops, were winning battles on all fronts. In October the German war machine ground to a halt with the realization that further fighting would accomplish nothing. The Austrian army disintegrated as its Czech, Polish, Hungarian and Croat soldiers deserted. Throughout the empire, long-desired national independence was finally being realized. Yet Zemlinsky's gaze remained fixed on a wounded Vienna: "To be sure, I cry for poor Vienna too. It is terrible that this magnificent city, with its great potential, talent, culture, *real* culture, is collapsing, to be reduced to a provincial city."[1] Bitter though his Viennese experiences had been, none were so devastating as to kill his love for the Austrian capitol. But Zemlinsky's instincts were right. With the Empire dissolved and the borders redrawn, imperial Vienna was reduced to little more than the "provincial capital of a tiny, near-bankrupt alpine republic".[2] As a crucible of modernist culture and thought, Vienna's glory days were over, and Europe's foremost intellectuals and artists began looking elsewhere for stimulating air. Within a few years Germany was refashioned into the Weimar Republic. As its capital Berlin grew in size and scope, it became recognized as the modern Metropolis, usurping Vienna's position as the hub of modernism for the German-speaking world. As it did for so many of Europe's leading intellectuals and artists, Berlin eventually beckoned Zemlinsky. But first Zemlinsky was to endure nine more years in Prague.

[1] Weber (1995), 201.
[2] Michael Haas, personal correspondence with the author.

Chapter 7

Freedom and Fading Dreams

This is more than just a lost war. A world has come to an end.

Walter Gropius[1]

AGAINST THE BACKDROP of the final days of the War to End All Wars, the Deutsches Theater opened its doors for the 1918/19 season by hosting the Czech premiere of Eugen d'Albert's two-year old opera *Die toten Augen*. Despite the relentless battles tearing Europe apart, Zemlinsky continued to challenge himself, his company and his audience. Finally, the war did end. On November 28, seventeen days after the formal armistice agreement, Zemlinsky led his Philharmonic in a fitting performance of Mozart's "Prague" Symphony, along with music of Bruckner and Dukas. With the war now over, Zemlinsky and the theater began adding a healthy dose of contemporary scores to the roster — Philharmonic concerts in the first few seasons after the war included music of Bartók, Debussy, Finke, Korngold, Krása, Schoenberg, Stravinsky and Webern, in addition to productions of operatic works by Hindemith, Schreker and Puccini.[2] Mahler's music also continued to play an important role in Zemlinsky's life and that of the city. The previous season had ended with performances of *Das klagende Lied* and *Das Lied von der Erde*, presented on a concert commemorating the seventh anniversary of Mahler's death, and this season would include performances of the First and Seventh Symphonies.

---

[1] Quoted in Taylor (1977), 210.

[2] While Puccini's name is not normally associated with "modern" music, *Il tabarro* and *Suor Angelica* were but two years old when Zemlinsky directed them in Prague.

But the new season was accompanied by a host of serious transitional concerns. Zemlinsky was not only left with a "decimated" chorus but one consisting of "the eldest singers, that is, not the best of age groups".[1] Furthermore, the theater was loosing its director. Heinrich Teweles was leaving for another local institution, the *Prager Tagblatt*, a daily German-language newspaper, and Leopold Kramer had been named his successor. In Vienna, where Zemlinsky and Kramer had been colleagues, Kramer had proven himself a capable actor. As a director, however, Zemlinsky believed Kramer was out of his element and jeopardized the institution to which Zemlinsky had given the last seven years of his life. The scenario was so distasteful to Zemlinsky that he again wrote Schoenberg of his willingness to leave Prague at any price.[2] His relationship with Teweles, a consistent supporter of Zemlinsky's undertakings, had been largely exemplary, and even when tensions ran high, as they did towards the end of Teweles's tenure, the two men were able to iron out their differences. To his credit, before leaving, Teweles recommended Zemlinsky be promoted from the position of first *Kapellmeister* to that of *Opernchef*, placing him in charge of all matters musical. But Zemlinsky believed that, in Kramer, the theater was inheriting an incompetent leader. Although Kramer lacked Teweles's vision and knowledge of serious music, Kramer was not nearly as incompetent as Zemlinsky perceived him to be. Despite inevitable periods of friction, Zemlinsky's diplomatic skills ultimately prevailed, and the two men gradually established positive working relations.

More critical, however, was the political backdrop beyond the theater's walls. Within weeks of the season's start, the independent Republic of Czechoslovakia was declared. For the first time in nearly four centuries, the country was out from under Austrian rule and free to determine its own destiny. As a member of the defeated Central Powers, on the other hand, Austria was made to forfeit vast amounts of land, and the newly organized borders resulted in Czechoslovakia's inheriting nearly eighty percent of the Empire's industry. As a result, large ethnic populations formerly under Habsburg rule, including Hungarians, Ruthenians, Slovaks and Poles, became Czechoslovakia's concern, and Prague was soon seething with ethnic tension. Fortunately, Tomáš Garrigue Masaryk, a leader determined to incorporate rather than alienate a diverse population dissatisfied with Czech political and economic domination, was soon at the helm of the new government.[3]

---

[1] Weber (1995), 333.

[2] Ibid., 199.

[3] Masaryk had been an advocate of Czech independence even before the start of World War I and upon its outbreak left the country to avoid being arrested and imprisoned for

One of the most difficult and immediate battles Masaryk faced was how to maintain a state of harmony among such a diverse ethnic population. The solution, Masaryk believed, lay in the government's ensuring full protection and representation to every ethnic group in the country. "This profound reality, which no one of good faith and free from prejudice could seriously have contested, fully justified the presence of the Bohemian Germans in the new Czechoslovakian state."[1] Nevertheless, many Austrians shuddered at the idea of the Czech government determining their fate. Zemlinsky was among those who had concerns about the future of Prague's German population, not to mention that of the Deutsches Theater.[2] The writer Max Brod sympathized with the Czech cause, but he nevertheless feared "a long winter of lawlessness and mob violence against Jews and Germans".[3] If not for the swift establishment and competent leadership of the Czech National Council, the Czechs might have exacted revenge on the Austro-German population who had inflicted hundreds of years of hardship and misrule upon them, culminating with the deprivations of a war they did not start.

But even a man of Masaryk's moral integrity and vision could not simply erase generations of hatred, fear and anti-Semitism overnight. In November 1920 three days of anti-Jewish and anti-German protests exploded in the city, during which time the Estates Theater, so long associated with German productions, was overrun by Czech street mobs and subsequently commandeered as their headquarters. German-language newspaper offices were sacked, "Jewish-looking" victims were attacked in the streets, Hebrew manuscripts were burned in front of the AltNeu Synagogue and the Jewish Town Hall was overrun. Franz Kafka wrote that he had "spent all afternoon out in the streets bathing in Jew-hatred", and heard the Jews referred to as *prašivé plemeno*, a filthy brood.[4] With no intention of waiting for the racial climate to stabilize, thousands of Jews began the exodus for Palestine. Fortuitously, Zemlinsky had left for Vienna just as the

treason. His travels took him to Switzerland, Italy and England, where he actively sought support for Czechoslovakian independence, and by 1918 the American president Woodrow Wilson was siding with his cause. On October 18 Masaryk stood on the steps of Philadelphia's Independence Hall and proclaimed Czech freedom. Recognized by the Allies as head of the Provisional Czechoslovak government, Masaryk returned to an independent homeland. In January 1919 Czechoslovakia was officially proclaimed a republic at the Paris Peace Conference, and the following year Masaryk was elected his country's first President, a position he retained for the next fifteen years.

[1] Tapié (1971), 397.
[2] Weber (1995), 201.
[3] Pawel (1984), 373.
[4] Ibid., 408.

rioting broke out, and by the time he returned to Prague several days later the demonstrations had been quelled and the city's prevailing peace was restored.

Incidents of this nature were unsettling but rare, and fortunately did not shake the otherwise strong sense of optimism flowing through the streets of the newly created Czechoslovakia. By the mid-1920s the country had made significant strides, cutting unemployment and reducing shortages of goods. Opportunities were especially plentiful in the field of education, as new universities and technical schools opened. Music and the arts were revived, and Zemlinsky was appointed director of the newly founded Deutsche Akademie für Musik und darstellende Kunst, the German Academy for Music and Applied Arts. Masaryk also ensured that the doors of the Deutsches Theater remained open and that the institution received the support of government subsidy, a significant symbol of good will by a government determined to guarantee its German citizens a healthy cultural atmosphere. Zemlinsky, personally affected by these events, later acknowledged the theater's indebtedness to the new President:

> My memories of the Deutsches Theater's most difficult period will always be connected to the illustrious appearance of President Masaryk. It is thanks to his interest in art and his unswerving support of the theater, which was held together during a very perilous time, that things were able to continue at the same level, perhaps even able to continue at all.[1]

Zemlinsky recognized that this was a crucial time for action and so as Director of the new music academy — for which he earned a mere 100 Kč a month[2] — he helped bolster local cultural life and ensured a future for the next generation. The school's faculty included the prominent violinist Henri Marteau and the pianist Conrad Ansorge, but Zemlinsky's visibility and rich pedagogical background made him a logical choice to head the program. By 1921 Zemlinsky's conducting class numbered thirteen students,[3] and in the years that followed he had the occasion to help mold a number of gifted composers, among them Hans Krása, whose life was tragically ended in the gas chambers of Auschwitz.

Zemlinsky's approach to teaching continued much as it had before. For analysis he often turned to Schubert songs and Beethoven sonatas and quartets, while technically he stressed the role of the bass line, which he believed helped determine the shape of a given phrase. Formal logic remained at the core of

---

[1] From an article entitled, "A. Zemlinsky, Masaryk und das Neue Deutsche Theater", *Neuer Morgen* (March 1, 1930), 8, quoted in Weber (1977), 32–33.

[2] Beaumont (2000), 289. 100 Kč was worth about $20 in 1920, equivalent to about $220 in 2010. See the sources cited at p. 15 n. 2.

[3] Weber (1995), 220.

Zemlinsky's approach, as it had when Alma Schindler numbered among his students. "A solid grasp of form is mandatory," he told her, "preparatory to being able to compose freely",[1] and though he impressed upon his students the need to be "pulled" by a given progression, he also encouraged individual search for distantly related chords and relations of pitches. Years later, Erich Korngold recalled being impressed by Zemlinsky's promotion of modern harmonies and, above all, of his guarding against arbitrary choices.[2]

Although teaching harmony and composition had long been part of the standard curriculum of European musical institutions, the development of a conducting pedagogy was a relatively recent phenomenon. Zemlinsky's conducting class at the Akademie was therefore something of a novelty.[3] Like his contemporaries, Zemlinsky was largely self-taught, and his lack of formal conducting instruction contributed to his personal teaching method. Instead of commencing by teaching hand motions associated with a particular time signature, for example, or instructing with the help of a mirror, Zemlinsky delved immediately into score study with his students. He was convinced "that one could not teach conducting via a routine but rather only through musical stimulation, and that he did by way of a unique manner".[4] Peter Herman Adler, who studied with Zemlinsky at the Prague Academy, recalled how Zemlinsky stressed a thorough knowledge of the music itself:

> For him the teaching did not consist so much of technical details or tricks, the way conducting is taught today, but rather through discussion of the score. He spoke first and foremost about the music while technique was approached incidentally. Within the domain of opera, the enormous influence that Gustav Mahler had exerted on him was certain. We spoke, for example, about Mahler's [approach to Beethoven's] "Fidelio," and he explained the extraordinarily slow tempo that Mahler had taken in the quartet of the first act. Then we attempted it with Zemlinsky at the piano and found it to be nearly impossible. He always said to us, "the better you know the music, the better a conductor you will be." Everything depended upon that. He was in the habit of sitting at the piano and inviting the students to comment upon what they heard.[5]

---

[1] AZ/AMW.

[2] See Korngold (1921), 230–32.

[3] As stated in Chap. 1, a *Kapellmeisterschule* had only been integrated into Vienna's Conservatory curriculum in 1909.

[4] Heinsheimer (1987), 17.

[5] Ibid.

It would be difficult to overemphasize the importance Zemlinsky placed upon score study. He felt "each composition must be fully comprehended from a melodic, harmonic, formal and orchestral standpoint prior to conducting it", and so dismissed teaching the rudiments of conducting until this knowledge was gained. "It was for this reason that he stressed the assiduous analyses of the classics and the symphonies of Schumann, Schubert and Brahms",[1] while also believing that a conductor's skill was crucially linked to pianistic ability, particularly as it related to score reading.

While his approach to teaching conducting may have been unique, his goal was no different from that of his composition lessons — to encourage self-discovery and bring out the student's natural abilities. To do this required freeing his students from preconceived ideas or influences, an approach published in *Der Auftakt*, the music newspaper of the German-speaking population in Czechoslovakia:

> My teaching method is different from other known styles in the sense that my students must take everything that they have regarded up until then as good or necessary, and then *unlearn it* [*verlernen*], in other words *learn afresh* what their talent deems necessary for their independent development. Only they can be entirely free of conventionalism and prevail who have passed through and mastered everything.[2]

Heinrich Jalowetz later noted that along with his seemingly inexhaustible productivity and the joy he derived from his work, Zemlinsky always found time as a pedagogue.[3] When Zemlinsky conducted works by students of the Academy during the 1924 Prague Music Festival, he must have recalled fondly the dedication J. N. Fuchs had shown towards him more than thirty years earlier.

Among the cultural institutions that sprang up in Czechoslovakia just after the war was the Šak Philharmonic, an ensemble founded by Vladislav Šak in 1919 to provide an alternative to the well-entrenched Czech Philharmonic. In April and May 1921 Zemlinsky appeared as the orchestra's guest conductor, the first time in recent memory that a German conductor and a Czech orchestra had shared the same stage.[4] Despite Šak's best intentions and the abilities of his

---

[1] Quoted in Clayton (1995), 304.
[2] Fleishmann (1921), 222.
[3] See Jalowetz (1921), 203.
[4] See Ludvová (1997), 5–7.

orchestra, Zemlinsky's concerts proved among the last ever performed by the "Bohemian Philharmonic", which folded at the end of the season. Still, a critical component of post-war relations had been achieved: a bridge separating the ethnic divide was spanned, and Zemlinsky was the first across.

In 1922 Zemlinsky appeared as a guest of the Czech Composition Society, where he lectured on the state of new Czech music, an event that helped forge a fruitful and enduring relationship with the Czech musical community. An invitation to guest-conduct followed from Václav Talich, conductor of the Czech Philharmonic, the country's premier musical institution. Zemlinsky led that esteemed ensemble for the first time the next season in a performance of Mahler's Sixth Symphony, and returned frequently thereafter.[1] Zemlinsky endeared himself to Czech audiences and consistently filled the hall to capacity at a time when, owing to the flurry of musical activity competing in the Czech capital, Prague musicians were accustomed to performing for near-empty houses. Furthermore, not only was Zemlinsky the first German conductor ever to receive an invitation to appear before this orchestra, but some Czech conductors subsequently "modeled themselves after his example and deferred to his authority without reservation".[2]

War had taken such a toll on both the Deutsches Theater and the Czech National Theater that the two organizations had little choice but to combine resources for concerts requiring large forces. While pragmatic, the solution was also unprecedented, and it came about because of Zemlinsky's diplomatic acumen and the high esteem in which he was held across town. Not only did the two theaters begin to share players, but Otakar Ostrčil, chief conductor of the Czech National Theater, began consulting with Zemlinsky about matters of composition and conducting.[3] Zemlinsky's interest in new music, in particular the work of Mahler, left a lasting impression on the Czech conductor, who subsequently led performances of Mahler's Fifth and Ninth Symphonies as well as *Des Knaben Wunderhorn*. He was also the first Czech to conduct *Das Lied von der Erde*. Zemlinsky was equally committed to the Czech musical cause. Until then, the music of Bedřich Smetana, so strongly associated with the aspirations of the

---

[1] The symphonies of Mahler remained the focal point of Zemlinsky's association with the Philharmonic. By the time of his final appearance on the Czech stage, on December 3, 1937, he had conducted *Das Lied von der Erde* and all but symphonies Four, Five and Seven.

[2] Adler (1923), 144.

[3] As late as 1927 the two ensembles continued to collaborate, as demonstrated by a June 1 performance of Mahler's Symphony no. 8, which utilized two German choirs, a strengthened Czech Philharmonic, six soloists from the Deutsches Theater and one from the Czech. See Biba (1992), 57.

Czech people, had never been heard on Prague's German stage. That ended in 1924 when Zemlinsky celebrated the hundredth anniversary of the composer's birth with a production of Smetana's *Der Kuss* (*Hubička*).[1] Performances of Smetana's *The Bartered Bride* and Janáček's *Jenůfa* soon followed.

There had once been a time when Zemlinsky gladly dedicated countless hours to societies whose missions promoted the cause of modern music. His commitment to the works of his contemporaries was unfailing and passionate, but now life's demands consumed him, leaving little time for the organization and administration of such pursuits. Schoenberg, meanwhile, was boldly forging ahead, undaunted by war or the struggles he had repeatedly faced in Vienna. In November 1918, the month of the armistice that ended World War I, Schoenberg founded the Verein für musikalische Privataufführungen (Society for Private Musical Performances) in Vienna. Two years later he brought his ensemble to Prague for four performances. Inspired by what he heard, a local clerk and an amateur violinist by the name of Georg Alter attempted to establish a similar organization in the Czech capital. But Alter's initial attempts to involve Zemlinsky produced a tepid response — despite the years that had elapsed, Zemlinsky no doubt remembered the volume of work such undertakings demanded, not to mention the struggles encountered building an appreciative audience for this music. But when Schoenberg's ensemble returned for a performance of *Pierrot lunaire* a year later, Zemlinsky had a change of heart. The electric performance, which Zemlinsky described as an "unqualified great success",[2] suggested Prague was ready to embrace such an undertaking.

The following spring, the Prague Verein für musikalische Privataufführungen was founded. At its charter meeting, Zemlinsky was elected president of the Prague Verein, Alter secretary, and Schoenberg honorary president. Thanks to the competent management of the gifted writer, conductor and publicist Erwin Stein, and to Anton Webern, who also led many of the rehearsals, the Verein contributed significantly to Prague's cultural landscape, despite surviving only three years.[3] Modeled closely on Schoenberg's Viennese society of the same name, the Prague chapter sought to further the cause of contemporary music through well-balanced programming and obligatory repeat performances. To ensure that the Verein maintained a consistently high level of performance,

---

[1] March 20, 1923.

[2] Weber (1995), 228.

[3] Schoenberg's Vienna-based organization also lasted only three years, from 1918 to 1921.

rigorous preparation for each program was the standard. Applause, demonstrations or disapproval would not be tolerated, as all performances were private and critical reviews prohibited. And as a policy, no single "school" was permitted to dominate its programs. Rather, offering a wide variety of styles, the Verein strove to present its audiences with a true sense of the present state of contemporary western music.

Issues of programming and concert duration dominated much of Zemlinsky and Schoenberg's correspondence during this period. Zemlinsky, of course, had the last word about artistic matters in Prague, but Schoenberg's experiences with the Vienna Verein made him an invaluable resource. To avoid appearances of furthering his own cause, Zemlinsky intended to limit performances of his music, as Schoenberg had done in Vienna. With the Vienna Verein, Schoenberg compensated by offering up an abundance of Max Reger — his music appeared forty-two times in a single season — a decision Schoenberg justified by claiming that "Reger must in my view be done often; 1, because he has written a lot; 2, because he is already dead and people are still not clear about him (I consider him a genius)."[1] Genius or not, Zemlinsky was not inclined to follow suit. He argued that while Schoenberg's Viennese Society performed weekly, the Prague concerts were of a more isolated nature, and too much Reger, or anyone else for that matter, would not go down well with its members. Above all, Zemlinsky did not want to risk losing his audience, for whom "the concerts were not inexpensive and who want to become familiar with as much as possible".[2]

For Erwin Stein, a critical juncture had been reached: "If one is not allowed to perform Zemlinsky, Schoenberg, or Reger, with what is one to produce modern programs??!!"[3] The answer was found in balance and variety, which involved programming the music of composers active beyond the Austro-German frontier. But agreement on which modern composers to program was not assured. Zemlinsky, for example, found the music of Darius Milhaud — whose *Le Bœuf sur le toit* was performed twice during the 1922 season — to be insignificant, but Schoenberg again felt otherwise:

> Now as to the "insignificant" Milhaud, I don't agree. Milhaud strikes me as the most important representative of the contemporary movement in all Latin countries: polytonality. Whether I like him is not to the point. But I consider him very talented. But that is not a question for the Society, which sets out *only to inform*. It was actually primarily on your own

[1] Letter to Zemlinsky of October 26, 1922. Schoenberg (1965), 80.
[2] Weber (1995), 237.
[3] Ringer (1990), 168.

account that I did Milhaud once again, hoping that he would interest you.[1]

In the end, a diverse list of international names ultimately found their way onto the Prague Verein's programs during the organization's brief three-year existence: Bartók, Debussy, Eisler, Kodály, Krenek, Milhaud, Pfitzner, Poulenc, Prokofiev, Ravel, Schnabel, Schulhoff, Stravinsky and Szymanowski. Yet despite all efforts to the contrary, the Verein remained partial to the Viennese. Berg and Webern were repeatedly performed, as was Zemlinsky.[2] Above all, the music of Reger and Schoenberg was most often programmed — eight times each — despite Schoenberg's initial intentions of keeping his own music to a minimum.[3] Indeed, Schoenberg had been present from the very start — the society's inaugural concert on May 25, 1922, included *Pierrot lunaire*, along with the Cello Sonata of Debussy. Zemlinsky, ironically, had been unable to attend the performance. By then he had already left for Cologne, where, three nights later, Otto Klemperer was scheduled to lead the premiere of Zemlinsky's latest opera.

Work on *Der Zwerg* had begun in 1918, but the opera's genesis dated back to at least 1911, the year the publication of Franz Werfel's *Der Weltfreund* sparked the literary movement known as Expressionism. That same year, Franz Schreker agreed to draft a libretto for Zemlinsky about "the ugly man", a theme Zemlinsky wished to explore in sound. Schreker was the ideal resource. He had not only penned his own libretto to his highly successful opera *Der ferne Klang*, he had since composed incidental music to Oscar Wilde's play *The Birthday of the Infanta*, a story about a princess's cruel treatment of a dwarf, for a pantomime production at Vienna's *Kunstschau* Garden Theater. Schreker thus possessed everything Zemlinsky required — first-rate musicianship, acute understanding

---

[1] Weber (1995), 240.

[2] During the Verein's 1922/23 season, four of Zemlinsky's unpublished songs were performed — most likely *Die Beiden, Noch spür ich ihren Atem, Hörtest du denn nicht hinein* and *Harmonie des Abends*, along with his Maeterlinck songs. The season that followed included the Second String Quartet, op. 15, in a performance by the Amar Quartet, with Paul Hindemith, violist.

[3] The pianist Eduard Steuermann performed his own transcription of Schoenberg's Chamber Symphony, op. 9, in addition to the Piano Pieces, opp. 11 and 19; Zemlinsky conducted the Five Orchestral Pieces, op. 16; finally, a program from October 10, 1923, consisted of the Eight Songs, op. 6, the newly composed Piano Pieces, op. 23, the Piano Suite, op. 25, and *Das Buch der hängenden Gärten*, op. 15, featuring Marya Freund, who came from Paris specifically for the performance.

of the relationship between text and music, and familiarity with the world of social alienation.

Whether or not Zemlinsky ever considered composing his own libretto, he ultimately came to the conclusion that his music would be better served by having someone of Schreker's experience involved. At the outset, Schreker seemed equally open to the idea of an artistic collaboration and commenced work on a libretto about the hunchback Alviano Salvago's fated love of a beautiful painter. Once into the project, however, Schreker's attitude quickly changed:

> The more I worked on it, the more abhorrent, the more unbearable I found the thought that not I, but another would compose the music to [*Die Gezeichneten*], music that was already taking firm shape and form within me. And it seemed to me as if, along with the libretto, I was giving him my musical self, as if I were selling my innermost soul, my very life. And I decided I would fight for the libretto. It wasn't necessary. My colleague in Apollo was a reasonable man and understood me without my having to say too much.[1]

As a substitute for *Die Gezeichneten*, which Schreker subsequently completed himself, Zemlinsky's colleague proposed drafting a libretto based on Edgar Allen Poe's *The Masque of the Red Death*. Zemlinsky, long a fan of Poe's writing, was initially in agreement with Schreker's suggestion, but the project never materialized, nor did any others despite further discussions.[2] Zemlinsky would go on to conduct performances of Schreker's operas *Der ferne Klang* and *Der Schatzgräber* in Prague, and Schreker, in turn, would offer Zemlinsky an appointment at the Berlin Hochschule in 1929, but there was to be no operatic collaboration between the two men.

There Zemlinsky's "ugly man" project sat until 1918, the same year incidentally that Schreker's *Die Gezeichneten* received its premiere in Frankfurt, when a young man by the name of Georg Klaren sent Zemlinsky a sample of his writing, presumably hoping to interest Zemlinsky in some sort of partnership. Zemlinsky knew little or nothing about Klaren personally, save perhaps that he had been or still was a student of linguistics at the University of Vienna, but Zemlinsky liked what he read, and the two men soon began considering ideas for a libretto.[3] They quickly settled on a tale of "animal magnetism" by

---

[1] From an article by Schreker, entitled, "Über die Entstehung meiner Opernbücher", quoted in Hailey (1993), 65.

[2] Evidently the two had also considered an adaptation of Selma Lagerlöf's book *Herr Arnes penningar* (*Herrn Arnes Schatz* in German). See Hailey (1993), 65.

[3] Weber (1995), 194.

Honoré de Balzac,[1] entitled *La Peau de chagrin*, and Zemlinsky sketched out musical ideas on and off for the next year. But work on what they subsequently renamed *Raphael* progressed slowly — presumably neither was fully convinced of the possibilities of the material. In July 1919 Zemlinsky finally set down his pen and proposed they turn their attentions to a story that had lain at the back of his mind for years — the same short story that Schreker had set over a decade earlier, Wilde's *The Birthday of the Infanta*. Klaren consented and prepared a text, and Zemlinsky immediately set to work.

Inspiration for Wilde's story sprang from a 1656 painting by Diego Velàzquez entitled *Las Meninas* (The Ladies-in-Waiting). In the painting, the daughter of King Philip IV and Queen Mariana of Spain, the Infanta Margarita, poses for her portrait, surrounded by courtiers, two dwarfs and a dog. In the background, a mirror reflects the royal parents back to the viewer. In Wilde's narrative, the mirror serves to reveal the truth, both as it pertains to the Dwarf's grotesqueness and the grotesque Spanish court, which was "always noted for its cultivated passion for the horrible".[2] Along with other stories from the same collection, which Wilde entitled *A House of Pomegranates*, *The Birthday of the Infanta* explores themes of social issues, particularly humanity's cruelty. It was, unfortunately, a subject with which Wilde was all too familiar. And though *The Birthday of the Infanta* remained a minor work within Wilde's *œuvre*, it reflected vital autobiographical elements of the author's life: "Wilde may very well have been projecting his own stigma, his own sense of being a 'court jester', onto the dwarf who does not know he is a monster."[3]

The tale is set in a Spanish court, where celebrations are being planned for the birthday of the Infanta, Donna Clara. The festivities begin as the court's subjects pay their respects to the spoiled Infanta, while the poor are served slices from an enormous birthday cake. Among the Infanta's presents, and the one she prefers over all, is a Dwarf. The hunchbacked creature, a charcoal burner's son with bristly red hair, has been caught in the forest during a hunt and arrives in a cage as a gift from the Sultan. Donna Clara and her playmates make fun of the Dwarf, who we soon learn has never seen his own image and is thus unaware of his grotesque appearance. When he is jokingly invited to choose one of the girls as his bride, the Dwarf chooses the Infanta, who subsequently taunts and torments, plays and dances with him, as he quickly falls in love with his "bride". With the Infanta gone, Ghita, the Infanta's maid, gently attempts to console the

---

[1] Balzac's short story of 1831 was influenced by lectures of Anton Mesmer that Balzac had attended at the Sorbonne.

[2] Pine (1995), 179.

[3] Ibid., 180.

Dwarf about the reality of the situation. He then glimpses his image in a mirror and for the first time is confronted with his hideous physical appearance. As he screams in horror, the Infanta rushes back. Overcome by her beauty, the Dwarf again professes his love for her, but she tells him he is only a wild animal and nothing but her plaything. Overwhelmed with shock and grief, the Dwarf collapses to his death. After pouting over her "broken" gift, the Infanta returns to her party.

Wilde's tale appealed to Zemlinsky and Klaren for markedly different reasons. For Zemlinsky, the Dwarf embodied "the ugly man", the persecuted outcast. It was a theme Zemlinsky had begun to explore with *Der Traumgörge* and with which he could personally identify on a number of levels, dating back to his early courtship with Alma Mahler. Alma, of course, struggled with Zemlinsky's physical appearance and in her memoirs years later she cruelly referred to him as a "hideous gnome".[1] But the physical comparison, despite being repeatedly drawn, ignores deeper and more compelling connections, such as Zemlinsky's struggles to find acceptance within critical Viennese musical society, or his feelings of being isolated and forgotten in Prague. Thus, Zemlinsky could sympathize with the plight of Wilde's Dwarf, whose self-worth society appeared incapable of recognizing.

By contrast, Georg Klaren's interest in Wilde's story was purely objective. He saw possibilities of interpreting Wilde's drama through the eyes and mind of Otto Weininger, a Viennese whose unique and troubling theories about human sexuality and psychology had long been of interest to the young writer.[2] Among those theories that appeared in Weininger's posthumously published book *Geschlecht und Charakter* (Gender and Character) was the idea that humans comprised a mixture of masculine and feminine elements. It was a concept Klaren found fascinating and that subsequently became central to his preparation of the libretto.

In Klaren's hands, significant modifications were made to Wilde's story. The Dwarf has, for example, gained a reputation as a performer, and six years have been added to the Infanta's age, most likely to intensify her erotic allures, although her actions — she is childish, naïve and cruel — remain those of Wilde's 12-year-old Princess. Much of Wilde's rich atmosphere has also been jettisoned, presumably for reasons of economy. Gone, for example, is the king's melancholy

[1] Mahler-Werfel (1958), 13.

[2] Weininger's disturbing theories of genius, human sexuality and religion, along with the nature of his death — Weininger shot himself in 1903, in the same house where Beethoven had died — made him a *cause célèbre* in his native Vienna and stimulated interest in the larger psychoanalytical world.

over his dead wife, and the fact that the king's brother, Don Pedro, is suspected of murdering her. And with the exception of the Dwarf's song and dance, the detail of Wilde's colorful pageant in celebration of the Infanta's birthday — from a mock bullfight to a performance by Egyptian musicians — is entirely absent. Naturally, adapting a work for the stage demanded careful decisions about what to save and what to discard, and considerations made on the basis of artistic merit — length, suitability, musical value and so on — were paramount,[1] but Klaren's alterations affected the text's emotional depth and psychological complexity. In Klaren's version, for example, we know next to nothing about the Dwarf's own background prior to his having arrived at the court as a birthday gift. On the other hand, the dynamics between the Infanta and the Dwarf are fueled through Weininger-inspired interpretation. Wilde's Infanta has become a *femme fatale* figure, whose beauty and dominance tilt the Dwarf's bisexuality in favor of his feminine side, thus rendering him weak and submissive in her presence. And Klaren's Dwarf now represents "every man", his ugliness symbolic of — according to Weininger — every man's sensation of inferiority toward women. In other words, the Dwarf is now hers to do with as she sees fit.

Klaren went on to publish his personal thoughts about the dynamics between the Infanta and the Dwarf in an article published for the *Kölnische Zeitung*, which unfortunately only appeared weeks after the opera's premiere.[2] The librettist also claimed that Zemlinsky modified his libretto without his consent. Zemlinsky's concern was, of course, how best to wed words and music to one another. Whatever his feelings regarding Klaren's Weininger-inspired interpretation, Zemlinsky's greater intent was to produce a score that magnified the text and educed the drama's extremes of emotions. The result was one of the most powerful and impressive scores Zemlinsky ever created.

Der Zwerg was not Zemlinsky's only opera to dramatize the theme of the social outcast, but it was the only one to explore the subject tragically and unflinchingly. In the words of Hans Keller, *Der Zwerg* "shies away from neither the Princess's thoughtless cruelty nor the foolishness of the Dwarf's infatuation with physical beauty".[3] A tale of such intensity would seem to have offered Zemlinsky the logical place to take a bold musical leap, had he been so inclined: it is

---

[1] Klaren confessed, "It is a very unenviable task, writing librettos! Goethe already warned Eckermann of it. If the reworked text fails to impress, it is the fault of the book, and if it succeeds, the audience finds the music deserving of merit." *Kölnische Zeitung* (June 17, 1922).

[2] Georg Klaren, "Der Zwerg und was er bedeutet". *Kölnische Zeitung* (June 17, 1922). The article was Klaren's attempt to explain his intentions, since, as he states, he was never asked to contribute to the program book for the premiere.

[3] Keller (1994), 153.

a story rife with cruelty and insensitivity, where even Ghita's grace and goodness find no opening. But despite his own demonstrations of progressive musical
thought in works such as the Second String Quartet, and his familiarity with
the *avant-garde* scores of his contemporaries, Zemlinsky evidently believed
that the anguish of Wilde's story could be captured without making musical
sacrifices. The score of *Der Zwerg*, therefore, adheres largely to a post-Romantic
musical idiom and is even organized along traditional lines, flowing effortlessly
between through-composed recitative and arioso. Zemlinsky's tonal palette remains equally conservative, even to the extent of relying on time-tested modes
of major and minor for dramatic effect. As the Dwarf casts his eyes on the Infanta for the first time, for example, his highly expressive lines sigh and cascade
in a plaintive duet with the English horn above the orchestra's minor tonality.
A brief shift to A major accompanies the Dwarf's confession that the woman before him "is not of this world", before immediately dropping back to the minor
mode. When the Dwarf inquires whether this is the Princess, the harmony rocks
mysteriously between A major and A minor, but Don Estoban's answer, "She
stands before you", is unaccompanied and fails to conclusively disclose either
mode. In the eyes (and ears) of the Dwarf, the Infanta remains suspended in
another world.

    That Zemlinsky had no intentions of pushing musical boundaries is further
demonstrated by his reliance on a sophisticated network of leitmotifs, which he
used to represent ideas both concrete (such as the rose presented to the Dwarf)
and abstract (such as the Dwarf's love for the Infanta). As with Wagner, many of
these motifs operate on an almost subconscious level. When Ghita is alone with
the Dwarf, for example, her concern for his welfare prompts her to reveal to him
his true nature. Shadowed by the oboe, Ghita sings about the Dwarf's goodness,
but the repeating three-note motif heard in the orchestra, a derivative of the
Infanta motif heard in the opera's opening phrase, suggests that the Dwarf's
thoughts are with the Princess and that he is oblivious to Ghita's sympathy. In
contrast to Ghita stands the Infanta, whose flippant teasing attitude Zemlinsky
captures with bland, cold phrasing, and whose vocal skips and leaps reflect her
frivolousness. Zemlinsky captures a similar dichotomy with the two male characters of the opera, the chamberlain, Don Estoban, whose music is impersonal
and simplistic — an indication of his formal and rather aloof demeanor — and
the Dwarf, a confused, troubled personality whose lines, ranging from lyrical to
intensely chromatic, perfectly mirror the gamut of emotions to which he suc-
cumbs.

    There are, of course, moments of intense horror and hysteria that Zemlinsky
powerfully portrays with unorthodox vocal leaps and bold harmonies, devices

that serve to anchor the opera to its expressionistic roots. The Dwarf's hideousness — his limp and awkward gestures, for example — is brilliantly captured with growling trombones and crude string glissandos. And in the history of opera, there may be no more crushing climax than that which occurs when the Dwarf comes face to face with his own image. Yet for all the intensity Zemlinsky brought to Wilde's tragic tale — Alban Berg found the opera "so harrowingly tragic as to be hardly bearable"[1] — in the end the score to *Der Zwerg* reflected the extent to which Zemlinsky remained linked to his musical origins.

Owing to Zemlinsky's conducting schedule, work on *Der Zwerg* had essentially been limited to two successive summers spent in the mountain villages in north-eastern Czechoslovakia. In 1919 a rainy summer was spent in Spindelmühle, and a portion of the following summer was spent in Bad Liebwerda (Lázně Libwerda), where Zemlinsky set to work on the opera's orchestration. Zemlinsky had earned his time off. The exhausting final weeks preceding the summer included a nearly sold-out performance of Schreker's *Der ferne Klang* in June and a set of guest conducting appearances in the town of Reichenberg (Liberec), the capital of a temporarily independent German state located near the northern border of Czechoslovakia. When Zemlinsky returned to Prague in the fall, his energies were split between the theater and preparations for the opening of the Deutsche Akademie für Musik und darstellende Kunst. *Der Zwerg*'s orchestration, therefore, was not completed until January 4, 1921, at which time Zemlinsky's decade-long obsession with the tragedy of the ugly man was finally laid to rest.

More than another year elapsed before *Der Zwerg* received its premiere, and in the meantime his opera *Kleider machen Leute* was reborn. Despite its disappointing premiere at Vienna's Volksoper ten years earlier, Zemlinsky always believed in the work's potential and for years had entertained thoughts of its revision. By 1919, unable to let the work languish any longer, Zemlinsky wrote his publisher that, "Kleider machen Leute won't leave me in peace . . . Why should such a really good, original work as this lie around for so long?"[2] A hoped-for 1921 performance in Munich failed to materialize, but, with a production slated for Prague in the year that followed, Zemlinsky and the librettist Leo Feld set about reworking the opera in depth. Major revisions now occupied him from spring until the year's end, during which time he composed seven insertions, heightening its overall dramatic potential while whittling its three acts down

[1] Grun (1971), 329.
[2] Undated letter to UE, located in the Vienna Stadt-und Landesbibliothek/Musiksammlung, quoted in Rode-Breymann (1995), 276.

to two. On April 20, 1922, *Kleider machen Leute* received its Prague premiere under Zemlinsky's direction. The critic Max Graf of the *Prager Tagblatt* captured the highly successful event:

> The poetic world of Gottfried Keller had a stimulating effect on Alexander Zemlinsky, a musician of such high musical culture and great artistic abilities. He is a young modernist, a musician with soul, who with the tip of his musical quill paints his motives on staff paper . . . In its new version premiered yesterday, the work had a stunning success.[1]

A little more than a month later, the curtain finally rose on *Der Zwerg*, when it received its world premiere in Cologne on May 28 under the baton of Otto Klemperer. In a city whose audiences were traditionally wary of novelty, Zemlinsky's music proved triumphant, and the public greeted the composer and the singers with stormy applause, recalling both to the stage a dozen times. Reviews in the days that followed acknowledged the power and beauty of Zemlinsky's score. The critic of the *Kölnischen Volkszeitung* went so far as to proclaim *Der Zwerg* "artistically superior to almost all modern works that had been presented on the Cologne operatic stage in recent years . . . Here is passion and ardor, a music of genuine feeling."[2] Not surprisingly, the Prague press had only glowing words to relay back home. Ernst Rychnovsky called *Der Zwerg* Zemlinsky's most musically and dramatically concentrated work to date, while Felix Adler waxed euphoric:

> Zemlinsky has delivered a work of such convincing uniformity and such strong inspiration, overpowering in moments of passionate ecstasy, so gripping in tenderness and the utmost feeling for lyrical expression, that there is certainly very little in the realm of contemporary opera that can compare with it. Here a great success has been achieved — it is the work of a master.[3]

Zemlinsky continued to work actively both in the pit and on the stage. Aside from his operatic commitments during the 1922/23 season, he gave five Philharmonic concerts in a period rich with Mahler symphonies. With his own Philharmonic Zemlinsky directed the Ninth and Eighth Symphonies in January and May respectively, and in April he formally inaugurated his association with the Czech Philharmonic with two performances of Mahler's Sixth. Then, at the start

---

[1] *Prager Tagblatt* (April 21, 1922), quoted in Mahler (1972), 241.

[2] *Kölnischen Volkszeitung* (May 30, 1922).

[3] *Prager Tagblatt* (May 30, 1922) and *Bohemia* (May 31, 1922).

of June, he left for Berlin to conduct his Maeterlinck Songs at an Austrian Music Week festival. Although the concert also included music of Bittner, Schoenberg and Berg and Webern's *Passacaglia*, op. 1, which Zemlinsky had conducted to great acclaim in Prague the previous December, Zemlinsky's songs, according to Berg, "enjoyed the greatest success of the evening. The audience wouldn't stop applauding until the last song was repeated."[1]

Zemlinsky's Berlin excursion proved well timed. Just weeks earlier the Staatsoper's director, Leo Blech, had resigned, so Zemlinsky was provided the opportunity to learn what was transpiring at first hand. Now 51, he was among those being considered for the post, along with Otto Klemperer, Bruno Walter and Erich Kleiber, a clear indication that Zemlinsky ranked among the best conductors of his generation. For Zemlinsky, the prospect of taking up residence in Berlin was thrilling, and in July he wrote to Schoenberg that issues of competition had been surmounted. Negotiations now rested solely on matters of salary:

> I am currently involved in very serious negotiations with the Berlin Staatsoper. It appears that there is but *one* more obstacle left, nevertheless one of great significance — *the salary*. Considering the collapsing value of the mark, it is questionable if they can even offer me close to what I *must* demand. The coming days will bring a decision.[2]

Despite Zemlinsky having finally found a ticket out of Prague, runaway inflation now forced him to consider the matter carefully. Not so long ago he had proclaimed his willingness to leave the Bohemian capital at any price, but the state of the German mark had since become too precarious for the middle-aged conductor to simply ignore.

Zemlinsky's precautions were well founded. All belligerent countries were facing hardship, but the crisis of Germany's economy had reached "catastrophic and ruinous proportions".[3] The country had failed to meet its World War I reparation obligations — 132 billion gold marks, then worth over $31 billion, equivalent to about $400 billion in 2010[4] — and in January 1923 the government of France chose to interpret Germany's default as an intentional act of

---

[1] Brand (1987), 325. Berg went on to note that the strong performance was at least partially a result of Zemlinsky's two-hour rehearsal that morning, which left barely enough time to rehearse Berg's music.

[2] Weber (1995), 251.

[3] Palmer (1992), 786.

[4] See http://en.wikipedia.org/wiki/Reichsmark and http://www.minneapolisfed.org/community_education/teacher/calc/hist1800.cfm (both accessed March 16, 2010).

provocation. In response, the French army sent troops into the industrial Ruhr valley, where they ruthlessly took control of the mines and industries for the Allied powers. In an act of passive resistance, the German workers countered with general strikes, and, although productivity was brought to a standstill, the Weimar government was then forced to print new money in order to provide benefits for its workers. German inflation, already severe, now spiraled completely out of control. The historian Peter Gay has vividly summarized Weimar's tragic situation:

> the disruption of trade, the disastrous decline in tax payments, all consequences of the Ruhr occupation, were more than the mark could stand. The Reichsbank tried to help, but its reserves were near depletion, and in April 1923 the dam burst: the currency dropped daily, and inflation reached fantastic dimensions — by October 1923 not millions, or billions, but trillions of marks were needed to buy a loaf of bread or mail a letter. Farmers refused to ship produce, manufacturing reached an all-time low, there were food riots, workers hovered near starvation, millions of bourgeois lost all their savings, while speculators grew rich. The resulting economic dislocation and psychological upheaval only strengthened the already pervasive distrust of the Weimar Republic.[1]

Zemlinsky was forced to weigh a dream long denied against an uncertain future. As things stood, Zemlinsky's demands were unlikely to be met, and he knew it. There was the option of accepting less favorable terms, in the belief that his contract could be renegotiated once the economy stabilized, but that was leaving too much to chance. In the end Zemlinsky did nothing except hope and wait for news to arrive from Berlin. As he did, the opportunity slipped away. Whether for reasons of salary, politics or both, Kleiber ultimately won the appointment. Zemlinsky and Berlin would have to wait.

Berlin was not the only affair to occupy Zemlinsky's attentions during the summer of 1923. At home that same July, Ida underwent two and a half hours of "radical" hysterectomy surgery.[2] By August, however, Ida's health had recovered sufficiently to allow them to travel to the picturesque town of Altaussee, in the beautiful Austrian lake district where the Zemlinskys had spent so many summers. Amidst beautiful surroundings, Ida convalesced and Zemlinsky

---

[1] Gay (1968),154.
[2] Weber (1995), 251.

found adequate time to compose. When not caring for Ida, Zemlinsky worked to complete the orchestration of the *Lyrische Symphonie*, which he had begun drafting in April of 1922. But in September unsettling news disrupted the Zemlinsky's summer idyll. While vacationing in the town of Traunkirchen, Mathilde had become seriously ill, so Schoenberg was returning with her to Vienna for testing. Toward the end of the month Schoenberg informed Zemlinsky that Mathilde's condition was critical. The doctors, however, could do little for her, and a short time later Mathilde died of renal failure.

It should have been a season of hope. *Der Zwerg's* successful Cologne premiere had sparked interest in Vienna, and the opera was currently planned for a November production at the Hofoper, now known as the Staatsoper. But prospects of work in Berlin had fallen through and Ida had health issues of her own, and with the death of his sister Zemlinsky was now the sole surviving member of his family. Mathilde's death had left him too shaken even to attend her funeral. Prospects of a Vienna triumph should have buoyed such a dark period in his life, but joys of returning to the city of his birth were tempered by apprehension. Several years earlier he had written Alma,

> I will, as you likely already know, conduct *Das Lied von der Erde* on 18 February in Vienna. I am greatly looking forward to it but nevertheless come with mixed emotions for Vienna. Probably the honored music critics will use the opportunity to attack me again.[1]

Zemlinsky needed to be reunited with old friends, but he knew the critics could not be counted among them.

Zemlinsky arrived in Vienna late in November for the final rehearsals, but there was little to inspire confidence that *Der Zwerg* would rescue Zemlinsky from becoming irrelevant in Vienna. Alban Berg was in attendance, but despite being greatly moved by what he heard, he remained critical of the production overall:

> The opera won't have any big success. There is a lot in it that's undramatic, and the dramatic part itself is so harrowingly tragic (like the first entrance of the dwarf) that it is hardly bearable. What a pity considering the wonderful music. Of course the production too is second-rate. Even Oestvig, who's best of all, hasn't grown into his part yet. The minor parts are third-rate. The female chorus thin, rather inaudible; so the whole of the first part is almost boring. Staging, direction, decor (Roller), all bad to my mind. But despite all that and the stiff conducting (Alwin), one can

[1] AZ/AMW.

still get great pleasure from large parts of it, thanks to the wonderful flow of glorious melody. Incidentally, the music isn't too easy to understand (because there's so much polyphony). I am looking forward to Saturday, sitting in a seat behind a column, and just following the score.[1]

In the hours following the dress rehearsal, Zemlinsky, Berg, Schoenberg and others retired to the Opera Restaurant. It was a bittersweet reunion, with the entire company on edge, no one more so than Zemlinsky, who burned a hole in the tablecloth with his cigarette. Schoenberg, likewise, was in an "appalling cantankerous mood . . . like a dead weight on the whole company".[2] The following afternoon everyone met again, this time at Schoenberg's house, where according to Berg the mood was anything but celebratory: "Not [a] very happy atmosphere, as always these last weeks. In fact the whole afternoon and evening was one long argument."[3]

The long shadows that had settled over Zemlinsky's circle in the fall of 1923 parted just long enough for *Der Zwerg* to catch a glimpse of sunlight — the performance had fared better than Berg had predicted. Afterward, Zemlinsky headed to the luxurious *Meissl und Schadn*, where his circle was joined by Georg Klaren, Adolf Loos and Josef Turnau, the chief producer of the Staatsoper. Karl Oestvig, who sang the title role, arrived drunk. Schoenberg's mood was temporarily improved, and, according to Berg, the entire company remained until after midnight and then headed off to another café, where they reminisced and celebrated until nearly two o'clock in the morning.[4]

Zemlinsky at first regarded the production "a great success",[5] but the reviews told a somewhat different story. On November 25, one day following the Viennese premiere, Julius Korngold's critique appeared. Among the most influential and most highly feared of Vienna's critics, Korngold's reviews were among the most anticipated, but his critique of *Der Zwerg* barely addressed the music. Instead, Korngold focused on Klaren's libretto.[6] By saying nothing,

---

[1] Grun (1971), 329. Karl Alwin was active at the Vienna Staatsoper from 1920 to 1938, at which time he immigrated to Mexico, where he remained until his death in 1941.

[2] Grun (1971), 330.

[3] Ibid., 333.

[4] Ibid., 332.

[5] Weber (1995), 340.

[6] *Neue Freie Presse*, November 25, 1923. Although Julius Korngold had once held Zemlinsky in high regard, Korngold's general disdain for contemporary composers probably resulted in his now placing Zemlinsky in the enemy camp. On page 114 of his memoirs, entitled *Postludes in Major and Minor*, Korngold wrote: "I fully shared Mahler's esteem of Alexander von Zemlinsky, then thirty-four years old. High refinement and brilliant artistry singled him

Korngold said everything. Erwin Schaeffer of the *Wiener Zeitung* struggled with the opera in general. Schaeffer acknowledged Zemlinsky's sensitivity and individuality but confessed that in an opera house "one awaits and desires less psychologically complicated plots, more graspable events and dramatic effects".[1] In other words, *Der Zwerg* simply wasn't good entertainment.

There were others who came to Zemlinsky's defense, such as Elsa Bienenfeld, who found Zemlinsky's opera

> the most cultivated and honest that we have heard in a long time . . . One does not often hear such an ingenious and finely worked score. There are not many operas, in which the ensemble's voices are carried forth with such delicacy, which is so elegantly orchestrated and the tender voices are handled with such grace and naturalness. One does not often hear themes of such nobility as those so abundant in this one act opera.[2]

But Bienenfeld's accolades meant little in light of Korngold's words, or lack thereof. In Vienna, *Der Zwerg* had failed to triumph.

The entire experience colored Zemlinsky's complex relationship with his home. Filled with enduring love for the city, yet stung by its critics, he sensed that his musical star had faded, and he feared he was becoming *persona non grata*. Only a few years earlier Zemlinsky's name had been completely omitted from a major article in the *Musikblätter des Anbruch* summing up the current state of new Viennese music,[3] an insult made all the more injurious since Zemlinsky's compositions had been advertised in detail on the journal's back page! Though he was not inclined to correct biographical errors, this oversight was more injurious, and an exasperated Zemlinsky took the article's author to task: "My name was the only one missing . . . I don't understand grounds for such

out as the most promising talent among Vienna's younger composers. Vienna, however, had also bestowed on him a certain degree of seductive indolence which jeopardized his full development and full success . . . In 1900 Mahler brought him into the limelight by performing his fairy-tale opera 'Es war einmal' and it remained 'Once Upon a Time'; nothing similar followed. Zemlinsky had been the theory teacher of his brother-in-law Arnold Schoenberg who, in turn, initiated him in his revolutionary ideas. So, like Mohammed's coffin, Zemlinsky began to float between heaven and earth, between Schoenberg's veiled sky and the solid ground of classical tradition." Information generously shared with the author by Mrs. Ernst W. Korngold and Kathrin Korngold Hubbard.

[1] *Wiener Zeitung* (November 27, 1923).

[2] *Neue Wiener Journal* (November 28, 1923).

[3] Specht (1921), 245–56 . Among the nearly two dozen composers listed in Specht's article were Alban Berg, Erich Korngold, Arnold Schoenber, Franz Schreker and Karl Weigl, names intimately associated with Zemlinsky.

an insult. Am I not Viennese? Authentically so in every respect? Isn't the very fact that my name has been forgotten itself proof that I genuinely belong to Vienna?"[1] And now Korngold's silence seemed to suggest that Zemlinsky wasn't needed there anymore. He had once lamented to Alma that "everyone should and does know that my heart has always been in Vienna and that I long to return to work there — but nobody thinks of me . . . "[2] The Staatsoper production of *Der Zwerg* suggested that he had not yet been totally effaced from the city's musical life, but moderate success was not enough to counteract the indifference and disloyalty Zemlinsky had suffered there. Zemlinsky would never entirely abandon the dream of one day returning to Vienna and picking up where he had left off years ago. But as he boarded the train for his return trip to Prague and watched the city fade from sight, it was clear that Vienna had less than ever to offer him.

[1] Biba (1992), 76.
[2] AZ/AMW.

Chapter 8

Lyrical Farewells

> This summer I've been composing something in the style of *Das Lied von der Erde*. I still have no title for it. It consists of seven related songs for baritone, soprano and orchestra, to be performed without interruption. I continue with the orchestration.[1]

WHEN ZEMLINSKY SENT these lines to his publisher Emil Hertzka, he had been at work on his symphony for five months. Seven months later, on August 29, 1923, the orchestration complete, he penned the final double bar and dated the manuscript. What would prove to be Zemlinsky's symphonic magnum opus had taken just under a year to compose. He also now had a title for it — the *Lyrische Symphonie*, the Lyric Symphony. Zemlinsky's most recent symphony, his Second Symphony in B-flat, had been composed twenty-five years earlier and was a classical work that exuded hints of Brahms and Dvořák. For the Lyric Symphony, a quarter century later, Zemlinsky drew inspiration from Bengali poetry, the human voice and Mahler. The resulting work showed great breadth, grandeur and emotional depth, and was unlike anything he had ever conceived.

When the Bengali poet Rabindranath Tagore came to Prague for the first time in 1920, he was met by a public familiar with and passionate about his work — his poetry had been translated into Czech before any other European language.[2] Zemlinsky, like other German readers, first encountered Tagore's

---

[1] Quoted in Lichtenfeld (1976), 101.

[2] The translation was the product of Vincent Slesny, Professor of Indology at Charles University. Professor Moritz Winternitz made Tagore's work available for the first time to the German population of Czechoslovakia. See Zbavitel (1961), 365.

sensuous images through Hans Effenberger's 1914 translation, *Der Gärtner* (The Gardener), and found himself captivated by the melodic nature and mystical allure and eroticism of the poetry. Zemlinsky arranged seven of the poems in three groups, aiming for the greatest dramatic intensity and charting a course for the full emotional range of unfolding love: the first two texts represent expressions of desire, the next two symbolize the fulfillment of this desire, and the last three depict freedom, separation and finally resignation.

The Lyric Symphony was Zemlinsky's first symphonic work to reveal a unique and individual voice, but, as he acknowledged, Mahler's *Das Lied von der Erde* had been at the back of his mind from the start. Both works commence with a motto theme and are held together by a series of orchestral interludes. And while the texts themselves have little in common, Mahler's reliance on eighth- and ninth-century Chinese lyrics and Zemlinsky's choice of Tagore's romantic texts color each composer's work with images of exotic, distant cultures and lands. However, while the lyrics chosen for *Das Lied* view events from afar, through memory bathed in sadness with an expectation of death, the Lyric Symphony speaks to the immediacy of flesh-and-blood sensations with an eye towards life. In other respects, similarities to Mahler's *Das Lied* are largely superficial. As compared to the six distinct movements of *Das Lied*, for example, the seven movements of the Lyric Symphony flow from one to the next and grow out of their close association with the texts — in the words of Oncley, each movement is "lyrically conceived".[1] And unlike Mahler, who infused his songs with Eastern color, Zemlinsky made no attempt to "localize" his composition, even if he willingly incorporated Tagore's musical metaphors.

Despite being separated from the Second String Quartet by some eight years, the Lyric Symphony shares critical connections with Zemlinsky's former chamber work. In each case, years elapsed since previous compositions of consequence for either medium, years that provided Zemlinsky with the necessary perspective to hone his individual musical voice. Thus, while both his quartet and symphony reflect intense personal expressions and emotional extremes, each also represents significant musical strides. In the Lyric Symphony, the structural formality that governed his earlier work is shed in favor of greater formal freedom, and the poetry plays as much a role as Zemlinsky's developmental procedures in determining shape and structure. Key signatures and their relationships within and between movements remain vital, but Zemlinsky frees himself from the classical constraint of operating within any larger overriding tonality. Zemlinsky replaces the abstract world of the four-movement sym-

---

[1] Oncley (1975), 324.

phony with a voyage of the soul in sound, where music gradually moves from the ethereal world of F-sharp minor to the tranquil stability of D major.

Along with Zemlinsky's powers of expression, his mastery of motivic development reaches its zenith in this symphony. For nearly forty-five minutes Zemlinsky spins a world of longing, attainment and loss from the symphony's opening cell and several subsequent motifs, all which influence the ethos regarded as vital to the work as a whole:

> The overall mood of the 7 songs, with their pre[lude] and interludes, all of which are based upon the same seriously deep, passionate character, must be perfectly evident for its true comprehension and performance. The basis for the entire symphony is provided in the prelude and first song. All the other pieces, despite individual differences in character, tempo, and so on, must comply with the shading of the first.[1]

The prelude opens with a brief burst of timpani followed by the motto — a dotted-eighth–sixteenth–half-note cell that is immediately varied over the next several bars. The modifications of the opening cell coalesce to form a chorale fanfare — a solemn, darkly orchestrated theme whose absence of leading tones weakens the F-sharp minor tonality and lends the introduction a mystical, quasi-religious air. It is from this idea that the majority of the prelude is constructed, but an impassioned secondary idea, played by the strings and mocked by the trumpets, soon follows in the wake of a powerful climax of the chorale. With the symphony's basic material established, Zemlinsky progresses to the songs and the drama begins to unfold.

With the baritone entrance the motto theme gains poetic meaning: "I am restless, I am athirst for far away things", and later, "I am a stranger in a strange land", words that held particular import for Zemlinsky, whose gaze was trained beyond Prague to Vienna as his ties to that grand city became increasingly tenuous. Because the inescapable motto infuses nearly every aspect of the texture — from the lyrical vocal lines and accompanimental rhythms to the ostinato passagework — any subsidiary ideas are ephemeral; even the impassioned secondary theme from the prelude appears but once, well into Tagore's fifth stanza.

With *Mutter, der junge Prinz* (Mother, the young prince) based on Tagore's poem about a young girl's hopeless attempt to win a young prince, Zemlinsky brings the mystical world of desire down to earth. Conceived of as a symphonic scherzo, Zemlinsky warns that the second movement should "not be too fleeting or conceived of as superficial". Nevertheless, teasing violin solos and playful

---

[1] Zemlinsky (1924), 10–11.

offbeat rhythms provide levity and brighten its somber successor. The song is a study in contrasts, not merely with respect to the movements that surround it but also internally. Set in A major and brilliantly orchestrated, Zemlinsky brandishes his powers of invention with a host of ideas spun from opening notes of the violin solo, itself a derivative of the symphony's motto cell. Each idea is provided a distinct character, the most memorable being the *cantabile* theme introduced in the song's second stanza. Flavored by the world of operetta with which Zemlinsky is altogether familiar, he sets the words "I know well he will not glance up once at my window" in the remote key of D-flat, a symbol of the vast distance separating the prince from the girl who seeks in vain to win his attention. The orchestral interlude at the song's conclusion builds to a feverish climax, briefly recalling the motto before settling in to the next movement.

Zemlinsky moves into the world of erotic love and fulfillment with the third song of the cycle, *Du bist die Abendwolke* (You are the evening cloud). He personally regarded this movement as his symphony's *Adagio*, but hoped to avoid any sense of nostalgia: "under no circumstances should it take on the feel of a delicate, languishing love song. Indeed, this song must hold fast to the deepest yearning and spirituality of the first song."[1] Much of the movement is densely scored, an exploration of a seemingly endless variety of orchestral textures and colors — the chromatic wash of the harp, the distant thunder of the gong, or the flutter tonguing of horns. It is only with the words "Du bist mein Eigen" ("You are my own") that stillness descends over the entire ensemble. Among the most tender lines Zemlinsky ever composed, this lilting refrain resonated deeply with Alban Berg, who quoted this passage in his Lyric Suite, a work encoded with references to his illicit love affair with Hanna Fuchs-Robettin. In June 1924, Berg wrote Zemlinsky about the deep impression his Lyric Symphony had made: "With this work a decade of love for your music has been brought to fulfillment . . . From the fullness of my heart and head allow me to thank you, esteemed master, for this work."[2]

At the epicenter of the composition stands the poem, *Sprich zu mir, Geliebter* (Speak to me, my love). Cast in Zemlinsky's "expressive" key of D minor, the music projects an ethereal and impressionistic aura entirely unique in Zemlinsky's repertoire. The intensity of the previous movement gives way to relaxation and transparency, an atmosphere established at the outset with the string duet. Juxtaposing the soprano's expressive vocal intervals with static layers of orchestral carpeting, unconventional *glissandi* and slithering ostinato patterns,

---

[1] Zemlinsky (1924), 10–11.
[2] Weber (1995), 308.

Zemlinsky achieves a sensuous mood evocatively depicting the mystical, nocturnal world of the lovers.

Befrei' mich von den Banden (Free me from the bonds) heralds the final phase of the journey. In a burst of orchestral sound the baritone suddenly escapes from his lover's embrace and attempts to regain his senses. Save several bars underscoring the confession of love, Zemlinsky pushes the music relentlessly forward. When it shudders to a stop, nothing is left but an E pedal in the bass, the fabric that binds the two briefest songs of the cycle together. For some four minutes the mysterious pedal continues unabated, over which the soprano moves in a Schoenbergian world bereft of tonal gravity. At this point, Zemlinsky's orchestration is the least complex and the most haunting of the entire cycle. Tethered to nothing but a static bass, the singer's tormented lines "Whom do I try to clasp in my arms?" arguably constitute the most disturbing and harmonically free passage ever written by Zemlinsky. With the singer's dramatic departure, Zemlinsky turns back to the motto theme of the first movement, and after driving the music to a nearly unbearable level of intensity, offers a final quotation of the impassioned secondary theme before allowing the music to come to rest.

The final song, *Friede, mein Herz* (Peace, my heart), resides comfortably in the warmth of D major. With pain and parting now subsumed by resignation, Zemlinsky's orchestral and vocal phrasing unfold slowly while the voice, in marked contrast with what came before, moves smoothly within a limited, comfortable range. At several points throughout this expressive epilogue Zemlinsky pays homage to Gustav Mahler—in particular, the expressive string writing introducing the words "Stand still, O Beautiful End", the unapologetic glissandi, and the oscillation between the major and minor modes all point to the world of his revered mentor. The symphony's opening prelude finds its counterpart here, with nearly half of the movement given over to the orchestra. A climax built of various themes surrenders to a final review of the motto theme, before the brass slide back into the comfortable realm of D major. The symphony's final bars then fade away, unresolved.

With his Lyric Symphony, Zemlinsky bade farewell to Mahler, the last progenitor of the Romantic symphony, and closed a chapter in his musical career. It was the last time he allowed himself the luxury of writing on so grand a scale:

Stand still, O Beautiful End, for a moment, and say your last words in silence. I bow to you and hold up my lamp to light you on your way.

Zemlinsky hoped to premiere his Lyric Symphony in June of 1923, during Berlin's Austrian Music Week, but with the work still months from being finished, its unveiling was postponed and the Maeterlinck songs performed instead, conducted by Zemlinsky's former Deutsches Theater colleague Paul Pella. The delay proved fortunate. The Lyric Symphony was consequently first heard in Prague, under the auspices of the recently founded International Society for Contemporary Music (ISCM). Prague was a far better fit than Berlin. Not only was Prague and its press appreciative of the work's Mahlerian associations, Zemlinsky was able to prepare his own ensemble, thereby guaranteeing his score was performed flawlessly the first time.[1]

Another world premiere had also lain at the forefront of Zemlinsky's mind for over two years — Schoenberg's expressionistic monodrama, *Erwartung*. Over a decade old, the score had lost none of its emotional intensity and eeriness, yet despite its 1917 publication, *Erwartung* had never been heard. Intent on premiering this work, Zemlinsky had been maneuvering to make it happen at least since August of 1922, but among the many obstacles faced was securing first performance rights, which Schoenberg had evidently promised to the Frankfurt Opera's director Ernst Lert.[2] Neither Schoenberg nor Zemlinsky placed much stock in Lert's ability to see it through — the director's attempts to arrange for performances of *Erwartung* in Frankfurt and Leipzig had failed, as had his promise to premiere Zemlinsky's *Der Zwerg* three years earlier[3] — but Schoenberg was not willing to risk a legal battle. Emil Hertzka, *Erwartung's* publisher, was best suited to handle the affair, and so was called in to help resolve the situation. Negotiations proceeded slowly, but eventually *Erwartung* was cleared for the Prague premiere.[4] Other issues, such as Schoenberg's role in the performance and his remuneration, remained. Schoenberg initially considered conducting the work himself but then learned that theater director Leopold Kramer would only cover travel expenses. Schoenberg was financially unable to agree to such conditions, and so if there was to be no stipend, then he preferred no payment and no baton at all. He would sooner come for free and have Zemlinsky conduct. At least then he would be ensured a convincing performance of the work:

[1] When Universal Edition published the full orchestral score in 1926, the first printing contained so many mistakes that a list of errata had to be included. Furthermore, Heinrich Jalowetz had not been credited with the piano reduction, so this too had to be subsequently added, as did the correct year of Jalowetz's reduction — 1924, not 1923, as originally printed.

[2] Weber (1995), 241.

[3] Ibid., 336.

[4] For more on the subject of the *Erwartung* negotiations, see Wurstbauer (1984), 75–96.

I want without fail to come to the performance of "Erwartung" and find
it humiliating that your Herr Kramer, who can pay fees to Strauss and
others, offers me only my expenses. I should under no circumstance accept this. If Herr Kramer can make a profit out of me, then let him pay
exactly as much as everyone else. If he cannot make a profit out of me,
then I shall gladly come without receiving any recompense, for the sake
of seeing you and yours. Of course, I should then be delighted if you
would conduct, for not only is it very instructive and pleasant for me to
hear my works conducted by you, and to be able to attend your rehearsals, but I also realize how valuable it is when someone of your authority,
your standing with the orchestra and the public, identifies himself with
the work, while I am all the more at the mercy of the wild beasts because
they would think your not conducting meant you had refused: "Even his
own brother-in-law doesn't like the stuff!"[1]

Schoenberg's request to turn the baton over to his brother-in-law probably
came as a relief to Zemlinsky — *Erwartung* stood a better chance of success
under his direction (as Schoenberg recognized), and it solved the question of
finances. The remaining issue was selecting the soprano soloist, a role that demanded both formidable technique and dramatic stage presence. The part was
finally entrusted to Marie Gutheil-Schoder, the soprano who premiered Schoenberg's Second Quartet in 1908. Disappointingly, by the time all the details were
ironed out, the opportunity for a 1923 *Erwartung* premiere was lost. Zemlinsky
eventually adopted a new course of action. He decided to lead two world premieres during the summer of 1924 — his own Lyric Symphony and Schoenberg's
Erwartung.

The months leading up to the summer festival found Zemlinsky wrapped up
in a number of other important projects at the Deutsches Theater. In February
1924, for instance, Zemlinsky led the Czech premiere of Schreker's six-year-old
opera *Der Schatzgräber*,[2] and on March 20 he deepened his commitment to the
Czech musical cause with the first of several performances of Smetana's *Der
Kuss*. The production, in celebration of Smetana's centenary, marked the first
time a Smetana opera had ever been mounted at the Deutsches Theater. Winter
also brought renewed hopes of bringing Schoenberg back to conduct. The two
again exchanged a flurry of letters, attempting to finalize programming and
remuneration details, but little progress was made. Beyond expenses, which
included a first-class hotel, Schoenberg requested a modest honorarium to

[1] Schoenberg (1964), 84.
[2] Premiered February 2, 1924.

compensate for the time and money he would lose while in Prague, and he again invoked the name of Strauss as a point of comparison: "Do you think it's right that I have to renounce everything that Strauss receives in Prague?"

Zemlinsky again found himself uncomfortably caught in the middle. He fully sympathized with Schoenberg's position yet was keenly aware of the theater's limitations. Writing to Schoenberg, Zemlinsky explained why his demands were impossible:[1]

> Concerning this matter there are limits — even if God himself wanted to conduct here. I can tell you nothing else except we're "economizing". Honorariums such as Bohnen,[2] Strauss, etc. once received from us have not existed for a long time, nor at that time were they as large as you claimed.[3]

Schoenberg accepted his brother-in-law's explanation regarding an honorarium, and at the close of the month wrote that he could forego the money if Kramer, the theater's director, sent him a personal invitation.[4] No formal invitation was forthcoming, and, as time ran out, another opportunity to bring Schoenberg to Prague was squandered.

In the summer of 1922 Salzburg played host to the International Society for Contemporary Music (ISCM) festival, the first post-war event of its kind dedicated to the cause of new music. Over twenty composers traveled to the charming Austrian town, long associated with Mozart, among them Bartók, Hindemith, Webern and Milhaud. Its success led to the festival becoming an annual event, held throughout Western Europe, the Soviet Union and America, in an effort to break down barriers and champion new music, "regardless of aesthetic trends or the nationality, race, religion or political views of the composer".[5] In 1924, Prague was hosting the third orchestral ISCM summer festival, and Zemlinsky was in the spotlight. At last he had the ideal venue to premiere Schoenberg's *Erwartung* and his own Lyric Symphony.

Although Zemlinsky preferred the recognition associated with having his scores conducted by others, such experiences had, more often than not, been

---

[1] Weber (1995), 260.

[2] Michael Bohnen, German bass-baritone active in Europe and at the Metropolitan Opera, New York.

[3] Weber (1995), 261.

[4] Ibid., 263.

[5] Quoted in Haefeli (1980), 275.

disappointing. There were exceptions, of course — in Cologne, for example, Zemlinsky had found Klemperer's approach to *Der Zwerg* "magnificent".[1] But Prague was Zemlinsky's domain, and, although Zemlinsky was confident that his Lyric Symphony did not present formidable problems for a conductor,[2] it nevertheless required an expert hand. Like the symphonies of Mahler, the Lyric Symphony was a work of extremes — delicate chamber music and powerful *tuttis*, and unless led by someone of great skill, the music's nuance and beauty could be sacrificed and the singers swallowed up in a whirlwind of sound. It is no coincidence that this was the only time Zemlinsky provided a series of remarks about how his music was constructed and how it should be executed.[3]

Schoenberg's nightmarish *Erwartung* was an entirely different animal. First, there was its subject matter — a woman waits anxiously in the forest at night for her lover, only to stumble over his bloody corpse. Schoenberg's score captured the extremes of her tormented psyche in highly expressionistic tones, as it evolves from terror to tenderness. Then there was the score itself. Schoenberg acknowledged that his music "appears so unusual on the page that even the best musicians are unable to form any idea of the sound and the effect",[4] and even Mahler had struggled to make sense of what he saw written down. For Zemlinsky, *Erwartung* presented challenges that appeared "almost insurmountable" when first encountered, difficulties he believed contributed to the infrequency of performances in the years that followed. Yet he was determined to surmount the obstacles, believing that "the greatest of these are overcome when two artists, a singer and a conductor, who are both convinced of the great worth of the work, devote themselves entirely to the work's preparation".[5] Hoping that others might embrace the challenges *Erwartung* provided and benefit from his own experience with the work, Zemlinsky left an account of his strategy. At the earliest stages he set about working with small groups of players — flutes and oboes; clarinets and bassoons; the horns alone; trumpets, trombones and percussion; first and second violins; violas, celli and contrabasses — since experience told him that rehearsing the orchestra *en masse* would likely lead to confusion and frustration, if not outright revolt. This course, regardless of its impact on his workload, produced efficient rehearsals and resulted in the individual parts' being accurately learned. Zemlinsky knew, in the long run, the strategy would produce a more satisfying performance.

[1] Weber (1995), 233.
[2] Zemlinsky (1924), 10–11.
[3] Ibid.
[4] Quoted in Auner (2003), 100.
[5] Zemlinsky (1927), 44–45.

Zemlinsky then began to build up the ensemble, first adding the strings and harp, then the brass and percussion, and finally the entire orchestra, without voice. With the parts so well learned,

> just two unstaged rehearsals (voice with orchestra) sufficed before the actual staged rehearsals commenced. Since the work has a running time of only a half hour, a lot could be accomplished in a normal three-hour rehearsal, so that ultimately three staged rehearsals were enough to bring about a clear and impressive performance. To lessen certain difficulties in the voice, I arranged to have a harmonium placed in the hollow of the stage normally used by the prompter, which gave her occasional pitches without disturbing the listener at all.[1]

The Lyric Symphony, by contrast, presented few difficulties for either soloists or orchestra and none comparable to those encountered in Schoenberg's score. One month prior to its unveiling, Rudolph Stephan Hoffmann, one of Zemlinsky's staunchest advocates, offered the public a general overview of Zemlinsky's newest work in the journal *Musikblätter des Anbruch*, which included the following words:

> The seven tight scenes suggestively unroll the story of a love that dies away with separation, having barely begun to smolder . . . There are many Songs of the Earth, and this is one of them. Its spiritual relationship to Mahler is indisputable, as is Zemlinsky's own personality, thus unmistakable and important impressions arise. It is a beautiful, unique and wonderfully stirring work, whose greatest worth lies in the nobility of its unprecedented and impressive melodic song.[2]

The Lyric Symphony's premiere took place on June 4, one day following the death of Prague's literary son Franz Kafka, which may have added to the poignancy of the performance. After all the vacillations, Schoenberg agreed to participate, conducting a Chorale Prelude of Bach's he had arranged a few years before, although it is unknown if Kramer compensated Schoenberg for his efforts. But the night belonged to Zemlinsky. Among the critics who glowed about Zemlinsky's latest opus was Paul Stefan of the *Musikblätter des Anbruch*. Stefan considered Zemlinsky's songs of love and leave taking even more distinct than Mahler's in *Das Lied von der Erde*, and praised Zemlinsky's melodic invention and the music's overall structure and shaping. "Such abundant lyrical

---

[1] Zemlinsky (1927), 44–45.
[2] Hoffmann (1924), 199–200.

beauty is a rarity", Stefan concluded, "and is something that should be cultivated everywhere with the greatest effort."[1]

But Zemlinsky had little time to savor the moment. Two days later he reclaimed the podium for the world premiere of Schoenberg's *Erwartung*. Zemlinsky's painstaking rehearsals had borne fruit and the premiere was his reward
— *Erwartung* was met with colossal jubilation.[2] No greater show of support was
forthcoming than that provided by Schoenberg's student Alban Berg:

> I know that there is no orchestra in the entire world that could perform
> this score with such clarity and creative classic simplicity; furthermore,
> that this is due not so much to the orchestra itself as to its conductor,
> who possesses something that has not been possible since Mahler, namely,
> the expertise of both the composer and of the man who has achieved his
> mastery through decades of association with a single body of sound as
> its director.[3]

For Berg, the opportunity to hear Zemlinsky's music or experience his work
on the podium was a rare pleasure, all too infrequently encountered. Prague,
however, was well accustomed to the efforts of its venerated music director. One
year earlier, Felix Adler had expressed his appreciation for what Zemlinsky had
done for the city, particularly as it related to his work with contemporary composers: "If Prague today is oriented toward the modern, if Schoenberg, Debussy,
Stravinsky, Webern and Berg find ears as prepared and ready as elsewhere, then
it is due to the methodical clear-sightedness of Zemlinsky's work."[4]

Zemlinsky now stood at the height of his musical powers and had arguably achieved the zenith of his fame. He commanded a unique musical voice,
and the compositions that followed in the wake of the Lyric Symphony, among
them the Third String Quartet, the *Symphonische Gesänge*, his opera *Der Kreidekreis* and the Sinfonietta, reveal a composer continuing to challenge himself
musically. As Zemlinsky matured and excelled, Prague benefited immeasurably
from his efforts. Under Zemlinsky's watch, the city's musical life attained unprecedented heights, the community remained abreast of contemporary musical
trends, and Zemlinsky's dedication to the Prague Academy helped establish it
as an invaluable resource for Czechoslovakia's next generation of musicians.

Still, Zemlinsky made no secret of wishing to be free of Prague. Despite plentiful resources at the theater, not to mention the job security it provided him, he

---

[1] Stefan (1924), 254.

[2] Ibid.

[3] Weber (1995), 310.

[4] Adler (1923), 144.

felt increasingly cut off from the west. But if he were to find work elsewhere, he would need to do so soon, while his renown and critical acclaim were at their summit . For the 53-year-old conductor, there could be no more thoughts about salary or rank.

With the third ISCM festival now behind him, Zemlinsky returned to the world of chamber music, and in the space of only a few weeks composed his Third String Quartet, published subsequently as his op. 19. Work on the quartet commenced on August 21, the day Schoenberg announced plans to marry Gertrud Kolisch, younger sister of the violinist Rudolf Kolisch. Mathilde had been dead barely ten months and already Schoenberg was remarrying, but the quartet conveys little of how Zemlinsky felt upon hearing the news. Whatever he was going through, by September 13 the quartet was finished. Zemlinsky had never composed so much in so short a time. Perhaps he believed it best to simply to look ahead.

Zemlinsky's newest chamber work does just that. It is efficient, playful, ironic, and emotionally detached. It lacks key signatures and tonal centers and reveals Zemlinsky pressing toward the austere language known as *Neue Sachlichkeit* or New Objectivity,[1] a style associated with the Weimar Republic of the 1920s, one that rejects Romantic sentimentality and the hyper-emotionalism of Expressionism in favor of a more detached approach. Most likely inspired by recent events at the ISCM, Zemlinsky heads off in a new direction with the Third Quartet, even though its outlines suggest Zemlinsky was looking backward, not forward. In contrast to the unconventional two-movement scheme found in his Second Quartet of nine years earlier, in his op. 19 Zemlinsky returns to the traditional four-movement design. But the classical architecture of each movement — sonata form, theme and variations, ternary song form and rondo[2] — merely serves as a framework within which Zemlinsky experiments with new musical techniques.

Zemlinsky's opening *Allegretto* definitively demonstrates his intent to continue mining the resources of motivic development common to both his Second

[1] Gustav Hartlaub is credited with inventing the phrase, with respect to a 1925 exhibit of post-Expressionist work by Otto Dix, George Grosz and others at the Mannheim Kunsthalle.

[2] Heinrich Jalowetz's analysis of the quartet was included with Universal's publication of the score. In it, he classifies the finale as a rondo, but the movement might just as well be interpreted as a sonata-allegro or sonata rondo, on account of its rather formal exposition, a development that focuses on principal material — which Jalowetz regards as transitory and subsidiary — and its faithful recapitulation of both the exposition's themes.

String Quartet and the Lyric Symphony. But former romantic indulgences are now replaced with the quest for efficiency. With his opening violin subject — a few descending chromatic pitches followed by a rhythmic step upward — Zemlinsky demonstrates what he learned from his lifetime preoccupation with developmental techniques, drawing a host of ideas from a minimal amount of material. For example, out of the descending scale Zemlinsky constructs a slow, relaxed secondary theme. From this rhythmic gesture, which is itself a variation on the quartet's two opening notes, Zemlinsky spins extended passages of high energy and derives the jaunty figure that brings the exposition and the entire movement to a close.

With the Theme and Variations, Zemlinsky continues to do more with less, wringing maximum material from the minimal primary idea. The *Allegretto's* rhythmic cell is reduced to its essence and stands isolated in the opening bar, punctuated by the detached dissonant accompaniment. The figure is repeated once, its pitches then quickly expanded and compressed. Throughout the course of the seven variations, the only recognizable entity is this single rhythmic idea, a cell that quickly disintegrates into *glissando*, *ponticello* and *pizzicato* textures. Toward the close of the seventh variation, the idea resurfaces as a cry or plea, before quickly exiting the stage in the fleeting, mysterious coda.

The concentrated *Romanze* offers a qualified respite from the two movements that surround it. While essentially lyrical in character, the syncopated and disjointed melody is pitted against a static, somber accompaniment. As the movement progresses, the melodic intervals become increasingly wider until they finally transform into desperate leaps spanning more than two octaves. If there is any place in Zemlinsky's quartet that hints at his emotions surrounding Mathilde's death and Schoenberg's precipitate remarriage, it is in this desperate climax, whose intensity stands in stark opposition to the movement's otherwise dispassionate atmosphere.

The *Burleske* opens with a muscular rondo theme in the cello, reminiscent of the opening of the last movement of the Quartet, op. 15. It begs for a contrapuntal response, a challenge taken up briefly by the other members of the ensemble before being dropped for less serious options. Two distinct ideas follow the pizzicato transition: a grotesque dance played by the viola, cut short by the cello, and a charming, off-kilter Viennese melody played by the violin. All four players assert their fragmented ideas until the cello takes control and starts the proceedings afresh. Eventually, the folk tunes are revisited after which all four players join in a unison transformation of the rondo theme, reducing it to a flurry of sixteenth notes that drive the quartet to its frenetic conclusion.

The ink was barely dry before the Wiener Streichquartett began rehearsing for the work's premiere, scheduled to take place in Leipzig within weeks. Anton Webern, on hand for a rehearsal in Vienna, relayed to Zemlinsky in Prague that the ensemble was working energetically, despite the music's enormous difficulties. Webern added his own thoughts about the quartet: "How unimaginable this richness, this beauty, the sonic effects — entirely overwhelming."[1]

Zemlinsky dedicated the quartet to his old friend and long-time colleague Friedrich Buxbaum,[2] cellist and founder of the Wiener Streichquartett. Buxbaum's ensemble gave a sparkling premiere of the Quartet on October 27. Reviewing the effort, the critic of the *Musikblätter des Anbruch* acknowledged Zemlinsky's consummate ability and subtly noted the challenging nature of Zemlinsky's mature style:

> Here no harmonic possibilities are shied away from; in the final analysis each is somehow tonally resolved (or rescued). With its four, tight, masterfully connected movements, which include a Theme and Variations, a Romanze, and a Burleske that gives way to a stormy conclusion, it constitutes nothing less than a defense [*Apologie*] of the traditional forms, requiring a hand as masterful as Zemlinsky's to control.[3]

Two years later Alban Berg was far more effusive in his praise of the work. One day after the the Sedlak-Winkler Quartet performed the quartet in the Musikverein's intimate chamber hall, Berg wrote enthusiastically:

> I must say that it was quite a good performance. If the Sedlak-Winkler Quartet didn't play with the greatest delicacy or verve . . . they nevertheless brought great warmth, aristocratic clarity, clean intonation and insight, so that the work could and did achieve its full effect. It was undeniably the most successful work of the evening (which also included Bachrich, Prokofiev and Hindemith) . . . Speaking for myself, I can only say that I count it among the most beautiful works of the last century, that I love every measure of this music with all my heart . . .[4]

---

[1] Weber (1995), 301.

[2] Buxbaum's relationship to Zemlinsky and his music dated back to their days together at the Conservatory. In 1894 Buxbaum shared the stage with Zemlinsky for the premiere of the latter's Cello Sonata and was involved with the premieres of each of Zemlinsky's string quartets in the years that followed, first in 1896, as a member of the Fitzner Quartet performing Zemlinsky's First Quartet and then again in 1918, when the Rosé Quartet premiered the String Quartet no. 2. In May of 1926 Buxbaum performed Bloch's *Schelomo* with the Philharmonic under Zemlinsky's direction.

[3] *Musikblätter des Anbruch* (1925), no. 1, 4.

[4] Weber (1995), 317–18.

Despite Berg's obvious adulation of Zemlinsky and his talent, Zemlinsky had never programmed any of Berg's music, though he repeatedly programmed other composers within their circle, including Schoenberg and Webern. That changed in May of 1925, when Zemlinsky led Berg's *Wozzeck-Bruchstücke* (*Wozzeck* Fragments), the concert suite of music from his nihilistic, atonal opera *Wozzeck*.[1] Berg arrived in Prague early enough for some of the rehearsals and was impressed with the technical command and the emotional depth displayed by Zemlinsky's orchestra. As for Zemlinsky's interpretive skills, Berg later wrote, "Zemlinsky is a colossal chap. How he gets hold of the Fragments, even at the piano. With such passion it makes it even more thrilling — if that's possible."[2] Berg's visit to the Czech capitol proved doubly significant, for it was during his time in Prague that he made the acquaintance of Hanna Fuchs-Robettin, sister of Franz Werfel and sister-in-law of Alma Mahler Werfel. Berg's love affair with Fuchs-Robettin, which found expression in the composer's *Lyric Suite*, lasted until Berg's death in 1935.

By the 1924/25 season, however, projects of this nature at the theater were more the exception than the norm. Whereas the institution once prided itself on its challenging programming, it had recently succumbed to lighter fare, an indication perhaps of financial concerns or simply complacency by an administration resting on its laurels. Whatever the case, Prague's German Theater had lost its edge. Because the house received only a minimal state subsidy — unlike the Czech National Theater, which received millions from the state — it could not survive, much less thrive, without intelligent management, successful programming and unwavering patronage. To Zemlinsky's credit, under his direction the Philharmonic continued to blend adventurous programming with the classics — the 1924/25 season included works of Debussy, Schoenberg and Dukas along with Beethoven, Mozart, Chopin and Berlioz. He also continued to champion the music of Mahler, performing two movements from the unfinished Tenth Symphony in December and Mahler's First Symphony the following April. And in March, Zemlinsky devoted an entire evening to works of

---

[1] In November of 1926 Otakar Ostrčil led the Czech premiere of Berg's *Wozzeck* — sung in Czech — at the Czech National Theater. In preparation, Ostrčil worked closely with both Berg and Zemlinsky. The first two performances went smoothly but at the third performance, a traditional subscriber event that included a large number of conservative, middle-class concertgoers, Berg's opera encountered strong opposition. In what became known as the "*Wozzeck* Affair," Ostrčil was forced to cancel the performance in the second act, after whistling gave way to a half hour of continued disruption, despite police being stationed throughout the theater. See Locke (2006), 200–206.

[2] Grun (1971), 338.

contemporary Czech composers — Ullmann, Schulhoff and Schimmerling. But
the theater's operatic repertoire had become mundane; apart from introducing
Dukas's *Ariane et Barbe-bleue* and Strauss's *Intermezzo* to Prague audiences,
little was new. Zemlinsky's appearances in the pit also declined, but he alone
was not responsible for the institution's lack of vision. For this, Leopold Kramer
was also accountable.

Erich Steinhard, a critic who had followed the Deutsches Theater most
closely over the past several years and been a strong supporter, now became
one of its most vehement critics. Steinhard assailed the theater's management —
especially Zemlinsky — for lacking vision and consistency:

> Let's bumble on! The opera division of the Prague Deutsches Theater
> seems to adhere to this motto even today. The scandalous cancellation
> of *Meistersinger* last season remains too fresh in our memory not to
> reconsider this case as proof that the leadership of the opera has not
> done the least to alter its lack of direction. Despite the bad experiences
> brought about by guest appearances, nothing is done to avoid perform-
> ances which up to the last minute remain uncertain whether or not they
> will take place and when the whole matter goes astray, the opera director
> calls in sick and leaves the theater to its fate. Who is responsible for the
> management of the opera? The public . . . has a right to know. Once and
> for all, it should be clarified if the title of opera director does nothing
> but provide us with the unfortunate experience of all too infrequently
> encountering Zemlinsky on the podium or whether with this title comes
> responsibility for whatever happens at the opera.[1]

In a subsequent article Steinhard was more to the point: "Does there exist a contemporary direction [*einen zeitgemässen Zug*] at the Prague Deutsches Theater
1924–25? Answer: No."[2]

Though severe, Steinhard's intentions were honorable — he remained
a staunch advocate of Zemlinsky, hence his desire to experience more of his
work. He simply hoped to rouse the theater from its slumber. The fact that the
Deutsches Theater righted itself so quickly suggests that the administration
took Steinhard's message to heart. In the meantime, others stepped forward
to express their support of Zemlinsky's work, among them the composer and
conductor Victor Ullmann, a member of Zemlinsky's Deutsches Theater staff
since 1920 and thus well positioned to reaffirm Zemlinsky's invaluable contri-

---

[1] Steinhard (1924), 230.
[2] Steinhard (1925), 259.

butions to the Prague musical community. Cognizant of Zemlinsky's diminishing theater appearances, Ullmann understood the significance of Zemlinsky's pursuits and even corrected a published report that erroneously stated that Hindemith's opera *Sancta Susanna* had never been performed outside of its Frankfurt premiere: "It is unknown to him [Paul Bekker] and to probably the majority that Zemlinsky conducted all three of Hindemith's operas shortly after their Frankfurt premiere, which included a particularly excellent performance of *Sancta Susanna*."[1] Though few were listening, Ullmann was proclaiming to all that Zemlinsky's "incomparable rehearsals and conducting art" demanded recognition and acclaim, yet still they continued to escape the attention of the west. The words written by Louis Laber were equally encouraging and supportive. Laber, as stage manager of the Deutsches Theater, was intimately familiar with Zemlinsky's work behind the scenes but, as his essay reveals, also had first-hand knowledge of the environment's limitations:

> With unfailing energy and without growing tired, this conductor succeeds in producing performances of the highest quality . . . despite often having average materials from which to operate. From the first rehearsal to the performance's final chord, he has everything under control and disciplined, and with a point-blank hypnotic authority [*geradezu hypnotischen Gewalt gezwungen*] gives everything of himself. It is no exaggeration when one says: Prague opera is Zemlinsky.[2]

Still, Steinhard's criticism that Zemlinsky's operatic commitments waned could not be denied. He had, for instance, begun to travel for guest performances at every opportunity — in 1925 Zemlinsky led successful concerts in Rome,[3] and the following season conducted in Barcelona, before embarking on a grand tour of Spain, with visits to Madrid, Toledo, Seville and Granada. And while Zemlinsky could never be accused of laziness — the fourteen-plus rehearsals he had dedicated to *Erwartung* proved otherwise — he was increasingly willing to delegate performances to his staff. In Zemlinsky's absence, other younger conductors were seen at the theater with growing frequency, among them Erich Steckel, an intelligent and able opera conductor who frequently stepped in at the last moment, and the recently appointed William Steinberg, who, as

---

[1] Ullmann (1925), 88. Indeed, on March 3, 1923, Zemlinsky conducted a Hindemith triple bill: *Mörder, Hoffnung der Frauen*, *Das Nusch-Nuschi* and *Sancta Susanna*.

[2] Laber (1925), 263.

[3] On January 18, 1925, Zemlinsky conducted music of Gluck, Korngold and R. Strauss at the Rome Augusteo and repeated the program seven days later. Program in possession of the Moldenhauer Archive, Harvard University.

a representative of a newer, more flamboyant school of conducting, quickly captured the hearts of the Prague public. In particular, Steinberg's performances
of Wagner and the Italian opera repertoire made a strong impression on both
his musicians and the public, while the critics found his enthusiasm a welcome
relief to the theater's lethargy. On the podium Steinberg was showy and vigorous, the antithesis of Zemlinsky; if he lacked his elder colleague's experience, he
compensated with youthful energy.

The events contributing to the decline in the Deutsches Theater's reputation
were quickly corrected and the house was soon back on track. On October 18,
1925, Zemlinsky and company unveiled Smetana's quintessential Czech opera,
The Bartered Bride, for the first time in the theater's history. Zemlinsky's interpretation was so mesmerizing that the audience and critics were won over from
the opening downbeat. At the conclusion of the overture, the public jubilantly
demanded an encore, an unheard-of phenomenon that Zemlinsky refused to
honor. The performance struck home with the Czech critic Iša Krejčí of *Rudé
právo*, whose unequivocal love of Smetana's music was matched only by his
admiration for the work's conductor:

> On Sunday the *Bartered Bride* celebrated its premiere in the Deutsches
> Theater. The success was extraordinary. First and foremost was the work
> itself deserving of merit, for with the exception of Mozart operas, there
> is little in the world's literature that can compare to it. Second was the
> excellent performance under the direction of Alexander Zemlinsky. I am
> a frequent visitor of the local German scene but I can safely affirm that
> (with the exception of *Don Giovanni*) I have never witnessed such a high
> level of performance, albeit Zemlinsky's efforts always demonstrate the
> highest caliber . . .[1]

The season also ushered in new productions of Strauss's *Salome*, Weber's
Der Freischütz and Mozart's *Don Giovanni* and *Die Entführung aus dem Serail*,
as well as the Deutsches Theater premiere of Janáček's *Jenůfa*. On February 4
the theater hosted a showing of a filmed version of Strauss's *Der Rosenkavalier*,
which Zemlinsky and his orchestra accompanied live.[2] And in May, Zemlin-

---

[1] Quoted in Mahler (1972), 242.

[2] Teweles had been showing movies at the Estates Theater since as early as 1911, in hopes of
shoring up his audience, but Zemlinsky's 1926 performance marked the earliest use of Edison's
projector at the Deutsches Theater.

sky led a new performance of Korngold's *Violanta* on a double bill that commenced with Steinberg conducting *Der Zwerg*.[1] When Zemlinsky took to the pit after the intermission, the Prague audience erupted into thunderous applause; Prague still valued Zemlinsky's artistry even if the much younger Steinberg was rapidly becoming the darling of the public.

Successful negotiations between Emil Hertzka and the Berlin Städtische Oper, the former Deutsches Oper in Charlottenburg, led to performances of *Der Zwerg* there in November.[2] Although Zemlinsky's music was not unfamiliar to Berliners, he had yet to gain any degree of loyalty from the city's audiences or press. *Der Zwerg* was thus met without partiality, and the results were disheartening. Reviews of the opera were lukewarm at best, with critics reproaching tenor Karl Oestvig's performance and diction, Klaren's libretto and Zemlinsky's score, the latter singled out as "too sensitive, too tender in its affect to win the hearts of the masses".[3] Bruno Walter, musical director of the Städtische Opera, felt that *Der Zwerg* might have suffered by sharing the program with Charles Raymond Maude's ballet *The Last Faun*, "a combination whose artistic essence made for a very poor fit".[4] More likely, Zemlinsky's score, powerful though it was, failed to deliver anything new or radical in a city that fancied itself as progressive. Whatever the reason, Walter wrote to Universal Edition that the opera fell short of expectations and, without going into further detail, informed the publishing house that he could not commit to an extended run. After only two performances, *Der Zwerg* was removed from the season's offerings.

Zemlinsky the composer may have failed to triumph in Berlin, but as a conductor he remained highly regarded by those at Berlin's premier institutions. Several years earlier he was offered the musical directorship of Charlottenburg's Deutsches Opernhaus,[5] and thereafter entered into negotiations with Berlin's Staatsoper. Ultimately, Berlin's staggering post-war economic struggles convinced Zemlinsky to remain in Prague, where he and his family continued to

---

[1] Only minutes prior to the opera's start, Oestvig, the tenor from the Vienna Staatsoper who had sung the opera's title role in the Vienna premiere, canceled because of sickness. The Prague tenor Franz Fellner stepped in and experienced a tremendous success in the performance. See Mahler (1972), 243.

[2] A letter to this effect by Hertzka to Zemlinsky, March 11, 1924 (Moldenhauer Archive, Harvard University). Fritz Zweig conducted the Berlin premiere on November 22, 1926.

[3] Ernst Biebig, *Magdeburger Zeitung* (November 25, 1926), quoted in Hajek (1988), 145.

[4] Ibid., 146.

[5] Beaumont, citing "Tan", states the offer appeared in the journal *Bohemia*, but nothing more is known about the offer. See Beaumont (2000), 294.

live free of financial worry. Berlin, however, had not forgotten him, and in 1926 the capital of the Weimar Republic called again.

Berlin was now home to a new, independent opera house, the Oper am Platz der Republik, an establishment overseen by Leo Kestenberg, musical advisor to the Prussian Cultural Ministry. At the end of August, Kestenberg offered the post of music director to the conductor Otto Klemperer, and in the months following his acceptance Klemperer set about selecting his staff. Zemlinsky was an obvious choice — he was seasoned, devoted to new music, and possessed a knowledge of the theater second to none. Klemperer also knew that what Zemlinsky desired more than anything was to leave Prague, so an offer was soon on the table. Years earlier, Zemlinsky had come to Prague hoping to find the opportunities and appreciation that eluded him in Vienna. The Czech capital had made good on its promises, but by 1926 little remained for him to accomplish there. Klemperer's invitation, therefore, required minimal consideration. Long weary of Prague's limitations and provincial isolation, and unwilling to forsake another offer from Berlin, Zemlinsky accepted.

In Berlin, Zemlinsky looked forward to new and exciting musical experiences, but the appointment carried risk and uncertainty. The city was home to two established opera companies, and, despite Berlin's penchant for experimentation, nobody knew how yet another operatic institution would fare in less than prosperous times. Zemlinsky would also no longer control programming. Although he had the right to request specific repertoire, Klemperer would have the last say. As a subordinate, Zemlinsky would also relinquish the privileges, responsibilities and benefits he had come to expect and enjoy over the past sixteen years in Prague. But in return, Zemlinsky was offered a fresh musical start and the possibility for a new future in a vital, vibrant European city, two opportunities for which he desperately hungered. With luck, Berlin would prove worth the wait.

Zemlinsky's final season in Prague reflected his undiminished dedication to contemporary programming. Between November 1926 and June 1927, he challenged himself and his audiences with performances of Mahler's Seventh Symphony, Weill's *Quodlibet*, de Falla's *Nights in the Gardens of Spain*, Hindemith's *Cardillac* and music from Pfitzner's *Palestrina*. Then, during the final weeks of the season — his last ever as a musical director — Zemlinsky led works by two composers linked closely with his career: Mahler and Mozart. On June 1 he conducted the Czech Philharmonic in a performance of Mahler's Eighth Symphony, the work that had ushered in Zemlinsky's dedication to Mahler over fifteen years earlier. The following day the Czech Communist newspaper *Rudé právo* reflected on the evening:

> On Wednesday the first of June, the long-time director of the local German Opera, Alexander Zemlinsky, took his leave from the Prague-German public with a performance of Mahler's Eighth Symphony. Both events were a great experience for the entire musical community of Prague, irrespective of one's nationality, for Zemlinsky himself, as with the works that he brought us, always meant a great deal for the entire Prague music scene during the last two decades . . . Zemlinsky also brought us a new conception of the duty of a conductor. And thus we also became familiar with totally new musical worlds. Above all, his Mozart and Beethoven appeared to us in an entirely new light. Out of all this arose the most important conductor of our generation, Otakar Ostrčil, whose personality is different than Zemlinsky's, but whose maturation as a conductor is impossible to imagine without Zemlinsky's liberating influence. Finally, Zemlinsky also showed us new paths with regard to repertoire. It came during a time when everyone's attention was already directed toward Richard Strauss; but we already lived for another, a master at that time unrecognized — Gustav Mahler . . . It was therefore greatly meaningful that on this evening Zemlinsky presented Mahler's magnificent Eighth Symphony. And, of course, he conducted it as only he was capable of.[1]

Zemlinsky's interpretations of Mozart had been equally lauded over the past decade and a half, so much so that some credited Zemlinsky with having created a 'Mozart style.' Nor was his affinity for Mozart limited to the operas. One Prague critic remarked that Mozart's G minor Symphony, K. 550, as conducted by Zemlinsky, was an "exemplary model exhibition, as Mozart should be interpreted".[2] Zemlinsky's June 24 performance of *Le nozze di Figaro* was therefore a fitting farewell to both his listeners and the members of his Deutsches Theater ensemble. The mood was one of "solemnity and sorrow".[3] Zemlinsky had provided Prague with countless performances at the highest possible level, set the standard for music-making throughout the city, fostered an interest in contemporary music, bridged the gap between the German and Czech musical communities and dedicated himself to the next generation of composers and conductors. Now, after sixteen years, it was time to exit the scene. After the

---

[1] Quoted in Mahler (1972), 244–45.

[2] Quoted in Vysloužil (1995), 244.

[3] Ibid.

extended ovation that concluded his farewell performance of *Figaro*, Zemlinsky took the stage for the last time and offered these modest words of farewell:

> Everything that I have to say, I have already said during my many years of artistic activity in Prague here on the conductor's podium. If I have succeeded in achieving the satisfaction of the public, then I am happy.[1]

His opera company responded with a personal letter of appreciation, signed by all the members of his ensemble:

> Alexander Zemlinsky,
> Our highly honored opera director;
> with memories of friendship from
> his opera ensemble.
> Prague, 24 June, 1927

Over the course of the following weeks, approbation from the public and the press continued. Erich Steinhard, who had only two years earlier attacked the Deutsches Theater for its apparent indifference to its responsibilities, now wrote:

> Whenever Zemlinsky appeared on the podium, he did so with a score dissected down to its smallest details, with an original and thoroughly digested interpretation, and with a temperament that conquered the masses. The citizens of Prague regret his parting.[2]

But of all the sentiments concerning Zemlinsky's accomplishments, none was more fitting or prophetic than the tribute that Schoenberg had paid his friend, colleague and brother-in-law in 1914, three years after his accepting the Prague post:

> It is unfortunate that you are not famous and thank God you are not. I don't know if one can remain so true if one is famous and so I don't know if I should wish that on you. However, I am convinced that you will always remain the same and that more than anything you will create a Mecca [*ein Mekka schaffen*]. For my closest students and me, Prague is a Mecca even now. Whenever we want to hear music we will make a pilgrimage there, or wherever you might be.[3]

---

[1] Mahler (1971), 257.

[2] Quoted in Ludvová (1997), 7.

[3] Weber (1995), 113

Now, thirteen years later, it was Zemlinsky who was preparing the pilgrimage to *his* new Mecca.

By late August, the contents of the Havlíčkova apartment were packed and ready, scores boxed up and the piano shipped north. On August 31, Zemlinsky, his wife and daughter caught the train bound for Berlin. The seasons of hoping and waiting were over.

To conquer Berlin was to conquer the world.

Carl Zuckmayer

PART III
Berlin and the Aftermath

Chapter 9

The Berlin Experiment

> The future of Germany is being tentatively anticipated by Berlin. The man who wants to gather hope should look there.
>
> Heinrich Mann[1]

I N EARLY SEPTEMBER 1927, the Zemlinskys disembarked at Berlin's Anhalter station and headed to the district of Tiergarten, where they took lodgings in a boarding house located at In den Zelten 17.[2] One of the finest addresses within the city before the war, the street outside was still popular for its cafés and bars. From this nucleus spread Berlin's distinctive districts, among them Charlottenburg due west, at that time the home of Schoenberg, and Schöneberg to the south, neighborhoods Zemlinsky would eventually call home. But for now, the quarters at In den Zelten had much to offer — Zemlinsky was just minutes by foot from the Oper am Platz der Republik, and Ida and Hansi could visit the nearby zoo or stroll along the Spree river, which ran nearby.

The Berlin of 1927 was a markedly different place than the one Zemlinsky had encountered a few years earlier, when concerns about the city's failing economy deterred him from relinquishing the security and stability of Czechoslovakia. As late as 1923, post-war inflation left Berliners demoralized, hungry and unemployed, but by the year's end the city's crippling inflation was under control. With its economy stabilized, a measure of optimism and confidence returned, and the path was paved for Berlin's *goldenen Zwanzigerjahren*, the

---

[1] Quoted in Gay (1968), 132.

[2] In den Zelten, literally "In the tents", was named for the site where, early in the preceding century, Napoleon's army had established its headquarters upon arriving in Berlin.

Golden Twenties, the era of renewal. It was this Berlin that met Zemlinsky upon his arrival at the start of September 1927.

With the incorporation of its suburbs, Berlin now ranked among Europe's largest cities, and was home to two centers, one commercial, the other governmental. The writer Christopher Isherwood, who came to Berlin two years after Zemlinsky, described both:

> the cluster of expensive hotels, bars, cinemas, shops round the Memorial Church, a sparkling nucleus of light, like a sham diamond, in the shabby twilight of the town; and the self-conscious civic centre of buildings round the Unter den Linden, carefully arranged. In grand international styles, copies of copies, they assert our dignity as a capital city — a parliament, a couple of museums, a State bank, a cathedral, an opera, a dozen embassies, a triumphal arch; nothing has been forgotten.[1]

A cultural and intellectual magnet, Berlin attracted some of Europe's premier architects, scientists, writers and artists, among them Albert Einstein, who moved to the Berlin suburb of Dahlem at the invitation of the physicist Max Planck;[2] the author and political activist Heinrich Mann, appointed to Berlin's Academy of Arts; and the Viennese-born film maker Fritz Lang, whose futuristic film *Metropolis* opened to Berliners in January 1927. With the influx of creative and scholarly icons came the progressive institutions with which they were associated. Berlin was home, for example, to the newly-founded Psychoanalytical Institute, where the revolutionary theories of Freud steadily gained influence, and claimed the intellectual left-wing literary journal *Die Weltbühne*, an outlet for political satire, poetry, fiction and social commentary. Edited by Carl Ossietsky, who went on to win the Nobel Peace Prize but died from a combination of tuberculosis and abuses suffered in a Nazi concentration camp, *Die Weltbühne* was the principal vehicle during the Golden Twenties for Karl Kraus, Thomas Mann, Walter Benjamin, Alfred Döblin and Kurt Tucholsky.

Alongside Berlin's thriving cultural life was a seedier side, fostering the decadent lifestyle depicted by Ernst Ludwig Kirchner and George Grosz in their unsettling portraits of streetwalkers and sinister bar-room characters, a city Hitler would come to refer to as "that sinful Babel."[3] As the writer Stefan Zweig recalled,

---

[1] Isherwood (1963), 186.

[2] It was in Berlin that Einstein formulated his general theory of relativity (1916) and won the Nobel Prize for Physics (1921) for his work on the photoelectric effect.

[3] Quoted in Shirer (1960), 68.

All values were changed, and not only material ones; the laws of the State were flouted, no tradition, no moral code was respected. Berlin was transformed into the Babylon of the world. Bars, amusement parks, honkytonks sprang up like mushrooms . . . Along the entire Kurfürstendamm powdered and rouged young men sauntered and they were not all professionals; every high school boy wanted to earn some money and in the dimly lit bars one might see government officials and men of the world of finance tenderly courting drunken sailors without any shame. Even the Rome of Suetonius had never known such orgies as the pervert balls of Berlin, where hundreds of men costumed as women and hundreds of women as men danced under the benevolent eyes of the police.[1]

Czech-born Willy Haas, who co-founded the Berlin-based weekly *Die literarische Welt*, was infatuated with the city's energy and verve:

I loved the rapid, quick-witted reply of the Berlin women above everything, the keen, clear reaction of the Berlin audience in the theater, in the cabaret, on the street and in the café, that taking-nothing-solemnly yet taking-seriously of things, that lovely, dry, cool and yet not cold atmosphere, the indescribable dynamic, the love for work, the enterprise, the readiness to take hard blows — and go on living.[2]

Music, whether in the cabaret or the opera house, was flourishing in Berlin. The city had supplanted Vienna as the musical capital of the German-speaking world and was now home to a number of Zemlinsky's composer friends and colleagues, among them Arnold Schoenberg, Franz Schreker and Paul Hindemith, and world-class conductors like Bruno Walter, Erich Kleiber, George Szell and Wilhelm Furtwängler. With its fervent demand for refined music, Berlin boasted three opera houses. First and foremost was the 1,200-seat Staatsoper Unter den Linden, the opera house that had chosen Kleiber over Zemlinsky several years earlier. The rival Städtische Oper in Charlottenburg had opened in 1912 and could accommodate an audience of 2,300. Finally, there was the Oper am Platz der Republik, the Opera on Republic Square, which, as the youngest of the three institutions, had the most at stake.

The Oper am Platz der Republik began life in 1844 as a magical winter garden for popular music. Its founder, Joseph Kroll, had bourgeois society in mind when he established his trendy meeting spot — a locale for masked balls and waltzes — under the trees of the nearby Berlin Zoo. In 1852 a larger hall, capable

---

[1] Zweig (1964), 313.
[2] Quoted in Gay (1968), 129.

of accommodating a Wagnerian opera, was added. Shortly before World War I, plans for an even more splendid opera house were set in motion, the Neues Königliche Opernhaus, but war brought the project to a halt and then reduced the theater to ruins. Amidst Berlin's post-war, avant-garde climate, the Winter Garden site was regarded as an ideal location for a new institution that would offer opera and other guest performances. Rebuilding began in 1919, and on January 1, 1924, the new hall, built of wood with a seating capacity of 2,200, was reopened as the Oper am Platz der Republik. Film stars and popular singers were frequent performers, either on the small stage or in the elegant upstairs ballroom. As described by Otto Friedrich,

> Negroes in gold braid held open the doors, and the customers not only could watch trapeze artists swinging across a star-flecked blue ceiling but could eat sausages and drink beer and smoke cigars (all of which were forbidden at the circus) while they watched. And there were singers and dancers — Caroline "La Belle" Otero came from Paris to perform at the Winter Garden, and another one of the stars was a young dancer named Mata Hari.[1]

More commonly referred to as the Kroll Oper, the hall was initially the second home of the Staatsoper Unter den Linden while its own house underwent renovation. Under the directorship of Heinz Tietjen, who, as *General-Intendant*, oversaw all three of Berlin's opera houses, it was decided that the Kroll should have its own company. Leo Kestenberg of Berlin's Cultural Ministry oversaw the Kroll's establishment and, consistent with his designs for music reform, intended that the new institution should serve Berlin's working class and act as a home to experimental operatic productions. Kestenberg selected Otto Klemperer as the Kroll's music director simply on the basis of reputation and ability, not out of a deeper consideration for any modernist leanings he may have had. Klemperer was no revolutionary, as was, for example, the theater's dramaturg, Hans Curjel. Rather, his intention was to cultivate "good theater; not avant-garde theater, but good theater".[2] As a conductor who had recently held posts in Wiesbaden and Cologne, Klemperer was known to command respect from those around him, and, while he was hardly prepared for the massive amounts of bureaucracy that lay ahead, his natural sense of authority resulted in great allegiance from his colleagues. In the words of Curjel,

> His severe and unaffected [*unverwachsenes*] music making, his freedom

---

[1] Friedrich (1995), 291.
[2] Heyworth (1985), 58.

from any sort of self-aggrandizement or other vanity, his eschewal of musical and personal gush were greatly esteemed. The authenticity of his music making, the self-control with which he conducted, instead of, like others, behaving as though he were officiating at High Mass, were a great example to us.[1]

Granted *carte blanche* to hand select his conducting team, Klemperer opted for an impressive group whose diversity of age and experience resulted in a well-balanced and versatile company. Appointed First Kapellmeister, Zemlinsky was the most seasoned conductor of the Kroll team, Klemperer included. Following on the heels of his Prague directorship, Zemlinsky's extensive conducting experience and practical knowledge of the theater made him invaluable; he quickly became acknowledged by the press as 'the musical conscience' of the organization. Even Klemperer deferred to him frequently, trusting his colleague's well-honed skills and wealth of knowledge, later describing Zemlinsky as "an extraordinarily sympathetic and considerate colleague".[2]

Fritz Zweig, Second Kapellmeister, was a former Kapellmeister of the Städtische Oper, and as such was no stranger to Berlin's musical landscape. Zweig proved to be the traditionalist of the group, the conductor least committed to performing music of their contemporaries. He "remained largely aloof from the intellectual currents and conflicts that eddied around the theater. Essentially a *musikant*, Zweig's literal views of stagecraft led him to regard innovative productions with suspicion if not with downright distaste."[3] Outwardly, Zweig appeared the antithesis of everything for which the Kroll stood. Yet Zweig was an accomplished conductor and superb diplomat, so often it was he who smoothed ruffled feathers when artistic tempers flared.

Two of Klemperer's other choices proved highly influential with respect to the institution's commitment to contemporary culture. Ewald Dülberg, the colleague closest to Klemperer, was initially placed in charge of the theater's visual department and expected to design its most important productions. Dülberg, however, was a perfectionist by nature and lacked the flexibility demanded of theater life. Yet ultimately it was tuberculosis, not the theater's imposing demands, that forced him to resign prematurely. The youngest member of the group was the producer Hans Curjel. The company's leading intellectual, Curjel's ideas about modern art and his commitment to the new generation of German composers proved fundamental to the Kroll's modernist undertakings.

---

[1] Curjel (1975), 19.

[2] Heyworth (1983), 249.

[3] Ibid., 250–51.

To set the Kroll apart from Berlin's more established opera companies, Klemperer and his administration planned to provide the city with a healthy mix of contemporary operas and unconventional productions of standard repertoire, such as *Madama Butterfly* and *Les Contes d'Hoffmann*.[1] The Kroll had no intention of catering to public taste, evidenced by only two operettas ever being performed at the theater: *Die Fledermaus*, to which Zemlinsky brought his musically unequaled interpretation, and Offenbach's *La Périchole*, adapted by Karl Kraus. To ensure that even the standard repertoire was approached from a contemporary perspective, artists like Giorgio de Chirico, Oskar Schlemmer and László Moholy-Nagy were engaged for set designs. The results were often startling examples of contemporary art, as revolutionary for their aesthetic qualities as for their use of resources like iron, wire, copper and lacquer — materials never previously employed in stage design.

The Kroll's overriding musical philosophy was objectivity — the music would speak for itself. Original texts were consulted and musical re-workings, such as Mahler's *Fidelio*, were cast aside. *Fermati*, *ritardandi*, *accelerandi*, and above all *rubati* — tempo notations with no musical basis that had slowly crept into standard practice — were systematically eliminated, while *secco* recitatives traditionally extracted from operas such as Rossini's *Il Barbiere di Siviglia* were dutifully reinserted.[2] Such "authentic" interpretations were occasionally met with strong criticism. For a performance of *Der fliegende Holländer*, for example, Klemperer used Wagner's original 1844 score and borrowed the original orchestral parts from Zurich, with the intention of performing the opera as it was first conceived.[3] But because audiences and critics were familiar only with Wagner's later revised version Klemperer's efforts were poorly received. Nevertheless, the Kroll philosophy persevered. Bad taste was avoided at all costs. The company strove for clarity and exactness, and limits were placed on the number of operas undertaken, with the intention of assiduously preparing and rehearsing each production.[4]

Whether Zemlinsky could adapt to his new role in a new city was uncertain.

---

[1] In retrospect, as an institution the Kroll proved progressive not so much because of its emphasis on modern works but for the open-mindedness with which the music was presented. As regarded its repertoire, the company incorporated a good deal that was not avant-garde, and in the relatively short time the theater was in existence it staged no more modern music than any other major house.

[2] Curjel (1975), 43.

[3] Heyworth (1983), 279.

[4] Despite employing some talented vocalists, the level of singing at the Kroll could not match that of either Berlin's two other opera houses, as the critics were quick to point out.

No longer responsible for shaping an institution's artistic profile, he would now follow the directions of a man fourteen years his junior and vie for critical acclaim among impressive names like Walter, Szell and Klemperer, younger men who already enjoyed celebrated status in prestigious European music capitals. At the peak of his career, a 56-year-old Zemlinsky would attempt to reinvent himself in one of the largest metropolitan cities in the world.

In January of 1926 Arnold Schoenberg had moved to Berlin for the third and last time. He was now teaching six months out of the year at Berlin's Prussian Academy of Fine Arts[1] and traveling frequently as a guest composer or conductor of his music. Sixteen years had elapsed since Schoenberg and his brother-in-law lived in such close proximity, but scheduling conflicts now replaced distance as the impediment to personal contact. When the Zemlinskys first arrived in Berlin, for instance, Schoenberg was heading to Vienna to attend the premiere of his Third String Quartet, and connecting in the months that followed appears to have been a struggle. Attempting to catch up with Schoenberg on a day in mid-October, Zemlinsky set out for Schoenberg's apartment but arrived over two hours late. Weary of waiting, Schoenberg sent Zemlinsky a humorous message suggesting they consult with Berlin resident Albert Einstein in hopes of securing a *rendezvous*:

> I'm truly sorry that we can't meet. However, it seems that we don't have a mutually agreeable time. Perhaps Einstein might help in this regard; and we might, by adding our motion to the concept of time, be able, theoretically, to find the best possible opportunity where and when we might have an encounter, since apparently our orbital rotations defy a precise mathematical pinpointing. So, what should we do? I really would like to see you! If a true appointment won't work, perhaps we should try once with a false one.[2]

The letter was among the last exchanged by the two men. Their correspondence, dating back to 1901, had broken off only temporarily over the years, but had become increasingly rare as of late and by the time of Zemlinsky's Berlin appointment had nearly ceased altogether. Although the ever-widening divergence of their respective compositional styles and philosophies might have

---

[1] Schoenberg received a lifetime appointment and a generous stipend, both of which the Nazis would annul. In the meantime, Schoenberg's responsibilities were ideal. He had only to commit to half a year, and then only to promising students, whom he taught at home.

[2] Weber (1995), 272–73.

contributed to the decline in correspondence, Schoenberg saw no reason that musical differences should be a source of friction: "I have written differently from Mahler and Zemlinsky, but never felt any need to take up opposition to them."[1] The fact that Schoenberg nominated Zemlinsky for a position at the Academy of the Arts two years after his brother-in-law's arrival in Berlin also attests to the enduring strength of their friendship and dedication.[2] Their limited correspondence from this period most likely stems from several factors unrelated to a falling out, among them the increasing use of the telephone[3] and the fact that they now lived in the same city — a personal visit now required a short ride on the electric train. Moreover, much of the Zemlinsky–Schoenberg correspondence over the previous decade revolved around concert negotiations and the choice of repertoire, particularly as concerned programming at the Deutsches Theater. In Berlin, such decisions were no longer Zemlinsky's to make, so correspondence of that nature ceased. Since the start of their relationship, their mutual love and respect always trumped whatever friction arose, and there is no reason to believe that their friendship was any less committed in Berlin.

The Kroll officially opened its doors on November 19, 1927, but because the Staatsoper was undergoing renovations, both companies shared the Kroll facilities, making for a number of difficult months. On four evenings a week the Staatsoper performed, on the remaining three the Kroll Opera held court, and both institutions suffered for lack of adequate rehearsal time. Only in April of the following year did the Staatsoper return to its Unter den Linden premises, leaving the Kroll ensemble sole use of its house for the first time since its inception.

It was within these less-than-ideal working conditions that Zemlinsky made

[1] Schoenberg (1965), 121. Nevertheless, Schoenberg had become increasingly impatient with anyone who dismissed his twelve-tone approach to composition. A year before coming to Berlin, Zemlinsky attended the ISCM festival in Venice and on the return trip shared a train compartment with Schoenberg's student Hanns Eisler. Eisler, then in the throws of rebelling against his teacher's theories, made numerous comments to Zemlinsky about his disillusionment with Schoenberg's approach and with twelve-tone music in particular. When word got back to Schoenberg, presumably from Zemlinsky himself, Schoenberg unleashed a flurry of letters, denouncing Eisler for having had such a discussion with Zemlinsky, who Schoenberg regarded as someone with whom such remarks were "likely to meet with a very favorable reaction". See, for example, Weber (1995), 271.

[2] The nomination was ultimately denied.

[3] Zemlinsky's name first appeared in the Berlin telephone directory in 1931. His phone number was listed as Cornelius 35 10.

his Kroll debut, with a production of Smetana's *Der Kuss*. Reviews of the performance, which took place a little over one week after Klemperer's opening night production of *Fidelio*, were not entirely unfavorable, but neither were they rich in praise. One of the most positive critiques came from Hanns Eisler of the Berlin Communist organ *Die rote Fahne*. Eisler, who earlier had studied composition with Schoenberg, extolled the virtues of Zemlinsky but had harsh words for the singers — a criticism leveled repeatedly at the Kroll by the Berlin press — and the man responsible for hiring them:

> Alexander Zemlinsky, Klemperer's colleague, is a wonderful musician, perhaps one of the best presently living in Berlin. The performance, so excellently prepared, resulted in fine, clean, noble music making, the likes of which one has not heard for a long time in this city, the city of conductors. The singers were adequate but nothing more than that . . . (it is incomprehensible why Klemperer, who has at his disposal such rich resources, could have engaged such an ensemble) . . . but it was the outstanding leadership of Zemlinsky that resulted in such a fresh and gratifying evening.[1]

But Eisler, both a friend and advocate, was hardly unbiased. A more objective review came from Max Marschalk, of the *Vossische Zeitung*, who considered the Kroll off to a disappointing start:

> The performance remained mediocre throughout and one can honestly say that this was the second disappointment afforded by the Kroll ensemble . . . One sensed the musical experience of the conductor, Alexander von Zemlinsky, but little else . . . Despite the honest performance, the weak work failed to warm the audience, whose reception of it can only be described as friendly at best.[2]

Another review pitted Zemlinsky's work in Prague against the level expected in the musical Mecca of Berlin. The critic of *Die Musik* took aim at Prague's provincialism and warned Zemlinsky to remember that he was no longer working in a remote corner of the world:

> Smetana's opera, with which Alexander Zemlinsky made his Kroll debut,

---

[1] *Der rote Fahne* (November 29, 1927).

[2] *Vossische Zeitung Berlin*, Nr. 279 (November 29, 1927). The *Vossische Zeitung* was among Berlin's oldest newspapers, but its liberal nature — referred to as *liberaldemokratisch* in German — led to its being shut down in 1934.

could actually not have any success under such circumstances. What succeeded in Prague must not necessarily also please in Berlin.[1]

Zemlinsky had been officially welcomed to the German capital.

While the Kroll may have harbored progressive ideals, little of the early repertoire allocated to Zemlinsky could be considered avant-garde. As the theater's opening season continued, Zemlinsky was slated to lead productions of Puccini's decade-old *Il trittico* and Weber's *Der Freischütz*. Puccini's three one-act operas were not Zemlinsky's forte, and Weber's seminal German Romantic masterpiece, though a defining work in Zemlinsky's earlier years, would not have kindled much excitement at this stage of his career. The theater was staging modern repertoire like Hindemith's *Cardillac*, Krenek's *Der Diktator*, Schreker's *Der singende Teufel*, Stravinsky's *Petroushka* and *A Soldier's Tale*, but none were on Zemlinsky's roster. The Kroll was well into its second season before Zemlinsky was offered more unusual fare in an evening devoted to contemporary French composers. Even so, most of the productions with which he was entrusted — *Les contes d'Hoffmann*, *Bartered Bride*, *Rigoletto*, *Butterfly*, *Fledermaus* and Charpentier's *Louise* — while sometimes boldly staged, afforded Zemlinsky little musical challenge.

The Kroll programs also included orchestral showcases, advertised as "Klemperer Concerts", although Zemlinsky and Zweig were also involved. These concerts likewise failed to offer Zemlinsky anything new, though he did have an orchestra with well-seasoned players at his disposal, many of whom had performed under maestros such as Richard Strauss and Karl Muck. The Kroll's philosophy of allegiance to the score evidently carried over to these symphonic programs as well. Max Strub, a member of the orchestra, recalled a performance of Bach's D major Orchestral Overture under Klemperer:

> On hand was the original score whereby we observed the tied bow markings. I still hear the *Air*, as the strings began to play without drawing a vibrato, playing only with an intensive, inner motion . . . I see Klemperer before me on the podium, with a minimum of motion, but the expressive concentration appeared to demand his entire spiritual and physical energy.[2]

In principle, these orchestral concerts also placed a premium on new music. Krenek's 1928 *Little Symphony* was programmed, as was Weill's radio cantata *Der Lindberghflug* and the *Kleine Dreigroschenmusik*, music from *The*

---

[1] *Die Musik* (February 1928), 376.

[2] Curjel (1975), 44.

Threepenny Opera that Weill arranged as an orchestral suite at Klemperer's suggestion. Stravinsky not only appeared as soloist in his own piano concerto, but his *Les Noces*, considered a highly radical work at the time, was part of an all-Stravinsky concert. Likewise, Hindemith performed as soloist in his own viola concertos op. 36 no. 5 and op. 48. Yet Zemlinsky's first orchestral concert, on April 12, 1928, consisted only of standard fare: Cherubini's *Anacreon* Overture, Mendelssohn's Violin Concerto (with Bronislav Hubermann as soloist) and Mahler's First Symphony. In Prague, a Zemlinsky performance of a Mahler symphony was an event guaranteed to elicit rave reviews. In Berlin, the critics were unimpressed. Zemlinsky's Mahler was criticized for its dryness and lack of nervous tension, qualities that Prague audiences never associated with their conductor. Walter Hirschberg wrote that Zemlinsky

> directed the Mahler Symphony with the taste of a good musician, and (apart from a certain stiffness) with the security and caution of an experienced conductor, but he failed to penetrate the depth of the work. He knows what he wants and attempts to produce flow and vitality, but the result lacks the shape and conviction of the great conductors . . . the special details that grab the listener seldom find their way into Zemlinsky's interpretation.[1]

Although Hirschberg duly notes that Zemlinsky was greeted with a strong ovation, the contrast with the Prague press could not have been more acute. After fifteen years in the Czech capital, the complaint was that Zemlinsky was not seen on the podium frequently enough! In Berlin, he was accused of lacking depth.

For a newcomer attempting to carve out a niche in one of the world's great conducting arenas, such stinging criticism was devastating, but descriptions like "stiffness" and "caution" suggest something more was involved. Zemlinsky was far too seasoned a conductor and too familiar with this music to be careful or superficial in his approach, especially with an orchestra that possessed so much collective experience. Zemlinsky had long been regarded as "a conductor for the ears, not the eyes",[2] and perhaps his economy of means on the podium struck some Berliners as rigid. The possibility also exists that Zemlinsky was simply growing tired. But Zemlinsky's perceived lack of involvement or "stiffness" might also have sprung from his attempt to imbue his interpretation with the

---

[1] Quoted in Mahler (1971), 258.
[2] Quoted in Biba (1992), 76.

neue Sachlichkeit, the quest for intellectual objectivity that was at the heart of the Kroll philosophy.

While Zemlinsky had his own reputation to consider, a far more menacing problem for the theater had arisen. In 1928, right-wing parties of the state parliament, the *Landtag*, brought motions to the floor to resolve the "Jewish matter" within Prussian state theaters. Strictly speaking, it wasn't simply that Jews had become too numerous and influential for the welfare of Berlin's cultural community; rather, institutions such as the Kroll were also fostering decadent, Bolshevist tendencies. For the moment there was no solution and parliament took no specific action, but it was clear that the Kroll was regarded by some in power as a breeding ground for subversive culture and should be carefully monitored.

Berlin was not the only city encountering hostility in the face of modernism. In Leipzig, for instance, the 1926 premiere of Ernst Krenek's *Jonny spielt auf*, an opera about the adventures of a black violinist that incorporated a mixture of styles, genres and sounds never before heard in the opera house, including jazz bands, car horns and sirens, set off a demonstration by conservatives who denounced the work's "Jewish-Negro perversities" (though Krenek was not Jewish). At the 1927 Vienna premiere, *Jonny* was again met by aggressive Nazi sympathizers but was nevertheless deemed a triumph. Fortunately for the Viennese-born Krenek, his home town was not yet consumed by the flames of Nazi hatred that would engulf it less than a decade later. His opera went on to play to over a hundred cities, proving that, for the moment, Krenek could still find success.

In Berlin, the press took up where the Bundestag left off, denouncing the tasteless events taking place in its newest opera house. The *Völkische Beobachter*, the National Socialist organ, had already criticized the Jewish influence at the Kroll by attacking Klemperer for his failure to plumb the depths of Beethovenian emotion with his opening *Fidelio* performance.[1] Now the *Signale für die musikalischen Welt*, another well-known conservative voice, accused the Kroll of musical "destruction and disintegration" and assailed the state for financially supporting the entire endeavor.[2]

The Kroll's inaugural season had not yet ended, but signs of strain had already emerged. Externally, criticism had been mixed, with the right-wing

---

[1] Heyworth (1983), 261.

[2] *Signale für die musikalischen Welt*, quoted in Heyworth (1983), 278.

press doing what it could to erode the young theater's reputation. Internally, the institution's music chief was suffering health issues related to his work. Klemperer had assumed an awesome task and probably underestimated the effort demanded of him. There were the day-to-day intricacies of theater life with its myriad administrative responsibilities, performances whose critical success depended upon an inconsistent stable of singers, and the ever-daunting challenge of balancing traditional and more adventurous repertoire and scenic designs. By the season's close Klemperer was deeply depressed and suffering from headaches, sleeplessness and growing self-doubt. In March 1928 Klemperer left for the Côte d'Azur, where he considered relinquishing the theater's directorship. At the end of April he returned and one month later announced his resignation as director. Replaced by Ernst Legal, a former theater director, Klemperer now assumed the role of *Generalmusikdirektor*, a position that allowed him to continue shaping the Kroll's artistic ideals free of administrative burdens.

Among the greatest challenges the Kroll faced was how to increase revenue. Leo Kestenberg had initially hoped unique productions and affordable prices would appeal to the masses, but disappointing ticket sales suggested public indifference. Many of those who came were unsure of what to make of it all. On May 21, Zemlinsky led a performance of *Der Freischütz*, but in place of traditional lush forest scenery, the curtain rose on a stark expressionist set designed by Ewald Dülberg. The audience was not impressed. Subjecting Weber's quintessentially German opera to such modernism, especially during a period of growing nationalist sentiment, was more than even a progressive Berlin audience could accept. With the inaugural season winding down Klemperer led a production of Hindemith's *Cardillac* at the end of June, with the sets again designed by Dülberg. But this combination too failed to illicit enthusiasm. All things considered — the theater's administrative shake-up, its tenuous budget, a less-than-stellar company of vocalists and the fact that the right-wing press was vociferously attempting to bring down the entire enterprise — the Kroll was off to an inauspicious start.

The Kroll's second season got underway with a run of rather traditional operatic fare that included works of Smetana, Puccini and Weber. On September 5, 1928, Zemlinsky led a performance of Strauss' *Salome*. Music had come a long way in the decade since Zemlinsky's stellar 1910 Vienna Volksoper premiere of the work, but the opera continued to present formidable musical and theatrical demands. Zemlinsky proved up to the challenge. Two days later the *Berliner Börsen-Courier* proclaimed that, "Under Zemlinsky's sovereign direction the orchestra performed with polished bravura. Even the textures most well known for their complexity were clearly voiced. The tonal subtlety and refined charm of the artful score resounded with sensuous fascination."[1] Since Zemlinsky's days in Vienna, critics had applauded his ability to elicit clarity from the densest of orchestral textures; now Berlin too recognized his discerning artistry.

But the Kroll seemed incapable of sustained success. Two days before Christmas, Zemlinsky led the Kroll premiere of Johann Strauss jr.'s *Die Fledermaus*, the first in a string of lackluster performances. The entire production was vilified. The cold January air of 1929 provided little relief from the heat that continuously assaulted the theater. When Klemperer opened the New Year with a production of Wagner's *Der fliegende Holländer*, hypersensitive nerves were set on end. Police were stationed around the theater just in case trouble broke out. Like *Der Freischutz*, the *Dutchman* was a German classic, but Klemperer and his colleagues were not swayed by expectations. Dülberg's sets were models of stark efficiency, the Dutchman was beardless, Senta's companions were dressed in skirts and blouses — in short, Wagner's staging had been stripped beyond recognition. In the aftermath, the critics maligned Klemperer for what they deemed yet another desecration of their birthright:

> What Herr Klemperer has done with this soiling of German opera . . . can no longer be excused as mere wrong-headedness. It is an irresponsible attempt to destroy, and to that there can only be one answer, "Out with the pest."[2]

As Klemperer's biographer Peter Heyworth points out, the Kroll production of *Dutchman* left such a black mark on the Berlin collective consciousness that it was singled out by the Nazis during a Düsseldorf exhibit of degenerate music in 1938. There it had the honor of being designated one of the Weimar Republic's most ignominious artistic undertakings.[3]

For Zemlinsky, home life offered little respite from the struggles he and his Kroll colleagues faced. Since coming to Berlin, his wife Ida had been diagnosed with leukemia, and in January her health began deteriorating rapidly. With each passing day Zemlinsky faced the increasing prospect of her death. Ida's life in Berlin had been difficult from the start. Apart from their daughter Johanna (Hansi), she had no strong personal connections or professional distractions other than those involving her husband, and her health had not been good for years.

Almost nothing is known about Zemlinsky and Ida's life together, either

---

[1] *Berliner Börsen-Courier* (September 7, 1928).

[2] Quoted in Heyworth (1983), 282.

[3] Ibid., 283.

before or during the years they lived in Berlin. Even Zemlinsky's letters throw little light on Ida's personality, interests or their relationship. When she is mentioned at all in correspondence, it is usually only to relay greetings or express good wishes. From a traditional view, Ida was the ideal wife and mother. Until her illness, she had provided stability and consistency, regardless where the couple found themselves, and by tending to day-to-day cares, Ida granted her husband greater time and energy for his work. With Ida's declining health, however, their roles reversed; Zemlinsky was now the caregiver and support system.

In January 1929 Zemlinsky was busy at the Kroll with preparations for the upcoming premiere of Offenbach's *Les contes d'Hoffmann*, but, when not in rehearsal, he was with Ida. By this time she had been moved to the nearby Charité, but the doctors could do little but administer morphine for her pain. On January 29, Ida, aged 48, took her last breath. In a letter to Schoenberg, Zemlinsky wrote that Ida "deserved a better lot. Hansi and I are now very lonely, and I feel it a thousand times more than I would have thought."[1] After Ida's death, Zemlinsky and his 21-year-old daughter left the boarding house for Tile-Wardenberg-Strasse 29, in the western part of the district of Tiergarten, where Hansi assumed charge of domestic affairs.

Back at the Kroll, the Bauhaus artist László Moholy-Nagy was commissioned to design the sets for a highly experimental production of *Les contes d'Hoffmann*. Moholy-Nagy created a modernist vision of Offenbach's dream world, utilizing machinery, shadows, photomontage and film, in an exploration of both the human and the mechanical. He later spoke of his breathtaking geometric shapes as having been designed "to create space from light and shadow . . . Everything is transparent and all the transparent surfaces work together to make an organized and well perceptible space arrangement."[2] As adventurous as anything the Kroll ever fashioned, Moholy-Nagy's designs featured visible joint fittings, the use of surreal automatic figures, steel furniture and shifting movable sets, resulting in a "new Romantic, whereby fantasy was ignited and the improbable was allowed to roam about".[3] By now, Zemlinsky and his colleagues were well conditioned to the affront likely to result from mixing the sacred with the profane — the marriage of an operatic staple with cutting-edge Bauhaus design seemed engineered to drive a lasting wedge between those who appreciated the company's contemporary adventurous spirit, and those who regarded the production as confirmation of the Kroll's decent into decadence.

---

[1] Weber (1995), 273.
[2] Moholy-Nagy (1938), 197.
[3] Curjel (1975), 50.

Determined not to cave in to public opinion, the Kroll mounted a production that was brilliant, *avant-garde* and entirely uninhibited.

The criticism that followed the February 12 premiere was refreshingly positive. Finally, it seemed, Berlin was waking to the artistic value of upgrading a classic like Offenbach's warhorse for the twentieth century. In a critique entitled, "An Interesting Night at the Opera", Adolf Weissmann portrayed the Kroll's unprecedented approach as a beautiful and intelligent experiment. Unlike Wagner, whose operas Germans held sacrosanct, Offenbach provided perfect fodder for the Kroll's modernist pursuits. Weissmann counted the evening as "one of the most interesting of my experiences".

> Whoever loves the transformation of the theater, whoever loves the music, must see it. Just as a spell is cast on the eyes, so are the ears hardly to be deprived. . . . Every beer-loving Philistine is bound to be disappointed by the absence of the traditional beer or wine tavern: the construction does not reflect the possibility to sit comfortably. Light flashes from beer mugs. Stairs coil up to where Lindorf sits. And everything is placed in the black night of shadows.[1]

Every aspect of the design seemed to challenge the viewer's expectations, yet Weissmann argued that contemporary art, architecture and film were striking out in new directions, so serious theater could not stand still. As for Zemlinsky's musical direction, Weissmann judged it a total success:

> On the podium Zemlinsky is generally all too little appreciated. Here, amidst such an experiment for the eyes, the security of his musical instinct and the assurance and flexibility of his direction delivered the music at its fullest. Such was clearly evident by the heartfelt ovation he received with his three curtain calls.[2]

Oscar Bie, who likewise acknowledged the important risks the theater was taking, also praised Zemlinsky's work. Though he regarded Moholy-Nagy's stagecraft as lacking a necessary organic quality, Zemlinsky's musical direction earned high praise: "Zemlinsky makes it very beautiful, brilliant, cheerful and yet melodically melancholy."[3] Naturally, there were also a few detractors who immediately dismissed anything that assaulted their sensibilities. One scathing

---

[1] *Berliner Zeitung* (February 13, 1929).

[2] Ibid.

[3] *Berliner Börsen-Courier* (February 13, 1929).

and bigoted review, by the anti-Semitic critic Paul Zschorlich, foreshadowed
the precipitous decline in store for both the Kroll and Germany:

> The Klemperer ensemble, which consists mainly of aliens, is bit by bit
> devouring the entire repertory. It presents the best-loved operas "accord-
> ing to the spirit of the times", that is, according to the Jewish spirit. We
> observe this spirit in Klemperer's deeds, in the collaborators he chooses,
> in his artistic attitudes and in his affinity to the Soviet potentates, from
> whom he earns so well on guest appearances . . . The three-quarters Jew-
> ish public was once again delighted by the evening . . . Klemperer and
> Legal would do well . . . to declare their cultural bolshevist undertaking
> a "Jewish Opera". What goes on in it has nothing to do with German
> artistic spirit.[1]

At present Berlin still harbored enough enlightened critics to counter the sinister
stabs of men like Zschorlich. But with anti-Semitism and xenophobia on the
rise, the Kroll could expect the stream of literary venom to continue if it maintained its present course.

Zemlinsky's seasonal schedule at the Kroll was significantly lighter than that
to which he was accustomed in Prague, even with the demands of productions
like the Offenbach. Consequently, he took advantage of offers that helped fill the
gaps and provided additional sources of income. In February 1928, he traveled
to Leningrad for three performances, the success of which led to an offer of appointment as director of the city's State Opera. While doubtless flattered and
perhaps even tempted by the offer, Zemlinsky could not abdicate his position
in one of Europe's most culturally dynamic cities. It had taken him too long to
make his way to Berlin, and Russia was simply too far away.

Back in Berlin, Zemlinsky accepted a part-time post conducting the student
chorus at the Staatliche Akademische Hochschule für Musik, following an invitation by Zemlinsky's Viennese colleague Franz Schreker. Schreker, who taught
composition and had served as the music director of the Hochschule since 1920,
oversaw a faculty that included Hindemith as a professor of theory and composition, George Szell, who taught score reading, the violinist Carl Flesch, the cellist Emanuel Feuermann and the pianist Arthur Schnabel.[2] Schreker provided
Zemlinsky with a contract that ran from November 1928 until September 30
the following year.[3] For directing the mixed choir and instructing the choral

---

[1] Quoted in Heyworth (1983), 286.

[2] Hailey (1993), 121.

[3] The contract was not renewed until 1931, at which time Zemlinsky took over Szell's score-
reading class.

conducting students and oratorio soloists, Zemlinsky earned 525 Reichmarks ($125 in 1929, worth about $1,590 in 2010)[1] and was granted four weeks' vacation. As choir director, Zemlinsky conducted only a single concert, on February 28, 1929, which featured the Berlin premiere of Kodály's *Psalmus Hungaricus* and the first German performance of Janáček's Glagolitic Mass.

In 1929 a volume of poetry appeared in German translation under the title *Afrika singt: Auslese neuer afro-amerikanischer Lyrik* (Africa Sings: A Selection of New Afro-American Lyrics). The anthology consisted of works by poets of the Harlem Renaissance, among them Langston Hughes, Claude McKay, Jean Toomer, Frank Horne, Fenton Johnson and Countee Cullen, and it quickly captured the attention of a handful of composers, Zemlinsky among them.[2] Whether remembering dark Harlem or painting a Georgia lynching, the poems captured a world an ocean away, but even in translation the theme of oppression struck a sympathetic chord with Zemlinsky. Having had neither the leisure nor the impulse to compose for several years, Zemlinsky now began considering the possibility of setting several of the poems to music, perhaps along the lines of the Lyric Symphony, but without the lush atmosphere of his earlier work. Instead, he took his cue from the jazz-inspired "American" sound and the detached, anti-romanticism of the *neue Sachlichkeit* as practiced by composers such as Hindemith, Schreker, Weill and Krenek. With the summer free of conducting obligations, Zemlinsky returned to composition and let the radically new Harlem poetry spark his creative thought. The *Symphonische Gesänge*, Symphonic Songs, was the result.

Externally, Zemlinsky's latest opus displays undeniable connections to the Lyric Symphony of six years earlier. Zemlinsky again embeds a group of seven songs within an orchestral fabric and takes as inspiration poetry that speaks of distant lands and peoples. Harmonically, both works are directed toward the key of D major, and each is organized around tight motivic cells. There, however, the parallels cease. Unlike its predecessor, there are no discernable motifs that run through the Symphonic Songs, although various organizing features do unify the seven songs. The texts, for example, are loosely organized on an arch principle: the two outer movements, *Lied aus Dixieland* and *Arabeske* sing of death by hanging; the second and the sixth, *Lied der Baumwollpacker* and

---

[1] See the sources cited at p. 193 n. 4 above.

[2] Fritz Kramer, Eric Zeisl, Wilhelm Grosz and Kurt Pahlen were likewise drawn to the Harlem poets.

Afrikanischer Tanz, a song and a dance, represent the African slave experience from day to night; the third and fifth, *Totes braunes Mädel* and *Erkenntnis* are songs of farewell; and *Übler Bursche*, at the collection's epicenter, stands as a dark, unapologetic confession.

Rhythm remains a driving force throughout the collection, a consequence of the poetry's African-American origins and Zemlinsky's occasional attempt to incorporate his own modified jazz idiom. In the second, third, forth and fifth songs, Zemlinsky repeatedly relies on some variation of an anapest rhythm (short-short-long), typically two equal eighth notes followed by a longer note of varying length. Elsewhere, too, rhythmic gestures and patterns dominate the texture, as is evident in *Übler Bursche* or in the driving figures found at the opening of *Arabeske* (which also incorporates the mandolin as a substitute for the ubiquitous guitar or banjo). Nor does Zemlinsky limit himself to the rhythms provided by a battery of percussion including tom-toms, woodblocks and xylophone. Instead, he frequently involves the lyrical instruments of the orchestra as extensions of the percussion family through the use of *col legno* string writing (tapping the strings with the wood of the bow), stopped horns and *staccato*, punctuated woodwind chords.

Aiming for a restrained and streamlined quality, Zemlinsky eliminates all nonessentials. In contrast to the Lyric Symphony, he neither embellishes the orchestral lines with virtuosic decoration nor provides the work with orchestral interludes. The result is a score a fraction of the Lyric Symphony's length. Vocally, Zemlinsky replaces his prior predilection for expressionistic vocal leaps with smaller intervals, and confines the singer's phrases to a more limited range. Sonorities, like those found in the wind-dominant opening of the *Lied der Baumwollpacker*, remain unforgivingly dark, while Zemlinsky's ambiguous harmonies, tone clusters and tendency to operate in various keys simultaneously masks any overt tonality. Zemlinsky's trademark lyricism does occasionally break through, particularly in slower moments such the English-horn writing of the *Lied aus Dixieland*, but at no point does Zemlinsky attempt to summon up a nineteenth-century idiom. Rather, his overall approach remains cool, dry and controlled.

Beyond the seduction provided by the Harlem poets and a desire to tap into the musical world around him, Zemlinsky's renewed impulse to create was also fired by his blossoming affair with a young singer. Zemlinsky had known Louise Sachsel for many years. Her family had come to Prague from Podwołoczyska, Galicia (now Pidvolochys'k, Ukraine), while Louise was still a young girl and by her early teens her gifts as both a painter and singer were evident. Unsure which to pursue, she had enrolled at the Prague Academy of Fine Arts in 1918 as a student of both art and music. Louise eventually came to the attention of Zemlinsky, who agreed to take her on as a vocal student early in 1919. Later that fall, when he learned of her artistic gifts, he also sat for a portrait. In 1920 Louise left for Vienna, where she continued her music studies at the Conservatory, now renamed the Akademie für Musik und darstellende Kunst (the Academy of Music and Performing Arts). Music, she decided, would be her calling, although her passion for painting endured throughout her life. By 1924 Louise was back in Prague and singing at the Deutsches Theater, but her roles were limited and her appearances on stage infrequent. The precise nature of Louise and Zemlinsky's relationship during this period is impossible to know, but it seems likely matters had developed beyond the realm of pure professionalism. Zemlinsky's interest in the young singer was understandable. Twenty-nine years his junior, Louise was attractive and talented and came from an established Jewish family. Her father, Ludwig Sachsel, was a former lieutenant in the Austro-Hungarian army who had since become an affluent businessman. But Zemlinsky was married and a highly visible figure in and around the theater and he wasn't about to jeopardize either institution. Their relationship, if one existed, remained discreet.

During Louise's two seasons with the Deutsches Theater, Zemlinsky could have ensured that more work came her way, but always circumspect in his professional life, he did not. Louise returned to Vienna, and found employment at the Volksoper. Here too her appearances were fleeting and her tenure brief. Zemlinsky was by this time a resident of Berlin, and his energies were consumed by his work at the theater and caring for his ailing wife. But by 1929, everything had changed. Ida was gone, and Zemlinsky, long accustomed to female companionship, decided to pursue Louise seriously.

In August, the couple traveled together to Juan-les-Pins on the French Riviera. By the time they arrived, Zemlinsky had set four of the Afro-American poems to music — Cullen's *A Brown Dead Girl*, and Hughes's *Danse Africaine*, *Song for a Dark Girl*, and *Disillusion*. With Louise at his side, he turned out three more with impressive speed: Toomer's *Cotton Song*, Horne's *Arabesque*, and Hughes's *Bad Man*. A fresh look at his initial setting of *Song for a Dark Girl* showed it to be too brief, so Zemlinsky expanded the song significantly before commencing to orchestrate the entire set. By the time he returned to Berlin to begin preparations for the coming season, the Symphonic Songs were finished.

Zemlinsky wasted no time trying to spark interest for his latest opus with his long-time Viennese publisher, Emil Hertzka, but repeated entreaties led nowhere. Despite Zemlinsky's longstanding association with Universal Edition, the firm was now concentrating its resources on a younger body of composers like Kurt Weill and Ernst Krenek, men whose music all but guaranteed returns on their investment. If Zemlinsky could wait it out until the current economic crisis turned around, then perhaps there was hope, but until then, Hertzka would make no commitment.[1] Zemlinsky had no better luck finding a performance venue. With stage music presently all the rage in Europe's major cities, there was no interest in a serious orchestral piece of this nature. Zemlinsky had to wait until 1935 before his long-time colleague Heinrich Jalowetz led the premiere for Radio Brno. It was the first and last time the composition was heard in its entirety during Zemlinsky's lifetime. A performance in Germany was by then out of the question, now that the country was under the control of the National Socialists, for whom Jewish composers and African-American subject matter were anathema. And the southeastern Czechoslovakian town of Brno was too remote to spark interest in the score anywhere else. Zemlinsky's Symphonic Songs, like their composer, became a victim of circumstance.

Within two months of Zemlinsky's putting the final touches on the Symphonic Songs, Berlin suffered a pair of fateful events that triggered its irreversible demise. The first occurred with the death on October 3, 1929, of Germany's Chancellor and Foreign Minister Gustav Stresemann. Stresemann was responsible for Germany's recent economic stabilization, and he even inspired hope that his government could make good on war reparations to the Allies (although in fact on the one hand the reparations were cancelled in 1932 and on the other the repayment of the loans raised to make earlier payments, resumed after World War II, remains incomplete in 2010). His death signified the end of an enlightened German government. Alfred Hugenberg, the Krupp armament and media magnate, seized the opportunity to gain ground with his Nationalist party, which had opposed Stresemann and his peace-keeping policies. As the city mourned Stresemann's death, Hugenberg, accompanied by his orator, a 40-year-old Bavarian named Adolf Hitler, fiercely campaigned against war reparations, a punishment they saw as having reduced the German *Volk* to a state of slavery. Their platform failed to gain sufficient support and was rejected by the Reichstag, but Hitler had learned much from the experience. His future plans for the Reich would prove far more exhilarating and would quickly galvanize his fellow countrymen to action.

Stresemann's absence created a gaping void and left the country vulnerable.

---

[1] In 1974 Louise Zemlinsky renewed conversations with Universal Edition about the *Symphonische Gesänge*. Three years later they were published as Zemlinsky's op. 20.

In the words of the historian Peter Gay, his death signaled a significant turning point in the country's political history:

> Stresemann should not be sentimentalized; nor should we exaggerate the power of one man in the turbulent stream of history — there were forces at work in New York and Paris and Berlin that Stresemann would have been powerless to stem. Yet his death was a grievous loss; it was, if not the cause, at least a sign of the beginning of the end.[1]

The forces to which Gay alludes were not political but economic, and as Berlin headed into the last week of October, it now faced a more immediate menace than Hitler. On October 24 the New York Stock Exchange collapsed, taking world markets with it. The result was massive unemployment, which in Germany had been steadily increasing since the spring. For its own protection, Germany began minimizing exports. In order to recoup losses, foreign markets began recalling the loans Germany depended on, further devastating its economy. With each passing day, Germany was losing capital and security and sinking further into the abyss of debt.

With a blind eye to the problems in Germany, at the end of the month Zemlinsky was in Vienna to lead a concert of his music for Radio Vienna. He had designed a diverse program revealing to his fellow Viennese the wealth of his emotional and stylistic range, one that left no question about his versatility as a composer or conductor: excerpts from his operas *Kleider machen Leute* and *Der Zwerg*, the final movement of the *Lyrische Symphonie* and four songs from the recently completed Symphonische Gesänge. Of the works performed, only the songs were unknown, and the entire performance was in Zemlinsky's hands, where his music fared best. Judging by the tone of a letter written to Alban Berg shortly after Zemlinsky returned to Berlin — he had spent a "wonderful, relaxing evening" at Berg's home — Zemlinsky's Viennese experience was one of the more satisfying of recent years.[2] If it was accompanied by the angst or expectation previously associated with a major premiere, there is no record of it.

It was during this period that Zemlinsky also embarked upon several recording projects with the orchestras of the Berlin Staatsoper, the Städtische Oper-Charlottenburg and the Berlin Philharmonic Orchestra. His work in Berlin's studios continued until the year 1932 and was followed by two recordings with Vienna's Konzertorchester in 1935. His recordings of arias by Verdi and Puccini, as well as recordings of Czech songs and arias, give little indication of

[1] Gay (1968), 158.
[2] Weber (1995), 324.

his abilities, since the singers naturally steal the limelight. But Zemlinsky also recorded a collection of overtures by Mozart (*Così fan tutte*, *Don Giovanni* and *Die Entführung aus dem Serail*), Beethoven (*Fidelio*), Rossini (*La gazza ladra*), Weber (*Der Freischütz*) and Johann Strauss (*Die Fledermaus*), in addition to Smetana's *Die Moldau* and overtures by Friedrich von Flotow, Louis Aimé Maillart and Jaromir Weinberger.[1] This series attests to Zemlinsky's extraordinary interpretive skills. Whether leading Mozart or Maillart, Zemlinsky renders definitive versions, and these recordings are strong evidence of his ability to illuminate every aspect of the music, from the clarity of the phrasing to the logic of the score's formal structure.

The 1929/30 Kroll season began with Zemlinsky on the podium. On September 27, 1929, the veteran conductor of a diverse array of modern scores delivered three one-act French works never before heard in Berlin: Ravel's *L'Heure espagnole*, Milhaud's *Le Pauvre Matelot* and Ibert's *Angélique*. The evening also celebrated the Kroll debut of the young Czech singer Jarmila Novotná, who went on to become a member of the Vienna Staatsoper and New York's Metropolitan Opera House. In a critique by Hans Stuckenschmidt, Zemlinsky was singled out for his spiritual and intellectual ability to draw out every nuance of each score,[2] but otherwise the evening fell short of the Kroll's expectations in generating enthusiasm for the French modernists. Mozart and Marschner followed, though Klemperer also failed to win over the press. At the close of December, Zemlinsky conducted a new production of Smetana's *The Bartered Bride*, which Hugo Leichtentritt of *Die Musik* found highly satisfying. But, as the press had previously reminded Zemlinsky, this was Berlin, not Czechoslovakia, and a Bohemian folk opera, no matter how successfully carried off, was not going to put the Kroll on a better footing.

As the German economic noose tightened, all aspects of day-to-day life became constricted. The Ministry of Culture began reducing spending, and between the years 1928 and 1933 Berlin's theater subsidy was cut nearly in half and theaters began closing down. As the youngest and the most controversial among the city's opera houses, the Kroll had become a lightning rod for vitriolic opponents like Pastor Julius Koch, who regarded the house as an outlet for cultural Bolshevism. Koch, delegate of the Deutschnationale Volkspartei, the

---

[1] The original pressings are in the possession of the Yale University Collection of Historical Sound Recordings. In 1986, Koch-Schwann reissued many of these works on compact disc (CD 310 037).

[2] Quoted in Curjel (1975), 274.

German National People's Party, was of the opinion that the theater was making a "conscious attempt to destroy Christian, German culture by replacing it with Jewish pessimism".[1] Despite claims of artistic merit, integrity and vision, the Kroll was under siege from two sides. It was at the mercy of a government struggling to right itself economically and forced to defend itself against powerful opponents who, amidst the rising tide of Aryan sentiment, were convinced it was fostering a Judeo-Negro epoch of Prussian art. It was a fight the Kroll could not win.

[1] Quoted in Quander (1992), 184

Chapter 10

Closing Doors

For Zemlinsky, the year 1930 began promisingly. On the fourth day of the New Year he married Louise Sachsel, one month after her conversion to Protestantism and a few weeks shy of the first anniversary of Ida's death. Like Schoenberg seven years earlier, Zemlinsky remarried quickly after his wife's death, whether from loneliness, a desire to move on, or true love mixed with a disregard for appearances. Living in the midst of progressive Europe, the usual customs did not apply. The couple, along with Zemlinsky's daughter, soon packed up the contents of their apartment at Tile-Wardenberg-Strasse 29 and moved south to Pariser-Strasse 19, in the Berlin district of Charlottenberg.

In March Zemlinsky returned to Prague to help celebrate President Masaryk's 80th birthday. Along with the music of Smetana, Zemlinsky was scheduled to lead the Czech Philharmonic and Prague's Deutsche Männergesangverein in Beethoven's Ninth Symphony, his great testament to brotherhood and peace. Not so long ago Zemlinsky had sought to foster healthy relations between Prague's Czech and German musical communities, but since his departure European politics had intervened. Arriving in the Czech capital in 1930, Zemlinsky learned that relations between the two communities had become so strained that the Czech choral society felt it a matter of national honor to sing in its own tongue. As matters stood, the female soloists planned to sing in Czech and the males in German. Not since 1920, when Prague's Estates Theater was overrun by a Czech street mob, had Zemlinsky encountered such animosity between the two cultures. Nevertheless, Zemlinsky handled the situation with his usual diplomatic aplomb, conducting the music of Beethoven while disassociating himself with matters political, stating, "It makes absolutely no difference in what language one sings if one sings beautifully."[1] The results he left for the audience to judge. According to the critic of the *Prager Presse*, the bilingual production was hardly even noticeable![2]

Once back in Berlin, Zemlinsky discovered that his Prague appearance had rankled his German superiors and that Heinz Tietjen, supervisor of Berlin's opera houses, had temporarily suspended him from the Kroll, an order that most likely originated in the German Foreign Office. To avoid becoming embroiled in politics, Zemlinsky quickly drafted a letter of apology and was reinstated shortly thereafter. Both the suspension and reinstatement made the headlines back in Prague:[3]

> *Nicht suspendiert . . .*
> *Ruhige Beurteilung der Zemlinsky-"Affaire" in Berlin*
>
> *Suspension lifted . . .*
> *Peaceful resolution to the Zemlinsky "affair" in Berlin*

Zemlinsky resumed his Kroll duties as if nothing were amiss. In May he led a sensual and dramatic production of *Rigoletto*, and in June he was scheduled to share the pit with Klemperer in a program featuring a pair of Schoenberg one-act monodramas, *Erwartung* and *Die glückliche Hand*.

Schoenberg's music had yet to be programmed at the Kroll — Klemperer was no admirer of his music — but the Kroll was in dire need of something contemporary. In March, Krenek's *Leben des Orest* had been pulled after its unsuccessful reception, but Klemperer had rejected Weill's *Aufstieg und Fall der Stadt Mahagonny* and Schoenberg's *Von heute auf morgen* as replacements. Nonetheless, Schoenberg's prominence and proximity as a resident of the city made him a logical choice, so Klemperer reluctantly settled on a Schoenberg double bill, though, as the historian Peter Heyworth noted, there was "no reason to suppose that he embarked on the task with enthusiasm".[4] Zemlinsky took charge of *Erwartung*, a work he knew better than anyone else save Schoenberg himself, and Klemperer oversaw its companion piece, the autobiographical *Die glückliche Hand*, a curious 'drama with music' for two silent actors, one singer and orchestra.

Oskar Schlemmer, a Bauhaus designer who had designed sets for operas by Hindemith and who had followed Schoenberg's work for years, was engaged for

---

[1] *Prager Presse* (March 25, 1930), 4.

[2] *Prager Presse* (March 23, 1930), 8.

[3] *Prager Presse* (March 26, 1930), 1.

[4] Heyworth (1983), 330.

both works, but, by the time consultations with Schoenberg began, less than a month remained until opening night. The sets were finished two days before the June 7 performance, but the complex synchronization of *Die glückliche Hand*'s colored lighting was still not functioning properly in one of the final rehearsals. In haste, a second rehearsal was called for eleven o'clock in the evening and lasted until four in the morning.

Not surprisingly, the reviews were mixed. Hans Stuckenschmidt of the *Berliner Zeitung*, perhaps more familiar with Schoenberg's music than any other critic, hailed Zemlinsky's interpretation as the product of an intellectual musician of the highest order,[1] and other critics extolled Zemlinsky's ability to build intensity and draw out the score's fabulous colors. Not everyone, however, was enamored with what they heard. Paul Zschorlich, memorable for his vitriolic, racially motivated review of *Hoffmann*, now proclaimed *Die glückliche Hand* as "diseased and poisonous as cocaine".[2] Four days later Zweig filled in for an ailing Zemlinsky, substituting Milhaud's *Le Pauvre Matelot* for *Erwartung*. *Die glückliche Hand* was heard only once more before it was pulled from the program. And after just two further performances of *Erwartung*, it suffered a similar fate and joined *Die glückliche Hand* in the Kroll archives. Years later, Klemperer looked back on the events, remarking, "It was right in a cultural sense to give these works at the Kroll. In another way it was nonsense. I never saw the theater so empty."[3]

Consistently poor attendance eroded confidence at the theater, and as one disappointment followed another, morale suffered and internal friction rose. Externally, matters were even more disheartening — the government had decided to withdraw its Kroll subsidy after one more season. Yet even that was one season too many for the right-wing Deutschnationale Volkspartei, which called for the doors to close immediately. In the Landtag and in print, writers and other members of Berlin's intelligentsia came to the theater's defense. The author Thomas Mann and the music historian Alfred Einstein (cousin of the physicist) argued for the theater's intellectual worth and pleaded for the government to preserve its already modest budget — after all, the defenders argued, of Berlin's three operatic institutions the Kroll cost the least to run. The defense, though noble, was Sisyphean; the entire company sensed that time was running out.

With another disheartening season in the books, Zemlinsky returned to composition, the precious summer months providing a temporary escape from

---

[1] Quoted in Curjel (1975), 289.

[2] Ibid., 292.

[3] Heyworth (1985), 79.

the Kroll's shaky existence. Several years earlier he had begun work on a new opera based on Gottfried Keller's legend *Der schlimm-heilige Vitalis*. He had eventually completed substantial drafts for the project, which he called simply *Der heilige Vitalis*, but despite the success Zemlinsky had with Keller's *Kleider machen Leute*, he now decided that Keller's tale was an operatic dead end. In 1930, he started afresh, this time with the vagabond poet and writer Klabund as his inspiration.

A pseudonym for Alfred Henschke, Klabund had become a popular source for the German theater during the last decade. A prolific poet and author of nearly a hundred books, Klabund early on attracted the support of his fellow authors and publishers. As a teenager he was incorrectly diagnosed with pneumonia — he was actually suffering from tuberculosis — and so was relieved of military duty during World War I because of his weak lungs. As a result, he took cures in Switzerland, during which time he began translating Chinese poetry. In 1923 Klabund came to the attention of Elisabeth Bergner, a Viennese actress, who commissioned an adaptation of Li Xingdao's classic fourteenth-century drama *Hui-Lan Ji*, as translated into French by Stanislas Julien. A year later, the work complete, the Frankfurt Schauspielhaus paid Klabund an advance royalty, enabling him to be treated by a specialist, though by now his tuberculosis had spread to his larynx, rendering him unable to speak. Despite his threatening illness, Klabund lived long enough to witness the overnight success of his play *Der Kreidekreis* (The Circle of Chalk), which played extensively throughout Germany and received an extended run at Prague's Deutsches Theater during Zemlinsky's tenure. Sadly, in May 1928, at the age of 37 and at the height of his powers, Klabund succumbed to tuberculosis.[1]

Two years later Zemlinsky set to work crafting a libretto from Klabund's drama. After decades of theater work and substantial involvement with librettists, Zemlinsky now possessed the confidence to undertake the project himself. By midsummer he was at work on the short score, and for two years he composed nothing else. In October 1932, nearly three years after they were married, Zemlinsky presented the completed score to Louise as a belated wedding gift.

Based on a masterpiece of the thirteenth- and fourteenth-century Yuan dynasty established by Kublai Khan, *Der Kreidekreis* revolves around the pretty Haitang, whose family is caught in a web of extortion spun by the mandarin Ma. Unable to pay his taxes, Haitang's father hangs himself, and her brother,

---

[1] By the time of his death, Klabund had written over a hundred books, had penned over 2,200 poems of all types, including sonnets, elegies and ballads, and had been actively translated.

Chang-Ling, becomes a revolutionary. Destitute, Haitang's mother sells her daughter into prostitution. Pao, the prince of a noble family, falls in love with Haitang and bids for her, but he cannot match the sum Ma is willing to pay.

At the start of the opera's second act, Ma's childless wife Yu-Pei learns that she is to be eliminated from Ma's will because Haitang has given birth to a son. Yu-Pei poisons Ma, and points the finger of blame at Haitang, paying off "witnesses" to bolster her case, all the while maintaining that the child is hers. Haitang is sentenced to death, but she is granted a stay of execution when Pao, who has since attained the rank of Emperor, suspends all death sentences as his first act of justice. Pao brings both women together and, placing the child between them in the middle of a circle of chalk, declares that whoever can pull the baby from the circle is the rightful mother. As Yu-Pei begins to pull the child away, Haitang relinquishes her grip so as not to cause him harm. Her true compassion proves her innocence and maternal rights, and exposes Yu-Pei's guilt. Pao then confesses to having seduced Haitang as she slept during her first night in the mandarin's house. Haitang's dream is now reality: her child is elevated to the rank of prince and she to Empress.

As was now common practice for Zemlinsky, he attaches distinct musical types to each character, underscoring and distinguishing their individual personae. Tong, the teahouse proprietor, speaks or sings in measured rhythms, reflecting the cool, calculated manner of an executioner-turned-businessman, while the Mandarin and Judge are given purely speaking roles, lending each the air of dispassion so characteristic of *neue Sachlichkeit* sensibility. In stark contrast stand Chang-Ling, Prince Pao and Haitang, whose lyrical expressions afford them a level of compassion denied the others. Yet Zemlinsky's deft hand and the opera's social implications cannot elevate these characters above a fairy-tale stereotype, whether wicked (the Mandarin) or compassionate (Prince Pao). Even Haitang remains one-dimensional; despite existing in her own spiritual plane, her transformation from concubine to Empress comes with the intervention of the *deus ex machina*, not through self-examination.

Despite the rags-to-riches story line of *Der Kreidekreis* and its fairy-tale ending, the opera is distinguished from all of Zemlinsky's earlier work through its reliance on a variety of powerful themes — good versus evil, rich versus poor, the brutality of the ruling class, rebellion, victimization, suicide and revolution. The story's focus on social order and morality, however stereotyped, places it squarely within the prevailing operatic zeitgeist, resulting in the timeliest of all Zemlinsky's operas.[1] The form and style of the opera also suggest Zemlinsky's

[1] Ernst Toch's *Der Fächer*, another *Zeitoper* with a Chinese subject, received its 1930

attempt to keep pace with his contemporaries, particularly Kurt Weill and Berthold Brecht, whose *Threepenny Opera* had burst onto the Berlin scene two years before Zemlinsky set to work on *Der Kreidekreis*. The latter opera's jazz associations, its combination of song, spoken dialogue and melodrama (spoken voice with orchestral accompaniment) and even its themes of social criticism all point to Brechtian dramaturgy and, arguably, to Berlin nightlife. The theatrical aspect of the work also provided the ideal vehicle for Zemlinsky to exploit his love of song, though neither Haitang's soulful "On the bank behind the willows" at the close of the opera's first scene, for example, or Pao's spirited "I am an adventurer", near the start of scene ii, was destined to capture the public's attention like Brecht and Weill's *Mack the Knife* or *The Alabama Song*.

From the first scene Zemlinsky is in territory far removed from anything he had ever composed. Tong, the teahouse/brothel proprietor, speaks directly with the audience, accompanied by the soft swing of the saxophone. The atmosphere is seedy and mysterious, and, if not for the libretto's indication that the scene opens in a teahouse, it could just as easily play in a smoky Berlin cabaret. Musically, however, *Der Kreidekreis* displays strong connections to Zemlinsky's work of recent years. Like the *Symphonische Gesänge* and the Third Quartet, Zemlinsky continues his reliance on tight motivic cells, static ostinato patterns and *neue Sachlichkeit* restraint, while on a harmonic level the opera charts a course parallel to the Symphonic Songs, moving from D minor to D major, a symbol of the plot's transcendence from darkness to light. On a looser level, *Der Kreidekreis* might also be seen as the conclusion of an exotically-inspired triptych, one that began with the sensual Bengali poetry found in the Lyric Symphony and passed through the dark, emotionally intense Afro-American experience as intoned by the Harlem poets.

No single style dominates Zemlinsky's score. Faced with a host of wide-ranging dramatic components, including the Chinese setting, social allegory, oppression and a fairy-tale ending (which must have appealed to him greatly), Zemlinsky incorporates a pastiche of styles — the jazz-inspired nightclub music heard at the outset, for example, or the chinoiserie that he juxtaposes with a military march in the middle of the third act. And though he occasionally draws on flutes, gongs and pentatonic scales for local color, Zemlinsky has no illusions of re-creating an authentic music of the Far East. Similarly, the sound

premiere in Königsberg. As the music historian Christopher Hailey points out, a similar social thread runs through other works of the time, including Hindemith's *Mathis der Maler*, Schreker's *Der Schmied von Gent*, Schoenberg's *Moses und Aron*, Krenek's *Karl V* and arguably the era's best known indictment of social corruption, Brecht and Weill's *Dreigroschenoper* (The Threepenny Opera). See Hailey (1993), 260.

he associated with American jazz is stylized and filtered through his European musical vernacular. Through Zemlinsky's pen, the context becomes cool, restrained and almost expressionless.

By the third act, however, the *neue Sachlichkeit* objectivity that has dominated Zemlinsky's score begins yielding to the warmth and expressiveness of an earlier style. Hints are audible in the Prelude, where Zemlinsky introduces the chief judge Chu-chu with mockingly dry counterpoint and Strauss-inspired parody, complete with teasing *glissandi* and blaring French horns. Later, as Haitang allows her child to be pulled from the circle, Zemlinsky faces the dilemma of how to address the climax and the resolution's extremes of emotion in musical terms. Finding his previous, detached style inadequate for capturing the ecstatic nature of the *denouement*, and having regained his post-Romantic voice, Zemlinsky sweeps all vestiges of restraint aside. His orchestra and singers now surge ahead with unapologetic abandon — Haitang's reunification with her child is awash in the lush, golden hues of operetta, and Pao's proclamations of joy are imbued with brilliant orchestration, remnants of Zemlinsky's Strauss-inspired days. Through two acts, the menacing atmosphere of *Der Kreidekreis* and the music of Berlin shaped Zemlinsky's musical thought, but in the end it was the magic of Klabund's fairy tale and Zemlinsky's lyrical roots that ruled the day.

On September 14, 1930, with the country in the grip of depression, Germans streamed to the polls to elect a new parliament. Starving and desperate, the population threw their support behind the Nazi party, which received 18 percent of the vote. Overnight, it was transformed from the smallest to the second largest party in Germany, and now commanded 107 seats in the Reichstag. Nazi storm troopers dressed as civilians and celebrated the victory by smashing Jewish storefronts and plundering restaurants. Under the leadership of Hermann Göring, the elected Nazi officials began undermining proceedings in the Reichstag, while outside Nazi agitators fanned the flames of fear and contributed to the rolling tide of street violence.

Amidst such an atmosphere, it was no surprise that the Kroll's 1930/31 season got off to a rocky start. The season was scheduled to commence with an updated version of *Il barbiere di Siviglia*, conducted by Fritz Zweig, but the premiere had to be postponed when internal conflicts erupted over the production. Janáček's opera *From the House of the Dead*, which had yet to receive a German premiere, was also put on ice in the wake of anti-German uprisings in Prague. A new production of *Tristan und Isolde*, to be conducted by

Klemperer, was completely scrubbed. Despite the string of setbacks, the Kroll conductors attempted to mount a quadruple bill juxtaposing several works of the twentieth-century: Ravel's *L'Heure espagnole* (Zemlinsky), Weill's *Kleine Dreigroschenmusik* (Klemperer), Debussy's *Jeux* (Zweig) and Hindemith's *Hin und zurück* (Klemperer). This effort was abandoned when it failed to ignite any interest.

After such a bleak beginning to what was expected to be its final season, Zemlinsky's December performance of Charpentier's *Louise* finally found success. The music critic Alfred Einstein, who had lobbied in support of the Kroll, hailed the performance as "continued proof of Zemlinsky's ability to capture all aspects of the music, from its finest nuances to its fullest sound" and hoped that all who were to decide the theater's fate in the coming days had been in attendance.[1] Zemlinsky carried his good fortune over into February when he led a production of *Madama Butterfly*. Moholy-Nagy's set designs, which previously had proven unsettlingly bold and experimental, were now praised for their naturalistic effect as the critics applauded the sliding stage, the bamboo structures and the running fountain. Although Einstein found Zemlinsky's interpretation "somewhat German", he acknowledged the warmth and colors he achieved,[2] while Oscar Bie of the *Berliner Börsen-Courier* felt that Zemlinsky had rarely achieved anything so beautiful and extolled the maestro's feel for "the candour and freedom of the canto-style".[3] It was perhaps the first time Zemlinsky ever garnered critical praise from opposing views!

Within weeks the Kroll's future was officially determined. Not surprisingly, this season would be the last. With the city's theater deficit continuing to rise, there was no support for continuing to subsidize a third opera house, particularly one so controversial. And so, the government formally passed the bill sealing the Kroll's fate. Members of Klemperer's entourage had been present at the Landtag for the pronouncement, and as Klemperer set off for home, Nazi thugs attacked in a conscienceless and brutal celebration of the news. It was only by jumping into a passing taxi that Klemperer managed to thwart the attack.[4]

The end came quickly. Zemlinsky's previous successes at the Kroll now held little meaning. The theater's dismantling was accompanied by a rapid decline in production standards. Preparation time was minimized and rehearsals, whether for operas or concerts, were curtailed. In one instance, Klemperer received the score of Webern's Opus 21 symphony just two weeks before its intended

[1] Quoted in Curjel (1975), 300.
[2] Ibid., 308.
[3] Ibid., 309.
[4] Curjel (1975), 82.

performance date, yet went ahead with the concert as scheduled. The Webern was greeted with laughter. Verdi's *Falstaff*, which opened in April, was similarly treated with half-hearted effort, although this time it was the designer Dülberg who was given too little time to prepare properly. With Dülberg unwilling to commit himself under such circumstances, Klemperer hired an unknown from Moscow's Central Children's Theater, whose operatic inexperience resulted in designs the critics chastised as tasteless and vulgar.[1] Klemperer's conducting was equally lackluster, but he no longer cared — he had already accepted a five-month engagement at the Teatro Colón in Buenos Aires. After leading two more performances of Verdi, the Kroll's apathetic music director packed up and headed for South America, abandoning the Kroll two months before its official closure.

In May, after much delay, the Kroll staged a fitting performance of Janáček's *From the House of the Dead*. The house was half empty. On July 3, 1931, at the conclusion of a performance of Mozart's *Figaro*, the curtain came down for the last time. A unique chapter in Berlin's musical and cultural life was finished. In response to a standing ovation, the entire Kroll ensemble assembled on stage: singers, orchestra, conductors, staff — everyone except Klemperer, who was now half a world away. With Leo Kestenberg's experiment officially dead, the conductor, who was then entering his prime and in high demand, had cut his losses and moved on. The Kroll experiment was over, and Klemperer's abandonment of the project in its final hours is but a footnote to the Kroll's failure.

The Kroll's fall prophesied a bleak future. Although cultural sophistication and innovation had been considered hallmarks of 1920s Berlin, these qualities were now regarded by the growing right as the socially disruptive effects of modernist decadence. Other progressive institutions soon met the same fate. One year after the Kroll went dark, the Bauhaus, Germany's leading avant-garde architecture and design school, was closed. Hoping to save the school, its director, Ludwig Mies van der Rohe, relocated from the Dessau location to an abandoned Berlin telephone factory, but his efforts were futile. A few months later the doors were permanently locked. And in March 1933, the newspaper *Die Weltbühne*, a forum for leftist and socialist thought, published its final edition before its presses were shut down. There was no longer a place for such ideas in the new world order.

In the weeks following the Kroll's closure, Heinz Tietjen, who oversaw all of Prussia's opera companies, set about finding alternative positions for those still under Kroll contract. To the 60-year-old Zemlinsky, Tietjen offered Klemperer's

[1] Heyworth (1983), 370–71.

former post as General Music Director of the Staatstheater in Wiesbaden.[1] In an earlier time, Zemlinsky would have taken on such a challenge eagerly, in spite of all the sacrifice and demands such a position entailed, but those days were now behind him. Moreover, Wiesbaden was provincial, and Zemlinsky had become protective of the time conducting spirited away from composing. After more than thirty years in the service of one institution or another, Zemlinsky decided that Wiesbaden was unlikely to bring him further musical gratification. Having no assurance that he would ever conduct again, Zemlinsky declined Tietjen's offer.

Momentarily opting to remain in Berlin, Zemlinsky accepted a contract at the Hochschule to take over a score-reading class previously taught by George Szell. Zemlinsky had long been aware of the younger conductor, whose formative years had mirrored Zemlinsky's — Szell's prodigious gifts as a composer and pianist had been similarly nurtured during his youth in Vienna, and he had since established himself among Europe's conducting elite. Professionally, Szell's career moved in a similar orbit to Zemlinsky's. Moreover, following an engagement as an opera coach at the Berlin Staatsoper, Szell had worked under Zemlinsky in Prague, albeit for only a single season, in 1919/20. In Prague, Zemlinsky openly acknowledged Szell's promising abilities to Alma, and expressed his willingness to help out his younger colleague, despite having little in common with him:

> There is much ado in the press about Szell, an inexperienced, capable and cold conductor with an excellent memory, because he accompanied Strauss on tour and because he is smooth, versatile, socially well-connected and knows how to be on good terms, but not on too good terms, with everyone. (Please, this is just between us! Szell knows a lot of jokes, and otherwise I am on very good terms with him. I don't know what he says about me but I remain entirely on his side and do all I can to further his interests.)[2]

Three years before Zemlinsky moved to Berlin, Szell returned as principal conductor of the Staatsoper and professor at the Hochschule, but in 1929 he left again for Prague, where he took up Zemlinsky's former position at the Deutsches Theater. Their mutual reversals of fortune — Europe's doors were opening for Szell just as Zemlinsky's were closing — could not have escaped Zemlinsky's notice.

[1] Biba (1992), 106.
[2] AZ/AMW.

Zemlinsky's Hochschule appointment lacked prestige, but it paid a professor's salary and required only about ten hours of work per week.[1] During this period Zemlinsky continued to travel to Prague, where he guest-conducted on a regular basis, despite the mounting political tension between Germany and Czechoslovakia. As late as 1937 he was guest-conducting one to three times a year, typically standard repertoire but occasionally leading more modern fare: a Hindemith Viola Concerto with the composer as soloist in 1932, Novák's Serenade for Small Orchestra, op. 36, in 1934 and the Suite for Small Orchestra of Emil Hlobil in 1936. But in Berlin in 1931, Zemlinsky embarked upon one of the most significant and satisfying experiences of his years in the German capitol.

Kurt Weill and Berthold Brecht's radical portrayal of injustice, greed, and gluttony, *Aufstieg und Fall der Stadt Mahagonny* (Rise and Fall of the City of Mahagonny), seemed tailor-made for a Kroll production, but although Klemperer had flirted with the idea of bringing the *Singspiel* to the Kroll stage in 1927, in the end he was unable to come to terms with the work.[2] When *Mahagonny* at last received its world premiere in Leipzig in March of 1930, a scandal reminiscent of Zemlinsky's Vienna days erupted. The brouhaha was not simply an issue of disgruntled conservative concertgoers. Rather, *Mahagonny* also affronted fascist Brownshirts. Klemperer, reportedly in attendance, left the theater speechless.[3]

Mahagonny finally played in Berlin in 1931, largely owing to the efforts of an impresario by the name of Ernst Josef Aufricht. Aufricht single-handedly raised enough money to rent the Theater am Kurfürstendamm, contract an orchestra, and hire a number of popular actors, including Lotte Lenya. Weill, impressed by Zemlinsky's extensive knowledge of the theater, requested Zemlinsky be engaged to conduct. By December of 1931, when rehearsals were in full swing, Weill knew he had made the right choice. Writing to Universal Edition, he exclaimed that Zemlinsky was "rehearsing from nine in the morning till one at night. Zemlinsky is really first class!!!"[4]

A blitz advertising campaign assured that *Mahagonny's* December 21 Berlin premiere would be a success. Karl Kraus promoted the production during his popular *Theater der Dichtung* (Theater of Poetry) series, where he recited excerpts. The non-traditional theatergoer was lured with the proposition that the boxing champion Max Schmeling would appear in the boxing scene.[5]

[1] Class was held only two days a week, on Tuesdays and Fridays, beginning at 3:30 pm.
[2] See Heyworth (1983), 295.
[3] Heyworth (1985), 78.
[4] Quoted in Schebera (1995), 164.
[5] Schebera (2004), 29.

Schmeling's cameo proved to be nothing but hype, but the performance exceeded everyone's expectations, as did the returns at the box office. During the next several weeks the work played to capacity. Its success is attributable to several factors, all of which came together at just the right time in Berlin's history: a powerful work of art, a stellar cast, a public hungry for artistic revolution amidst growing fascist resistance to modern art, and Alexander Zemlinsky, whom the musicologist Theodor Adorno regarded as "making the decisive difference":

> One must admit that Zemlinsky's conducting makes all the difference
> . . . He has finally freed Weill's music from the misunderstanding of
> élan, jazz, and devilish entertainment, and has shown its true essence:
> its smoldering, shrill, then again deadly sad, fading background, sharply
> contoured to reveal all the cracks and gaps, which a song-seeking public
> prefers to ignore; above all, in the sound he wrests from the wretched
> batch of instruments, which possesses an expansive power that leaves
> behind the diffuse sound of many larger orchestras; such is the sound
> when realized by Zemlinsky.[1]

By the time *Mahagonny* closed in Berlin early in 1932, the production had set a new record for contemporary musical theater, with an uninterrupted run in excess of forty performances.

In the weeks that followed, Zemlinsky fulfilled commitments in Leningrad and Prague. When he returned to Berlin, he resumed work at the Hochschule. His class roster from April of 1932 numbered twenty-five students, among them a pupil by the name of Bernhard Heiden. Heiden soon fled to the United States, eventually settling in Bloomington, Indiana. Years later he recalled that Szell and Zemlinsky "had one thing in common — they were unbearable!" Both were chain smokers that incited fear in their students, none of whom consequently wanted to be the first to enter the smoke-filled classroom. Heiden recalled Zemlinsky's penchant for biting remarks. "Is that all?" he would ask when they had executed the task set before them. Heiden remembered Zemlinsky's appearance as slight, even breakable, yet he was "very democratic in the destruction of all his students". While Zemlinsky may have been committed to the next generation, teaching at the Hochschule on a part-time basis must have been trying, especially coming on the heels of his recent professional misfortunes and the overall deterioration of cultural life he witnessed all around him. As Heiden told it:

[1] *Musikblätter des Anbruch* (1932), no. 2–3, 53–54.

There were two pianos in the room. They were not pleasant lessons and I'm sure he didn't want to teach. Imagine, all his life he wanted to compose, and he never quite had the opportunity to be one hundred percent a composer. Szell and Zemlinsky wanted to prove how much they knew and how much better they were, especially Szell. You came out of the lesson feeling as though you'd been through the wringer. Szell was a hard act to follow and he [Zemlinsky] might have been the only one who could.[1]

By the summer of 1932 Germany was once again knee-deep in recession. Thousands of small businesses failed, six million people were out of work, and Marxism was a growing threat, with Berlin in chaos. In June, President Hindenberg appointed Franz von Papen chancellor of Germany. Papen then called for new parliamentary elections, in hopes of winning a majority in the Reichstag. Instead, on July 31, the National Socialists won the day, garnering 230 seats, catapulting them to the largest and most powerful party in Germany. Several weeks later Papen's coalition dissolved when a majority in the Reichstag gave it a vote of no confidence, forcing yet another election in November. This time the Nazis lost seats. Although still the largest party in the Reichstag, the Nazis were nearly bankrupt, and Hindenburg declared his unwillingness ever to make Hitler chancellor. Joseph Goebbels, who had headed up Hitler's campaign, appeared beaten, and jotted in his diary that "All chances and hopes have quite disappeared."[2]

But the New Year ushered in a series of unanticipated events. Nationalist, conservative and anti-republican factions came to Hitler's aid, believing that together they could temper Hitler's lust for power while collectively staving off the country's growing discontent and the rising Communist threat. At the same time, intrigues within Hindenberg's cabinet led to several downfalls, including the resignation of the chancellor, General Kurt von Schleicher. In January 1933, Hindenberg, 85 years old, desperate and exhausted, gave in and appointed Hitler chancellor of a new coalition. That month, Zemlinsky presented Louise with the finished copy of his score to *Der Kreidekreis*, and at the start of February, Zemlinsky traveled to Prague to lead the Czech Philharmonic in music of Weber, Mozart and Smetana.

In the afternoon of February 17, 1933, a detachment of fifteen uniformed

---

[1] Bernhard Heiden, personal interview with the author.
[2] Friedrich (1995), 378.

Brownshirts stormed into the Berlin Academy of Arts during exam time, hauled four Jewish and Marxist professors out of their classrooms and into the street and proceeded to beat up any students who attempted to defend them.

Hitler quickly eradicated all expectations of shared power, and called for a new election, hoping the Nazi party would regain valuable votes. One week before the election, the Reichstag went up in flames. When Parliament reconvened within the walls of the defunct Kroll, Hitler, with no proof, blamed the fire on the Communists.[1] Even with the Red Scare and voter intimidation by Hitler's Brownshirts, the Nazis won only 44 percent of the vote, necessitating another coalition government. Still, once unified with the Nationalists, the Nazis now controlled 52 percent of Parliament.[2] By the end of March, Hitler was officially in control, astonishingly not through force but rather as the result of the democratic process.

On March 1, Max von Schillings, whose opera *Mona Lisa* Zemlinsky had conducted in Prague years ago, and who now served as president of the Academy of Art, announced in a faculty meeting that the Jewish musical influence must end. Schoenberg, who was in attendance, resigned immediately and left for Paris with his family, where he reconverted to Judaism. By the end of October, the Schoenbergs were in America.

Whereas Universal Edition had passed on publishing Zemlinsky's Symphonic Songs of 1929, by 1933 the Viennese publisher was again working on Zemlinsky's behalf and arranged for *Der Kreidekreis* to receive its world premiere in various German cities simultaneously, including Berlin, Frankfurt, Nuremberg and Cologne. In Berlin, the premiere was to be led by Klemperer—disenchanted with the musical life of Buenos Aires, he had returned to the Staatsoper. The April premiere was the single light flickering on the horizon for Zemlinsky, but in mid-March, as Hitler was ascending to power, Zemlinsky got word that his opera was on hold. The Reich had yet to establish its "official" policy regulating what could and could not be performed, but already its intent was clear where Jews and Jewish music were concerned. Before January, the attacks came by way of the Nazi press and through the disruption of concerts. By February and March, members of the Sturmabteilung (SA) began invading opera houses and threatening conductors. Klemperer and the Staatsoper drew attention in February with an unorthodox interpretation of Wagner's *Tannhäuser*, which

[1] Friedrich (1995), 383.
[2] Palmer (1992), 826.

Goebbels considered a travesty and which was marred by cries of disgust from attending Nazis. Before another Klemperer concert, a caller threatened to disrupt the performance, which was then cancelled outright "for reasons of public safety".[1] In view of these events, Heinz Tietjen refused to allow Klemperer or the Staatsoper to take unnecessary risks, writing to Klemperer in March that the choice to postpone *Der Kreidekreis* was "primarily preventative".[2] Universal Edition expected the other theaters around Germany to follow suit.[3]

Zemlinsky's letters to Universal during this period reflect frustration and anxiety. Zemlinsky knew that complications were inevitable in performance, but the current problems were new and sinister, and Zemlinsky was at a loss how to deal with them. What, Zemlinsky wanted to know, was the exact nature of the situation: "Are the problems with the libretto — the music — myself?"[4] For the moment, nothing was certain, except that Zemlinsky's case was not unique. Already in 1932 Ernst Toch's opera *Der Fächer* had been shut down in mid-rehearsal when storm troopers wrested the baton from the conductor's hand. Berthold Goldschmidt's opera *Der Gewaltige Hahnrei*, on the other hand, went more quietly. Scheduled for Berlin's Städtische Oper in 1933 following its successful Mannheim debut, it was simply cancelled with no explanation.[5] In Dresden, the music director Fritz Busch was manhandled in rehearsal and subsequently resigned. Although not Jewish, Busch was openly and vehemently opposed to Hitler and the Nazi Party. The Jewish conductor Bruno Walter, physically barred from conducting in Leipzig, requested police protection for a concert with the Berlin Philharmonic. Rather than honor his request, the authorities replaced Walter.[6] For Zemlinsky, Universal still held out hopes that his opera would premiere in mid-November, but because the new regime did not expect to have its people and policies in place before the end of April, the Staatsoper could make no decisions until it got the green light.

On April 7 all non-Aryans automatically lost their official positions when Hitler's government issued the Law for the Restoration of the Professional Civil Service. The list of composers, performers and conductors immediately dismissed was extensive. It included Klemperer at the Staatsoper and Schoenberg and Schreker at the Academy of Arts (Schreker had already been forced

---

[1] Meyer (1991), 23

[2] Quoted in Heyworth (1983), 415.

[3] Letters in the possession of Universal Edition.

[4] Letter to Universal Edition, April 10, 1933.

[5] Information generously provided by Michael Haas.

[6] See Meyer (1991), 23. Richard Strauss agreed to act as Walter's replacement, but only if his fee was donated to the orchestra.

to resign as director of the Hochschule the previous year). Schoenberg and Klemperer went on to find success beyond Germany's borders, but within a year of his dismissal Schreker was dead, the result of a stroke brought on by the event. Shortly after, Goebbels — now Reich Minister for Public Enlightenment and Propaganda — began restructuring Berlin's cultural scene.[1] Bernard Heiden recalled famous faculty being replaced by unknown Nazis who "came out from everywhere". With them arrived "incredibly bad textbooks" and the conductor and musicologist Fritz Stein, newly appointed to replace Schreker at the Hochschule.

In mid-April Zemlinsky left for Vienna, possibly to investigate a part-time position with the Wiener Konzertorchester, the Vienna Concert Orchestra. He arrived at the Pension Columbia, where he listed himself as an irregular or part-time (*Unterparteien*) resident of the city.[2] By 1933 residency applications required a declaration of religious affiliation, be it ethnic or practiced, and on Zemlinsky's Viennese document, "Israel.[itisch]" was typed.[3] Zemlinsky probably did not declare himself "Israelitisch" — it seems highly unlikely, considering his Protestant conversion and the climate of growing anti-Semitism — but must have had no choice in the matter. We cannot know for certain, but the end result was the same. Vienna's officials designated Zemlinsky a Jew.[4]

Hermann Scherchen's Wiener Konzertorchester was only two years old, but it filled a unique niche — it consisted largely of previously unemployed Viennese musicians and was dedicated largely, though not exclusively, to the cause of new music. However lofty his goals, Scherchen's experience and abilities kept them well grounded. He had helped found the ISCM, had assisted Schoenberg with preparations for *Pierrot lunaire* in 1911 and had founded the journal

[1] Goebbels' profound understanding of both these elements made him a powerful figure, as has been well documented. In 1938 he remarked, "The language of sound is sometimes more compelling than the language of words . . . music is an art that penetrates to the very depth of the soul." See Taylor (1997), 282.

[2] Berlin remained Zemlinsky's permanent residence until the end of September, at which time Louise, presumably unaccompanied, returned to Berlin and officially withdrew her family's residency status there. NLZ (Ab 1).

[3] Documents in the possession of the Wiener Stadt- und Landesarchiv.

[4] Zemlinsky would subsequently correct this oversight by declaring himself "Evangelisch" (Protestant) on similar *Meldezetteln* from 1933, 1934 and 1938. Still, while Zemlinsky may have no longer considered himself Jewish, others did, as is confirmed by the entry of his name in the 1941 edition of the *Lexikon des Juden in der Musik*. See Stengel (1941), 403–4. Zemlinsky's name was among those left out of the first edition (1938).

Melos, a forum dedicated to new music.[1] The writer Elias Canetti remembered Scherchen's approaching new music as a challenge to both his players and his audience:

> What interested him above all was to study and master a new composi-
> tion and — most important — to put it over, in other words, to present it as
> perfectly as possible to a public that had no related experience, to whom
> such music was unfamiliar, repellent and ugly. First he had to coerce the
> musicians, compel them to play this music as he wanted it played. Once
> he had the musicians in hand, the resistance of the public — the greater,
> the better — remained to be broken down.[2]

Scherchen, however, decided it was time to move to Switzerland, and he wondered if Zemlinsky might be interested in taking his place. Zemlinsky was as familiar as anyone with the risks a new musical enterprise entailed, particularly one dedicated to the cause of new music. But coming to Vienna seemed no more risky than remaining in Berlin — and, at the very least, the Konzertorchester might enable Zemlinsky to regain his footing in the city. So, on April 28, Zemlinsky wrote to Fritz Stein, requesting to be released from his Hochschule duties. Stein willingly consented.[3]

Less than two weeks later, Berlin university students began burning books by Jewish authors, stolen from libraries throughout the city. Setting them ablaze, they danced around the flames, crying, "Burn Karl Marx, burn Sigmund Freud." Heinrich Heine, whose pages were among those turning to embers and rising as ashes above the city, had once written, "Wherever they burn books, sooner or later they will also burn human beings."[4] By contrast, for Joseph Goebbels the experience was liberating:

> German men and women! The era of exaggerated Jewish intellectualism
> has come to an end! . . . You are doing the right thing at this late hour,
> consigning to the flames the intellectual garbage of the past. It is a strong,
> great and symbolic act . . .[5]

Zemlinsky returned to Berlin briefly to tie up loose ends. During his last

---

[1] Scherchen would go on to lead premieres of music by Berg, Webern, Roussel, Dallapic-cola, Stockhausen, Varese, Henze, Blacher and Xenakis.

[2] Canetti (1999), 619.

[3] Communication in the possession of the Hochschularchiv der Hochschule der Künste Berlin.

[4] Friedrich (1995), 385.

[5] From Goebbels' speech recited at the Berlin book burning, May 10, 1933.

days in the German capital, he had hoped to learn something about the future of *Der Kreidekreis*, but its fate still rested in the hands of Goebbels. Zemlinsky said his goodbyes and then headed to the Anhalter railway station, where he and his family had arrived six years earlier.[1] The musical promise and expectation of those days had long since been replaced by discouraging events and the dark shadows of politics; the Berlin on which he had pinned his hopes for a new future had failed him at almost every level. Whatever thoughts accompanied his departure, it is likely Zemlinsky believed he was leaving the Nazi threat behind him. After years of hoping, waiting and dreaming, he was finally coming home to Vienna.

[1] The Zemlinskys' final address in the city, where they had been living since 1931, was at Landshuter-Strasse 26, in the district of Schöneberg.

Chapter 11

Homecoming

T HE VIENNA TO WHICH Zemlinsky returned was a radically different city from the one he had left twenty-two years earlier. The once proud capital of the monarchy had been reduced to a fraction of its former glory with the disintegration of the Empire following World War I and the failure of world markets after the New York stock-market crash of 1929. Economically, Austria was in shambles, since a large part of its former manufacturing industry was now located in Czechoslovakia and Yugoslavia. With the country's former sources of food and coal also outside its post-war borders, production had dropped by 40 percent and unemployment was snowballing.

The city's physical landscape had also changed significantly, particularly in neighborhoods beyond the Ringstrasse, now dotted with new apartments. Among the initiatives undertaken by the Social Democratic government of 1922 was a massive housing project, launched to help alleviate shortages (particularly for the working class) and curb diseases like tuberculosis exacerbated by poor or non-existent housing. Throughout the 1920s, some 63,000 new municipal apartments went up, including superblocks, designed by the architects Adolf Loos and Josef Hoffmann, with indoor plumbing — still a novelty for the masses — stone-floored kitchens and wooden-floored rooms; or Karl Ehn's Karl-Marx-Hof, a veritable self-contained city, enclosing 1,382 apartments, laundries, co-operative food stores, kindergartens and even medical and dental facilities for its working-class inhabitants. Meanwhile, the urban middle class was throwing its support behind the German Nationalists, and there was a growing sentiment to unite with Germany.

The republic's first experiment with an elected government soon failed, as Austria continued to wallow in economic distress. In 1932, Engelbert Dollfuss was installed as the head of a new coalition cabinet, one uniting Christian Socialists with Agrarians, whose principal aim was to bring Austria's desperate economic situation under control. But with the victory in Germany of the National Socialists, Dollfuss soon faced a growing Nazi threat. Undaunted by his diminutive stature — Dollfuss stood less than five feet tall — or his political enemies, Dollfuss first attempted to stave off anti-governmental agitation by suspending parliamentary government. Then, in June of 1933, Dollfuss dissolved the Nazi party entirely, which merely intensified Nazi terrorism and fueled anti-Semitic activity. Nazi sympathizers soon roamed the streets, ransacking the university, Jewish coffee houses and businesses. Dollfuss was now ruling by decree.

Musically, Vienna was only marginally better than what Zemlinsky had left in Berlin, but only because Nazi policy was yet to determine the fate of Vienna's musicians and cultural climate. Given the current climate, there was little reason to celebrate his return. Indeed, he slipped back into the city practically unnoticed. He and Louise took an apartment located at Mariannengasse 28, to the south of the Volksoper, just doors away from the house where Gustav Mahler had died, but it's not known if Zemlinsky attempted to renew past acquaintances before the couple left again for the summer. Hoping to put some distance between themselves and the volatile environments of Berlin and Vienna, they headed for the Swiss village of Montagnola, a picturesque town overlooking Lake Lugano. There, Zemlinsky found peaceful surroundings and fresh creative energy. Inspired by August Eigner's *Und einmal gehst du*, a poem that cast autumn as a metaphor for old age, Zemlinsky delicately set Eigner's lyrics within a loosely tonal framework:

> There is no reason to hesitate, no reason to turn back . . .
> everyone must at some point set out on it:
> the journey into his personal autumn.

The twelve-line song would have taken only a few hours to write; yet it was all that Zemlinsky composed during their stay. Instead, he used the time for rest and reflection, enjoying Louise's company and the beauty of Montagnola and their surroundings. Nevertheless, the skeletal song and Eigner's text served as a prelude to Zemlinsky's Six Songs, op. 22. As with the Eigner, the collection of songs that Zemlinsky composed in the cold January following that summer was an exploration into the autumn of life, a theme with ever growing relevance.

When Zemlinsky returned to Vienna he was offered enough work to divert his mind from the disquieting dilemma of his and Austria's future. The first order of business was the world premiere of *Der Kreidekreis*. Because the German production was still in limbo, Zemlinsky's former student Robert Kolisko, the principal conductor of the Zurich Stadttheater, requested that he lead the premiere. A Swiss production was not likely to lead to future performances in mainstream Europe, nor would the opera be accompanied by simultaneous performances elsewhere, but Zemlinsky no longer was concerned with such details. Matters were hastily arranged, and the Zurich premiere of *Der Kreidekreis* was scheduled for October 14, 1933.

Hoping to cure Austria's economic woes and keep Austria free of German annexation, Chancellor Dollfuss secured a loan from the League of Nations by guaranteeing that Austria would not enter into political or economic union with Germany. Dollfuss had meanwhile thrown his cards in with Benito Mussolini, who recognized the value of Austria's serving as a buffer between Germany and Italy and who could provide Austria with much-needed military support. These events further agitated Austrian Nazis, and on October 3 a Nazi bullet narrowly missed Dollfuss.

Within days of the assassination attempt, Zemlinsky returned to Switzerland, this time without Louise. In Zurich, he initially harbored concerns about the quality of the production, but when the curtain finally rose all worries were laid to rest. As reported as far away as New York, the performance was an unqualified triumph:

> [Zemlinsky's] latest work, produced here at the Zurich National Opera House on Oct. 14, may prove his greatest artistic and popular success . . . Already at the opening performance, after the first act, there was a great ovation, while later on the composer was called repeatedly to the stage and the success of his work was extraordinary. Zemlinsky's "Kreidekreis" seems to be one of the best German operas of the last ten years.[1]

The critic of Switzerland's *Neue Zürcher Zeitung* was equally enamored:

> Zemlinsky is an immensely refined and distinctive colorist . . . a master to the highest degree who never sinks to the level of mere routine, but rather, loves stylistic and formal originality. Zemlinsky writes music that is not only distinctly unique but music that is also truly and deeply sensitive. [His] score, bearing the characteristics of chamber music . . . holds delights of rich, colorful nuance, delights which in the final analysis seem to result equally from the brilliant treatment of the transparent, discrete and tactful orchestral accompaniment.[2]

---

[1] *New York Times* (November 8, 1933).

[2] *Neue Zürcher Zeitung* (October 16, 1933), quoted in Hajek (1988), 161.

And three days after the opera's premiere, the *Neue Zürcher Nachrichten* reviewer wrote that not "since Berg's *Wozzeck* has such a well-composed opera created such a strong impression; upon leaving the theater one trembled and felt blessed by the art . . . this was one of the most beautiful performances at the Zurich State Theater that I can remember coming to pass."[1]

Zemlinsky, returning from Zurich with his star ascendant, now trained his focus on the Konzertorchester. While still savoring his *Kreidekreis* victory he led the ensemble on October 22 in music of Beethoven (Leonore Overture no. 3 and Symphony no. 5) and a set of Mahler songs. It was a consciously conservative program, one that would neither alienate his audience nor jeopardize the institution's shaky finances. Zemlinsky's years in Vienna had taught him to take seriously the city's love for its past, and he made it a point not to program modern works to the exclusion of the classical canon. Three concerts were ambitiously scheduled for the following month: Bach's Brandenburg Concerto no. 4, Hindemith's *Konzertmusik* for piano, two harps and brass, and Brahms' Symphony no. 4 (November 12); Mahler's *Das Lied von der Erde* (November 16); and Weber's Oberon Overture, Franz Schmidt's *Beethoven Variations* for piano and orchestra, and Schumann's Symphony no. 4 (November 26).

Toward the end of the year Zemlinsky finally received the long-awaited good news: *Der Kreidekreis* had been given the go-ahead to play in Germany. Opera houses across Germany scrambled to put things in order, and in the first few months of 1934 the floodgates were thrown open. Productions were staged in Stettin (January 16), Coburg (January 21), Nuremberg (January 25) and Graz, Austria (February 9). On January 23, Berlin witnessed the first of over twenty performances, and at the Cologne premiere a few days later the opera realized overwhelming success.[2] Productions in Bratislava and Prague followed toward the year's end. Throughout Germany, the reviews were, predictably, widely divergent. Many critics praised Zemlinsky's technique, his control and his colors. The Berlin critic H. H. Stuckenschmidt wrote, "one would have to be struck blind and deaf in order not to recognize the high level and high artistic worth of this (consciously restrained) music."[3] But mixed with the praise were other more scathing reviews, such as the vitriolic criticism of Fritz Brust of the *Allgemeine Musikzeitung*: "It is undoubtedly true that *Der Kreidekreis* does not gain depth by repeated listening."[4] Considering Germany's volatile sociopolitical

[1] *Neue Zürcher Nachrichten* (October 17, 1933), quoted in Hajek (1988), 160.

[2] K. H. Ruppel, "De Kreidekreis in der Staatsoper", *Kölnische Zeitung* (January 26, 1934).

[3] H. H. Stuckenschmidt, "Der Kreidekreis in Berlin", *Berliner Zeitung* (January 24, 1934).

[4] Fritz Brust, "Zemlinskys 'Kreidekreis' in der Staatsoper", *Allgemeine Musikzeitung* (January 1934).

climate, such polarized views were to be expected, and Zemlinsky and others would have undoubtedly discerned the anti-Semitic nature of the press that attacked his music because of his heritage. In spite of the occasional harsh word, at the age of 63 Zemlinsky was finally on the verge of realizing international acclaim.

The feeling was short-lived, as open doors quickly closed. In Stettin the chief of police, who had heard about the opera at second hand, canceled all subsequent performances. Shortly after, the rest of Germany followed suit. *Der Kreidekreis* was soon branded as *entartete Musik* — degenerate music unfit for German society. The classification was part of a larger program, overseen by Josef Goebbels, to purge the Reich of anything that threatened to pollute the purity of German culture. This program targeted music of all composers with Jewish lineage, dead or alive; among them Mendelssohn, Mahler, Schoenberg, Schreker, Weill and Korngold. The classification, however, did not stop with Jewish music. The designation *entartete* also encompassed anything the Reich deemed abnormal, Marxist, decadent, or simply a threat to the future welfare of German music or the German *Volk*. It included the work of Hindemith and Berg and any other composer who maintained connections with the Jewish world. And, of course, no music was tolerated that contained an objectionable racial identity, be it jazz or stage works involving Jewish or African characters.

The Reich's *entartete* classification also spilled over to modern art and literature, whether it was by Jews or it contained anything regarded as depraved, distorted or in any other way indecipherable. The list of banned artists contained well over a hundred names, from Marc Chagall and Oskar Kokoschka to the Bauhaus designer Laszlo Moholy-Nagy, and encompassed major artistic innovations, from Cubism, Fauvism and Post-impressionism to Dada, all falling under the "degenerate" umbrella. Over 5,000 works were seized and over 650 paintings, along with music and books, were gathered and featured in a traveling exhibition of *entartete Kunst*. The spectacle opened in Munich and moved on to other cities in Germany and Austria, assuring the German *Volk* that their Aryan culture had been cleansed of these unhealthy and undesirable influences.[1]

In Zemlinsky's case, the ban on *Der Kreidekreis* was not just a result of his Jewish heritage. The opera had thrust Zemlinsky to the epicenter of the Reich's ban; he was simultaneously composer, conductor, teacher, colleague and friend of many who fell victim to the *entartete* decree. The opera may have played

---

[1] Following the exhibition, Goebbels ordered a second, more thorough search, bringing the combined seizure of art to some 16,558 works. See Baron (1991).

behind an Oriental scrim, but its themes — prostitution, destitution, decadence, and above all governmental oppression — were particularly abhorrent to the Nazis. Zemlinsky's association with other known "degenerates", among them Schoenberg, Hindemith and Schreker, not to mention his Kroll associations, only further doomed his work. In arguably the most heartbreaking moment of Zemlinsky's career, *Der Kreidekreis* was struck from the repertoire at the very moment it appeared destined to triumph. Zemlinsky was never again presented with such an opportunity. In a life already plagued by more than its share of disappointments, this was surely among the hardest to endure.

Civil war broke out in Austria in the second week of February 1934. Following Dollfuss's decree that all parties except his would be dissolved, the National Socialists responded with a massive railroad, water and electricity strike, with the intent of breaking Dollfuss's authoritarian regime. As lights went out and the streetcars came to a halt, the chancellor called out the *Heimwehr*, the military arm of the Austrian right wing, with orders to suppress the uprising whatever the cost. Howitzers and mortars soon began assaulting the workers and their neighborhoods, with the fighting fiercest around the superblocks, particularly the Karl-Marx-Hof. During three days' time, government soldiers killed or wounded more than 2,000 workers. Stefan Zweig regarded the event as "no less than the suicide of Austrian independence".[1]

On May 1 Dollfuss instituted a new absolutist constitution; Austro-Fascism had crushed the Social Democrats. Still, Dollfuss' autocratic decrees were powerless to stave off the Nazi threat, a movement growing stronger daily. New members were actively recruited from all social strata, including civil servants, the police and the army. Then, on July 25, 1934, a second attempt on Dollfuss' life achieved what the first had failed to do — Austrian Nazis shot Dollfuss at close range and he subsequently bled to death. Although Western powers did nothing to slow the Nazi *Putsch*, Mussolini intervened. "Il Duce", not yet the Hitler ally he would soon become, mobilized Italian forces on the Austrian frontier to deter German aggression, and for a few short years Austrian independence remained secure.

By September 1934, Zemlinsky was no longer associated with the Vienna Konzertorchester. A posting in the music periodical *Anbruch* listed Paul Breisach, a conductor with the Städtische Oper in Berlin, as the ensemble's per-

---

[1] Zweig (1964), 385.

manent director and educator (*Erzieher*) for the 1934/35 season.[1] Whether
Zemlinsky stepped down of his own accord or was asked to resign for political
reasons is not known. All that is certain is that his first season with the orchestra
was also his last.

Released from all long-term professional engagements, Zemlinsky composed
leisurely, and the resulting flurry of activity surpassed anything he had exhibited for many years. Over the course of the next several years, Zemlinsky either
completed or made substantial progress on works in every genre, including
lieder, chamber music, choral and orchestral works, and opera. The first music
Zemlinsky composed following his return to Vienna was a set of six songs begun
in January 1934, while he awaited productions of *Der Kreidekreis* around Germany. After his previous forays into the exotic worlds of Tagore and the Harlem
poets, Zemlinsky now came home to Goethe and Christian Morgenstern and
set six of their poems to music — brief, tightly-knit reflections on the journey of
the soul. Zemlinsky never undertook their publication — they were published
posthumously in 1977 — but he regarded them as a unit and performed them as
such, and he personally designated them as his opus 22.

The collection opens with a gentle setting of *Auf braunen Sammetschuen*,
whose velvety evening Zemlinsky captures with an ascending pentatonic vocal
line in G-flat that tenderly unfolds against a gently pulsating piano accompaniment. A series of falling chromatic tones draw the ethereal opening back to the
weariness of earth before the cycle begins again a step higher. It is only with the
words "Sei ruhig" (be calm) that the piano's eighth notes find momentary rest.
Then, sinking back to G-flat, Zemlinsky allows the upward arching line from
the song's outset to bring Morgenstern's poem to a tranquil close.

Zemlinsky sets Morgenstern's *Abendkelch voll Sonnenlicht*, a poem of heartache and nightfall, in slow triple time but places the weight of each bar on the
second beat, lending the song the quality of an odd, intoxicated waltz. Intense
chromaticism and angular vocal lines create a further sense of disorientation,
with any feel for goal-oriented motion completely abandoned. Zemlinsky completes the picture with an almost total avoidance of tonal gravity, suspending
the music in a haze of seemingly unrelated pitches, and it is only at the two
major cadence points of the text where Zemlinsky offers even a glimpse of resolution. The effect is most acutely felt in the closing bars, where Zemlinsky allows

---

[1] *Musikblätter des Anbruch* (1934), no. 7, 156. In his single season with the orchestra, Bre-
isach revealed a passion for adventurous programming. In addition to performing works by
Krenek and Schreker, Czechoslovakia's Václav Tálich was invited to direct music of Berg and
Schoenberg, and Nicolai Malko conducted music of Bartók, Skriabin, Stravinsky and Adolf
Heller.

himself the luxury of a dominant–tonic relationship by suspending the word "sinken". But even this impression proves illusory, as the bitonal chords of the final bar wash away the tonal reference, leaving the poetry's secret unresolved.

Zemlinsky casts aside the fragile, transparent world of previous songs in favor of hardier textures and an energetic spirit to adequately capture the rallying call of Goethe's *Feiger Gedanken bängliches Schwanken* — misfortune must be countered by firm resolve. Vigorous Brahms-inspired arpeggios[1] at the outset introduce a series of impassioned vocal phrases that rise steadily in pitch and intensity over the course of the first four lines, a pattern that Zemlinsky repeats in the poem's second stanza. Over the course of the song's brief fifteen measures, Zemlinsky drives his music relentlessly forward until the closing bars, where he slackens the pace and draws out the words "kräftig" (strong) and "zeigen" (flaunt), paving the way for the song's heroic E-flat resolution.

Zemlinsky's *Elfenlied* offers momentary levity to the otherwise somber tone of the collection. While linked to its predecessors by its nocturnal theme, Zemlinsky shifts from the previously serious depictions of midnight, portrayed in *Auf braunen Sammetschuhen* and *Abendkelch voll Sonnenlicht*, to a world of elves who dance and sing at night while their human counterparts sleep soundly. Zemlinsky opens Goethe's nocturnal *Elves' Song* with a static rocking ostinato (B-flat–G-flat) in the piano's bass register, suggesting the still, midnight air of humankind. In contrast stands the magical world of the elves, which Zemlinsky aptly depicts with nimble arpeggiated chords and playful polytonal filigree in the piano's brilliant upper register. The song closes with an added refrain, now slowed considerably, allowing for a final presentation of the opening ostinato.

Morgenstern's *Volkslied* follows, a poem of love and loss that takes its place in the collection with its final lines: "O world, your delicacies / are not for me, for me!" The song is characterized by its languid rocking gesture that binds it unmistakably to the preceding *Elfenlied*. Zemlinsky pivots lazily between the unrelated keys of D major and F major, but relies on pentatonic scale patterns (reminiscent of *Der Kreidekreis*) and simple rhythmic figures to carry across the message of folk song. The music moves along innocently enough until those moments where Zemlinsky interrupts the flow by interjecting varying degrees of dissonance to underscore the ultimate plight of the lovers — beneath the "uns" (us) at the close of the first stanza, for example, or following the word "Glück" (happiness) at the conclusion of the third stanza, where an unprepared chromatic descent negates the moderator's conviction of happiness. Zemlinsky's set-

---

[1] Brahms's setting of the same text (*Beherzigung*), scored for solo choir as part of his Songs and Romances, op. 93a, bears no resemblance to Zemlinsky's composition.

ting of the word "nicht" (not) in the penultimate stanza of the song is the most unsettling. Here, a jarring piano dissonance brings home the reality of a love that cannot be.

Throughout most of Morgenstern's *Auf dem Meere meiner Seele*, the singer and pianist seem determined to remain in two separate worlds, the flurry of piano counterpoint continually at odds with the chromatically charged vocal lines. Against the undulating, *moto perpetuo* accompaniment, Zemlinsky's impassioned yet tonally free vocal line is held together by a single strand — the incessant recurrence of a terse rhythmic motive borrowed from the singer's initial entrance. At the start of the final verse, Zemlinsky momentarily incorporates the voice into the contrapuntal fabric by twice juxtaposing an ascending vocal line against a wave of descending piano cascades. Then, in a final burst of energy, the piano surges upward only to give way to the unexpected key of E major, bringing the entire collection to a jubilant conclusion.

Sporadic though they were, performance opportunities for Zemlinsky did arise. In May 1934, for example, the Vienna Symphony commemorated the fiftieth anniversary of Smetana's death with a program dedicated to the Czech master in the Great Hall of the Musikverein. Zemlinsky, whose well-known association with Smetana's music dated back to his Prague days, was invited to be guest conductor for the event. Zemlinsky also maintained his close ties to the city of Prague, visiting there several times that year. On three occasions he led the Czech Philharmonic in programs weighted heavily toward Mozart, Beethoven and Mahler, and in November he led the Prague Radio Orchestra in an all-Zemlinsky program that included his *Lyrische Symphonie*, Maeterlinck Songs, and selections from *Kleider machen Leute* and *Der Kreidekreis*.

Though Zemlinsky had no permanent position, the instability of his musical life at present posed little concern to him or Louise. Knowing they could depend on income from her family if matters became desperate, the couple began making plans to leave their apartment in the Mariannengasse. In 1934 a plot was purchased in the Viennese suburb of Grinzing, an area well known for its popular *Heurigen* or wine taverns, and work on a new house commenced. Louise planned to make the drive to and from the city in their recently purchased Ford.[1]

In June, Zemlinsky and Hansi departed for Marienbad, a well-known spa some 455 kilometers north-east of Vienna, while Louise oversaw work on the

---

[1] Weber (1995), 326.

Grinzing home. Located at Kaasgrabengasse 24, the single-level, Bauhaus-inspired structure featured a sort of temple hall as its center. The Zemlinsky's new home was hardly the last word in visual opulence, but it was definitely *en vogue*, having been designed by Josef Hoffmann's student Walter Loos. Neighbors included Sigmund Freud, Egon Wellesz and the writer Elias Canetti — reflecting the suburb's popularity with Vienna's artists and cultural elite — and Zemlinsky's boyhood friend and one-time student, Hugo Botstiber, whose father had founded the Polyhymnia Society so many years ago.[1] The location of their new house was especially appealing because of its proximity to the grave of Mahler, affording Zemlinsky frequent visits to the resting place of the late composer.

Zemlinsky continued to compose prodigiously, and by the start of July yet another composition was concluded, the Sinfonietta, op. 23. Zemlinsky had not written solely for orchestra since his B-flat symphony of thirty years ago, when as a young composer he sought to carve out a place for himself in Vienna. But for the past several months, Zemlinsky took advantage of uninterrupted stretches of time and gave himself freely to the Sinfonietta's composition. Gone, however, were the days of conforming to antiquated molds or obeying Conservatory rules, and though he could not bring himself to abandon his pedigree completely, he found a middle ground to express himself in a modern, yet accessible and personal language. Zemlinsky set himself strict parameters — he cast the work in three movements, kept the size of his orchestra modest,[2] and adhered to the classical ideals of clarity and restraint. Otherwise, he incorporated everything he had come to understand about orchestral composition: a mastery of form and counterpoint, virtuosic handling of orchestral forces, a severe economy of means. His score reflected the astringent language of the times, shot through with Zemlinsky's hallmark lyricism and wry humor. And it was all packed into less than twenty-five minutes. In a world becoming more menacing by the day, Zemlinsky turned inward and reveled in the mastery of his craft.

In his younger days in Vienna, Zemlinsky stressed to his students the significance of distinctly contrasting themes. The divergent material found at the outset of the first movement (*Sehr lebhaft*), a tight four-note motive brimming with Beethoven-like energy offset by an oscillating theme characterized by falling fifths, offers abundant proof that he continued to adhere to this traditional approach. The secondary theme is also a model of efficiency: by introducing it

---

[1] See Hilmar (1990), 113, and Beaumont (2000), 410.

[2] The score calls for two flutes, two oboes, two clarinets, two bassoons, four horns, three trumpets, three trombones, percussion, and strings.

as a variation of the four-note cell — which he now expands to the octave — and incorporating a portion of the introduction into mid-phrase, Zemlinsky exhibits the economical prowess he flaunted in his youthful chamber music. But beyond matters of technique, Zemlinsky also infuses the *Sehr lebhaft* with what Berg called "that genuine Zemlinsky-sound",[1] fashioning passages of great warmth, such as those found in the solo trumpet lines, the expressive string writing and the *gemütlich* Viennese *Ländler* at the movement's center.

Zemlinsky opens the *Ballade* with a series of imitative phrases in the winds and lower strings that solemnly introduce the building blocks for the rest of the movement: two pitches, then three, then a rocking two-note motive that brings the introductory procession to a close. The imitation is now carried over into the clarinet and oboe, whose yearning theme — spun from the former rocking figure — suggests the sound of street musicians Zemlinsky had heard as a youth in Leopoldstadt. Further transformations of the opening bars now occur, including a series of mocking gestures in the upper winds and a nostalgic violin phrase culminating in a two-octave *glissando*. The B-minor key signature is canceled at the start of the second section, where Zemlinsky forges a haunting atmosphere from a mysterious, pendulating ostinato that continues in various permutations until the movement's closing bar. Initial themes and keys then return as the ostinato ascends through the winds, concluding the movement in a shimmering haze. Berg, who heard the Sinfonietta in a radio broadcast in June 1935, regarded the *Ballade* as the high point of the entire work.[2]

The anxious *Rondo* comprises several ideas, each drawn loosely from the jaunty "tick-tock" pattern at the opening, a *pizzicato* figure that returns to distinguish the movement's three major sections. Following the spry introduction, the woodwinds enter with the principal theme, marked by two quick false starts and a long, unwinding answer that trips downward and spills into a passionate secondary idea shared by the strings and trumpets. A *tutti* outburst of the principal material then gives way to another pair of themes, a plaintive melody played by the oboe and echoed by the strings, and a cantabile theme dominated by the violins. The tick-tock ostinato nervously ushers in the movement's compact middle section, a whirlwind of contrapuntal activity where Zemlinsky virtuosically juggles several of these ideas at any given moment. The compact development comes to a head with the violins stubbornly locking in at half-tempo, until the ostinato — played by the bassoon — signals the concluding portion. After a quick review of the themes, the orchestra builds to a jubilant

---

[1] Weber (1995), 326.

[2] Ibid.

climax before evaporating, as the exhausted ostinato slows to a standstill. Following a brief flute cadenza, Zemlinsky rallies his forces a final time, driving the work to its brilliant closing bars.

Life, meanwhile, continued under the illusion of normality. Zemlinsky polished off two more songs, *Das bucklichte Männlein* and *Ahnung Beatricens*,[1] in December 1934 and January 1935 respectively. On February 13 he appeared in concert as pianist, accompanying the singer Julia Nessy in a program of songs by masters old (Peri, Cavalli, Scarlatti) and new (Debussy and Schoenberg). The recital, which took place in the small concert hall of the Musikverein, also included a premiere of Zemlinsky's recent lieder, the complete Six Songs, op. 22 (four of which had debuted in Prague the previous April). The journal *Anbruch* reported that Zemlinsky's art of keyboard accompanying was unsurpassable.[2]

A few days later Zemlinsky left for Prague, to attend the February 19 premiere of the Sinfonietta under the baton of Heinrich Jalowetz (Universal Edition had since accepted the work for publication). The next day, Zemlinsky crossed town to lead the Czech Philharmonic as a last-minute replacement for Václav Tálich.[3] He then returned to Vienna and his writing desk.

Intent on making up for years of lost time, Zemlinsky continued to compose at a feverish pace, revisiting another genre long absent from his portfolio — psalm composition. He had set psalms twice, a curious undertaking for someone with so little interest in religion *per se*. But Zemlinsky's previous attraction to the texts stemmed from specific needs, whether spiritual (Psalm 83, a means of coming to terms with the death of his father) or pragmatic (Psalm 23, a concert piece for Schreker's Philharmonic Chorus). Now, as Zemlinsky experienced the euphoria accompanying his recent string of premieres in the face of dark politics and an uncertain future, he looked for text that reflected his life. Psalm 13 — "How long wilt thou forget me, O Lord?" — was the ideal vehicle. With its transcendence from the anguish of abandonment to the exaltation of salvation, Zemlinsky found the expression he needed to offer his own hymn of thanks.

The work opens in darkness, without melody or harmony, offering only the dull drone of a D pedal, the hollow thud of the timpani and the listless strains of a clarinet ostinato. The optimism found in the Sinfonietta is initially replaced with heavy anguish, which Zemlinsky realizes with a directionless wind *cantus*

---

[1] Both songs were published with Zemlinsky's op. 22 by Mobart in 1977.

[2] *Musikblätter des Anbruch* (1935), no. 1, 26. The review appears to precede the recital!

[3] The program included an orchestral adaptation of the *Art of the Fugue* of Bach, a composer Zemlinsky had never actively programmed.

firmus, winding cello lines, and a wailing violin lament. The chorus enters, weighed down with sorrow, as their chromatic, contrapuntal lines complete the picture of a lost soul: "How long must I bear this pain in my soul and have grief in my heart all day?" The overall pitch and volume begins to build but the energy quickly collapses and the bleak strains of the opening return.

Zemlinsky now heightens the work's intensity by juxtaposing textures, first homophonically — "How long will my enemy exalt over me?" — and then by building to a dramatic climax with contrapuntal passagework for the entire ensemble. The tension turns quickly inward, as *ponticello* strings slithering chromatically over a C-sharp pedal in the brass and timpani evocatively portray life's passing: "I sleep the sleep of death." The battle is renewed with the orchestral interlude that follows, as Zemlinsky brings the various motives into direct conflict, playing them off one another in a wave of contrapuntal turbulence.

In a majestic chorale, the orchestra, organ, and chorus join together for a triumphant, E-flat major proclamation of God's mercy, followed by a brief dance of exaltation before relaxing into an extended passage evoking the mystical strains of ancient Israel: "I will sing unto the Lord." Now begins the transition to the concluding hymn of praise, proclaimed first by a majestic brass fanfare and swirling winds, and finally by the unison chorus, as the crowning D major orchestral glory of the Psalm's climatic closing bars overwhelms even the chorus. In the final measures, Zemlinsky transforms the bleak opening meters into a triumphant apotheosis, an affirmation that despite years of disappointment and neglect, perhaps a world still existed that could recognize value in what he had to offer.[1]

Zemlinsky put the finishing touches on the Psalm in the first days of April 1935. On June 4, he led the Vienna Symphony in a live radio broadcast of his Sinfonietta. Berg, who listened to the transmission, wrote Zemlinsky that the signal was both strong and without interference, and described the work's unmistakable color and the "true Zemlinsky sound, which was audible with every phrase".[2]

During the summer of 1935 Zemlinsky became absorbed with yet another

[1] Various performances of Zemlinsky operas were then occurring: *Der Kreidekreis*, for example, received its Prague premiere under Georg Szell's direction in December of 1934 and was repeated several times throughout the 1934/35 season, while *Kleider machen Leute* received a fully staged production in Zurich that season as well. Such performances, however, were of an increasingly isolated nature.

[2] Weber (1995), 326.

project, this one dating back to the days of Herodotus. The story, which the French writer André Gide adapted in 1901 and which was subsequently translated into German four years later,[1] revolves around King Candaules, a foolish king who entrusts his wife Nyssia to the fisherman Gyges. With the aid of a magic ring that renders its wearer invisible, Gyges seduces the Queen with Candaules' consent, but when Gyges confesses his act to the Queen, she demands Candaules' death. Gyges rashly follows her orders and slays the King. Overcome by his deed, Gyges pulls the ring from his finger and drops to his sovereign's side, only to be proclaimed by Nyssia heir to her slain husband's throne. As a potential opera, the story had much in its favor, including a blood-and-thunder plot and the requirement of a minimum of singers and set changes. If there were concerns about the plot's underlying sexuality, the matter didn't dissuade Zemlinsky from moving forward with his plans. Zemlinsky, presumably with Louise's aid, began constructing a libretto at the start of summer. In July, work on the short score began in earnest. And by September 15, Act I of *Der König Kandaules* was complete.

That very day the Nuremberg Laws went into effect in Germany, legally distinguishing Jews from non-Jews. With the Reich Citizenship Law, all Jews were stripped of their citizenship, and marriage between Jews and Germany's non-Jews became illegal. Believing that the purity of German blood was "essential for the further existence of the German people",[2] the Reich also passed the infamous Law for the Protection of German Blood and German Honor. Strict regulations were placed on Jewish marriages, relationships, employment, and even patriotic observances (Jews, for example, were forbidden to raise the national flag). Subsequent amendments would clarify the definition of what constituted "Jewish blood".[3]

Work on *Kandaules* suffered constant interruption nearly from the start. Within days of finishing the first act, Zemlinsky headed to Zurich for the Swiss premiere of *Kleider machen Leute*. From there he was off to Brno, where he led a series of highly successful performances of Mozart's *Le nozze di Figaro* at the

---

[1] André Gide's verse drama, *Le roi Candaule*, was translated into German in 1905 by Franz Blei, librettist of Hindemith's opera *Das Nusch-Nuschi*.

[2] Sax and Kuntz (1992), 406.

[3] For a description of the racial policies, see United States Chief Counsel for Prosecution of Axis Criminality (1946), 1417-PS. Racial policies aside, Zemlinsky's name was entered in the 1941 edition of *Lexikon des Juden in der Musik*, which reminded its readers that Zemlinsky also championed the 'degenerate' music of his brother-in-law, Arnold Schoenberg. See Stengel and Gerigk (1941), col. 403.

Landestheater.[1] Zemlinsky fit in time for *Kadaules* whenever possible, but when Alban Berg died on Christmas Eve, work on the opera came to a complete stop.

Months earlier, Berg had developed a painful abscess on his back, apparently the result of an insect bite, and in the weeks and months that followed the infection worsened, the pain increased and blood poisoning set in. Berg finally checked in to a Vienna hospital, but it was too late. Following an unsuccessful blood transfusion, the composer died on December 24, 1935, at the age of 50. His death came as a shock to the Viennese musical community, particularly as Berg himself had not realized the seriousness of his condition. Zemlinsky's contact with Berg had been sporadic since Zemlinsky's return to Vienna, largely because Berg lived on the Wörthersee, miles from the city. Nevertheless, Berg's death affected Zemlinsky greatly, and in the days after Berg's death, *Kandaules* was put aside and Zemlinsky commenced work on a new string quartet.

Since the mid-1920s Zemlinsky's relationship to Berg had grown from collegial to one of genuine friendship. Before coming home to Vienna, Zemlinsky had enjoyed spending time with Berg when he was in town on business, and each developed an admiration for the other's music. Zemlinsky took Berg's Lyric Suite — itself influenced by his own Lyric Symphony — as an organizational model and built his new quartet around a similar six-movement structure. Like Berg, Zemlinsky grouped the work in pairs of movements, a novel plan in light of the "single" overriding movement of the Second Quartet and the Third Quartet's return to the traditional four-movement scheme of his youthful Quartet in A major. In this Fourth (and final) Quartet, Zemlinsky establishes thematic connections between movements and moves *attacca* from one directly into the next; but he also creates associations by way of similarities of mood — movements I, III and V are slow and reflective, whereas movements II, IV and VI are fast and virtuosic. Taken as a whole, the Fourth Quartet, op. 25, represents a lyrically heightened approach to the genre, as opposed to the austerity exhibited in his Third Quartet, as if this tribute to Berg required a magnitude of emotional expression unattainable with an astringent vocabulary.

The first movement (*Präludium*) commences with a solemn, timeless chorale marked *senza espressione*, with echoes of an ancient, E-minor tonality. Over this static carpet of sound an equally sober violin enters, whose lyrical, improvised air eventually pulls the other members of the quartet into an increasingly active web of polyphony. At the *più adagio* Zemlinsky introduces a new theme, whose expressionistic leap of a minor ninth suggests the spirit of Berg

[1] Unidentified review of October 1, 1935. Moldenhauer Archive, Harvard University, folder HD bMS, Mus 261 (2011).

and which builds to a vigorous re-examination of the opening chorale. With a quick *glissando*, the instruments quickly slip back into the static opening and re-emerge transformed, while a series of ostinato patterns — a walking bass the most idiosyncratic of the group — join in support of the solo violin. After a final visit of the opening chorale, Zemlinsky gently closes the movement in E major.

The energetic *Burleske* is a virtuosic study of characters and textures, with Zemlinsky fully exploiting the technical limits of his ensemble. In four quick motions, the cello and viola warm to their task, launching into a *moto perpetuo* transformation of the *Präludium's* introductory motif, loosely imitated by edgy violin *pizzicati*. Zemlinsky then spins out a further set of variants, including a syncopated dance, a vigorous unison passage culminating *col legno* (played with the wood of the bow), and an expressive lyrical theme shared by the ensemble, relentlessly accompanied by the *moto perpetuo* figure. The tender D major trio recalls the ostinato passagework of the *Präludium* and offers gentle respite from the frenetic activity at its borders.

Although the *Adagietto* is characterized at the outset by its long winding lines, Zemlinsky slowly narrows his focus by concentrating on a pair of motives found at the outset — an expressive ascent of a fifth (violin) and its counterpart, a four-note turn (viola) that falls a fifth before righting itself. Both ideas are repeatedly compressed, inverted and expanded over the course of the next three minutes and become the sole points of interest as the movement's tension reaches its height. The movement's contrapuntal sobriety is immediately erased by the jaunty *Intermezzo*, which turns recent material into a bouncy theme with a foundation built of Bartók-inspired syncopation. As fragments begin to break off, the texture becomes increasingly polyphonic and the jagged theme develops a new linear identity, with both versions developed simultaneously. With an abrupt break, the ensemble unites for an extensive episode built around running sextuplets (*Animato*), which gets its start from the *col legno* passage of the *Burleske* and eventually pays passing tribute to the Presto from Schubert's Quartet in D minor, "Death and the Maiden". Zemlinsky then consigns the furious passagework to the background, where it serves as the accompaniment for a final review of the original dance.

Just months earlier Berg had confided his love for the "genuine Zemlinsky-sound". Now, as if in response, Zemlinsky acquiesces with an elegiac theme and variations (subtitled *Barcarole*), among the most overtly lyrical scores he composed in years. The mournful theme, which Zemlinsky gives to the cello alone, harbors no specific tonal center, but is nevertheless laid out in four clearly delineated phrases and, in stark contrast to Zemlinsky's Third Quartet, it remains fully identifiable throughout the course of the variations. Against a changing backdrop of moods and textures that includes the appearance of a gentle *Barcarole* rhythm in the third and final variation, the theme grows increasingly impassioned before returning calmly to the solo cello.

Until this point, Zemlinsky relied on counterpoint to provide textural contrast for a largely 'harmonious' composition, but the *Allegro molto* is built entirely upon polyphonic procedures. Out of the calm *Barcarole* Zemlinsky launches directly into a furious double fugue, whose primary subject harkens back to the *Burleske*. The counter subject, which enters following the cello's downward *glissando*, is drawn from the *Präludium's più allegro*, and throughout the exposition, the subject's jagged outlines become increasingly strident (the contours of the principal subject, meanwhile, grow rounder). At the coda (*più mosso*), a fugal *stretto* transforms the detached opening subject into a running pattern of triplets, and although the jagged second subject soon demands equal hearing, it is the primary subject that has the last word.

By April 1936, the Fourth Quartet was complete. As with his recently completed Psalm 13, there is no indication Zemlinsky had any particular designs for its future, although it's hard to imagine that something of such magnitude at this stage of his life could have been created simply for cathartic reasons. Whatever the case, as with the Psalm, Zemlinsky never had the opportunity to hear the work performed in concert, nor the privilege of seeing it in print. The Fourth Quartet first appeared in published form in 1974, Psalm 13 three years earlier.[1]

With the Fourth Quartet behind him, Zemlinsky picked up where he had left off with *Der König Kandaules*. *Kandaules* occupied him for the rest of 1936, and by the year's end the opera's final orchestration was nearly complete. In its present form, however, the score did not sit well with Zemlinsky, and he immediately commenced revising almost every bar of what only weeks earlier had appeared all but done. He sensed that the work lacked stylistic unity, a result of the string of interruptions to which it had been subjected, but, because Zemlinsky also came to regard the unfinished score as "ultra-modern",[2] impetus for the revisions may also have stemmed from a desire to adjust the tone accordingly. Whatever Zemlinsky's intentions, at some point he understood that the opera was unlikely to be performed any time soon in a German-speaking land, whether

[1] The Fourth Quartet, op. 25, received its premiere in 1967 (LaSalle Quartet), Psalm 13 in 1971.
[2] "Zemlinsky Comes to Live Here", *New York Times* (January 8, 1939). In reality, the music, an admixture of Zemlinsky-style lyricism set in a freely chromatic framework, was consistent with much of his recent work. The score does contain instances of bi- and polytonality, but overall it seems tame when compared to the work of some of Zemlinsky's contemporaries, such as the twelve-tone violin concerto Berg had completed just months before his death.

because of his Jewish roots, the story's sexual component, or Gide's publicly acknowledged homosexuality. So rather than simply spin his wheels, Zemlinsky set the score aside, perhaps hoping to take it up again at another, better time.

The threatening world of pre-war Germany was beginning to close in. Old colleagues were fleeing or making plans to do so. Schoenberg was in America; Berg, Schreker and Hertzka were no longer alive.[1] Alma, now married to the writer Franz Werfel, whose sonnet *Ahnung Beatricens* Zemlinsky had set at the start of 1935, still lived in Vienna, though she had recently lost her daughter Manon Gropius to polio (prompting Berg's dedication of his Violin Concerto "to the memory of an angel"). Zemlinsky's guest-conducting appearances were dwindling. He was no longer invited to conduct in or around Vienna. In 1936, for instance, his engagements were limited to Spain, where he conducted Smetana's *The Bartered Bride* and Dvořák's *The Jakobin* in Barcelona, and to several appearances in Prague, mostly for performances of Mahler, Mozart and Beethoven.[2]

Two poignant recollections of Zemlinsky from this period reveal a preoccupied and troubled man. The writer Elias Canetti encountered the musician frequently on the trolley, which stopped directly in front of Zemlinsky's Kaasgrabengasse address. Canetti, familiar with Zemlinsky's reputation as a conductor, often rode the trolley simply as a means of observation, and on occasion his gaze would fall on Zemlinsky without attracting notice. "The sight of him always intimidated me, I sensed his extreme concentration; his small, severe, almost emaciated face was marked by thought and showed no sign of the self-importance one would expect in such a conductor."[3] Hans Gál, a neighbor of Zemlinsky's, observed him in the Grinzing suburb, and described him thus: "He looked very old, very miserable, a broken man."[4]

In late March of 1937, Zemlinsky sat down to begin composing what forty years later would be published as his Twelve Songs, op. 27. Over the course of nearly five decades he had composed in excess of one hundred and twenty songs, whose musical range was as diverse as the poetry itself. His final twelve choices summed up his eclectic history with the genre: the Germans Goethe and Stefan George, the Americans Langston Hughes and Claude McKay of the Harlem Renaissance, and the 1,500-year-old Sanskrit masters Kalidasa and Amaru.

[1] Emil Hertzka had died in 1932.

[2] Mozart, Overture to the *Marriage of Figaro* and Piano Concerto in A Major, K. 488; Mahler, Symphony no. 9, February 12, 1936. Mahler, Symphony no. 8, May 25, 1936. J. C. Bach, Symphony in D Major; Hlobil, Suite for Small Orchestra, op. 7; Beethoven, Symphony no. 3, December 19, 1936.

[3] Canetti (1999), 797.

[4] From a BBC broadcast, quoted in Beaumont and Clayton (1995), 248.

The poems themselves were, on the whole, shorter than anything Zemlinsky had set before — brief but stimulating and eclectic texts that helped propel him beyond the stasis brought on by the *Kandaules* project, and which once again provided the impetus for a new, progressive means of expression.

Bearing the date March 31, George's *Entführung* was the first and longest song of the collection, a fitting start for what proved to be Zemlinsky's final compositional journey of consequence:

> Come with me, beloved child
> into the woods of far-off story,
> And as my gift keep
> Only my song upon your lips.

The song begins diatonically, but by the poem's second stanza Zemlinsky washes away any tonal reference with freely shifting harmonies, polytonality and the intense chromaticism common to much of the collection. Open-ended cadences further relax the formal contours of George's lines and suggest, along with the speed at which the overall collection was composed, that Zemlinsky's creative process was being governed, at least in part, by a stream of consciousness. The day after *Enführung*'s completion, Zemlinsky set Kalidasa's *Sommer*, a sensual, seven-line poem about the reawakening of the god of love, characterized by static dissonances and an accompaniment so transparent as to be almost non-existent. Two more Kalidasa settings followed on April 2, six-line miniatures that Zemlinsky continued to treat with delicate transparency — *Frühling*, a poem about love and desire colored with pentatonic flourishes and wide vocal leaps, and *Jetzt ist die Zeit*, a tightly knit, eighteen-measure song of fertility. On April 4 came *Die Verschmähte*, a poem by the Indian poet Amaru, where cold, economical counterpoint depicts a woman's rejection by her lover, and then Kalidasa's *Der Wind des Herbstes*, whose images of a sparkling crystal sea and luminous stars Zemlinsky portrays with right-hand piano arabesques.

In the second week of April Zemlinsky revisited the Harlem anthology *Afrika singt*. In Langston Hughes's *Elend*, a song punctuated by offbeats and falling vocal lines, Zemlinsky deftly portrays a woman jilted by her lover and comes as close as he ever would to capturing the sound of the blues. Then, returning to his own musical vernacular in Claude McKay's *Harlem Tänzerin*, Zemlinsky slowly transforms the *staccato* vocal rhythms and strident piano offbeats of the opening measures into passionate, expressive lines, as the narrator's focus moves from laughing youths to the swaying rhythms and the distant gaze of the sensual dancer at their center. On April 15 Zemlinsky offered a new setting of Hughes's *Afrikanischer Tanz* — which he had formerly set as part of the

Symphonische Gesänge — with energized rhythms and relentless ostinato patterns reflecting the beat of tom-toms and the dancer's stirring gyrations.

The final three poems of the collection are more in tune with the aging Zemlinsky of the quiet Viennese suburb of Grinzing. In *Gib ein Lied mir wieder*, Zemlinsky interprets George's fleeting, irretrievable images of an earlier day with disconnected vocal lines and an intensely chromatic yet weary piano accompaniment, lending an unmistakable air of sorrow to the text. Dated April 19, it was the last of the collection's twelve songs to be composed. *Regenzeit*, from April 2, mirrors the transparency and minimalist tendencies found in the earlier, seasonal Kalidasa poems, and the song's phrasing, which springs directly from the natural inflection and rhythm of the text, suggests that it too was composed quickly and instinctively. Inexplicably, Zemlinsky placed *Regenzeit* near the end of the collection. There is no such mystery concerning the location of *Wanderers Nachtlied*, Goethe's prayer for peace — though composed near the beginning of April, it fittingly closes the op. 27. Zemlinsky's setting is laden with fatigue, weighed down with weary piano chords and a vocal line that consistently comes to rest with tired, chromatically descending cadences, echoed in the piano's final notes. In setting Goethe's famous poem, Zemlinsky knowingly followed in the footsteps of two of his Viennese predecessors, Schubert and Wolf, but few poems could have better expressed his present state of mind or more clearly articulated feelings about an uncertain future:

> Ah, I am weary of being driven onward!
> To what end is all that pain and joy? —
> Sweet peace,
> come, ah, come into my breast!

As a conductor, two dates still remained on Zemlinsky's calendar, both in Prague. On December 3, 1937, he led the Czech Philharmonic in a program featuring the Schumann Cello Concerto, with Pablo Casals, and Mahler's Fourth Symphony. Zemlinsky's association with the Spanish cellist, exile and humanitarian dated back to 1912, when the two collaborated for the first time shortly after Zemlinsky's arrival in Prague. But it was Mahler's Fourth that brought Zemlinsky's long association with the Philharmonic to an end.

He returned to Prague at the start of January 1938, to lead a gala performance of *Carmen* in celebration of the Deutsches Theater's fiftieth anniversary. The American mezzo-soprano Risë Stevens played the role of Carmen, a role with which she later became closely associated. Stevens had first appeared in Prague two years earlier, when she made her début as Mignon in December 1936, and she returned to the Deutsches Theater frequently thereafter, with leading roles in operas from Mozart and Humperdinck to Wagner and Strauss. Stevens has distinct memories of Zemlinsky as a magnificent conductor, yet someone with whom she was unable to communicate personally, despite her great desire to do so:

> He didn't want to conduct Bizet, he wanted to conduct one of his own works, and I don't blame him. I remember that he was a very depressed man when he came to Prague. He wasn't very tall and he was very bent over. I remember that very well because I followed him and I tried to get him to speak with me, and he wouldn't. He was very depressed, very unhappy, and like so many in Prague, he found it very difficult to cope. If I'd only warmed up to him, but I couldn't. He would come into the rehearsal, go through the score sitting at the piano, and bingo, he was out. That was it.[1]

Stevens later recalled that he would not talk about anything. "He was getting itchy about getting away [from Europe], and luckily he did. I left and Hitler came through." Zemlinsky never ascended a podium again.

As January came to a close, the Vienna sky played host to an unsettling omen, the *aurora borealis*, which had not been seen in that city since the occupation of Napoleon's forces nearly 140 years earlier. Those who regarded the sign as an ominous premonition did not have long to wait until their fears were confirmed. One month later, the Austrian chancellor Kurt von Schuschnigg, who had succeeded the assassinated Engelbert Dollfuss in 1934, met with Adolf Hitler at the Führer's mountain retreat on Obersalzburg Mountain. Among other terms, Schuschnigg was forced to accept Arthur Seyss-Inquart, a Nazi official, as the Austrian Minister of the Interior. Had Schuschnigg rejected the terms, Hitler would have marched on Vienna within hours; but in the end, it was only the difference of a few weeks.[2] German units began rolling into the city on March 12, 1938. One day later, Hitler addressed the largest crowd ever assembled in Vienna, proclaiming the *Anschluss*, Austria's annexation by the German Reich. Three decades earlier, Hitler had come to Vienna to study art in the hope of making something of himself. Now the entire country was his. On April 10 the polling booths opened. Vienna's Jews stayed away, the Reich won 99 percent of the vote, and independent Austria was officially gone.

---

[1] Based on the author's personal interview with Risë Stevens.

[2] Back in Vienna Schuschnigg ordered a plebiscite to determine whether or not Austrians wished to remain independent of the Third Reich. When faced with a German invasion aimed at preventing the plebiscite, Schuschnigg resigned on March 11 and Seyss-Inquart was appointed chancellor. The following day German troops poured into the city.

Almost at once the arrests began. Seventy thousand people, including Christian Socialists, Social Democrats and anti-Nazi officials, were soon on their way to prisons and concentration camps. The police looked on encouragingly as Jews were harassed in the streets. Two weeks after the *Anschluss*, Hitler's second-in-command, Hermann Göring, announced that within four years Vienna would be *Judenrein*, cleansed of Jews: "The Jews do not like us. We do not like the Jews. They shall go."[1] Since Vienna's Jews made up 10 percent of the population in a country of approximately two million inhabitants, the Gestapo had its work to do, but it wasted little time. Jewish shops were soon looted, synagogues destroyed, homes targeted. One day during the occupation, two Nazis visited the Zemlinsky home under the pretext of needing Louise's help washing the floor of one of their barracks. After an extended discussion the soldiers left without her. Louise was aware that Nazis had begun seizing letters and documents, and, knowing they would soon return, she burned some eighty letters in their house. She also suggested that photos of Zemlinsky's Turkish-Muslim grandmother and Spanish-Jewish grandfather be destroyed, lest they betray his origins.[2] The time had come for the Zemlinskys to leave.

The attorney Alfred Indra, also the lawyer of Sigmund Freud, was contracted to negotiate a lease on their Kaasgrabengasse home. Until now the Zemlinskys had been in no hurry to join the *Auswanderern*, or emigrants, but a letter from Indra dated June 30 indicates a heightened sense of urgency:

> Dear Professor,
>
> I can fully empathize with your mood and I assure you that I feel particular compassion for you as a great artist, because I know from experience that sensitive people suffer particularly badly from the uncertainties of their situation. Therefore, you can be assured that I will do everything possible to help you as quickly as I can. However, I ask you to prepare yourself mentally for a period of three to four weeks; if I should be able to secure a settlement of this matter sooner that that, I would be most satisfied myself. However, I have very often seen that the acceptance of early deadlines, which then could not be met because of some circumstance, has had the most adverse effects on the nerves of those affected.
>
> Most sincerely yours,
> Alfred Indra, Attorney[3]

---

[1] Quoted in Fraenkel (1967), 468.

[2] Letter from Louise Zemlinsky to Peter Dannenberg, dated May 24, 1991, NLZ (Da 13).

[3] Moldenhauer Archive, The Houghton Library, Harvard University, bMS Mus 261(567) Indra, Alfred, folder 1.

The Zemlinskys were busy meanwhile setting things in motion, applying for exit visas and filing tax forms. Melanie Guttmann, Zemlinsky's childhood sweetheart and sister of his first wife Ida, was contacted in New York about her possible sponsorship of Zemlinsky and his family. Melanie, however, lacked the requisite financial resources, and, with no official sponsor, the Zemlinskys were left no alternative but to attempt immigration under the quota system, which sought to limit the number of refugees entering the United States each year. Fortuitously, the Zemlinskys found help in the person of Asa Friedmann.

Years earlier in Prague, Zemlinsky had taken Schoenberg's advice and hired a young singer by the name of Klara Kwartin. According to Kwartin, Schoenberg had been on hand for the audition and "urged Zemlinsky to give me a contract in the opera house then and there, before someone else grabs her".[1] Kwartin, the daughter of Zawel Kwartin, one of the century's greatest cantors, had three highly successful seasons at the Deutsches Theater (1924–27), during which time she also became a friend of Zemlinsky's. Contact between the two continued in the years that followed, and in 1927 Kwartin followed Zemlinsky to Berlin and sang at the Kroll. In the 1930s she immigrated to America, where she married a prominent New York radiologist by the name of Asa Friedmann.

Early in 1938 Friedmann came to the Zemlinskys' aid. In hopes of securing American visas for the Zemlinsky family, he took it upon himself to file affidavits and financial documents with the American Consulate in Vienna. In June, still awaiting a decision, Dr. Friedmann wrote to the State Department in Washington, D.C., stressing the significance of the Zemlinskys' immigration and the need for quick action. Willing to accept all charges for the cabling of information, Friedmann wrote:

> Professor Zemlinsky is an outstanding musical composer and conductor, formerly director of the Opera House in Prague and Berlin, a composer of many operas and a teacher of many of today's outstanding musicians. Professor Zemlinsky and his wife are independently wealthy in Europe but inasmuch as Mrs. Zemlinsky is Jewish they are probably suffering still more because of their wealth.[2]

At first it appeared that Friedmann's appeals would do little to expedite matters. Another two weeks elapsed before a cable from the Vienna Consul was sent to Washington stating that the Zemlinskys' status had been deemed satisfactory,

---

[1] Klara Kwartin-Friedmann to Clara Steuermann, May 11, 1977. Arnold Schönberg Center, Vienna (Kwartin-Friedmann Collection)

[2] Information provided by the National Archives, Washington, D.C.

but that present visa quotas would most likely push any final decision back to as late as the September or October of that year. On July 14, A. M. Warren, Chief of the U.S. Visa Division, informed Dr. Friedmann of the quota circumstances but assured him that "at such time as quota numbers shall become available for Professor and Mrs. von Zemlinsky's use, the Consul General at Vienna will accord as prompt consideration as possible to their visa applications."[1]

Arrangements concerning the house were finalized at the start of August. Indra leased the house to a Mr. Kurt Frick, who agreed to move in only after the Zemlinskys emigrated from the German Reich. Knowing that they could not remain in Vienna until their visas were issued, the Zemlinskys now planned to temporarily join Louise's family in Prague, a decision that necessitated obtaining Czech entry visas. On August 20 the Zemlinskys were notified about the processing of their *Reichsfluchtsteuer*, the tax levied on all emigrants, which amounted to one quarter of their savings.[2] Two days later, perhaps in need of a distraction, Zemlinsky began sketches for a quartet for clarinet and strings. With so much to be done and conditions hardly conducive to composing, it is not surprising that the work barely progressed beyond a skeletal stage. On September 7 the Zemlinskys were issued one-year passports, and three days later the family was in Prague. Zemlinsky would never again set foot on Austrian soil.

Two months later the Sephardic Synagogue of Zemlinsky's youth met its fate during the infamous and brutal *Kristallnacht*, the Night of Broken Glass, along with nearly every synagogue in Germany and Austria. The synagogue, whose history Zemlinsky's father Adolf had so beautifully documented in 1888, was first looted and then reduced to rubble. The historian Manfred Papo asserts that explosives must have been used to finish the job, as "fire alone would never have razed that solid building to the ground".[3]

Having taken refuge with Louise's mother Hanna, the Zemlinskys were granted a permit allowing them to remain in Prague until October 31, 1938, provided that Zemlinsky refrained from seeking employment.[4] October came and went without visa notification from the Viennese Consul, but on November 11 the appropriate documents were finally authorized. Knowing they would soon depart for America, efforts were made to convince Louise's mother Hanna to accompany her daughter and son-in-law to the New World, but even the argument that Czechoslovakia might share Austria's fate could not persuade the older woman to make the trip. And so, on December 2, 1938, the Zemlinskys

[1] Ibid.
[2] See Krones (1995a), 248.
[3] Fraenkel (1967), 346.
[4] Notice from the Prague Landesamt, NLZ (Ab 17).

bade Hanna goodbye and flew to Rotterdam. They then boarded the *S.S. Statendam*, and sailed first for Boulogne and then to Paris. On December 14 they embarked on their trans-Atlantic journey. Nine days later, on December 23, the Zemlinskys arrived in America.

Five years hence and safely on American soil, Louise received the dreaded telegram from her nephew Paul in Prague concerning her mother and her aunt Klara: "HANNA KLARA DEPORTED TOGETHER PROBABLY POLAND PARENTS VIA TEREZIN SIMILAR DESTINATION STOP ALL MISSING AFRAID LITTLE HOPE."[1] Paul's fears were justified. Louise's mother and aunt had perished in the camps.

[1] NLZ (Ac 15)

Chapter 12

"Zemlinsky Comes to Live Here"

> After one's sixtieth year unusual powers are needed in order to make an-
> other wholly new beginning. Those that I possess have been exhausted
> by long years of homeless wandering.
>
> Stefan Zweig[1]

T HE ZEMLINSKYS WERE MET with clouds and drizzle as they disembarked
at Ellis Island. Clearing customs, they proceeded to immigration, where
the waiting camera captured their images for identification. Bespectacled
and dressed in coat and tie, the 67-year-old Zemlinsky appears understandably
weary in his first American photograph, coming as it did on the heels of a trans-
atlantic ocean voyage prefaced by months of stress. Next to his photo on the immigration card, the first official document of his new life, Zemlinsky's country
of birth was labeled as Germany, his nationality as German, reflecting America's
de facto recognition of Germany's annexation of Austria.[2]

Having navigated through the first stage of American bureaucracy, Zemlinsky came face to face with Melanie Guttmann for the first time in forty years.
Melanie shepherded the family to the Hotel Hamilton on West 73rd Street, but
any details of their reunion, sadly, have been lost. Louise and Hansi had never
met Melanie, the sister of Zemlinsky's first wife and Hansi's aunt, but all were
grateful Melanie was there. Within days of their arrival, Zemlinsky enrolled in

---

[1] From Zweig's suicide note, reprinted in Zweig (1964), 437. Zweig took his own life on
February 23, 1942.

[2] Keyserlingk (1988), 57.

an English-language class for adults, and by February 1939 they were settled in an apartment at 46 West 83rd Street.

Zemlinsky was soon in touch with his one-time pupil and former assistant, Arthur Bodanzky, who had come to New York in 1915 and joined the ranks of the Metropolitan Opera as a specialist of the Germanic repertoire. By now a well-established resident of New York, Bodanzky did what he could to help his old friend restart his career in America. Within two weeks of Zemlinsky's arrival, Bodanzky arranged a luncheon date with Howard Taubman of the *New York Times*. Acting as interpreter, Bodanzky helped Zemlinsky navigate his way through the interview. Taubman, whose story "Zemlinsky Comes to Live Here" appeared in the *Times* on January 8, was interested in all aspects of Zemlinsky's life, not only his past but also his feelings about the state of new music and even his quest to learn English:

> He was evidently tackling the task scientifically. As he mastered a new word or phrase he would whisper it to himself, framing it between lips that were poised as carefully as those of a singer. Someone spoke the word "after." Mr. Zemlinsky repeated the word cautiously and smiled as Mr. Bodanzky nodded approval. "Somewhere between after and awfter, nein?" Mr. Zemlinsky asked reflectively, as if to carve it indelibly on his memory.[1]

Asked about Schoenberg's music, Zemlinsky hesitated before admitting, "I was studying the score of Schoenberg's recent work, his quartet for woodwinds, the other day.[2] I studied it measure for measure. To be frank, I do not understand it." It was a startling statement from the man who had once been one of Schoenberg's staunchest adherents, arguably his staunchest of all. Over the years Zemlinsky's loyalty to his brother-in-law, friend and colleague had repeatedly led to invitations and concerts of Schoenberg's music, first in Prague and later in Berlin. Now, Zemlinsky confessed he could no longer comprehend the music of the man whose cause he had once so ardently championed. Earlier, Zemlinsky had believed that one simply needed time to come to terms with the challenging nature of Schoenberg's music:

> I have infinite, boundless admiration for Mahler's work . . . it is my belief that before too long Mahler will be counted among the sacrosanct. I am not always of the same love for the late works of Schoenberg, although my immeasurable respect remains. I know from experience that with

---

[1] Howard Taubman, "Zemlinsky Comes to Live Here", *New York Times* (January 8, 1939).

[2] Zemlinsky meant the 1924 Wind Quintet.

those works that do not speak to me today, I can form a loving relationship tomorrow."[1]

But at sea in his new life in America, Zemlinsky could not see his way to tomorrow. Although the intimacy of their relationship had seen them through
many personal and professional trials, in the end their musical paths diverged
irreconcilably.

At lunch, Bodanzky also told Howard Taubman that Zemlinsky had a future
in America, teaching "composition, or conducting or harmony or counterpoint.
After all, such a musician can teach anything a musician needs to know." But
Zemlinsky had other ideas about his future; pedagogy, apparently, was not
among them. He now lived entirely to compose and turned first to resurrecting
Der König Kandaules. Again, Bodanzky seemed the logical resource. He possessed an intimate knowledge of Zemlinsky's music, and as musical director of
New York's Friends of Music, Bodanzky had presented the Maeterlinck Songs
in 1924 and Psalm 23 in 1928. In addition, he had gained valuable professional
perspective through his years at the Met. Surely Bodanzky would know if there
was a future for such an opera. Bodanzky read the libretto but was not encouraging — the nude scene alone, whether realized or imagined, would likely be the
opera's undoing. At Bodanzky's recommendation, *Kandaules* was shelved yet
again.

Soon another project surfaced, one involving the actor Walter Firner, brother
of Artur Feinsinger, a conductor who had worked under Zemlinsky in both
Prague and Berlin. Having recently arrived on American shores, Firner and his
wife Irma Stein were in search of a composer to set a libretto they had written jointly. Composed while in Europe, their work was based on the Homeric
legend of Circe, the sorceress who stirs Odysseus' passions and whose virginal
beauty transformed men into pigs. The Zurich State Theater had accepted the
project for production but the music had yet to be composed. Richard Strauss
had declined, possibly because of his unwillingness to endure any more med-
dling by Goebbels and the Nazi party, who had already admonished him for
collaboration with another Jewish author and librettist, Stefan Zweig. Now that
the Stein-Firners were in America, it quickly became apparent that Zemlinsky
was the composer they sought.

Zemlinsky was intrigued by the project for several reasons. Foremost, the
opera's subject matter, based on the wanderings of Odysseus, provided Zemlinsky with a return to the Greek mythological world he had abandoned with *Der
König Kandaules*. Centering upon the persona of the *femme fatale*, much like

---

[1] Undated letter to the *Musikpädagogischen Zeitschrift*, Vienna, quoted in Biba (1992), 106.

Kandaules, Eine florentinische Tragödie, and *Der Zwerg,* it was also a subject Zemlinsky knew well. And the likelihood of a Swiss performance was alluring. Zemlinsky had established relations with the Zurich theater's director, Karl Schmid-Bloss, during the highly successful production of *Kreidekreis* several years earlier, and Switzerland, a neutral country, remained a safe haven for Jews and the avant-garde.

Zemlinsky set to work immediately and by the end of March had completed a piano reduction for the first act of *Circe.*[1] But before much more progress was made, a new and unexpected opportunity arose. Bodanzky had recently introduced Zemlinsky to Max Dreyfus, a representative of the publishing firm of Chappell & Company. Max now approached Zemlinsky about composing popular songs.[2] Although not above composing for the Berlin cabaret years earlier, writing popular ditties for the masses was certainly not how Zemlinsky envisioned earning a living in his new life in America, or anywhere else for that matter. But with the family finances now shaky, Zemlinsky could not afford to be proud. Besides, such an opportunity might lead to other, more prestigious prospects. According to Hans Heinsheimer, a former employee of Universal in Vienna who later worked at G. Schirmer in New York, Dreyfus's offer came with a hitch — the songs were to be published under a pseudonym, a name with a safe, strong American ring: Al Roberts.[3] Zemlinsky agreed.

Work on three songs — *Chinese Serenade, My Ship and I* and *Love, I Must Say Goodbye,* again based on lyrics by Irma Stein-Firner — began at once, as did work on two school pieces, the *Jagdstuck* (Hunting Piece) for two horns and piano and a *Humoreske* for wind quintet. All were completed by July of 1939. When the songs were published one year later, for reasons unknown, Al Roberts never got the credit. Whether this had been negotiated by Zemlinsky or urged by someone else, Zemlinsky's real name graced the title pages.

Zemlinsky's health suddenly began to fail rapidly. After suffering a stroke that left him partially paralysed, he was beset with fainting spells throughout much of the second half of 1939, confining him to his bed for much of this time. Psychologically spent and physically broken, Zemlinsky moved around only with great difficulty. Work on *Circe,* which had barely progressed beyond a few hundred bars of the second act, was set aside and never taken up again. Since the middle of the year, Zemlinsky's colleague Arthur Bodanzky had also been

---

[1] Weber (1995), 279.

[2] Heinsheimer (1987), 13.

[3] Ibid. Inquiries to Warner/Chappell have failed to bring to light any contractual history between Zemlinsky and Chappell & Co.

ailing. When Bodanzky died from heart disease on November 23, Louise kept his death from her husband, fearing the news might crush him.

In the latter half of December, Zemlinsky received a visit from the conductor Fritz Stiedry, whose career had followed a path similar to Zemlinsky's, from Vienna's Volksoper to Berlin's Staatsoper. Stiedry had conducted the Leningrad Philharmonic before immigrating to New York, where in 1937 he assumed the directorship of the New Friends of Music orchestra. By 1946, Stiedry was a regular at the Met, specializing in Wagner and Verdi. While Zemlinsky and Stiedry had interacted little with one another in the past, in America Stiedry was sympathetic to his colleague's plight and came to visit. The energetic conductor Stiedry had known in Europe was gone by 1939, and in his place was a frail and wounded man. Yet Zemlinsky's faculties remained sharp. In a letter to Schoenberg, who was now living in California and teaching at the University of California, Los Angeles, Stiedry penned a vivid and insightful account of Zemlinsky's mental acuity, even in physical decline:

> A fortnight ago I saw Zemlinsky for the first time. He was sitting in his small bedroom at a table next to his bed, his left hand paralyzed, hidden shamefully under the table, his face not actually deformed but indeed strange. He spoke slowly, with occasional mistakes, but he spoke of everything and often with outstanding powers of recall. Since we all feared that my visit might excite him, it had been postponed. He knew nothing of Bodanzky's death, only that he was in the hospital with serious heart trouble . . . I left after half an hour and the following day his wife phoned me up. My visit had so pleased him that I was gladly invited to return. Because of two concerts my visit was postponed until last Thursday. On that morning his wife phoned me and in a shaky voice related to me that he had suffered another serious attack, was lying in bed and asked me to postpone the visit.[1]

Amidst concerns for Zemlinsky's health there was also cause for celebration. Several months earlier Louise's brother Otto had arrived from Europe, along with his business assets, both very welcome in the Zemlinsky home. Moreover, contact with the Schoenbergs had been re-established on American soil. Learning of Zemlinsky's health through his daughter Trudi in New York, Schoenberg had written immediately. Louise answered and brought Schoenberg up to date — her husband's health had improved to the point that he managed a few hours a day away from his bed and could walk in his bedroom a little, but everything

[1] Quoted in Beaumont and Clayton (1995), 254.

had to be undertaken with great care.[1] For the moment, however, Louise felt it best not to overwhelm Zemlinsky with the news of Schoenberg's letter. A second stroke followed, but Zemlinsky eventually found the strength to write to Schoenberg himself about his condition: "That which we experienced in Vienna and saw could only have resulted in a complete nervous breakdown."[2] Zemlinsky updated his old friend about others from their circle were also in poor health — Bodanzky (who Zemlinsky believed was still alive), Siegfried Theumann, a violinist and conductor who had taken part in the premiere of Zemlinsky's String Quartet in A Major, op. 4, who was dying of cancer, and Klemperer, who was undergoing surgery to remove a tumor from his right ear. Nevertheless, Zemlinsky held out hope to come west with the very first day of spring.

At the start of 1940 life appeared a bit less bleak. Schoenberg, thrilled with the thought of Zemlinsky's coming to California, assured his brother-in-law that the California air would do him well:

> I'm sure you'll be your old self again in no time, namely, the youngster you always were. Do you remember, in 1924, when you conducted my *Erwartung* in Prague, how we sprang over the guardrail into the orchestra pit, something the youthful oldies didn't dare do! I am absolutely sure that a week in the California climate will have us both jumping again.[3]

Schoenberg laid himself at his brother-in-law's disposal and expressed his willingness to help him find an apartment, inquiring how many rooms Zemlinsky desired and how much money he was willing to spend.

More signs promising a better life in America were evident in 1940. In February, the League of Composers presented "An Evening in Honor of European Composers Now Living in the United States", which included three Zemlinsky songs, *Entführung* and *Afrikanischer Tanz* from the op. 27 collection and *Abendkelch voll Sonnenlicht* from op. 22.[4] That same month, Zemlinsky informed Schoenberg he had heard a radio broadcast of Schoenberg's Second Quartet and his own Maeterlinck Lieder. Perhaps Zemlinsky had a future in America after all.

Following the advice of his doctor, Zemlinsky spent the next several months in the country, in hopes of becoming healthy enough to undertake the taxing journey to California. For the time being, however, the Zemlinskys remained in New York. Zemlinsky and Louise, and her brother Otto, who was also in poor

[1] Weber (1995), 274–75.
[2] Ibid., 276.
[3] Ibid., 278.
[4] Program in the collection of the Moldenhauer Archive.

health and no more fit to make the trek west than Zemlinsky, decided to build on some property in Larchmont, N.Y., about a half-hour's drive from Manhattan. In the meantime, leaving the city was in the best interest of both men, so the family moved to a Tudor-style house located at 68 Kewanee Road in New Rochelle. During the ensuing summer months, as both Otto and Zemlinsky enjoyed the fresh air and relaxed lifestyle of the small town, Louise oversaw work on their new Larchmont home, located just four and a half miles away.

Schoenberg was hard at work, but at long last, enjoying the fruits of his labors. In February he penned a letter to Zemlinsky, confessing that "One must work colossally hard in America if one is to earn one's bread — but it is indeed served up with a lot of very good butter."[1] In November, Schoenberg came to New York for a performance of *Pierrot lunaire* at Town Hall and it was during his visit that he was reunified with Zemlinsky for the first time since Schoenberg's abrupt departure from Berlin in 1933. Encouraged by what he saw, Schoenberg cabled home, "ZEMLINSKY BETTER THAN EXPECTED."[2]

In December, however, Zemlinsky took a turn for the worse. In the days following the bombing of Pearl Harbor, he suffered another stroke and was rendered nearly comatose. With Otto's health also deteriorating rapidly,[3] Louise found herself caring for two ailing men. Matters worsened when Otto passed away on Saturday, December 14. Grief-stricken, Louise handled the arrangements for Otto's cremation while continuing to nurse her husband. Zemlinsky's condition was so poor that he seems not to have known about the fate of his brother-in-law.

At 3:00 in the afternoon on December 29, Dimitri Mitropoulos led the Philharmonic Society of New York in a performance of Zemlinsky's Sinfonietta, along with music by Brahms, Chausson and Casella. In one of the few times of Zemlinsky's career, critics were united in their acclamation of his work. Olin Downes of the *New York Times* wrote:

> It was high time that a local audience should have been made acquainted with a score by the teacher and later the brother-in-law of Arnold Schoenberg and a composer credited with having exerted a lasting influence upon modern European music. It is clearly, wittily, cunningly wrought. It proved highly effective with the audience.[4]

---

[1] Weber (1995), 278.

[2] Ibid., 280.

[3] Quoted in Beaumont and Clayton (1995), 255.

[4] Olin Downes, *New York Times* (December 30, 1940).

And the *New York Sun* reported that

> Zemlinsky's music provided the deepest satisfaction. It has the surehand-
> edness which one would expect from a musician who was, among other
> things, Schönberg's teacher; but it also has a nub of quality, a kernel of
> expressiveness which are no common attributes of contemporary writ-
> ing. Though the work has no pretensions to superficial effectiveness, Mr.
> Mitropoulos made a remarkably resonant thing of it.[1]

Zemlinsky's music had triumphed, but it is doubtful he was conscious during the broadcast, or heard Louise read him the reviews and Schoenberg's cable
(he had tuned in from California): "JUST HEARD YOUR WONDERFUL SYMFONI-
ETTA [*sic*]. HOPE IT IS THE BEGINNING OF YOUR AMERICAN SUCCESS."[2] Because
of her husband's condition, Louise responded to Schoenberg's telegram, convey-
ing Zemlinsky's appreciation and deep admiration for his brother-in-law.[3]

Little is known about Zemlinsky's final year, but as Louise attended to him,
his health continued to decline and their time together neared its end. The attention demanded by the Larchmont home provided the only distraction. Over
the winter, as its old-world, gingerbread charm slowly took shape, Zemlinsky's
health steadily worsened; by March 1942, when the house at 81 Willow Avenue
was finally ready to become a home, it's doubtful if Zemlinsky was sufficiently
lucid to appreciate its quaint beauty. With his vital organs failing, he was reduced to a diet of pureed vegetables and fruit and was ministered to at home by
a Dr. Gustav Reiter. On March 13, 1942, pneumonia set in, the result of a cerebral
hemorrhage. Two days later, on March 15, Zemlinsky's life was over. He was 70
years old.

The *New York Times* obituary reported that Zemlinsky died early on the morning of the 16th,[4] but in truth he had been pronounced dead on March 15 at 8:15
pm. An unidentified obituary cited the Zemlinsky address as 81 Villa Avenue,
no doubt a result of Louise's accent — she would have pronounced Willow as
"Villow".[5] Both papers, along with the *New York Herald Tribune*, erroneously
published Zemlinsky's age as 69, not 70, most likely because Zemlinsky's date
of birth for years had been recorded in biographical entries and elsewhere as

[1] Irving Kolodin, *New York Sun* (December 30, 1940).

[2] Weber (1995), 279.

[3] Ibid., 279–80.

[4] *New York Times* (March 17, 1942), 21.

[5] NLZ (Ibb 3).

1872, something he had never bothered to correct. Zemlinsky was cremated on March 18 and his ashes buried at Ferncliff Cemetery in Hartsdale, N.Y., beside Louise's brother Otto.

In 1945, Louise Zemlinsky sold the Larchmont home and moved to an apartment on New York's East Side. She continued to paint and lived to witness the renaissance of her husband's music. In 1989, Louise established the Alexander Zemlinsky Fund, located in Vienna's Musikverein, where Zemlinsky had attended the Conservatory and where he frequently returned as composer and conductor. One year later she established the Alexander Zemlinsky Composition Prize at the Cincinnati College-Conservatory of Music. Louise died in 1992, at the age of 92. Years earlier Johanna, Zemlinsky's only child, had moved to Hampstead, N.C., a bedroom community just outside Wilmington. She died on November 30, 1972, at the age of 64.[1] Johanna never married.

In July 1985, Zemlinsky's remains were transferred to a grave of honor in Vienna's Zentralfriedhof, the Central Cemetery, where Beethoven, Schubert, and Brahms are also buried. The site was fitted with a marker bearing the following:

Zemlinsky

1872–1942

As the final insult of an indifferent world, an erroneous birth date had been etched into Zemlinsky's gravestone.[2] Still, for the very last time, Zemlinsky had returned to Vienna, the city of his birth, the city of his most conflicting emotions, and the city to which he was inextricably bound and from which he proved to be ultimately inseparable.

---

[1] Obituary in *Wilmington Morning Star* (December 2, 1972), 24.

[2] The date was eventually changed to reflect accurately the year of Zemlinsky's birth as 1871.

Epilogue

The Zemlinsky Revival

I N 1921 ARNOLD SCHOENBERG addressed the question of Zemlinsky's lack of renown as a composer at a time when Zemlinsky was savoring some of his greatest conducting triumphs in Prague. Aware of the challenges Zemlinsky was already facing as a composer, Schoenberg acknowledged that time alone would have the final say:

> Zemlinsky will first be appreciated as his mastery deserves when his librettist pleases the public. Only then will they see how hard it all is to understand, even when one has good ears and understanding. And some will also then understand why even I, who am not out of practice and despite the ebb and flow of friendship and loyalty, can only begin to grasp this beauty and profundity through repeated listenings. And I shall be excused for it, because by then people will hear his operas often enough also to perceive the music in them.
>
> But for that there is time: Zemlinsky can wait.[1]

And wait he did. Little notice was taken of Zemlinsky's contributions in the years following his death, and for decades Schoenberg's optimism did not come to pass.

Louise made some of the earliest attempts to generate interest in her late husband's music. A year after his death she wrote a number of conductors, among them Eugene Ormandy and Serge Koussevitzky: "May I take the liberty of approaching you with the idea of a possible performance . . . ? Needless to say, I would be very happy over any interest you may show in my husband's

---

[1] *Der Auftakt* (1921), nos. 14–15, 228–30.

works, and shall be delighted to let you see his manuscripts."[1] All her requests went nowhere. Zemlinsky's music was occasionally heard on European airwaves, however, and in 1955 *Der Kreidekreis* was even staged in Dortmund, but these were isolated events, curiosities, token nods to an overlooked composer.

It was only in 1960 that one of Zemlinsky's former students was actually in a position to help. Peter Herman Adler, who had studied with Zemlinsky at the Prague Academy for Music, arrived in America shortly after the Zemlinskys and later toured with the NBC Opera Company, serving as a co-conductor with Toscanini. In 1959 Adler was appointed Music Director of the Baltimore Symphony, and less than one year later Zemlinsky's music was on the orchestra's schedule. In November 1960 Adler led a performance of the Sinfonietta, and in April 1965 the conductor engaged William Warfield to sing the *Lied aus Dixieland* from the *Symphonische Gesänge*. But Adler's interest in Zemlinsky's music was a rarity. There were others, of course, who had known Zemlinsky in Europe and who had since attained conductorships of prominent American orchestras, men like William Steinberg in Pittsburgh and Boston and George Szell in Cleveland, the latter of whom had led the 1934 Prague premiere of *Der Kreidekreis*. Like many American orchestras, these ensembles were playing a considerable amount of new music, but Zemlinsky's scores weren't among them.[2] Adler alone dared to program Zemlinsky's music, and his efforts, sadly, had no lasting impact.

Ironically, it was a small ensemble with international appeal that is most often credited with sparking the Zemlinsky revival. Founded in 1949, the La-Salle String Quartet was among the foremost interpreters of the quartets of Schoenberg and the Second Viennese School, but until the early 1960s, Walter Levin, the ensemble's founder and first violinist, had been unaware that Zemlinsky had ever composed quartets, since none were in print or had been performed for decades. Then, around 1963, Levin happened across a score of Zemlinsky's Third Quartet during a routine visit to a Manhattan music store. Although Levin had only a vague notion of who Zemlinsky was, he had a sense that this music would be a natural fit for an ensemble committed to the scores of Zemlinsky's better-known contemporaries.

---

[1] Letter dated June 10, 1943, in the Koussevitzky collection of the Library of Congress.

[2] Indeed, between 1950 and 1965 American orchestras played works by 343 American composers, whether immigrant or native-born. For more on the repertoire of American orchestras, see Hevner (1973). The music of Gustav Mahler, meanwhile, was experiencing a renewal probably unprecedented in the history of Western music. With the celebration of the centennial of Mahler's birth in 1960, the interest in his music surged, aided in no small part by the work of Leonard Bernstein, whose Mahler performances developed a strong following. Soon Mahler's music was among that most frequently performed and recorded.

Individual quartet parts were not available in the early 1960s, so each member of the ensemble played from a copy of the score. According to Levin, he and his colleagues quickly became intrigued by the sound of the music:

> It had a tone entirely of its own. It was not avant-garde in any way but there was something sparse about it that attracted us. It was something that had to do with the post-WWI period in Germany, when there was an anti-Romantic feeling such as that found in Weill and *Mahagonny* and so forth. The Third Quartet was short, with a fabulous variation movement, and in every respect was both expressive and yet negative. It was not a work that painted a beautiful world — anything but. It represented very much what I think is the character and personality of Zemlinsky.[1]

Levin's enthusiasm for the music was bolstered by a discussion with Igor Stravinsky in Cincinnati, where the LaSalle ensemble was in residence. Though totally unfamiliar with Zemlinsky's work, Stravinsky remembered well Zemlinsky's prowess as a conductor and waxed enthusiastic about the ensemble's commitment to performing his music.

When the LaSalle quartet gave the American debut of the Third Quartet on March 16, 1964, it was the first time any of Zemlinsky's chamber music had been heard outside Europe. The ensemble then turned to Zemlinsky's demanding Second Quartet, which they eventually offered to record for Deutsche Grammophon (DG). But despite the ensemble's prior success with their recordings of Schoenberg, DG was wary of investing in Zemlinsky. According to Levin, nobody thought a string-quartet recording of Zemlinsky, a name totally unfamiliar to classical music audiences and record buyers, would sell, nor did DG want to import it to America. Eventually DG acquiesced, and in 1978 the first recording of Zemlinsky's chamber music was made. What happened next came as a complete shock, even to the LaSalle members themselves. Their recording became a best-seller and developed a cult following. The way was now paved for the LaSalle ensemble to record Zemlinsky's other quartets. The First and Third Quartets were recorded in 1980, the Fourth a year later. And in March 1981, the LaSalle quartet performed the entire quartet cycle over the course of four evenings at the Vienna Konzerthaus. The ensemble's pioneering efforts signaled the first major resurgence of Zemlinsky's music after his death and hinted that, if championed, it would gain a following.

At approximately the same time that the LaSalle String Quartet was recording Zemlinsky's quartets, Peter Ruzicka, a German musicologist, composer and

---

[1] Personal interview with the author.

conductor, and a man with a passion for Zemlinsky, was on a parallel course to record a number of Zemlinsky's large-scale compositions for the first time. In 1979 Ruzicka was appointed artistic director of the Berlin Radio Symphony Orchestra (RSO), and within a year of his arrival the orchestra recorded the *Lyrische Symphonie* and the Sinfonietta, issued as LPs on the Schwann label. Schwann and the RSO soon followed with *Eine florentinische Tragödie* and *Der Zwerg* (revised and retitled *Der Geburtstag der Infantin*, The Birthday of the Infanta).

Zemlinsky continued to inspire champions of his music. In 1981, for instance, the baritone Dietrich Fischer-Dieskau and the conductor Lorin Maazel recorded the *Lyrische Symphonie* for DG with the Berlin Philharmonic. Then came the conductor Riccardo Chailly. Though initially unfamiliar with Zemlinsky's music, he soon embraced Ruzicka's passion for the orchestral and operatic scores. In 1982, Chailly was appointed chief conductor of Ruzicka's RSO, and it was with that ensemble that he recorded *Die Seejungfrau* in 1986 and Symphony no. 2 a year later, both on the Decca label. When Chailly left Berlin to assume the post of principal conductor of Amsterdam's Royal Concertgebouw Orchestra, his dedication to Zemlinsky's music did not wane. In Amsterdam, Chailly made several significant Zemlinsky recordings, among them *Eine florentinische Tragödie* and the *Lyrische Symphonie*.

By now Zemlinsky's operas were experiencing a renaissance throughout Germany.[1] The revival was set in motion with a production of *Eine florentinische Tragödie* in Kiel in 1977. Three years later, *Der Traumgörge* was staged in Nuremberg. The next decade of Zemlinsky's resurrection belonged to Hamburg and Peter Dannenberg, chief dramaturg of the Hamburg Staatsoper. Dannenberg's repeated commitment to Zemlinsky productions soon established Hamburg as the new center for Zemlinsky opera. Between 1981 and 1988 *Eine florentinische Tragödie* and *Der Zwerg* were paired and performed twenty-four times, including traveling performances in Edinburgh and Vienna. Building on his

[1] Ironically, the institutions with which Zemlinsky worked most closely were among the slowest to stage modern productions of his operas. It was only in 1992 that the Prague State Opera (the former Deutsches Theater) finally produced *Eine florentinische Tragödie* and *Der Zwerg*, despite Zemlinsky's having spent sixteen years there. The first modern production of Zemlinsky at Vienna's Volksoper came only with its 1997 production of *Der König Kandaules*, and as of this writing the Vienna's Staatsoper's most recent staging of a Zemlinsky opera was its 1923 production of *Der Zwerg*. *Eine florentinische Tragödie*, meanwhile, was heard at the Theater an der Wien in 1985. It was not until 1993 that Zemlinsky's name reappeared on a Vienna Philharmonic program, when the orchestra re-created the infamous Scandal concert of 1913. A year earlier Zemlinsky was the subject of an exhibition sponsored by Vienna's Archiv der Gesellschaft der Musikfreunde, entitled *Bin ich kein Wiener? — Alexander Zemlinsky*.

success, Dannenberg turned next to *Der Kreidekreis*, which received fourteen performances between 1983 and 1985. Dannenberg left Hamburg's Staatsoper in 1987, but Ruzicka, Dannenberg's successor, carried on the institution's commitment to Zemlinsky. The Staatsoper remained at the forefront of the Zemlinsky operatic revival through 1996, the year it gave the world premiere of Zemlinsky's *Der König Kandaules*, in an orchestration by Antony Beaumont.

In the mid-eighties, as Zemlinsky's music was finding ever larger audiences, advances in digital recording and the advent of the compact disc resulted in significant changes in the recording industry. As recording and compact-disc production became less expensive, recording companies began investing in projects involving less well-known composers and compositions. Zemlinsky's music benefited directly from these changes. Late in the decade, for example, DG contracted a handful of some of the world's greatest vocalists, including Barbara Bonney and Anne Sofie von Otter, for world-premiere recordings of many of Zemlinsky's songs. But Zemlinsky's music played a role in an even more visible and ambitious recording project, one undertaken by a London/Decca recording producer by the name of Michael Haas.

In 1988 Haas became involved with Decca's plans to record all of Kurt Weill's stage works, a project for which the label had allocated £2 million. But early on, complications with the Kurt Weill Foundation led to the project's collapse. Haas, sensing a rare opportunity, suggested the London label use the funds for another purpose — to record music he had learned about through his Weill research, music the Nazis had branded degenerate. The result was Decca's *Entartete Musik* series, which the label officially launched under Haas's direction in 1993. A host of conductors, singers and German orchestras were contracted to record works by composers such as Erwin Schulhoff and Viktor Ullmann, who both perished in concentration camps, Schreker's student Ignace Strasfogel and Erich Wolfgang Korngold, Zemlinsky's one-time student who went on to become one of Hollywood's most successful movie composers. It was also under this critical series that a number of Decca's earlier Zemlinsky recordings were re-released, including Chailly's recordings of *Die Seejungfrau* and Psalm 13 from 1986, thus providing Zemlinsky's music with still broader visibility.

As late as 2000 the series was still going strong, but unfortunately the economic interests of the music industry began to trump artistic decisions. By now Seagram had at a huge cost acquired PolyGram — London/Decca's parent company — and then folded it into Universal Music, and no recording project, not even with financing, could be justified if there was no expectation of a significant profit at the end of the day. According to Haas, "Even meetings with Edgar Bronfmann, head of Seagram and the World Jewish Conference, did not help. The series never lost anything. Its problem was that it didn't make big profits!"[1] And so the project was killed off.

In the mid-1990s Zemlinsky's music found a new advocate in conductor James Conlon. During Conlon's thirteen-year tenure as General Musikdirektor of the Gürzenich Orchestra and the Cologne Opera, which began in 1989, Conlon established himself as one of Zemlinsky's staunchest champions. *Die Seejungfrau* and the Sinfonietta were the first Zemlinsky scores Conlon recorded. *Der Zwerg* came next. In the years that followed, Conlon and his colleagues recorded all of Zemlinsky's orchestral works, his music for chorus and orchestra, his symphonic lieder and three of Zemlinsky's operas. This series of recordings on the EMI label represents the most comprehensive collection of Zemlinsky's music recorded to date. In Paris, Conlon's production of *Der Zwerg*, the first in France, was so successful it was brought back a second time, and in Italy, Conlon's performances of Zemlinsky were firsts for two of the country's leading houses: La Scala in Milan and the Maggio Musicale Fiorentino in Florence. Conlon's commitment to the music of Zemlinsky and other "degenerate" contemporaries remains intense and unflagging. Conlon enthusiastically continues to familiarize audiences across the globe with Zemlinsky's work.

Zemlinsky's music is no longer the exclusive domain of major labels. Once only large companies such as EMI, DG, Schwann and Decca had the resources for recording projects of this nature. However, independent labels like Capriccio, Chandos, Koch, Jecklin and Pan soon began to pursue such projects. Indeed, it was on labels such as Koch and Capriccio that the operas *Sarema*, *Der Traumgörge*, *Es war einmal* and *Der Kreidekreis* were recorded for the first time. With the smaller labels filling the gaps, nearly all of Zemlinsky's music has found its way to compact disc. The diverse locations for many of the recordings reflect just how international Zemlinsky's appeal has become: operas recorded in France and Denmark, orchestral music captured in Bratislava, the songs committed to disc in Japan. As of this writing, fourteen professional ensembles have recorded Zemlinsky's string quartets, works once the exclusive domain of the LaSalle String Quartet. That various incomplete and unfinished scores have also been recorded is further testimony to Zemlinsky's present day appeal.

The surge of interest in Zemlinsky's music has similarly been reflected in the publishing industry. As the included work-list reveals, much of Zemlinsky's music was published for the first time only after his death, particularly in the 1970s and again in the 1990s. The extensive number of published scores, along with the availability of numerous manuscripts located in the Library of Con-

---

[1] Personal interview with the author.

gress, has greatly benefited both performers and scholars, the latter who have mined Zemlinsky's *œuvre* — songs, piano works, operas, chamber music, orchestral and choral works, and theater music — for books, dissertations, articles and symposia.

All of these events have enabled Zemlinsky's music to reach an ever-expanding audience. Owing to the increasing frequency of Zemlinsky performances around the world it is difficult to track them all, although those registered with Vienna's Universal Edition reflect the exponential growth his music has experienced over the past few decades. Between 1990 and 1999 Universal charted 202 performances worldwide, a number that more than tripled between January 2000 and December 2007.[1] The figures continue to grow, as do the venues. In 2008 Zemlinsky was heard in Annandale-on-Hudson,[2] Basel, Darmstadt, Dresden, The Hague, Jerusalem, Leipzig, Linz, Lleida, London, Los Angeles,[3] Madrid, Oslo, Saarbrücken, Santa Barbara, Songerborg, Vienna, and Walnut Creek, California. And at the time of this writing, Zemlinsky performances are scheduled in, among many other places, Adana, Athens, Barcelona, Gdansk, Nice, Osaka, Tokyo and Turku.

At the close of 2005 an original Zemlinsky manuscript turned up in a most unusual location: Sotheby's of London. A rare event for a Zemlinsky score, the auction was all the more interesting as it involved the sale of the Cello Sonata in A minor, a composition previously lost. The Sonata, whose whereabouts had been unknown even as late as 2000,[4] was expected to fetch in the region of $10,000 on the international market. The work had been performed only once, when Zemlinsky and the cellist Friedrich Buxbaum debuted the recently completed composition in the Vienna Musikverein in 1894. Then, for over a century, it disappeared and went unheard. With time, the British musician, broadcaster and journalist Fritz Spiegl and Peter Wallfisch, father of the celebrated English

[1] See www.universaledition.com/calendar#composer=796, using the search facility at the right side of the web page (accessed March 31, 2010).

[2] In the summer of 2007, Leon Botstein led performances of *Eine florentinische Tragödie* and *Der Zwerg* with the American Symphony at Bard College, deep in New York's Hudson Valley. The occasion marked the first time Zemlinsky's one-act operas had been heard together on American soil. It is understandable that any opera company or festival would carefully weigh the financial burden associated with such a production (in this case $1.2 million), particularly since Zemlinsky's music, despite its increasing popularity, still remains unfamiliar to many audience members.

[3] February 2008 marked the first Zemlinsky operatic performance by a major American company, when James Conlon and the Los Angeles Opera staged *Der Zwerg* alongside Victor Ullmann's *Der zerbrochene Krug*.

[4] Beaumont (2000), 476.

cellist Raphael Wallfisch, learned of the Sonata's existence and attempted to bring it to light, but it wasn't until 2005 that the score was finally published.

The hammer fell on the manuscript for £18,000,[1] or upwards of $32,000, definitive proof that Zemlinsky's music, even a relatively early composition, has gained monetary as well as historic value. Within months of its publication, cellists around the world scrambled for performance rights to the sonata, and in short order, three recordings of the work were released on commercial disc, further evidence of Zemlinsky's continuing rise in popularity.

In a letter to Franz Schreker, Zemlinsky once wrote, "You know, we — you, Schoenberg, I and others of like minds — will, for the time being, be able to win over only a small number of people, but good ones, for our endeavors."[2] Over time, the power and approachability of Zemlinsky's music has won over inestimable admirers. Zemlinsky no longer waits — his time has come.

[1] See http://www.sothebys.com/app/live/lot/LotDetail.jsp?sale_number=L05412&live_lot_id=215 (accessed March 26, 2010).

[2] Weber (1995), 331.

Afterword

N AN AGE of show business, commercial popular art, and commercialization of classical art, many serious artists' voices today are drowned out in a sea of noisy superficiality. Exactly a century ago, on the eve of the First World War and the disintegration of the European "world order", it was a very different world. High art enjoyed an exalted status, and though artists competed with each other, it was with a seriousness peculiar to its time.

Alexander Zemlinsky was born into that environment, lived and developed in it, and passed the very end of his life exiled from it. He was not buried under the cacophony of a media-dominated popular culture. He wrote his music, practiced his multidimensional art, and lived his life. The fact that his music met with less public success than that of many others and, in my opinion, less than it deserved, resided as much with his personality as with the confused and turbulent times. That he was forgotten completely after the Second World War has much to do with the massive destruction perpetrated by the Third Reich.

It is not necessary for me to recount Zemlinsky's life, as Marc Moskovitz has done just that. I feel I can, and should, recount my own very personal experience with his music. I do so not in the spirit of autobiography, but because my experience has given me insight into the core of the phenomenon of forgotten music. My knowledge of the composer and his music started from zero, the same point from which nearly everyone recently started, or still find themselves today.

The first part of my story is shared by the vast majority of musicians and music lovers in the world. I had spent my entire student years and approximately the first two decades of my professional life knowing only Zemlinsky's name and, initially, having a vague notion of his proximity to Mahler and later to Schoenberg. Never having heard any of his music, he meant no more than any other unknown figure from the past. Now, as I look back, it is a part of the tragedy of this lost music that, even I, as a practicing musician, who had spent every day since the age of 11 studying and learning the most diverse music, from

Bach through the contemporary music of the last decades, had never been exposed to his music nor even to a person who suggested that I should be. Mine is the common experience. If this is true for professional musicians, it is even more the case with the general listening public.

Toward the late eighties and early nineties, I started to hear Zemlinsky's name more often, especially in Germany. At some point in the early nineties *Die Seejungfrau* figured on a list of suggestions of rarely played works which the dramaturge of the Gürzenich Orchestra in Cologne had given me. I noted the name, but nothing more.

And then, by an extraordinary and fateful happenstance, after a performance at the Cologne opera and a late-night dinner, I switched on my car radio while making the short drive to my home. I was struck by the beauty and opulence of what I heard. I tried guessing what it was, and could not. When I arrived in front of my door, I was afraid to turn it off for fear of not learning what it was; it would have haunted me like the lost chord. The announcement was strongly to impact the next decades of my professional life: *Die Seejungfrau* by Alexander Zemlinsky.

So, I thought to myself, *that* is Zemlinsky. I recalled the list of suggested works, immediately set about to get a score and to program the work for the following season. But even then I could not know what was in store. I asked for several other scores at the same time, and started poring over them. Around this the time, the recording label EMI asked me what I might want to record. *Seejungfrau* was my first suggestion, and another work was needed to complete the disk. This obliged me to quickly familiarize myself with several other pieces for orchestra. I settled on the Sinfonietta; the length was perfect, and the balance between an early and a late work was ideal. The recording was made and well received.

I continued to research as much as I could. Extensive biographical material was hard to come by at that time, and scores were not always readily available. Shortly thereafter, sponsorship money became available to underwrite performances of works first played in Cologne. I jumped at the opportunity, knowing that *Der Zwerg* had been premiered at the Cologne Opera under the direction of Otto Klemperer.

Three live performances and two "patch" sessions later, the recording was produced, released and met with sufficient critical success that the decision was made with EMI to continue and to try to record the entire output of orchestral works and as many operas as possible. At the end of my thirteen-year tenure in Cologne, all of the orchestral works (including lieder and choral music) were done, as well as three of the eight operas.

How the recordings came to be is not particularly important. What *happened to me*, however, is an indication of what potentially could happen to anybody. Learning *all* of Zemlinsky's music, at least in two genres, had so permeated me that I found the same need to return to his music as I did for, say, Mozart, Mahler or Wagner. It had fulfilled at least two of the most important elements of what, in my mind, constitutes a classic: it has transcended its time, and acquaintance with it breeds the desire to hear it again and yet again.

For the musician, difficult pieces present a challenge, and mastering them provides one of the great satisfactions for any instrumentalist or conductor. When the task is done (if one can ever say that it is), an important point is reached. Is the piece still interesting in such a way that one thinks, "Now I am at the beginning"? Or, for whatever reason, does it seem that the deciphering of the mechanism and structure of the piece was, in fact, the end of the process? From this point on, it is a matter of personal preference. But to my mind music of ongoing significance belongs to the first group, and, after several years, it was clear to me that Zemlinsky's music was not only worthy of performance, it was worthy of repeated performances.

This last point is for me important. Unknown composers are often resisted through ignorance and lack of familiarity. Unfortunately, our classical musical institutions are heavily dependent on being able to sell their programs with well-known repertory. While there may be nothing wrong with that, it militates against the presentation of works by composers whose names are not familiar. Zemlinsky is such a case. He, like others, has fallen victim to clichés of our time: "If you haven't heard of it, it can't be good", "There are no lost masterpieces", etc. To these I would counter that though it is an axiom of our market-oriented society to assume that the best product will always float to the top, it simply does not apply to art. I invite anyone who thinks that there are no lost masterpieces to meditate on the ravages of war that have destroyed art and humanity since the dawn of civilization. They would be proposing, in effect (if they need one amongst thousands of examples), that only the pre-Columbian art we know is valuable and none of what was lost.

So it is with Zemlinsky. Unplayed music is the equivalent of lost art. It is irrelevant if a manuscript exists and the score is published if it is not performed and heard. Music lives in performance, and grows with repeated hearings. Zemlinsky was a highly significant figure in his time, equally adept as a composer, conductor, pianist and teacher. He struggled for recognition as a composer. He did not always get it, and his reticence, or indifference to self-promotion, contributed to his difficulties. But throughout history the "struggling artist" has been a staple, the norm rather than the exception. The intrinsic value of the music should be our only criterion for judgment, and this necessitates making its acquaintance in performance.

There are divergent viewpoints as to why Zemlinsky's music encountered resistance, and they are dealt with in this biography. One that consistently strikes me is that, living in a century in which reductionism and categorization played a powerful role, nobody knew where to place him. Too modern for the conservatives, and too resistant to the avant-garde, he did not fit into convenient categories. Of course, no artist or work of art is obliged to do so. A work of art has only to be consistent with its own essence. If that is confusing to others, so be it. Judging a category of works, or judging a work by its category, is to do it a fundamental injustice. No one could easily line up for or against Zemlinsky because he had a singular voice, to which he remained obstinately true.

He passionately loved the human voice, and the marriage of word and music. The vast majority of his works reflects this. When one counts the lieder, the operas, the choral works, the orchestral song cycles, one quickly sees that apart from the string quartets (which stand among his greatest works) there is not much left. As with many passions, he was to pay a price. His music could never serve as a vehicle for others. There was no piano literature, no concertos, and very little music for orchestra alone. Even his masterpiece (the Lyric Symphony), requires two great singers and cannot serve as a vehicle for the orchestra and conductor. This did not escape the attention of his publishers, who pushed him to produce the Sinfonietta so that, in their words, those conductors too vain to share the stage with others might champion his orchestral works. In fact, Dimitri Mitropolous' performance of the Sinfonietta with the New York Philharmonic was the only occasion one of his works was performed in the U.S. during his lifetime.

It is now easy to overlook that certain great composers in the twentieth century were largely ignored except for one or two well-known pieces. Sibelius is an excellent case in point. He was, for many, the composer of *Finlandia* and a violin concerto. His name travelled the world because virtuoso violinists played his concerto. It took well over half of the century before his prolific output was universally recognized. Had Zemlinsky written a violin or piano concerto, the story might have been different. Had he written symphonies or orchestral pieces that were relatively easy to produce, it might have been different. Had he had a better business sense, or ability for self-promotion, it might have been different.

But one thing is sure; the Nazi regime pounded the nail into the coffin. No struggling artist can overcome a public ban on his or her music. The Nazi suppression of Jewish artists finished the story. The post-war years, for deeply complex reasons, treated Zemlinsky (and many others) no better.

For musicians and musicologists, the complexity of his music, its technical structure, its examples of motivic development, are all worthy of study. The effort is highly rewarding. Like his Viennese contemporaries, he threaded the needle of the Brahms/Wagner polemics with his own synthesis. The compositional discipline of Brahms and the harmonic, theatrical and dramatic aspects of Wagner's genius were in no way lost on him. Schoenberg felt that Zemlinsky understood the exigencies of music theater better than anyone else in the twentieth century.

I admire and love all of this in his music, as I do his honesty and courage in remaining true to his own voice, in the face of resistance. He was a part of the avant-garde so long as it was consistent with *his* nature. But when it went forward, he went another way. It is not that he couldn't continue in the same direction as Schoenberg, because I am sure he was technically capable of anything. He *would* not. He was to pay for his convictions, both in his lifetime, and above all, in the post-war period of compositional orthodoxies.

This is the time to hear his music — all of it. With its deep humanity, passion, eroticism, fearless portrayal of ugliness and beauty, it captures the seismic (Adorno's metaphor) turbulence of his times, and renders it meaningful today. Judgments, if they must be made, should be based on a deep knowledge of his works, not on superficial acquaintance, a casual hearing or *a priori* opinions. Tokenistic performances of his works are useless (as they are for all music). Passionate, committed performances will eventually make their point.

My own experience has convinced me that his time will come, as Mahler said about himself and Schoenberg suggested about Zemlinsky. It may take another generation to penetrate the canon of works to which it belongs. It is new to many musicians and listeners, and therefore requires more familiarity with his vocabulary. But I have seen certain works (*Die Seejungfrau* and, above all, *Der Zwerg*) make their point powerfully even on the first hearing. I did not start the Zemlinsky crusade, I joined it. My mission is to rescue his music from the shipwreck of the twentieth century: to beat the Zemlinsky drum until others join in. That is happening now and will continue. I believe deeply in his genius and in his works. I have no doubts about either, and when I encounter resistance, I think of the testimony of Berg and Schoenberg. If Zemlinsky elicited the deep admiration of those two geniuses, I can feel confident that I am on the right track.

James Conlon
Milan, 2010

List of Works

Works are listed chronologically by genre, followed by date of completion and publisher (P). Works that did not progress beyond substantial drafts are not included.

Songs (for voice and piano unless otherwise indicated)

Die Nachtigal auf meiner Flur singt (unknown text source), 1888

O wär mein Lieb (unknown text source), 1888

Seven Songs (originally twelve), 1889–90, P Ricordi, 1995
    1. *Die schlanke Wasserlilie* (Heine)
    2. *Gute Nacht* (Eichendorff)
    3. *Liebe und Frühling* (Fallersleben)
    4. *Ich sah mein eigen Angesicht* (Vulpinus)
    5. *Lieben und Leben* (Pfleger)
    6. *In der Ferne* (Prutz)
    7. *Waldgespräch* (Eichendorff)

Three Songs, 1890, P Ricordi, 1995
    1. *Das Rosenband* (Klopstock)
    2. *Lerchengesang* (Candidus)
    3. *Abendstern* (Mayrhofer)

Des Mädchens Klage (Zusner), 1891, P Ricordi, 1995

Nebel (Lenau), c.1891

Mir träumte einst (Hilfreich), 1892

Der Morgenstern (Zusner), 1892, P Ricordi, 1995

Two Songs (Heyse), 1892, P Ricordi, 1995
    1. *Auf die Nacht*
    2. *Im Lenz*

Mädchenlied (Heyse), 1892

Die Trauernde (Treitschke), c.1893

Two Songs (Heine), 1892, ᴘ Ricordi, 1995
    1. *Frühlingslied*
    2. *Wandl' ich im Wald des Abends*

Die Nonne (Uhland), s, vc, pf, c.1894

Five Songs, 1895–96, ᴘ Ricordi, 1995
    1. *Orientalisches Sonett* (Grasberger)
    2. *Süsse, süsse Sommernacht* (Lynx)
    3. *Herbsten* (Wertheimer)
    4. *Nun schwillt der See so bang* (Wertheimer)
    5. *Der Tag wird kühl* (Heyse), 1897

Es muss ein Wunderbares sein (Redwitz), 1896

Klagend weint es in den Zweigen (Werthheimer), 1896

Lieder, op. 2, 2 vols., 1895–96, ᴘ Hansen, 1897
  Vol. 1
    1. *Heilige Nacht* (Feth)
    2. *Der Himmel hat keine Sterne* (Heyse)
    3. *Geflüster der Nacht* (Storm)
    4. *Der Liebe Leid* (from the Turkish)
    5. *Mailied* (Goethe)
    6. *Um Mitternacht* (Rodenberg)
    7. *Vor der Stadt* (Eichendorff)
  Vol. 2
    1. *Frühlingstag* (Siebel)
    2. *Altdeutsches Minnelied*
    3. *Der Traum: Es war ein niedlich Zeiselein* (children's song)
    4. *Im Lenz* (Heyse)
    5. *Das verlassene Mädchen* (Leixner)
    6. *Empfängnis* (Wertheimer)

Waldgespräch (Eichendorff), S, 2 hn, hp, str., 1896, ᴘ Ricordi, 2000

Gesänge, op. 5 , 2 vols., 1896–97, ᴘ Hansen, 1898
  Vol. 1
    1. *Schlaf nur ein* (Heyse)
    2. *Hütet euch* (Heyse)
    3. *O Blätter, dürre Blätter* (Pfau)
    4. *O Sterne, goldene Sterne* (Pfau)
  Vol. 2
    1. *Unter blühenden Bäumen* (Genischen)
    2. *Tiefe Sehnsucht* (Liliencron)
    3. *Nach dem Gewitter* (Evers)
    4. *Im Korn* (Evers)

Walzer-Gesänge nach toskanischen Volksliedern, op. 6 (Gregorovius), 1898, P Simrock, 1899

    1. *Liebe Schwalbe*

    2. *Klagen ist der Mond gekommen*

    3. *Fensterlein, nachts bist du zu*

    4. *Ich gehe des Nachts*

    5. *Blaues Sternlein*

    6. *Briefchen schrieb ich*

Irmelin Rose und andere Gesänge, op. 7, 1898–99 P Hansen, 1901

    1. *Da waren zwei Kinder* (Morgenstern)

    2. *Entbietung* (Dehmel)

    3. *Meeraugen* (Dehmel)

    4. *Irmelin Rose* (Jacobsen)

    5. *Sonntag* (Wertheimer)

Turmwächterlied und andere Gesänge, op. 8, 1899, P Hansen, 1901

    1. *Turmwächterlied* (Jacobsen)

    2. *Und hat der Tag all seine Qual* (Jacobsen)

    3. *Mit Trommeln und Pfeifen* (Liliencron)

    4. *Tod in Aehren* (v. Liliencron)

Ehetanzlied und andere Gesänge, op. 10, 1900–1901, P Doblinger [1901]

    1. *Ehetanzlied* (Bierbaum)

    2. *Selige Stunde* (Wertheimer)

    3. *Vöglein Schwermut* (Morgenstern)

    4. *Meine Braut führ' ich heim* (Jacobsen)

    5. *Klopfet, so wird euch aufgetan* (Lingen)

    6. *Kirchweih* (Busse)

Two Brettl-Lieder, 1901, P Ricordi, 1995

    1. *In der Sonnengasse* (Holz)

    2. *Herr Bombardil* (Schröder)

Eine ganz neu Schelmweys (Dehmel), c.1901 [lost]

Die Juli-Hexen (Bierbaum), 2 female voices, pf, c.1901 [lost]

Erdeinsamkeit (Eichendorff), middle voice and orchestra, 1901, P Ricordi (orch Beaumont), 1999

Four Songs, 1903–5, P Ricordi, 1995

    1. *Es war ein alter König* (Heine)

    2. *Über eine Wiege* (Liliencron)

    3. *Mädel, kommst du mit zum Tanz?* (Feld)

    4. *Schlummerlied* (Beer-Hofmann)

Maiblumen blühten überall (Dehmel), S, string sextet, c.1903, P Ricordi, 1997

Schmetterlinge (Liliencron), 1904

Five Songs (Dehmel), 1907, P Ricordi, 1995
1. *Vorspiel*
2. *Ansturm*
3. *Letzte Bitte*
4. *Stromüber*
5. *Auf See*

Two Ballads, 1907, P Ricordi, 1995
1. *Jane Grey* (Amann)
2. *Der verlorene Haufen* (Klemperer)

Der alte Garten (Eichendorff), middle voice and orchestra, 1908, P Ricordi (orch. Beaumont), 1999

Der chinesische Hund (Zemlinsky), voice and tambourine, 1908

Six Songs, op. 13 (Maeterlinck), 1910, 1913(*), P Universal Edition, 1914
1. *Die drei Schwestern*
2. *Die Mädchen mit den verbundenen Augen*
3. *Lied der Jungfrau*
4. *Als ihr Geliebter schied**
5. *Und kehrt er einst heim*
6. *Sie kam zum Schloss gegangen**
nos. 1, 2, 3, 5 orch. 1913, P Universal Edition, 1923
nos. 4, 6 orch. 1921, P Universal Edition, 1924

Four Songs, 1916, P Ricordi, 1995
1. *Noch spür ich ihren Atem* (Hofmannsthal)
2. *Hörtest du denn nicht hinein* (Hofmannsthal)
3. *Die Beiden* (Hofmannsthal)
4. *Harmonie des Abends* (Baudelaire)

Lyrische Symphonie, op. 18 (*see below under* Orchestral)

Und einmal gehst du (Eigner), 1933, P Ricordi, 1995

Six Songs, op. 22, 1934, P Mobart, 1977
1. *Auf braunen Sammetschuhen* (Morgenstern)
2. *Abendkelch voll Sonnenlicht* (Morgenstern)
3. *Feiger Gedanken bängliches Schwanken* (Goethe)
4. *Elfenlied* (Goethe)
5. *Volkslied* (Morgenstern)
6. *Auf dem Meere meiner Seele* (Morgenstern)

Das bucklichte Männlein (Des Knaben Wunderhorn), 1934, P Mobart, 1977

Ahnung Beatricens (Werfel), 1935, P Mobart, 1977

Symphonische Gesänge, op. 20, Bar (or Alto), orch, 1929, P Universal Edition, 1977
1. *Lied aus Dixieland* (Hughes)
2. *Lied der Baumwollpacker* (Toomer)
3. *Totes braunes Mädel* (Cullen)
4. *Übler Bursche* (Hughes)
5. *Erkenntnis* (Hughes)
6. *Afrikanischer Tanz* (Hughes)
7. *Arabeske* (Horne)

Twelve Songs, op. 27, 1937, P Mobart, 1978
1. *Entführung* (George)
2. *Sommer* (Kalidasa)
3. *Frühling* (Kalidasa)
4. *Jetzt ist die Zeit* (Kalidasa)
5. *Die Verschmähte* (Amaru)
6. *Der Wind des Herbstes* (Kalidasa)
7. *Elend* (Hughes)
8. *Harlem Tänzerin* (McKay)
9. *Afrikanischer Tanz* (Hughes)
10. *Gib ein Lied mir wieder* (George)
11. *Regenzeit* (Kalidasa)
12. *Wanderers Nachtlied* (Goethe)

Three Songs (Stein-Firner), 1939, P Chappell, 1940
1. *Chinese Serenade*
2. *My Ship and I*
3. *Love, I must say goodbye*

Piano Solo

Sonata, G major, 1887 [incomplete]

Sonata, C minor, 1890 [lost]

Three Pieces, 1891

Four Miniatures, *c.*1891

Two Pieces, *c.*1891

Two Pieces, four hands, 1891

Drei leichte Stücke, 1891 [lost]

Ländliche Tänze, op. 1, 1892, P Breitkopf und Härtel, 1892

Four Ballades, 1893, P Ricordi, 2000

Albumblatt, 1895, P Ricordi, 2000

Skizze, 1896, P Ricordi, 2000

Fantasien über Gedichte von Richard Dehmel, op. 9, 1898, P Doblinger, 1901

Menuett (from *Der Triumph der Zeit*), 1901, P Musik-Blätter, 3rd Jg., Nr. 20, repr. Ricordi, 1996

Three Pieces, four hands, 1903

Chamber

Romanze, D-flat major, vn, pf, 1889

Drei Stücke (Humoreske, Lied and Tarantell), vc, pf, 1891, P Ricordi, 2006

Terzet, str trio, 1892 [lost]

String Quartet, E minor, c.1893, P Ricordi, 1996

Piano Quartet, D major, 1894 [incomplete]

Sonata, vc, pf, 1894, P Ricordi, 2006

String Quintet, D minor, first movement 1894, finale 1896, P Ricordi, 2000

Serenade (Suite), A major, vn, pf, 1895, P Universal Edition, 1984

Trio, D minor, op. 3, cl/vn, vc, pf, 1896, P Simrock, 1897

String Quartet no. 1, A major, op. 4, 1896, P Simrock, 1898

String Quartet no. 2, op. 15, 1915, P Universal Edition, 1915

String Quartet no. 3, op. 19, 1924, P Universal Edition, 1925

String Quartet, 1927 [incomplete], P Ricordi, 1994

String Quartet no. 4 (Suite), op. 25, 1936, P Universal Edition, 1974

Hunting Piece, 2 hn, pf, 1939, P (as Jagdstück) Universal Edition, 1977

Humoreske, wind quintet, 1939, P Universal Edition, 1978

Choral

Vor der Stadt (Eichendorff), SATB chorus, 1893

Minnelied (Heine), TTBB chorus, 2 fl, 2 hn, hp, c.1895, P Ricordi, 2000

Frühlingsbegräbnis (Heyse), SB, SATB chorus, orch, 1896, P Ricordi, 2000

Frühlingsglaube (Uhland), SATB chorus, str, 1896, P Ricordi, 1995

Geheimnis (unidentified), SATB chorus, str, 1896, P Ricordi, 1995

Hochzeitsgesang (Jewish liturgy), cantor (T), SATB chorus, org, 1896, P Ricordi, 2000

Aurikelchen (Dehmel), SSAA chorus, 1898, P Ricordi, 1996

Psalm 83, SATB, SATB chorus, orch, 1900, P Universal Edition, 1987

Psalm 23, op. 14, SATB chorus, orch, 1910, P Universal Edition, 1911 (v.s.), 1922 (score)

Psalm 13, op. 24, SATB chorus, orch, 1935, P Universal Edition, 1971

Stage

Sarema (opera, lib. Zemlinsky, Adolf von Zemlinszky, Schoenberg, after Gottschall, *Die Rose vom Kaukasus*), 1893–95, P Berthé, 1899, repr. Ricordi, 1995

Es war einmal (opera, lib. Singer, after Drachmann), 1897–99, P Ricordi, 1990

Der Triumph der Zeit (ballet, Hofmannsthal), 1901 [incomplete]

Ein Lichtstrahl (mime drama with pf, Geller), 1901, P Ricordi, 2000

Der Traumgörge (opera, lib. Feld), 1904–6, P Ricordi, 1990

Kleider machen Leute (opera, lib. Feld, after Keller), 1907–9, P Bote & Bock, 1910; rev. 1922, P Universal Edition, 1922

Malwa (opera, lib. R.L., after Gorky), 1912–13 [substantial sketches]

Cymbeline (incidental music, Shakespeare), 1913–15, P Ricordi, 1996

Eine florentinische Tragödie, op. 16 (opera, lib. Wilde, trans. Meyerfeld), 1915–16, P Universal Edition, 1916

Raphael (opera, lib. Klaren, after Balzac, *La Peau de chagrin*), 1918 [substantial sketches]

Der Zwerg, op. 17 (opera, lib. Klaren, after Wilde, *The Birthday of the Infanta*), 1920–21, P Universal Edition, 1921

Der Kreidekreis (opera, after Klabund), 1930–32, P Universal Edition, 1933

Der König Kandaules (opera, Gide, trans. Blei), 1935–38 [comp. Beaumont, 1993], P Ricordi, 1996

Circe (opera, lib. Stein-Firner), 1939 [substantial drafts and sketches, piano-vocal score of first act complete]

Orchestral

Symphony, E minor, 1891 [incomplete]

Symphony no. 1, D minor, 1892–93, P Ricordi, 2000

Lustspiel Overture, 1895

Suite, *c.*1895

Symphony no. 2, B-flat major, 1897

Drei Balletstücke, from *Der Triumph der Zeit*, 1901–2, P Ricordi, 1992

Die Seejungfrau, fantasy for orchestra, 1902–3

Ein Tanzpoem, from *Der Triumph der Zeit*, 1904, P Ricordi, 1991

Lyrische Symphonie, op. 18 (Tagore, trans. Effenberger), S, Bar, orch, 1922–23, P Universal Edition, 1923 (v.s.), 1926 (score)

    1. *Ich bin friedlos, ich bin durstig nach fernen Dingen*

    2. *O Mutter, der junge Prinz*

    3. *Du bist die Abendwolke*

    4. *Sprich zu mir Geliebter*

    5. *Befrei mich von den Banden deiner Süsse, Lieb*

    6. *Vollende denn das letzte Lied*

    7. *Friede, mein Herz*

Symphonische Gesänge, op. 20 (*see above under* Songs)

Sinfonietta, op. 23, 1934, P Universal Edition, 1935

Discography

compiled by Jerome F. Weber

The works are listed alphabetically in six categories with the published books of songs listed before uncollected songs. Each recording is identified by performers, (date of recording), [timing]. The listing is chronological under each work. Each record issue is identified by format (i.e., LP, CD, Super Audio CD), record label, issue number — reviews. Reviews are useful for the information they contain, but the main purpose of the citation is to suggest the date of issue. Other composers found on the same issue are cited in [brackets], or a general disc title is cited in ["bracketed quotation marks"]. An asterisk (*) against the name of a chamber ensemble indicates that its members are identified at their first appearance under the category "Chamber". For the titles of songs in collections, see the List of Works above.

Reviews are cited primarily from US *Fanfare* (Fa.), UK *Gramophone* (Gr.), France *Diapason* (Dp.) and Germany *FonoForum* (Fono.). A few other reviews are cited from *The American Record Guide* (ARG) and *Klassik-heute* (Klassik). In the absence of a review, the first listing in the German *Bielefelder Katalog Klassik* (Biel.) is cited. The issue dates of Japanese records are cited from a Japanese general catalog. The data have been compiled from the records as issued, correspondence with labels and performers, and information supplied by librarians and reviewers who had access to the records. Warmest thanks are due to all who helped, most especially to James H. North (*Fanfare*) and Janet W. McKee (Library of Congress). Data entry closed on 1 January 2010.

Songs

Lieder, op. 2

(*I/1, 3, 7*) Steven Kimbrough (bar), Cord Garben, pf (rec. 1982) [2:23, 1:12, 1:43]
    LP: Acanta 40.23509 DX — Biel. 10/83; Fa. 3/84
    CD: Acanta 43509 — Dp. 7/88
    CD: Arts 47613-2 — Klassik 12/01; Gr. 11/02
(*I/2, 6; II/6*) Barbara Bonney (s), Cord Garben, pf (rec. 22–23 Feb. 1988) [1:23, 3:38, 2:42]

(*II/3; III/1, 3, 5*) Anne Sofie von Otter (ms), Cord Garben, pf (rec. 16–18 May 1988) [1:19, 1:14, 1:35, 2:02]

(*II/1, 7; III/2, 4*) Andreas Schmidt (bar), Cord Garben, pf (rec. 27–28 Jan. 1988) [2:39, 1:38, 1:44, 1:06]

    CD: D.G. 427348-2 [2] — Dp. 9/89; Gr. 10/89; Fono. 10/89; Fa. 7/90

    CD: Brilliant 9009 — 2009

(*III/4*) Bo Skovhus (bar), Helmut Deutsch, pf (rec. 10–11 Dec. 1994) [2:27]

    CD: RCA Victor 09026-68111-2 — Fono. 11/96; Gr. 12/96; Fa. 1/97

(*II/1, III/3*) Wendy Nielsen (s), Robert Kortgaard, pf (rec. 4–7 Aug. 1997) [2:36, 1:39]

    CD: Marquis 81265 — issued 2/01 [+ Dvorak, Tchaikovsky, Dohnanyi]

(*II/7*) Wolfgang Holzmair (bar), Imogen Cooper, pf (rec. 13–17 Oct. 1999) [1:21]

    CD: Philips 464991-2 — Gr. 2/03; Fa. 7/03 ["Eichendorff Lieder"]

(*II/1*) Jean Stilwell (ms), Robert Kortgaard, pf (rec. 12–13 June or 4–7 Sept. 2002)

    CD: CBC Records MVCD 1162 — issued 9/03 ["Kabarett"]

Gesänge, op. 5

(*II/1; III/2, 4*) Steven Kimbrough (bar), Cord Garben, pf (rec. 1982) [3:03, 0:43, 1:03]

    LP: Acanta 40.23509 DX — Biel. 10/83; Fa. 3/84

    CD: Acanta 43509 — Dp. 7/88

    CD: Arts 47613-2 — Klassik 12/01; Gr. 11/02

(*II/1–4, III/1–4*) Georg Jelden (bar), Hans-Dieter Wagner, pf (rec. 4–5 Oct. 1984 or 10 Mar. 1985) [2:27, 0:52, 2:11, 1:27, 2:01, 0:49, 1:30, 1:12]

    LP: Calig CAL 30842 — Fono. 4/86 [+ Korngold, R. Stephan, Schreker]

(*II/2*) Barbara Bonney (s), Cord Garben, pf (rec. 22–23 Feb. 1988) [1:09]

(*II/3*) Anne Sofie von Otter (ms), Cord Garben, pf (rec. 16–18 May 1988) [2:47]

(*II/1; III/4*) Hans Peter Blochwitz (t), Cord Garben, pf (rec. 14–16 Mar. 1988) [2:23, 1:15]

(*II/4; III/1, 2, 3*) Andreas Schmidt (bar), Cord Garben, pf (rec. 27–28 Jan. 1988) [1:15, 2:13, 0:45, 1:55]

    CD: D.G. 427348-2 [2] — Dp. 9/89; Gr. 10/89; Fono. 10/89; Fa. 7/90

    CD: Brilliant 9009 — 2009

(*III/1*) Bo Skovhus (bar), Helmut Deutsch, pf (rec. 10–11 Dec. 1994) [1:55]

    CD: RCA Victor 09026-68111-2 — Fono. 11/96; Gr. 12/96; Fa. 1/97

(*II/3*) Wendy Nielsen (s), Robert Kortgaard, pf (rec. 4–7 Aug. 1997) [2:54]

    CD: Marquis 81265 — issued 2/01 [+ Dvorak, Tchaikovsky, Dohnanyi]

(*II/1, 3; III/1, 4*) Violet Chang (s), Norman Shetler, pf

    CD: Aricord CDA 10506 — issued in Austria 2006 [+ Mahler]

Gesänge, op. 6

(*1, 4, 5*) Steven Kimbrough (bar), Cord Garben, pf (rec. 1982) [1:28, 0:46, 1:40]

    LP: Acanta 40.23509 DX — Biel. 10/83; Fa. 3/84

    CD: Acanta 43509 — Dp. 7/88

    CD: Arts 47613-2 — Klassik 12/01; Gr. 11/02

(*1, 3, 5, 6*) Barbara Bonney (s), Cord Garben, pf (rec. 22–23 Feb. 1988) [1:35, 1:00, 1:46, 0:59]

(*2, 4*) Anne Sofie von Otter (ms), Cord Garben, pf (rec. 16–18 May 1988) [1:26, 0:52]
    CD: D.G. 427348-2 [2] — Dp. 9/89; Gr. 10/89; Fono. 10/89; Fa. 7/90
    CD: Brilliant 9009 — 2009

(*1–6*) Miwako Matsumoto (s), Shoko Takeuchi, pf (rec. 1994)
    CD: Shinseido scw 5001 — issued in Japan 3/96 ["Viennese Rarities"]

(*1–6*) Hermine Haselböck (ms), Florian Henschel, pf (rec. June 2003) [1:35, 1:29, 1:01, 0:52, 1:50, 1:02]
    CD: Pan Classics PAN 10162 — Biel. 3/04
    CD: Bridge 9244 — issued 2/08

(*5*) José Carreras (t), Michael Lessky, Junge Philharmonie Wien [1:45]
    CD: Sony BMG 82876-81921-2 — issued 3/06; Gr. 1/08 ["Belle Epoque"]

(*1–6*) Diana Damrau (s), Stephan Matthias Lademann, pf (rec. live 13 Aug. 2005) [8:13]
    CD: Orfeo c 702061 B — Biel. 4/07 [+ Berg, Mahler, Strauss, Wolf]

(*1–6*) Judith Kopecky (s), Julia Tinhof, pf
    CD: Extraplatte EX 662-2 — issued 2006 ["Exiles"]

(*1–6*) Andrea Stadel (s), Rita Klose, pf [1:45, 1:39, 1:01, 0:58, 1:54, 1:02]
    CD: Bella Musica Antes AN 319248 — Biel. 2/09 ["Volkslieder"]

Gesänge, op. 7

(*2, 3, 5*) Steven Kimbrough (bar), Cord Garben, pf (rec. 1982) [2:11, 2:53, 0:57]
    LP: Acanta 40.23509 DX — Biel. 10/83; Fa. 3/84
    CD: Acanta 43509 — Dp. 7/88
    CD: Arts 47613-2 — Klassik 12/01; Gr. 11/02

(*2, 3*) Dietrich Fischer-Dieskau (bar), Aribert Reimann, pf (rec. 6 Feb. 1985) [1:34, 2:34]
    CD: Orfeo c 390951 — Fa. 7/96 ["Dehmel Lieder"]

(*3, 5*) Barbara Bonney (s), Cord Garben, pf (rec. 22–23 Feb. 1988) [2:48, 1:06]

(*1*) Anne Sofie von Otter (ms), Cord Garben, pf (rec. 16–18 May 1988) [1:29]

(*4*) Hans Peter Blochwitz (t), Cord Garben, pf (rec. 14–16 Mar. 1988) [3:08]

(*2*) Andreas Schmidt (bar), Cord Garben, pf (rec. 27–28 Jan. 1988) [2:28]
    CD: D.G. 427348-2 [2] — Dp. 9/89; Gr. 10/89; Fono. 10/89; Fa. 7/90
    CD: Brilliant 9009 — 2009

(*2*) Bo Skovhus (bar), Helmut Deutsch, pf (rec. 10–11 Dec. 1994) [1:57]
    CD: RCA Victor 09026-68111-2 — Fono. 11/96; Gr. 12/96; Fa. 1/97

(*3, 5*) Ruth Ziesak (s), Cord Garben, pf (rec. 12–14 Aug. 1996) [2:40, 1:03]

(*1*) Iris Vermillion (ms), Cord Garben, pf (rec. 12–14 Aug. 1996) [1:45]

(*2, 4*) Christian Elsner (t), Cord Garben, pf (rec. 12–14 Aug. 1996) [1:52, 3:06]
    CD: CPO 999455-2 — Gr. 1/98; Dp. 1/98; Fa. 3/98 [+ A. Mahler]

(*4*) Wendy Nielsen (s), Robert Kortgaard, pf (rec. 4–7 Aug. 1997) [2:55]
    CD: Marquis 81265 — issued 2/01 [+ Dvorak, Tchaikovsky, Dohnanyi]

(*1–5*) Britta Stallmeister (s). Christian Schulte, pf (rec. 29–30 Sept. 1999)

    CD: Ars Musici AMP 5086-2 — Biel. 10/00 [+ Berg, Boulanger, Szymanowski]

Gesänge, op. 8

(*1, 2*) Steven Kimbrough (bar), Cord Garben, pf (rec. 1982) [7:23, 4:07]

    LP: Acanta 40.23509 DX — Biel. 10/83; Fa. 3/84

    CD: Acanta 43509 — Dp. 7/88

    CD: Arts 47613-2 — Klassik 12/01; Gr. 11/02

(*2*) Anne Sofie von Otter (ms), Cord Garben, pf (rec. 16–18 May 1988) [4:22]

(*1, 3, 4*) Andreas Schmidt (bar), Cord Garben, pf (rec. 27–28 Jan. 1988) [7:23, 2:32, 4:11]

    CD: D.G. 427348-2 [2] — Dp. 9/89; Gr. 10/89; Fono. 10/89; Fa. 7/90

    CD: Brilliant 9009 — 2009

(*1*) Wendy Nielsen (s), Robert Kortgaard, pf (rec. 4–7 Aug. 1997) [7:38]

    CD: Marquis 81265 — issued 2/01 [+ Dvorak, Tchaikovsky, Dohnanyi]

(*3, 4*) Thomas Hampson (bar), Wolfram Rieger, pf (rec. live 18 Aug. 2005)

    CD: Orfeo C 708061 B — Biel. 2/08 ["Verboten und verbannt"]

Gesänge, op. 10

(*4*) Steven Kimbrough (bar), Cord Garben, pf (rec. 1982) [1:20]

    LP: Acanta 40.23509 DX — Biel. 10/83; Fa. 3/84

    CD: Acanta 43509 — Dp. 7/88

    CD: Arts 47613-2 — Klassik 12/01; Gr. 11/02

(*2*) Georg Jelden (bar), Hans-Dieter Wagner, pf (rec. 4–5 Oct. 1984 or 10 Mar. 1985) [1:55]

    LP: Calig CAL 30842 — Fono. 4/86 [+ Korngold, R. Stephan, Schreker]

(*1–6*) Ursula Zehnder (s), Theodor Künzi, pf (rec. June 1987)

    LP: Jecklin 259 — Biel. 3/89 [+ A. Furer, W. Grimm, J. Marx, Pfitzner]

(*5*) Barbara Bonney (s), Cord Garben, pf (rec. 22–23 Feb. 1988) [1:54]

(*1, 3, 6*) Hans Peter Blochwitz (t), Cord Garben, pf (rec. 14–16 Mar. 1988) [2:25, 2:26, 3:19]

(*2, 4*) Andreas Schmidt (bar), Cord Garben, pf (rec. 27–28 Jan. 1988) [2:13, 1:18]

    CD: D.G. 427348-2 [2] — Dp. 9/89; Gr. 10/89; Fono. 10/89; Fa. 7/90

    CD: Brilliant 9009 — 2009

(*2*) Bo Skovhus (bar), Helmut Deutsch, pf (rec. 10–11 Dec. 1994) [2:08]

    CD: RCA Victor 09026-68111-2 — Fono. 11/96; Gr. 12/96; Fa. 1/97

Gesänge, op. 13

(*2*) Friedrich Ofner (bar), Robert Schollum, pf (rec. 1968) [2:30]

    LP: Österreichische Phonothek ÖPh 10009 — ["Österreichische Musik des 20. Jahr-hunderts, vol. 5"]

(*4*) Hermann Prey (bar), Michael Krist, pf (rec. Oct. 1975) [2:23]

  LP: Philips 6599 401 in set 6747 061 [6] — Biel. 10/76 ["Lied Edition Prey 4: 20th Century"]

  CD: Philips 442706-2 [4] — Biel. 3/01

(*1–6*) Ursula Gerlach (a), Karl Michael Komma, pf (rec. 1976)

  LP: FSM Audite 63412 — Fono. 7/84 [+ Komma, Webern]

(*1, 2, 3, 5*) Dorothy Dorow (s), Massimiliano Damerini, pf (rec. live 1980) [2:44, 2:10, 2:30, 2:39]

  CD: Etcetera KTC 1044 — Gr. 8/89; Fa. 9/89; Dp. 9/89 [+ Marx, Schreker]

(*2, 4*) Steven Kimbrough (bar), Cord Garben, pf (rec. 1982) [2:25, 2:08]

  LP: Acanta 40.23509 DX — Biel. 10/83; Fa. 3/84

  CD: Acanta 43509 — Dp. 7/88

  CD: Arts 47613-2 — Klassik 12/01; Gr. 11/02

(*1, 2, 4, 6*) Christopher Norton-Welsh (bar), Charles Spencer, pf (rec. June–July 1983) [3:15, 2:01, 2:01, 4:21]

  LP: Preiser 120653 — issued 1983 [+ K. Weigl, A. Mahler, Schoenberg]

(*5*) Georg Jelden (bar), Hans-Dieter Wagner, pf (rec. 4–5 Oct. 1984 or 10 Mar. 1985) [2:31]

  LP: Calig CAL 30842 — Fono. 4/86 [+ Korngold, R. Stephan, Schreker]

(*1–6*) Anne Sofie von Otter (ms), Cord Garben, pf (rec. 16–18 May 1988) [3:11, 2:16, 1:46, 1:58, 2:52, 4:02]

  CD: D.G. 427348-2 [2] — Dp. 9/89; Gr. 10/89; Fono. 10/89; Fa. 7/90

  CD: Brilliant 9009 — 2009

(*1–6*) Anne Gjevang (a), Einar Steen-Nøkleberg, pf (rec. Sept. 1995) [3:29, 2:15, 1:58, 2:18, 3:05, 4:15]

  CD: Victoria VCD 19069 — Fono. 1/97 [+ Mahler, A. Mahler, Pfitzner]

(*2, 6*) Wendy Nielsen (s), Robert Kortgaard, pf (rec. 4–7 Aug. 1997) [2:54, 3:34]

  CD: Marquis 81265 — issued 2/01 [+ Dvorak, Tchaikovsky, Dohnanyi]

(*1–6*) Hermine Haselböck (ms), Florian Henschel, pf (rec. June 2003) [3:34, 2:22, 1:47, 2:04, 2:50, 3:50]

  CD: Pan Classics PAN 10162 — Biel. 3/04

  CD: Bridge 9244 — issued 2/08

(*1–6*) Janine Baechle (ms), Charles Spencer, pf (rec. 10–12 Jan. 2008)

  SACD: Marsyas MAR 1803-2 — issued 9/08 ["Chansons grises"]

— (*1–6*) orch. Zemlinsky

Glenys Linos (a), Bernhard Klee, Berlin Radio SO (rec. 2–3 July or 15 Sept. 1980) [4:00, 3:24, 2:28, 3:19, 2:14, 5:00]

  LP: Schwann VMS 1603 — Fono. 11/82; Fa. 11/82

  CD: Schwann Musica Mundi CD 11602 — Fa. 9/86

Felicity Palmer (s), Bernhard Klee, BBC PO (rec. 6 June 1986) [4:21, 3:14, 2:46, 3:26, 2:23, 5:03]

  CD: BBC Radio 15656 9185-2 — Biel. 3/98

Jard van Nes (a), Riccardo Chailly, Concertgebouw Orch Amsterdam (rec. Oct. 1989) [4:00, 3:02, 2:36, 3:03, 2:20, 4:27]

    CD: Decca 430165-2 [2] — Gr. 11/90; Dp. 1/91; Fa. 3/91 [+ Mahler 6th]

    CD: Decca 2894-30165-2 [2] — Biel. 3/91

Birgitta Svenden (ms), John Carewe, Nice PO (rec. July or Nov. 1990) [3:59, 2:41, 2:13, 3:06, 1:53, 4:09]

    CD: Forlane UCD 16642 — Dp. 2/92 [+ Elgar, Mahler]

Hedwig Fassbänder (ms), Vaclav Neumann, Czech PO (rec. live 29 Apr. 1992) [5:00, 2:48, 2:10, 3:00, 2:05, 4:55]

    CD: Supraphon 11 1811-2 — Gr. 7/93; Fa. 7/93; Dp. 3/95 [+ Reger op. 100]

Anne Sofie von Otter (ms), John Eliot Gardiner, Hamburg NDR SO (rec. live Jan. 1993) [3:53, 3:07, 2:39, 2:10, 3:17, 4:54]

    CD: D.G. 439928-2 — Gr. 3/97; Dp. 3/97; Fa. 7/97 [+ Mahler]

Cornelia Callisch (ms), Armin Jordan, Orch de la Suisse Romande (rec. 27 June to 1 July 1995) [4:06, 3:22, 2:52, 2:12, 3:27, 5:01]

    CD: FNAC Aria 592011 — Dp. 2/97; Fa. 5/97

Violeta Urmana (ms), James Conlon, Cologne Gürzenich Orch (rec. live 15–17 Nov. 1998) [4:17, 3:22, 2:28, 2:22, 3:19, 5:06]

    CD: EMI 5 57024 2 — Dp. 9/00; Gr. 11/00; Fa. 1/01

    CD: EMI 5 86079 2 [2] — Fa. 7/05

Dagmar Pecková (ms), Jiří Bělohlávek, Prague Philharmonia (rec. Sept. 1999) [20:24]

    CD: Supraphon SU 3417-2 — Gr. 7/00; Fa. 9/00; Klassik 12/00 [+ Brahms, Schoenberg, Wagner]

Eva Marton (s), John Carewe, Budapest SO (rec. 13–21 Sept. 1999)

    CD: Hungaroton HCD 31932 — Fono. 10/01 [+ Korngold, Schoenberg, Schreker]

Randi Stene (ms), Muhai Tang, Trondheim SO (rec. 14–18 June 2004) [4:15, 3:17, 2:56, 2:35, 3:10, 5:07]

    CD: Simax PSC 1249 — issued 6/07 [+ E. Schulhoff op. 26, 28]

— *(2, 5: arr. Erwin Stein)*

Wendela Bronsgeest (s), Reinbert de Leeuw, Schoenberg Ensemble (rec. Dec. 1980) [3:10, 3:36]

    LP: Philips 6514 134 — Fa. 9/82; Gr. 10/83 [+ Reger, Schoenberg]

Maria Riccarda Wesseling (ms), Pierre-Alain Monot, Nouvel Ensemble Contemporain (rec. 10–17 Aug. 2003) [2:55, 3:02]

    CD: Claves 50-2312 — Biel. 1/05 [+ Berg, Mahler, Schoenberg]

Lieder, op. 22 (including no. 6 *Auf dem Meere*)

(3, 4, 5, 6) Steven Kimbrough (bar), Cord Garben, pf (rec. 1982) [0:35, 1:30, 2:21, 0:53]

    LP: Acanta 40.23509 DX — Biel. 10/83; Fa. 3/84

    CD: Acanta 43509 — Dp. 7/88

    CD: Arts 47613-2 — Klassik 12/01; Gr. 11/02

(*4*) Barbara Bonney (s), Cord Garben, pf (rec. 22–23 Feb. 1988) [1:08]

(*1*) Anne Sofie von Otter (ms), Cord Garben, pf (rec. 16–18 May 1988) [1:45]

(*2, 3, 5*) Hans Peter Blochwitz (t), Cord Garben, pf (rec. 14–16 Mar. 1988) [2:09, 0:33, 2:13]

(*6*) Andreas Schmidt (bar), Cord Garben, pf (rec. 27–28 Jan. 1988) [1:03]
> CD: D.G. 427348-2 [2] — Dp. 9/89; Gr. 10/89; Fono. 10/89; Fa. 7/90
> CD: Brilliant 9009 — 2009

(*4*) Christiane Oelze (s), Eric Schneider, pf (rec. 1992) [1:19]
> CD: Berlin 1030-2 — Dp. 11/03 ["Goethe Lieder"]
> CD: Berlin 001331-2 — Biel. 1/05

(*2*) Dagmar Hesse (s), Antony Beaumont, pf (rec. 5 Oct. 1996) [1:41]
> CD: Thorofon CTH 2376 — Fono. 12/98; Fa. 3/99

(*1, 2, 5, 6*) Thomas Hampson (bar), Wolfram Rieger, pf (rec. live 18 Aug. 2005)
> CD: Orfeo C 708061 B — Biel. 2/08 ["Verboten und verbannt"]

Lieder, op. 27

(*4, 9*) Steven Kimbrough (bar), Cord Garben, pf (rec. 1982) [1:20, 0:50]
> LP: Acanta 40.23509 DX — Biel. 10/83; Fa. 3/84
> CD: Acanta 43509 — Dp. 7/88
> CD: Arts 47613-2 — Klassik 12/01; Gr. 11/02

(*7, 10*) Annette Céline (ms), Felicja Blumental, pf (rec. 1982) [2:16, 2:47]
> CD: Claudio CB 4837-2 — P 1999 ["Mozart to Weill"]

(*1–12*) Beverly Morgan (s), Christopher O'Riley, pf (rec. Dec. 1982) [1:45, 1:26, 1:00, 0:38, 2:21, 1:05, 1:46, 1:55, 0:52, 2:34, 0:47, 1:57]
> LP: Northeastern NR 215 — Fa. 3/86

(*7, 8, 9*) Jill Gomez (s), John Constable, pf (rec. 18–19 Feb. 1987) [2:06, 2:17, 0:53]
> CD: Unicorn-Kanchana DKP(CD) 9055 — Gr. 6/88; Fa. 11/88 ["Cabaret Classics"]

(*4, 5, 7, 11*) Barbara Bonney (s), Cord Garben, pf (rec. 22–23 Feb. 1988) [0:58, 2:00, 2:17, 0:39]

(*10*) Anne Sofie von Otter (ms), Cord Garben, pf (rec. 16–18 May 1988) [2:16]

(*1, 2, 3, 6, 8, 12*) Hans Peter Blochwitz (t), Cord Garben, pf (rec. 14–16 Mar. 1988) [2:27, 1:10, 0:49, 1:04, 1:51, 1:47]

(*9*) Andreas Schmidt (bar), Cord Garben, pf (rec. 27–28 Jan. 1988) [0:51]
> CD: D.G. 427348-2 [2] — Dp. 9/89; Gr. 10/89; Fono. 10/89; Fa. 7/90
> CD: Brilliant 9009 — 2009

(*7*) Cyndia Sieden (s), Steven Blier, pf (rec. 13–15 Feb. & 15 Mar. 1991) [2:37]
> CD: Koch 3 7086 2 — Fa. 3/93 ["Unquiet Peace"]

(*1, 7, 9*) Dagmar Hesse (s), Antony Beaumont, pf (rec. 5 Oct. 1996) [2:37, 2:10, 0:52]
> CD: Thorofon CTH 2376 — Fono. 12/98; Fa. 3/99

(*1, 2*) Sandrine Piau (s), Susan Manoff, pf (rec. July 2006) [2:17, 1:24]
> CD: Naïve V 5063 — Dp. 12/07; Gr. 2/08 ["Evocation"]

Three songs: Chinese Serenade; My ship and I; Love, I must say goodbye

Dagmar Hesse (s), Antony Beaumont, pf (rec. 5 Oct. 1996) [1:31, 1:05, 1:58]
    CD: Thorofon CTH 2376 — Fono. 12/98; Fa. 3/99

Abendstern

Iris Vermillion (ms), Cord Garben, pf (rec. 5–8 June 1993) [1:57]
    CD: Sony SK 57960 — Dp. 4/95; Gr. 6/95; Fono. 7/95; Fa. 9/95

Ahnung Beatricens

Barbara Bonney (s), Cord Garben, pf (rec. 22–23 Feb. 1988) [3:42]
    CD: D.G. 427348-2 [2] — Dp. 9/89; Gr. 10/89; Fono. 10/89; Fa. 7/90
    CD: Brilliant 9009 — 2009
Dagmar Hesse (s), Antony Beaumont, pf (rec. 5 Oct. 1996) [3:29]
    CD: Thorofon CTH 2376 — Fono. 12/98; Fa. 3/99

Der alte Garten (arr. Beaumont)

Andreas Schmidt (bar), James Conlon, Cologne Gürzenich Orch (rec. live 10–12 Oct.
    1999) [5:03]
    CD: EMI 5 57024 2 — Dp. 9/00; Gr. 11/00; Fa. 1/01
    CD: EMI 5 86079 2 [2] — Fa. 7/05

Ansturm

Kurt Widmer (bar), Jean-Jacques Dünki, pf (rec. 1985) [1:37]
    LP: Jecklin 594 — Dp. 5/85; Fono. 9/85; Gr. 1/86
    CD: Jecklin JD 594-2 — Fa. 3/89; Dp. 3/89; Fono. 3/89
Hans-Peter Blochwitz (t), Cord Garben, pf (rec. 25–26 May 1993) [1:19]
    CD: Sony SK 57960 — Dp. 4/95; Gr. 6/95; Fono. 7/95; Fa. 9/95

Auf See

Kurt Widmer (bar), Jean-Jacques Dünki, pf (rec. 1985) [1:55]
    LP: Jecklin 594 — Dp. 5/85; Fono. 9/85; Gr. 1/86
    CD: Jecklin JD 594-2 — Fa. 3/89; Dp. 3/89; Fono. 3/89
Hans-Peter Blochwitz (t), Cord Garben, pf (rec. 25–26 May 1993) [1:32]
    CD: Sony SK 57960 — Dp. 4/95; Gr. 6/95; Fono. 7/95; Fa. 9/95

Die Beiden

Ruth Ziesak (s), Cord Garben, pf (rec. 30–31 Mar. 1993) [3:12]
    CD: Sony SK 57960 — Dp. 4/95; Gr. 6/95; Fono. 7/95; Fa. 9/95

Das bucklichte Männlein (this replaced *Auf dem Meere* as no. 6 of op. 22)

Barbara Bonney (s), Cord Garben, pf (rec. 22–23 Feb. 1988) [2:54]
    CD: D.G. 427348-2 [2] — Dp. 9/89; Gr. 10/89; Fono. 10/89; Fa. 7/90
    CD: Brilliant 9009 — 2009

Thomas Hampson (bar), Geoffrey Parsons, pf (rec. Mar. 1989) [2:58]
  CD: Teldec 244923-2 — Fa. 7/90; Gr. 10/90
  CD: Teldec 2292-44923-2 — 1990 ["Lieder aus des Knaben Wunderhorn"]
Cyndia Sieden (s), Steven Blier, pf (rec. 13–15 Feb. & 15 Mar. 1991) [3:37]
  CD: Koch 3 7086 2 — Fa. 3/93 ["Unquiet Peace"]
Dagmar Hesse (s), Antony Beaumont, pf (rec. 5 Oct. 1996) [3:05]
  CD: Thorofon CTH 2376 — Fono. 12/98; Fa. 3/99

Erdeinsamkeit (arr. Beaumont)

Andreas Schmidt (bar), James Conlon, Cologne Gürzenich Orch (rec. live 10–12 Oct.
    1999) [12:13]
  CD: EMI 5 57024 2 — Dp. 9/00; Gr. 11/00; Fa. 1/01
  CD: EMI 5 86079 2 [2] — Fa. 7/05

Es war ein alter König

Iris Vermillion (ms), Cord Garben, pf (rec. 5–8 June 1993) [2:11]
  CD: Sony SK 57960 — Dp. 4/95; Gr. 6/95; Fono. 7/95; Fa. 9/95

Frühlingslied

Sandrine Piau (s), Susan Manoff, pf (rec. July 2006) [1:38]
  CD: Naïve v 5063 — Dp. 12/07; Gr. 2/08 ["Evocation"]

Gute Nacht

Iris Vermillion (ms), Cord Garben, pf (rec. 5–8 June 1993) [0:52]
  CD: Sony SK 57960 — Dp. 4/95; Gr. 6/95; Fono. 7/95; Fa. 9/95
Hermine Haselböck (ms), Florian Henschel, pf (rec. June 2003) [0:47]
  CD: Pan Classics PAN 10162 — Biel. 3/04
  CD: Bridge 9244 — issued 2/08

Harmonie des Abends

Ruth Ziesak (s), Cord Garben, pf (rec. 30–31 Mar. 1993) [3:49]
  CD: Sony SK 57960 — Dp. 4/95; Gr. 6/95; Fono. 7/95; Fa. 9/95

Herbsten

Iris Vermillion (ms), Cord Garben, pf (rec. 5–8 June 1993) [1:22]
  CD: Sony SK 57960 — Dp. 4/95; Gr. 6/95; Fono. 7/95; Fa. 9/95
Hermine Haselböck (ms), Florian Henschel, pf (rec. June 2003) [1:19]
  CD: Pan Classics PAN 10162 — Biel. 3/04
  CD: Bridge 9244 — issued 2/08

Herr Bombardil

Iris Vermillion (ms), Cord Garben, pf (rec. 5–8 June 1993) [1:33]
  CD: Sony SK 57960 — Dp. 4/95; Gr. 6/95; Fono. 7/95; Fa. 9/95

Hermine Haselböck (ms), Florian Henschel, pf (rec. June 2003) [1:39]
  CD: Pan Classics PAN 10162 — Biel. 3/04
  CD: Bridge 9244 — issued 2/08
Violet Chang (s), Norman Shetler, pf
  CD: Aricord CDA 10506 — issued in Austria 2006 [+ Mahler]

Hörtest du denn nicht hinein

Ruth Ziesak (s), Cord Garben, pf (rec. 30–31 Mar. 1993) [1:29]
  CD: Sony SK 57960 — Dp. 4/95; Gr. 6/95; Fono. 7/95; Fa. 9/95

Ich sah mein eigen Angesicht

Iris Vermillion (ms), Cord Garben, pf (rec. 5–8 June 1993) [1:08]
  CD: Sony SK 57960 — Dp. 4/95; Gr. 6/95; Fono. 7/95; Fa. 9/95
Hermine Haselböck (ms), Florian Henschel, pf (rec. June 2003) [1:17]
  CD: Pan Classics PAN 10162 — Biel. 3/04
  CD: Bridge 9244 — issued 2/08

In der Ferne

Hans-Peter Blochwitz (t), Cord Garben, pf (rec. 25–26 May 1993) [1:29]
  CD: Sony SK 57960 — Dp. 4/95; Gr. 6/95; Fono. 7/95; Fa. 9/95
Hermine Haselböck (ms), Florian Henschel, pf (rec. June 2003) [1:32]
  CD: Pan Classics PAN 10162 — Biel. 3/04; Bridge 9244 — issued 2/08

In der Sonnengasse

Iris Vermillion (ms), Cord Garben, pf (rec. 5–8 June 1993) [1:40]
  CD: Sony SK 57960 — Dp. 4/95; Gr. 6/95; Fono. 7/95; Fa. 9/95
Hermine Haselböck (ms), Florian Henschel, pf (rec. June 2003) [1:47]
  CD: Pan Classics PAN 10162 — Biel. 3/04
  CD: Bridge 9244 — issued 2/08
Violet Chang (s), Norman Shetler, pf
  CD: Aricord CDA 10506 — issued in Austria 2006 [+ Mahler]

Jane Grey

Andreas Schmidt (bar), Cord Garben, pf (rec. 5–8 June 1993) [4:51]
  CD: Sony SK 57960 — Dp. 4/95; Gr. 6/95; Fono. 7/95; Fa. 9/95

Letzte Bitte

Kurt Widmer (bar), Jean-Jacques Dünki, pf (rec. 1985) [1:25]
  LP: Jecklin 594 — Dp. 5/85; Fono. 9/85; Gr. 1/86
  CD: Jecklin JD 594-2 — Fa. 3/89; Dp. 3/89; Fono. 3/89
Bo Skovhus (bar), Helmut Deutsch, pf (rec. 10–11 Dec. 1994) [1:45]
  CD: RCA Victor 09026-68111-2 — Fono. 11/96; Gr. 12/96; Fa. 1/97

Liebe und Frühling

Ruth Ziesak (s), Cord Garben, pf (rec. 30–31 Mar. 1993) [2:06]
   CD: Sony SK 57960 — Dp. 4/95; Gr. 6/95; Fono. 7/95; Fa. 9/95
Hermine Haselböck (ms), Florian Henschel, pf (rec. June 2003) [1:40]
   CD: Pan Classics PAN 10162 — Biel. 3/04
   CD: Bridge 9244 — issued 2/08
Sandrine Piau (s), Susan Manoff, pf (rec. July 2006) [1:41]
   CD: Naïve V 5063 — Dp. 12/07; Gr. 2/08 ["Evocation"]

Liebe und Leben

Hermine Haselböck (ms), Florian Henschel, pf (rec. June 2003) [1:56]
   CD: Pan Classics PAN 10162 — Biel. 3/04
   CD: Bridge 9244 — issued 2/08

Lied der Circe (arr. Beaumont)

Dagmar Hesse (s), Antony Beaumont, pf (rec. 5 Oct. 1996) [3:18]
   CD: Thorofon CTH 2376 — Fono. 12/98; Fa. 3/99

Des Mädchens Klage

Ruth Ziesak (s), Cord Garben, pf (rec. 30–31 Mar. 1993) [3:33]
   CD: Sony SK 57960 — Dp. 4/95; Gr. 6/95; Fono. 7/95; Fa. 9/95
Miwako Matsumoto (s), Shoko Takeuchi, pf (rec. 1994)
   CD: Shinseido SCW 5001 — issued in Japan 3/96 ["Viennese Rarities"]

Mädel, kommst du mit zum Tanz? (later incorporated into Der Traumgörge)

Hans-Peter Blochwitz (t), Cord Garben, pf (rec. 25–26 May 1993) [1:50]
   CD: Sony SK 57960 — Dp. 4/95; Gr. 6/95; Fono. 7/95; Fa. 9/95

Maiblumen blühten überall

Susan Narucki (s), Schoenberg Quartet*; Jan Eric van Regteren Altena, 2 vla; Taco
   Kooistra, 2 vlc (rec. 14 Feb. 1994) [10:19]
   CD: Chandos CHAN 9772 [2] — Fa. 9/02; Dp. 10/02; Gr. 13/02
Edith Mathis (s), Antony Beaumont, Hamburg NDR SO str. (rec. 18 Apr. 1997) [9:06]
   CD: Capriccio 10740 — Fono. 12/97; Dp. 6/98; Fa. 11/98
Soile Isokoski (s), James Conlon, ensemble: Torsten Janike, Rose Kaufman, Mile Kosi,
   Urara Seo, Daniel Cahen, Sylvia Borg (rec. 16, 22–23 June 1998) [9:07]
   CD: EMI 5 57024 2 — Dp. 9/00; Gr. 11/00; Fa. 1/01
   CD: EMI 5 86079 2 [2] — Fa. 7/05
Juliane Banse (s), Vienna String Sextet: Erich Hörbarth, Peter Matzka, Thomas Riebl,
   Siegfried Führlinger, Rudolf Leopold, Susanne Ehn (rec. Feb. 2000) [7:50]
   CD: Pan Classics PC 10120 — Klassik 2/01 [+ Korngold op. 10]
Anneke de Wit (s), Doelen Quartet: Frank Groot, Laurens Van Vliet, Karin Dolman,

Hans Woudenberg; Anne Huser (2 vla), Wouter Mijnders (2 vlc) (rec. live 14 Sept. 2005)

    SACD: Cybele AB 003 [4] — issued 9/06 [+ Berg, Schoenberg]

Der Morgenstern

Ruth Ziesak (s), Cord Garben, pf (rec. 30–31 Mar. 1993) [3:05]
    CD: Sony SK 57960 — Dp. 4/95; Gr. 6/95; Fono. 7/95; Fa. 9/95

Noch spür' ich ihren Atem

Ruth Ziesak (s), Cord Garben, pf (rec. 30–31 Mar. 1993) [2:08]
    CD: Sony SK 57960 — Dp. 4/95; Gr. 6/95; Fono. 7/95; Fa. 9/95

Nun schwillt der See so bang

Ruth Ziesak (s), Cord Garben, pf (rec. 30–31 Mar. 1993) [1:34]
    CD: Sony SK 57960 — Dp. 4/95; Gr. 6/95; Fono. 7/95; Fa. 9/95
Hermine Haselböck (ms), Florian Henschel, pf (rec. June 2003) [1:24]
    CD: Pan Classics PAN 10162 — Biel. 3/04
    CD: Bridge 9244 — issued 2/08

Orientalisches Sonett

Hans-Peter Blochwitz (t), Cord Garben, pf (rec. 25–26 May 1993) [3:33]
    CD: Sony SK 57960 — Dp. 4/95; Gr. 6/95; Fono. 7/95; Fa. 9/95
Hermine Haselböck (ms), Florian Henschel, pf (rec. June 2003) [3:44]
    CD: Pan Classics PAN 10162 — Biel. 3/04
    CD: Bridge 9244 — issued 2/08

Das Rosenband

Hans-Peter Blochwitz (t), Cord Garben, pf (rec. 25–26 May 1993) [2:16]
    CD: Sony SK 57960 — Dp. 4/95; Gr. 6/95; Fono. 7/95; Fa. 9/95
Sandrine Piau (s), Susan Manoff, pf (rec. July 2006) [1:39]
    CD: Naïve V 5063 — Dp. 12/07; Gr. 2/08 ["Evocation"]

Die schlanke Wasserlilie

Iris Vermillion (ms), Cord Garben, pf (rec. 5–8 June 1993) [1:10]
    CD: Sony SK 57960 — Dp. 4/95; Gr. 6/95; Fono. 7/95; Fa. 9/95
Hermine Haselböck (ms), Florian Henschel, pf (rec. June 2003) [1:06]
    CD: Pan Classics PAN 10162 — Biel. 3/04
    CD: Bridge 9244 — issued 2/08

Schlummerlied

Barbara Bonney (s), Cord Garben, pf (rec. 22–23 Feb. 1988) [1:52]
    CD: D.G. 427348-2 [2] — Dp. 9/89; Gr. 10/89; Fono. 10/89; Fa. 7/90
    CD: Brilliant 9009 — 2009

Stromüber

Kurt Widmer (bar), Jean-Jacques Dünki, pf (rec. 1985) [3:01]
   LP: Jecklin 594 — Dp. 5/85; Fono. 9/85; Gr. 1/86
   CD: Jecklin JD 594-2 — Fa. 3/89; Dp. 3/89; Fono. 3/89
Bo Skovhus (bar), Helmut Deutsch, pf (rec. 10–11 Dec. 1994) [3:20]
   CD: RCA Victor 09026-68111-2 — Fono. 11/96; Gr. 12/96; Fa. 1/97

Süsse, süsse Sommernacht

Ruth Ziesak (s), Cord Garben, pf (rec. 30–31 Mar. 1993) [1:29]
   CD: Sony SK 57960 — Dp. 4/95; Gr. 6/95; Fono. 7/95; Fa. 9/95
Angelika Kirchschlager (ms), Helmut Deutsch, pf (rec. 23–29 Mar. 1999) [1:27]
   CD: Sony SK 61768 — Gr. 11/99 ["When Night Falls"]
   CD: Sony SK 64498 — P 1999
Hermine Haselböck (ms), Florian Henschel, pf (rec. June 2003) [1:22]
   CD: Pan Classics PAN 10162 — Biel. 3/04
   CD: Bridge 9244 — issued 2/08

Der Tag wird kühl

Hermine Haselböck (ms), Florian Henschel, pf (rec. June 2003) [2:53]
   CD: Pan Classics PAN 10162 — Biel. 3/04
   CD: Bridge 9244 — issued 2/08

Über eine Wiege

Iris Vermillion (ms), Cord Garben, pf (rec. 5–8 June 1993) [2:51]
   CD: Sony SK 57960 — Dp. 4/95; Gr. 6/95; Fono. 7/95; Fa. 9/95

Und einmal gehst du

Kurt Widmer (bar), Jean-Jacques Dünki, pf (rec. 1985) [2:28]
   LP: Jecklin 594 — Dp. 5/85; Fono. 9/85; Gr. 1/86
   CD: Jecklin JD 594-2 — Fa. 3/89; Dp. 3/89; Fono. 3/89
Andreas Schmidt (bar), Cord Garben, pf (rec. 5–8 June 1993) [2:55]
   CD: Sony SK 57960 — Dp. 4/95; Gr. 6/95; Fono. 7/95; Fa. 9/95

Der verlorene Haufen

Andreas Schmidt (bar), Cord Garben, pf (rec. 5–8 June 1993) [5:04]
   CD: Sony SK 57960 — Dp. 4/95; Gr. 6/95; Fono. 7/95; Fa. 9/95

Vorspiel

Kurt Widmer (bar), Jean-Jacques Dünki, pf (rec. 1985) [1:40]
   LP: Jecklin 594 — Dp. 5/85; Fono. 9/85; Gr. 1/86
   CD: Jecklin JD 594-2 — Fa. 3/89; Dp. 3/89; Fono. 3/89
Hans-Peter Blochwitz (t), Cord Garben, pf (rec. 25–26 May 1993) [1:58]
   CD: Sony SK 57960 — Dp. 4/95; Gr. 6/95; Fono. 7/95; Fa. 9/95

Waldgespräch

Andreas Schmidt (bar), Cord Garben, pf (rec. 5–8 June 1993) [2:37]
    CD: Sony sk 57960 — Dp. 4/95; Gr. 6/95; Fono. 7/95; Fa. 9/95
Hermine Haselböck (ms), Florian Henschel, pf (rec. June 2003) [2:46]
    CD: Pan Classics pan 10162 — Biel. 3/04
    CD: Bridge 9244 — issued 2/08

— *orch. Zemlinsky*
Edith Mathis (s), Antony Beaumont, Hamburg NDR SO (rec. 30 Nov. 1995) [6:59]
    CD: Capriccio 10740 — Fono. 12/97; Dp. 6/98; Fa. 11/98
Soile Isokoski (s), James Conlon, Cologne Gürzenich Orch (rec. 16, 22–23 June 1998)
    [7:25]
    CD: EMI 5 57024 2 — Dp. 9/00; Gr. 11/00; Fa. 1/01
    CD: EMI 5 86079 2 [2] — Fa. 7/05
Charlotte Margiono (s), Julian Reynolds, Brabant Orch (rec. Aug. 1999) [7:15]
    CD: Globe glo 5199 — Klassik 4/00; Fa. 5/00 [+ A. Mahler]

Wandl' ich im Wald des Abends

Andreas Schmidt (bar), Cord Garben, pf (rec. 5–8 June 1993) [2:24]
    CD: Sony sk 57960 — Dp. 4/95; Gr. 6/95; Fono. 7/95; Fa. 9/95
Sandrine Piau (s), Susan Manoff, pf (rec. July 2006) [2:17]
    CD: Naïve v 5063 — Dp. 12/07; Gr. 2/08 ["Evocation"]

Piano

Albumblatt

Siegfried Mauser, pf (rec. Dec. 1993) [3:57]
    CD: Virgin 5 45125 2 — Dp. 6/95; Gr. 9/95; Fono. 9/95
Silke Avenhaus, pf (rec. 5–7 July 2003) [2:46]
    CD: Naxos 8.557331 — Fa. 11/05

(4) Balladen

Siegfried Mauser, pf (rec. Dec. 1993) [19:34]
    CD: Virgin 5 45125 2 — Dp. 6/95; Gr. 9/95; Fono. 9/95
Silke Avenhaus, pf (rec. 5–7 July 2003) [4:02, 2:21, 3:14, 4:08]
    CD: Naxos 8.557331 — Fa. 11/05

(4) Fantasien, op. 9

Jean-Jacques Dünki, pf (rec. 1985) [3:37, 5:27, 3:16, 1:20]
    LP: Jecklin 594 — Dp. 5/85; Fono. 9/85; Gr. 1/86
    CD: Jecklin jd 594-2 — Fa. 3/89; Dp. 3/89; Fono. 3/89

Siegfried Mauser, pf (rec. Dec. 1993) [14:12]
  CD: Virgin 5 45125 2 — Dp. 6/95; Gr. 9/95; Fono. 9/95
Marco Rapetti, pf (rec. 2001)
  CD: Frame 9931/2 [2] — issued 4/02 ["Yearbooks of the 20th-Century Piano"]
Silke Avenhaus, pf (rec. 5–7 July 2003) [2:30, 3:23, 3:29, 1:27]
  CD: Naxos 8.557331 — Fa. 11/05

Fuge in G minor

Siegfried Mauser, pf (rec. Dec. 1993) [3:41]
  CD: Virgin 5 45125 2 — Dp. 6/95; Gr. 9/95; Fono. 9/95

Ein Lichtstrahl

Silke Avenhaus, pf (rec. 5–7 July 2003) [17:35]
  CD: Naxos 8.557331 — Fa. 11/05

(12) Ländliche Tänze, op. 1

Jean-Jacques Dünki, pf (rec. 1985) [0:41, 1:35, 2:02, 1:24, 2:24, 0:57, 1:34, 0:48, 1:10, 1:07, 1:08, 1:05]
  LP: Jecklin 594 — Dp. 5/85; Fono. 9/85; Gr. 1/86
  CD: Jecklin JD 594-2 — Fa. 3/89; Dp. 3/89; Fono. 3/89
Siegfried Mauser, pf (rec. Dec. 1993) [18:21]
  CD: Virgin 5 45125 2 — Dp. 6/95; Gr. 9/95; Fono. 9/95
Silke Avenhaus, pf (rec. 5–7 July 2003) [0:58, 1:22, 1:48, 1:14, 2:12, 0:48, 1:25, 0:52, 1:04, 1:00, 2:08]
  CD: Naxos 8.557331 — Fa. 11/05

Menuett

Silke Avenhaus, pf (rec. 5–7 July 2003) [1:10]
  CD: Naxos 8.557331 — Fa. 11/05

Skizze

Siegfried Mauser, pf (rec. Dec. 1993) [3:28]
  CD: Virgin 5 45125 2 — Dp. 6/95; Gr. 9/95; Fono. 9/95
Silke Avenhaus, pf (rec. 5–7 July 2003) [2:32]
  CD: Naxos 8.557331 — Fa. 11/05

Chamber

Humoreske

Belgian Woodwind Quintet: Jean-Michel Tanguy, fl; Louis Op 't Eynde, ob; Hedwig
  Swimberghe, cl; Herman Lemahieu, hr; Yves Bomont, bsn
  LP: Pavane ADW 7152 — Dp. cat. 9/84; Gr. 2/85 ["Three Centuries of Woodwind
  Quintets"]

Albert Schweitzer Quintet: Angela Tetzlaff, fl; Christiane Dimigen, ob; Diemut Schneider, cl; Silke Schurak, hr; Eckart Hübner, bsn

LP: Harmonia Mundi DMR 2013 — issued 1986; Biel. 10/87 [+ Danzi, Hindemith, Ligeti, Mozart]

LP: Harmonia Mundi 835131 — 1992

Aulos Woodwind Quintet: Peter Rijkx, fl; Diethelm Jonas, ob; Karl Theo Adler, cl; Dietmar Ullrich, hr; Ralph Sabow, bsn (rec. 1986) [4:18]

LP: Schwann VMS 1063 — Gr. 2/89 [+ Holst, Nielsen]

CD: Koch Schwann 310100 — Fa. 1/91 [+ Holst, Nielsen, Jolivet, Pierné]

Berlin Philharmonic Wind Quintet: Michael Hasel, fl; Andreas Wittmann, ob; Walter Seyfarth, cl; Fergus McWilliam, hr; Henning Trog, bsn (rec. 17–22 Nov. 1992) [4:29]

CD: BIS CD 612 — Fa. 9/94 [+ J. Foerster, K. Pilss (Pliss), C. Reinecke]

CD: King BIS KKCC 2154 — issued in Japan 8/94

Zemlinsky Quintett Wien: Heidrun Wagner-Lanzendörfer, fl; Andrea Krauk, ob; Kurt Franz Schmid, cl; Michael Gasciarino, hr; Gottfried Pokorny, bsn (rec. 1996) [4:05]

CD: ORF. 2000388 — issued 1997 [+ Danzi, Ligeti, Mozart, Damase]

CD: Preiser 114 — issued 2007

Hans-Udo Heinzmann, fl; Malte Lammers, ob; Walter Hermann, cl; Bernd Künkele, hr; Björn Groth, bsn (rec. 5 Oct. 1996) [4:04]

CD: Thorofon CTH 2376 — Fono. 12/98; Fa. 3/99

Vienna Wind Quintet: Hansgeorg Schmeiser, fl; Harald Hörth, ob; Helmut Hödl, cl; Martin Brahmböck, hr; Maximilian Feiertag, bsn (rec. 28 Apr. to 2 May 1997) [4:06]

CD: Nimbus NI 5542 — Gr. 4/98 ["Strauss in Vienna"]

Vento Chiaro: Joanna Goldstein, fl; Ana-Sophia Campesino, ob; Michelle Doyle, cl; Jason White, hr; Ellen Barnum, bsn (rec. 3–5 Jan. 2008)

CD: Ongaku 024-120 — Fa. 3/09 ["Music for Wind Quintet"]

Hunting Piece

Bernd Künkele, hr; Thorsten Schwesig, hr; Jürgen Lamke, pf (rec. 5 Oct. 1996) [5:23]

CD: Thorofon CTH 2376 — Fono. 12/98; Fa. 3/99

Quartet no. 1, op. 4

La Salle Quartet: Walter Levin, Henry Meyer, Peter Kamnitzer, Lee Fiser (rec. 5–10 Dec. 1980) [10:40, 4:10, 6:03, 5:31]

LP: D.G. 2741 016 [3] — Fono. 11/82; Dp. 12/82; Fa. 3/83 [+ H. Apostel op. 7]

CD: D.G. 427421-2 [2] — Dp. 6/89; Gr. 8/89; Fono. 8/89; Fa. 1/90 [+ same]

Vienna Quartet: Werner Hink, Hubert Kroishamer, Klaus Peisteiner, Fritz Dolesal (rec. 16–17 Apr. 1988) [12:24, 5:45, 6:54, 7:52]

CD: Camerata 32CM 99 — Fa. 11/90 [+ Berg, Webern]

Schoenberg Quartet: Janneke van der Meer, Wim de Jong, Henk Guittart, Viola de
    Hoog (rec. 14–15 Dec. 1993) [9:09, 4:41, 7:26, 5:31]
    CD: Chandos CHAN 9772 [2] — Fa. 9/02; Dp. 10/02; Gr. 13/02

Artemis Quartet: Heime Müller, Natalia Prichepenko, Volker Jacobsen, Eckart Runge
    (rec. 19–21 Nov. 1996) [26:42]
    CD: Ars Musici AMP 5076-2 — Biel. 3/98; Dp. 6/02 [+ Berg, Webern, Wolf]

Prazák Quartet: Václav Remeš, Vlastimil Holek, Josef Klusoň, Michal Kaňka (rec.
    Sept. 1997 and Mar. 1998) [11:29, 4:19, 6:50, 6:54]
    CD: Praga PRD 250107 — Dp. 9/98; Gr. 11/98

Artis Quartet Vienna: Peter Schuhmayer, Johannes Meissl, Herbert Kefer, Othmar
    Müller (rec. 15–18 Dec. 1997) [10:20, 4:01, 6:49, 5:10]
    CD: Nimbus NI 5563 — Gr. 11/98; Fono. 3/99; Dp. 12/99

Corda Quartet: Olga Nodel, Christiane Plath, Frauke Tometten Molino, Edith Salz-
    mann (rec. 22–24 June 1998) [11:14, 4:26, 6:41, 6:09]
    CD: Stradivarius STR 33564 — Dp. 11/00

Brodsky Quartet: Andrew Haveron, Ian Belton, Paul Cassidy, Jacqueline Thomas (rec.
    8–9 June 1999) [10:49, 5:04, 6:59, 6:54]
    CD: Vanguard 99208 — Gr. 4/00; Klassik 4/00 [+ Schoenberg, Webern]
    CD: Challenge Classics CC 72040 — issued 11/99

Castagneri Quartet: Jean-Marc Bourret, Martial Gautier, Daniel Vagner, Yovan Marko-
    vitch (rec. 8, 11 Jan. 2000) [12:24, 4:31, 7:04, 7:45]
    CD: Le Chant du Monde LDC 2781130 — Dp. 12/00; Fa. 3/01 [+ Brahms op. 51/2]

Zemlinsky Quartet: František Souček, Petr Střížek, Petr Holman, Vladimír Fortin
    (rec. 2007)
    CD: Praga PRED 350029 — Dp. 11/07; Gr. 12/07

Quartet no. 2, op. 15

La Salle Quartet* (rec. 5–8 May 1978) [3:27, 14:35, 5:48, 15:05]
    LP: D.G. 2530 982 — Gr. 4/79; Fono. 6/79; Dp. 7/80
    LP: D.G. 2741 016 [3] — Fono. 11/82; Dp. 12/82; Fa. 3/83; Gr. 2/84
    CD: D.G. 427421-2 [2] — Dp. 6/89; Gr. 8/89; Fono. 8/89; Fa. 1/90

Artis Quartet Vienna* (rec. 22–24 June 1989) [9:08, 7:13, 8:42, 11:10]
    LP: Orfeo A 194891; S 194901 — Biel. 10/90 [+ Schoenberg Qt. in D]
    CD: Orfeo C 194891; C 194901 — Gr. 7/90; Fa. 11/90; Dp. 11/90

Schoenberg Quartet* (rec. 1990) [10:00, 9:10, 5:50, 3:34, 11:21]
    CD: Koch Schwann 310118 — Fono. 2/92; Fa. 3/92; Gr. 3/92; Dp. 3/92

Artis Quartet Vienna* (rec. 15–18 Dec. 1997) [5:48, 11:42, 3:48, 4:22, 3:23, 9:14]
    CD: Nimbus NI 5563 — Gr. 11/98; Fono. 3/99; Dp. 12/99

Schoenberg Quartet* (rec. 30 June to 1 July 2000) [10:39, 9:19, 5:44, 16:00]
    CD: Chandos CHAN 9772 [2] — Fa. 9/02; Dp. 10/02; Gr. 13/02

Johannes Quartet: Frédéric Angleraux, Jérôme Meunier, Nicolas Mouret, Jean-
    Sébastien Barbey (rec. May 2001)
    CD: Assaï 222472 — Dp. 2/03 [+ H. Eisler, Webern]

Kocián Quartet: Pavel Hula, Jan Odstrcil, Zbynek Padourek, Václav Bernásek (rec. 18–19 Jan. 2003) [39:30]

    CD: Praga PRD 250193 — Dp. 7/03; Fa. 3/04

Casals Quartet: Vera Martínez Mehner, Abel Tomàs Realp, Jonathan Brown, Arnau Tomàs Realp (rec. 24–26 June 2004) [9:40, 2:40, 5:38, 3:13, 5:47, 5:17]

    CD: Harmonia Mundi Fr. HMI 987057 — Fa. 7/05; Gr. 7/05 [+ Debussy Qt.]

Quartet no. 3, op. 19

La Salle Quartet* (rec. 5–10 Dec. 1980) [7:07, 5:12, 4:37, 4:59]

    LP: D.G. 2741 016 [3] — Fono. 11/82; Dp. 12/82; Fa. 3/83; Gr. 2/84

    CD: D.G. 427421-2 [2] — Dp. 6/89; Gr. 8/89; Fono. 8/89; Fa. 1/90

Kroft Qt: Josef Kroft, Pavel Arazim, Jan Marek, Ladislav Pospisil (rec. 14–15 Dec. 1982) [7:38, 6:00, 9:50]

    LP: Supraphon 1111 3610 — 1985 [+ Berg, Webern]

Schoenberg Quartet* (rec. 1990) [8:04, 5:25, 5:49, 5:23]

    CD: Koch Schwann 310118 — Fono. 2/92; Fa. 3/92; Gr. 3/92; Dp. 3/92

Kocián Quartet* (rec. 1 Sept. 1995) [7:36, 6:12, 4:58, 5:06]

    CD: Praga PR 250092 — Dp. 3/96; Fono. 6/96; Fa. 7/96; Gr. 7/96

    CD: Praga PRD 250193 — Dp. 7/03; Fa. 3/04

Artis Quartet Vienna* (rec. 23–26 Mar. 1998) [7:31, 5:17, 4:17, 4:45]

    CD: Nimbus NI 5604 — Gr. 7/99; Fono. 11/99; Dp. 12/99 [+ J. Müller-Hermann]

Corda Quartet* (rec. 22–24 June 1998) [7:38, 5:44, 5:09, 5:46]

    CD: Stradivarius STR 33564 — Dp. 11/00

Schoenberg Quartet* (rec. 16–17 Jan. 2001) [8:51, 5:55, 5:32, 5:45]

    CD: Chandos CHAN 9772 [2] — Fa. 9/02; Dp. 10/02; Gr. 13/02

Zemlinsky Quartet* (rec. 2007)

    CD: Praga PRED 350029 — Dp. 11/07; Gr. 12/07

Quartet Movements

Schoenberg Quartet* (rec. 15 Feb. 1994) [7:28, 8:01]

    CD: Chandos CHAN 9772 [2] — Fa. 9/02; Dp. 10/02; Gr. 13/02

Katrin Schaitzbach, Mayumi Shimizu, vlns; Jakob (Jaap) Zeijl, vla; Michael Katzenmaier, vlc (rec. 5 Oct. 1996) [7:23, 8:04]

    CD: Thorofon CTH 2376 — Fono. 12/98; Fa. 3/99

Corda Quartet* (rec. 27–29 May 1996) [7:36, 7:28]

    CD: Stradivarius STR 33438 — Gr. 10/97; Dp. 7/98 [+ Schoenberg]

Prazák Quartet* (rec. Mar. 1998) [7:29, 7:26]

    CD: Praga PRD 250107 — Dp. 9/98; Gr. 11/98

Quartet no. 4, op. 25

La Salle Quartet* (rec. 14–19 Dec. 1981) [3:48, 4:58, 2:56, 4:11, 4:44, 3:09]

    LP: D.G. 2741 016 [3] — Fono. 11/82; Dp. 12/82; Fa. 3/83; Gr. 2/84

    CD: D.G. 427421-2 [2] — Dp. 6/89; Gr. 8/89; Fono. 8/89; Fa. 1/90

Schoenberg Quartet* (rec. 16–17 Dec. 1993) [4:05, 5:29, 2:52, 4:40, 5:19, 3:13]
    CD: Chandos CHAN 9772 [2] — Fa. 9/02; Dp. 10/02; Gr. 13/02
Lark Quartet (New York): Eva Gruesser, Jennifer Orchard, Anna Krueger, Astrid
    Schween (rec. 10–12 June 1995) [4:25, 4:45, 3:21, 4:21, 5:26, 3:09]
    CD: Arabesque Z 6671 — Fa. 7/96 [+ Schoenberg op. 7]
Prazák Quartet* (rec. Sept. 1997) [4:30, 5:08, 2:49, 4:07, 5:09, 3:07]
    CD: Praga PRD 250107 — Dp. 9/98; Gr. 11/98
Artis Quartet Vienna* (rec. 23–26 Mar. 1998) [3:45, 4:54, 2:51, 4:08, 4:49, 3:02]
    CD: Nimbus NI 5604 — Gr. 7/99; Fono. 11/99; Dp. 12/99 [+ J. Müller-Hermann]
Corda Quartet* (rec. 22–24 June 1998) [3:49, 4:59, 2:22, 4:50, 4:36, 3:27]
    CD: Stradivarius STR 33564 — Dp. 11/00

Quartet for Clarinet and Strings (fragments)

Walter Hermann, cl; Katrin Schaitzbach, vln; Jakob Zeijl, vla; Michael Katzenmaier,
    vlc (rec. 5 Oct. 1996) [2:11, 4:32]
    CD: Thorofon CTH 2376 — Fono. 12/98; Fa. 3/99

Quintet Movements

Corda Quartet*; Andrea Wennberg, 2 vla (rec. 27–29 May 1996) [13:37, 5:27]
    CD: Stradivarius STR 33438 — Gr. 10/97; Dp. 7/98 [+ Schoenberg]
Vienna String Sextet members* (rec. Feb. 2000) [13:04, 8:02]
    CD: Pan Classics PC 10120 — Klassik 2/01 [+ Korngold op. 10]

Serenade (Suite) in A major

Kamilla Schatz, vln; Silke Avenhaus, pf (rec. Feb. 1996) [2:16, 6:24, 3:43, 3:22, 4:49]
    CD: Discover International DICD 920397 — Biel. 10/98 [+ Bartók, Hindemith, Rudolf
    Moser]
Sergiu Schwartz, vln; Alec Chien, pf (rec. July 2002) [2:24, 6:21, 3:27, 3:29, 3:42]
    CD: Roméo 7220 — issued 1/03; Biel. 10/03 ["Poème mystique"]
Mirijam Contzen, vln; Herbert Schuch, pf (rec. 27–29 Nov. 2006) [2:27, 6:45, 4:06,
    3:42, 3:47]
    CD: Oehms OC 596 — Klassik 9/07 [+ Schubert, Brahms]
Elena Denisova, vln; Alexei Kornienko, pf (rec. 30 Aug. 2005) [2:17, 6:41, 3:42, 3:50,
    3:43]
    CD: Gramola 98776 — issued 12/05 [+ R. Fuchs, P. Singer]
Thomas Albertus Imberger, vln; Evgeny Sinaisky, pf (rec. 20–22 Apr. 2007) [2:28, 6:45,
    4:04, 4:06, 4:10]
    CD: Gramola 98833 — issued 5/08 [+ Goldmark, Korngold, Schoenberg]

Sonata for Cello (1894)

Raphael Wallfisch, vlc; John York, pf (rec. 30–31 May 2006) [11:22, 9:05, 8:58]
    CD: Nimbus NI 5806 — Gr. 5/07 [+ Goldmark, Korngold]

Discography   341

Johannes Moser, vlc; Paul Rivinius, pf (rec. 18 Dec. 2006) [10:44, 7:34, 7:49]
  CD: Hänssler 93206 — Gr. 10/07; Fa. 11/07 [+ Brahms, R. Fuchs]
Othmar Müller, vlc; Christopher Hinterhuber, pf (rec. 9–11 Apr. 2007) [9:58, 9:13, 8:24]
  CD: Naxos 8.570540 — Fa. 9/08; Dp. 11/08

Three Pieces for Cello (1891)

Othmar Müller, vlc; Christopher Hinterhuber, pf (rec. 9–11 Apr. 2007) [2:59, 3:27, 1:38]
  CD: Naxos 8.570540 — Fa. 9/08; Dp. 11/08
Raphael Wallfisch, vlc; John York, pf (rec. 30–31 May 2006) [2:46, 2:42, 1:42]
  CD: Nimbus NI 5806 — Gr. 5/07 [+ Goldmark, Korngold]

Trio in D minor (cl, vlc, pf), op. 3

Schubert-Weber Trio: Ernst Kindermann, cl; Günter Lösch, vlc; Siegfried Schubert-
    Weber, pf (rec. 4–19 Apr. 1980) [9:37, 7:51, 5:13]
  LP: FSM Brockhoff 53225 — Fono. 2/81 [+ W. Berger op. 94]
Chester Brezniak, cl; Richard Sher, vlc; Christopher O'Riley, pf (rec. Dec. 1982) [12:57,
    9:36, 5:34]
  LP: Northeastern NR 215 — Fa. 3/86
Eduard Brunner, cl; David Geringas, vlc; Gerhard Oppitz, pf (rec. 28 Jan. & 26 June
    1985) [14:37, 9:08, 5:19]
  LP: Tudor 73053 — Dp. 3/88 [+ Schoenberg op. 9]
  CD: Tudor 717 — Dp. 3/88; Fono. 4/88; Fa. 9/88
Danish Trio: Jens Schou, cl; Svend Winsløv, vlc; Rosalind Bevan, pf (rec. 1987) [10:50,
    9:12, 5:52]
  CD: Paula PACD 52 — Dp. 9/88; Fa. 11/88 [+ Brahms op. 114]
Kari Kriikku, cl; Martti Rousi, vlc; Arto Satukangas, pf (rec. May or Aug. 1990) [13:40,
    8:20, 5:26]
  CD: Ondine ODE 760 — Dp. 9/91; Fa. 11/91 [+ Bruch op. 83]
Walter Boeykens, cl; Roel Dieltiens, vlc; Robert Groslot, pf (rec. Feb. 1991) [15:15, 8:34,
    5:38]
  CD: Harmonia Mundi Fr. HMC 901371 — Dp. 1/92; ARG 3/92; Gr. 4/92
  CD: Harmonia Mundi Fr. HMA 1901371 — issued 1995 [+ Bruch op. 83]
Trio Zemlinsky: Thomas Friedli, cl; Annick Gautier, vlc; Patricia Thomas, pf (rec.
    11–13 May 1992) [13:10, 7:38, 5:35]
  CD: Claves 50-9217 — Fono. 4/93; Dp. 4/93; Fa. 5/93 [+ Bruch op. 83]
Amici Chamber Ensemble: Joaquin Valdepeñas, cl; David Hetherington, vlc; Patricia
    Parr, pf [14:27, 8:47, 5:28]
  CD: Summit DCD 151 — P 1993; Fa. 5/94 [+ Beethoven, Chan Ka Nin]
Trio Paideia: Hans Dietrich Klaus, cl; Claus Kanngiesser, vlc; Nerine Barrett, pf (rec.
    1996) [13:54, 8:05, 5:43]
  CD: Tacet 58 — Fono. 6/97; Fa. 7/99 [+ Brahms op. 114, P. Juon]

Ensemble Kontraste: Reiner Wehle, cl; Christoph Marks, vlc; Friederike Richter, pf
    (rec. 1997) [14:20, 9:20, 5:18]
    CD: Thorofon CTH 2368 — Fa. 7/99 [+ Brahms op. 114, W. Rabl op. 1]
Henk de Graaf, cl; Wladislav Warenberg, vlc; Daniel Wayenberg, pf (rec. Dec. 1998)
    [12:01, 7:38, 5:16]
    CD: WRPHO. F 6972 — issued 1999 [+ Beethoven, Glinka, Brahms]
Roger Salander, cl; Fritz Dolezal, vlc; Patrick Dheur, pf (rec. live 25 Feb. 2002) [13:56,
    8:57, 5:22]
    CD: ORF. CD299 — Fa. 9/07 [+ C. Frühling op. 40]
Ernst Ottensamer, cl; Othmar Müller, vlc; Christopher Hinterhuber, pf (rec. 9–11 Apr.
    2007) [13:29, 9:28, 5:47]
    CD: Naxos 8.570540 — Fa. 9/08; Dp. 11/08
The recording of the clarinet trio announced on Analekta is nonexistent.

— *arr. Zemlinsky for vln, vlc, pf*

Vienna Schubert Trio: Boris Kuschnir, vln; Martin Hornstein, vlc; Claus-Christian
    Schuster, pf
    LP: Pan 170012 — Gr. 12/87 [+ Grieg, Shostakovich]
Clementi Trio Cologne: Daniel Spektor, vln; Manuel Gerstner, vlc; Deborah Richards,
    pf (rec. Jan. 1987) [13:43, 8:44, 5:26]
    LP: Largo 5011 — Biel. 3/88 [+ Schoenberg op. 4]
    CD: Largo 5111 — Fa. 1/89, 3/92
Beaux Arts Trio: Isidore Cohen, vln; Peter Wiley, vlc; Menahem Pressler, pf (rec. June
    1992) [13:26, 8:45, 5:24]
    CD: Philips 434072-2 — Dp. 5/94; Gr. 6/94; ARG 9/94 [+ Korngold]
Dresdner Klaviertrio: Kai Vogler, vln; Peter Bruhns, vlc; Roglit Ishay, pf (rec. live 30
    Nov. 1995) [9:15, 7:07, 5:06]
    CD: International Physicians IPPNW-Concerts CD 17 — issued 1996 [+ Schubert op.
    99]
Vidor Nagy, viola; Jürgen Gerlinger, vlc; Carmen Piazzini, pf (rec. 15–16 Nov. 2004)
    [28:15])
    CD: Edition Hera 02119 — Fa. 5/08 [+ Beethoven, Brahms]
Vienna Piano Trio: Wolfgang Redik, vln; Matthias Gredler, vlc; Stefan Mendl, pf (rec.
    6–8 Dec. 2004) [12:13, 7:04, 5:14]
    CD: MDG. 342 1354 — Fa. 5/06 [+ Schoenberg, Mahler]

Choral

Aurikelchen

James Conlon, Mülheimer Kantorei (rec. 16, 22, 23 June 1998) [1:12]
    CD: EMI 5 56783 2 — Dp. 1/99; Fono. 4/99; Gr. 6/99; Fa. 7/99
    CD: EMI 5 86079 2 [2] — Fa. 7/05

Frühlingsbegräbnis

Deborah Voigt (s), Donnie Ray Albert (bar), James Conlon, Düsseldorf Musikverein
    Chorus, Cologne Gürzenich Orch (rec. live 18 Mar. 1997) [4:17, 2:39+4:01, 2:22,
    3:04, 1:50, 6:03]
  CD: EMI 5 56474 2 — Dp. 12/97; Fa. 9/98
  CD: EMI 5 56783 2 — Dp. 1/99; Fono. 4/99; Gr. 6/99; Fa. 7/99
  CD: EMI 5 75184 2 [2] — Biel. 10/03
  CD: EMI 5 86079 2 [2] — Fa. 7/05
Edith Mathis (s), Roland Hermann (bar), Antony Beaumont, Hamburg NDR Chorus
    and SO (rec. 16–17 Apr. 1997) [4:18, 5:21, 2:01, 3:07, 1:57, 5:57]
  CD: Capriccio 10740 — Fono. 12/97; Dp. 6/98; Fa. 11/98

Frühlingsglaube

James Conlon, Mülheimer Kantorei (rec. 16, 22, 23 June 1998) [4:25]
  CD: EMI 5 56783 2 — Dp. 1/99; Fono. 4/99; Gr. 6/99; Fa. 7/99
  CD: EMI 5 86079 2 [2] — Fa. 7/05

Geheimnis

James Conlon, Mülheimer Kantorei, Cologne Gürzenich Orch (rec. 16, 22, 23 June
    1998) [1:29]
  CD: EMI 5 56783 2 — Dp. 1/99; Fono. 4/99; Gr. 6/99; Fa. 7/99
  CD: EMI 5 86079 2 [2] — Fa. 7/05

Hochzeitsgesang

Lothar Blum (t), James Conlon, Mülheimer Kantorei; Romano Giefer, org (rec. 16, 22,
    23 June 1998) [3:21]
  CD: EMI 5 56783 2 — Dp. 1/99; Fono. 4/99; Gr. 6/99; Fa. 7/99
  CD: EMI 5 86079 2 [2] — Fa. 7/05

Minnelied

James Conlon, Mülheimer Kantorei, Cologne Gürzenich Orch (rec. 16, 22, 23 June
    1998) [5:04]
  CD: EMI 5 56783 2 — Dp. 1/99; Fono. 4/99; Gr. 6/99; Fa. 7/99
  CD: EMI 5 86079 2 [2] — Fa. 7/05

Psalm 13, op. 24

Riccardo Chailly, Ernst-Senff-Chor, Berlin Radio SO (rec. Mar. 1986) [13:43]
  LP: Decca 417450-1 — Gr. 6/87
  LP: Decca 6.43548 az — Fono. 7/87
  CD: Decca 417450-2 — Gr. 6/87; Dp. 6/87; Fono. 7/87; Fa. 11/87
  CD: Decca 444969-2 — Dp. 10/96
  CD: Decca 473734-2 [2] — Gr. 6/03

Karl Anton Rickenbacker, Berlin Radio SO and Chorus (rec. 8–10 Mar. 1994) [13:14]
  CD: Koch 3 1486 2; 231 486 2 – Gr. 7/99; Dp. 7/99

James Conlon, Düsseldorf Musikverein Chorus, Cologne Gürzenich Orch (rec. live
    18–21 Apr. 1998) [13:13]
  CD: EMI 5 56783 2 – Dp. 1/99; Fono. 4/99; Gr. 6/99; Fa. 7/99
  CD: EMI 5 86079 2 [2] – Fa. 7/05

Peter Ruzicka, Berlin Radio Chorus (rec. live 7 Mar. 2003) [15:21]
  CD: Profil PH 04036 – issued 2004 [+ Markevitch, Korngold, Bloch]

Psalm 23, op. 14

Riccardo Chailly, Ernst-Senff-Chor, Berlin Radio SO (rec. Sept. 1987) [10:55]
  CD: Decca 421644-2 – Gr. 3/89; Dp. 3/89; Fono. 5/89; Fa. 9/89
  CD: Decca 444969-2 – Dp. 10/96
  CD: Decca 473734-2 [2] – Gr. 6/03

Michael Gielen, Bratislava Phil. Cho., Baden-Baden Radio SO (rec. June 1988) [10:24]
  CD: Intercord 830879 – Biel. 10/90 [+ Reger op. 114]
  CD: Intercord 860911 – Dp. 2/94
  CD: Intercord 544052-2 – 1995

Karl Anton Rickenbacker, Berlin Radio SO and Chorus (rec. 8–10 Mar. 1994) [10:22]
  CD: Koch 3 1486 2; 231 486 2 – Gr. 7/99; Dp. 7/99

James Conlon, Düsseldorf Musikverein Chorus, Cologne Gürzenich Orch (rec. live
    18–21 Apr. 1998) [10:16]
  CD: EMI 5 56783 2 – Dp. 1/99; Fono. 4/99; Gr. 6/99; Fa. 7/99
  CD: EMI 5 86079 2 [2] – Fa. 7/05

— arr. Erwin Stein

Reinbert de Leeuw, Netherlands Chamber Choir, Schoenberg Ensemble (rec. May
    1981) [11:47]
  LP: Philips 411088-1 – Gr. 3/84 [+ Schoenberg]

Psalm 83

Karl Anton Rickenbacker, Berlin Radio SO and Chorus (rec. 8–10 Mar. 1994) [13:36]
  CD: Koch 3 1486 2; 231 486 2 – Gr. 7/99; Dp. 7/99

James Conlon, Düsseldorf Musikverein Chorus, Cologne Gürzenich Orch (rec. live
    18–21 Apr. 1997) [14:08]
  CD: EMI 5 56783 2 – Dp. 1/99; Fono. 4/99; Gr. 6/99; Fa. 7/99
  CD: EMI 5 86079 2 [2] – Fa. 7/05

Riccardo Chailly, Slovak Phil. Choir, Vienna PO (rec. 9–13 June 1998) [12:18]
  CD: Decca 460213-2 – Dp. 11/98; Gr. 1/99; Fa. 3/99 [+ Janacek, Korngold]
  CD: Decca 473734-2 [2] – Gr. 6/03

Stage

Cymbeline (incidental music)

Jaroslav Březina (t), Antony Beaumont, Czech PO, with members of the Bremen Shakespeare Company (rec. 14–19 May 2002) [3:48, 0:59, 2:14, 1:22, 0:19, 3:03, 0:42, 1:59, 0:53, 2:47, 8:22]
    CD: Chandos CHAN 10069 — Fa. 5/04

— suite

David Kübler (t), James Conlon, Cologne Gürzenich Orch (rec. 20–22 Oct. 1996) [4:46, 3:57, 1:18, 3:57, 3:16]
    CD: EMI 5 56474 2 — Dp. 12/97; Fa. 9/98
    CD: EMI 5 75184 2 [2] — Biel. 10/03

Es war einmal

Eva Johansson (s), *Princess*; Kurt Westi (t), *Prince*; Per Arne Wahlgren (bar), *Kaspar*; Aage Haugland (bs), *King*; Ole Hedegaard (t), *Suitor*; Guido Paevatalu (bar), *Commissioner*; Christian Christiansen (bs), *Commander, Herald*; Susse Lillesoe (s), *Lady in waiting*; Hans Graf, Danish National Radio SO and Chorus (rec. June 1987) [104:04]
    CD: Capriccio 60019-2 [2] — Fono. 2/91; Fa. 3/91; Dp. 3/91; Gr. 5/91

— prelude to Act 1

Antony Beaumont, Czech PO (rec. 17–19 Jan. 2001) [5:37]
    CD: Nimbus NI 5682 — Gr. 11/01
    CD: Chandos CHAN 10204 — Dp. 7/04; Fa. 1/05
James Conlon, Cologne Gürzenich Orch (rec. live 23–28 Aug. 2001) [5:29]
    CD: EMI 5 57307 2 — Dp. 5/02
    CD: EMI 3 72481 2 — 2007

— Zwischenspiele

James Conlon, Cologne Gürzenich Orch (rec. live 23–28 Aug. 2001) [5:04]
    CD: EMI 5 57307 2 — Dp. 5/02
    CD: EMI 3 72481 2 — 2007

Eine florentinische Tragödie, op. 16

Sigune von Osten (s), *Bianca*; Werner Götz (t), *Guido Bardi*; Heinz-Jürgen Demitz (bar), *Simone*; Friedrich Pleyer, La Fenice Theatre Orch (rec. live 4 Oct. 1980) [50:40]
    LP: (Fonit Cetra) Musica/Aperta LMA 3010 — Gr. 5/82; Fono. 10/82
Doris Soffel (ms), *Bianca*; Kenneth Riegel (t), *Guido Bardi*; Guillermo Sarabia (bs), *Simone*; Gerd Albrecht, Berlin Radio SO (rec. Oct–Nov. 1983) [52:25]
    LP: Schwann VMS 1625 — Dp. 2/85; Fa. 5/85; Fono. 5/85; Gr. 9/85
    CD: Schwann CD 11625 — Fono. 10/85; Gr. 12/85
    CD: Koch Schwann 314012 — 1989

Iris Vermillion (ms), *Bianca*; Heinz Kruse (t), *Guido Bardi*; Albert Dohmen (bar), *Simone*; Riccardo Chailly, Concertgebouw Orch of Amsterdam (rec. 25–29 Apr. 1996) [53:37]

    CD: Decca 455112-2 — Dp. 11/97; Gr. 12/97; Fono. 3/98; Fa. 5/98

    CD: Decca 473734-2 [2] — Gr. 6/03 [+ A. Mahler]

Deborah Voigt (s), *Bianca*; David Kübler (t), *Guido Bardi*; Donnie Ray Albert (bar), *Simone*; James Conlon, Cologne Gürzenich Orch (rec. live Mar. 1997) [55:43]

    CD: EMI 5 56472 2 — Dp. 11/97; Fono. 3/98; Fa. 9/98

Iris Vermillion (ms), *Bianca*; Viktor Lutsiuk (t), *Guido Bardi*; Albert Dohmen (bar), *Simone*; Armin Jordan, Radio France PO (rec. live 13 Sept. 2003) [60:26]

    CD: Naïve v 4987 — Dp. 10/04; Gr. 3/05

Kleider machen Leute

Hermann Winkler (t), *Wenzel Strapinski*; Edith Mathis (s), *Nettchen*; Wicus Slabbert (bs), *Melchior Böhni*; Hans Franzen (bs), *Adam Litumlei*; Stefania Kaluza (a), *Frau Litumlei*; Volker Vogel (t), *Polykarpus Federspiel*; Ueli Hunziker, *Schneidermeister*; Björn Jensson, *1 Schneidergeselle, Der Hausknecht*; Ulrich Simon Eggimann, *2 Schneidergeselle*; Rudolf A. Hartmann, *Amtsrat*; Peter Keller, *Ältere Sohn*; Ruth Rohner, *Frau Häberlein*; Jacob Will, *Jüngere Sohn*; Rainer Scholze, *Der Wirt*; Renate Lenhart, *Die Wirtin*; Kimberly Justus, *Die Köchin*; Sarianna Salminen, *Der Kellnerjunge*; Claudio Otelli, *Der Kutscher*; Ulrich Peter, *Ein Prologus*; Ralf Weikert, Zurich Opera Chorus and Orch (rec. live 29 June 1990 [98:03]

    CD: Koch Schwann 314069 [2] — Gr. 1/92; Dp. 2/92; Fa. 3/92; Fono. 4/92

— *waltz-intermezzo and Zwischenspiel*
James Conlon, Cologne Gürzenich Orch (rec. live 23–28 Aug. 2001) [4:15, 4:08]

    CD: EMI 5 57307 2 — Dp. 5/02

    CD: EMI 3 72481 2 — 2007

Der König Kandaules

James O'Neal (t), *King Kandaules*; Monte Pederson (bar), *Gyges*; Nina Warren (s), *Nyssia*; Klaus Häger (bs), *Phedros*; Peter Galliard (t), *Syphax*; Mariusz Kwiecien (bar), *Nicomedes*; Kurt Gysen (bs), *Pharnaces*; Simon Yang (bs), *Philebos*; Ferdinand Seiler (t), *Sebas*; Guido Jentjens (bar), *Archelaos*; Gerd Albrecht, Hamburg State PO (rec. live 18, 25 Oct. 1996) [127:42]

    CD: Capriccio 60071-2 [2] — Fono. 7/97; Gr. 9/97; Dp. 9/97; Fa 3/98

    CD: Capriccio 10724 (*prelude to act 3 and monolog "Mein Ring" only*)

Robert Brubaker (t), *King Kandaules*; Wolfgang Schöne (bar), *Gyges*; Nina Stemme (s), *Nyssia*; Mel Ulrich (bar), *Phedros*; John Nuzzo (t), *Syphax*; Jochen Schmeckenbecher (bar), *Nicomedes*; Randall Jakobsch (bs), *Pharnaces*; Georg Zeppenfeld (bs), *Philebos*; John Dickie (t), *Sebas*; Almas Svilpa (bs), *Archelaos*; Jürgen

Sacher (t), *Simias*; Peter Loehle (bs), *Der Koch*: Kent Nagano, Deutsches SO Berlin and Mozarteum Orch Salzburg (rec. live 28 July 2002) [131:21]

    CD: Andante AN 3070 — Fa. 7/05

— prelude to Act 3

Gerd Albrecht, Hamburg State PO (rec. June 1992) [5:54]

    CD: Capriccio 10448 — Fono. 10/93; Dp. 12/93; Fa. 1/94; Gr. 3/94

James Conlon, Cologne Gürzenich Orch (rec. live 23–28 Aug. 2001) [5:42]

    CD: EMI 5 57307 2 — Dp. 5/02

    CD: EMI 3 72481 2 — 2007

Antony Beaumont, Czech PO (rec. 14 Mar. 2003) [5:30]

    CD: Chandos CHAN 10204 — Dp. 7/04; Fa. 1/05

— monolog "Mein Ring"

Franz Grundheber (bar), Gerd Albrecht, Hamburg State PO (rec. June 1992) [6:01]

    CD: Capriccio 10448 — Fono. 10/93; Dp. 12/93; Fa. 1/94; Gr. 3/94

Der Kreidekreis

Renate Behle (s), *Tschang-Haitang*; Gabriele Schreckenbach (ms), *Mrs. Tschang*; Roland Hermann (bar), *Ma*; Siegfried Lorenz (bar), *Tschao*; Reiner Goldberg (t), *Emperor Pao*; Uwe Peter (t), *Tong*; Hans Helm (bar), *Tschang-Ling*; Gertrud Ottenthal (s), *Mrs. Ma*; Kaja Borris (ms), *Midwife*; Gidon Saks (bar), *Soldier*; Celina Lindsley (s), *Girl*; Warren Mok (t), *1 Coolie*; Bengt-Ola Morgny (t), *2 Coolie*; Peter Matić (speaker), *Tschu-Tschu*; Stefan Soltesz, Berlin Radio SO (rec. 12–16 Feb. 1990) [124:12]

    CD: Capriccio 60016 [2] — Gr. 1/92; Fa. 3/92

— prelude to Act 3

James Conlon, Cologne Gürzenich Orch (rec. live 23–28 Aug. 2001) [2:16]

    CD: EMI 5 57307 2 — Dp. 5/02

    CD: EMI 3 72481 2 — 2007

Sarema

Karin Clarke (s), *Sarema*; Lásló Lukas (bar), *Dscherikoff*; Norbert Kleinhenn (t), *Asslan*; Andreas Scheel (bar), *Amul Beg*; Juri Zinovenko (bs), *Prophet*; Nick Herbosch (bs), *Godunoff*; Florian Simson (t), *Herald*; István Dénes, Trier Theatre Chorus and City Orch (rec. live 2–4 July 1996) [104:30]

    CD: Koch 3 6467 2 [2]; 236 467 2 [2] — Gr. 3/97; Fa. 5/97

— overture

Thomas Dausgaard, Danish Radio SO (rec. 1 May 1997) [5:46]

    CD: Chandos CHAN 9601 — Fono. 8/98; Dp. 9/98; Gr. 9/98; Fa. 11/98

James Conlon, Cologne Gürzenich Orch (rec. live 23–28 Aug. 2001) [5:43]

    CD: EMI 5 57307 2 — Dp. 5/02

    CD: EMI 3 72481 2 — issued 2007

Der Traumgörge

Janis Martin (s), *Gertraud, Princess*; Josef Protschka (t), *Görge*; Pamela Coburn (s),
    Grete; Hartmut Welker (bar), *Hans, Kaspar*; Martin Blasius (bs), *Pastor*; Pater
    Haage (t), *Innkeeper*; Victor von Halem (bs), *Miller, Mathis*; Heinz Kruse (t),
    Züngl; Birgit Calm (s), *Innkeeper's Wife*; Gabriele Maria Ronge (s), *Marei*; Gerd
    Albrecht, Hessian Radio Choirs, Frankfurt Radio SO (rec. live Sept. 1987) [111:00]
    CD: Capriccio 10241-42 — Fono. 1/89; Fa. 3/89; Gr. 3/89; Dp. 5/89

Patricia Racette (ms), *Gertraud*; David Kuebler (t), *Görge*; Iride Martinez (s), *Grete*;
    Andreas Schmidt (bar), *Hans*; Zelotes Edmund Toliver (bs), *Miller, Mathes*; Ju-
    lian Rodescu (bs), *Pastor, Peasant*; Susan Anthony (s), *Princess*; Machiko Obata
    (s), *Dream Voice, Innkeeper's Wife*; Michael Volle (bar), *Kaspar*; Lothar Odinius
    (t), *Züngl*; Nathalie Karl (s), *Marei*; John C. Pierce (t), *Innkeeper*; James Conlon,
    Opernchor der Hochschule für Musik Köln, Cologne Gürzenich Orch (rec. live
    6–8 June 1999) [147:27]
    CD: EMI 5 57087 2 [2] — Gr. 4/01; Dp. 4/01; Fa. 9/01

Der Zwerg, op. 17

Soile Isokoski (s), *Infanta*; David Kuebler (t), *Dwarf*; Iride Martinez (s), *Ghita*; An-
    drew Collis (bs), *Major-Domo*; Juanita Lascarro (s), *1 Maid*; Machiko Obata (s),
    2 Maid; Anne Schwanewilms (s), *3 Maid*; Natalie Karl (s), *1 Gespielen*; Martina
    Rueping (s), *2 Gespielen*; James Conlon, Frankfurt Kantorei, Cologne Gürzenich
    Orch (rec. live 11, 13 Feb. 1996) [86:35]
    CD: EMI 5 66247 2 [2] — Dp. 1/97; Gr. 6/97
    CD: EMI 5 56208 2 [2] — Fa. 7/97

— *libretto revised 1981 by Adolf Dresen as "Der Geburtstag der Infantin"*
Inga Nielsen (s), *Infanta*; Kenneth Riegel (t), *Dwarf*; Béatrice Haldas (s), *Ghita*; Dieter
    Weller (bs), *Major-Domo*; Cheryl Studer (s), *1 Maid*; Olive Fredericks (s), *2 Maid*;
    Marianne Hirsti (s), *3 Maid*; Gerd Albrecht, RIAS Kammerchor, Berlin Radio SO
    (rec. Oct–Nov. 1983) [73:30]
    LP: Schwann VMS 1626 [2] — Fono. 8/84; Dp. 9/84; Gr. 10/84; Fa. 11/84
    CD: Schwann CD 11626 — Gr. 4/86; Fa. 5/86; Dp. 6/86
    CD: Koch Schwann 314013 — 1989

Orchestral

Ein Lyrische Symphonie, op. 18

Dorothy Dorow (s), Siegmund Nimsgern (bar), Gabriele Ferro, BBC SO (rec. 13–14 Apr.
    1978) [46:00]
    LP: (Fonit Cetra) Italia ITL 70048 — P 1978; Gr. 6/79
    CD: Fonit Cetra CDC 70 — Biel. 10/95
    CD: Fonit Cetra 0927-43405-2 — 2004

Elisabeth Söderström (s), Dale Duesing (bar), Bernhard Klee, Berlin Radio SO (rec. 30 June – 2 July 1980) [11:03, 7:00, 7:12, 8:01, 1:54, 4:40, 8:56]

    LP: Schwann VMS 1602 — Gr. 3/82; Fa. 3/82

    CD: Schwann Musica Mundi CD 11602 — Fa. 9/86

    CD: Koch Schwann 311053 — 1989

Elisabeth Söderström (s), Thomas Allen (bar), Michael Gielen, BBC SO (rec. live 18 Feb. 1981) [10:52, 6:35, 6:19, 7:55, 1:49, 4:23, 7:49]

    CD: BBC Radio 15656 9185-2 — Biel. 3/98

Julia Varady (s), Dietrich Fischer-Dieskau (bar), Lorin Maazel, Berlin PO (rec. 10–12 Mar. 1981) [10:08, 5:56, 6:15, 7:06, 1:56, 4:07, 8:25]

    LP: D.G. 2532 021 — Gr. 3/82; Dp. 3/82; Fa. 9/82; Fono. 11/82

    CD: D.G. 419261-2 — Fono. 4/87; Gr. 6/87; Fa. 9/87

    CD: Brilliant 9120 — Dp. 10/09

Julia Varady (s), Dietrich Fischer-Dieskau (bar), Lothar Zagrosek, Vienna ORF SO (rec. live 9 Aug. 1982) [46:25]

    LP: ORF. 120654

    CD: Orfeo C 535001 — Dp. 11/00; Fa. 3/01 [+ K. A. Hartmann]

Karan Armstrong (s), Ivan Kusnjer (bar), Bohumil Gregor, Czech PO (rec. 16 Dec. 1987, 19 Apr. 1988) [11:44, 6:54, 6:54, 7:58, 2:10, 4:54, 8:12]

    LP: Supraphon 11 0395-1 — © 1989

    CD: Supraphon 11 0395-2 — Fono. 9/91; Gr. 10/91; Fa. 3/92; Dp. 5/92

    CD: Denon COCO 75609 — issued 8/93; COCO 70768 — issued 12/05

Jirina Marková (s), Ivan Kusnjer (bar), Vladimir Válek, Prague Radio SO (rec. live 4 Nov. 1992) [9:56, 6:14, 6:09, 5:40, 1:48, 3:57, 6:12]

    CD: Praga PR 250092 — Dp. 3/96; Fono. 6/96; Fa. 7/96; Gr. 7/96

Alessandra Marc (s), Hakan Hagegard (bar), Riccardo Chailly, Concertgebouw Orch of Amsterdam (rec. Mar. 1993) [10:38, 7:14, 6:35, 7:52, 2:05, 4:36, 8:07]

    CD: Decca 443569-2 — Gr. 12/94; Dp. 12/94; Fono. 1/95; Fa. 7/95

    CD: Decca 473734-2 [2] — Gr. 6/03

Luba Orgonásova (s), Bo Skovhus (bar), Claus Peter Flor, Hamburg NDR SO (rec. 8–12 Sept. 1994) [11:33, 6:50, 7:08, 8:48, 2:03, 4:57, 8:57]

    CD: RCA Victor 09026-68111-2 — Fono. 11/96; Gr. 12/96; Fa. 1/97

Vlatka Orsanic (s), James Johnson (bar), Michael Gielen, SWF SO (rec. 21–23 Feb. 1994) [9:24, 5:55, 5:27, 7:29, 1:53, 4:02, 6:54]

    CD: Arte Nova 74321-27768-2 — Dp. 2/97; Gr. 10/97 [+ Berg]

Deborah Voigt (s), Bryn Terfel (bs-bar), Giuseppe Sinopoli, Vienna PO (rec. live June 1995) [10:56, 6:51, 7:11, 8:30, 2:13, 5:10, 8:20]

    CD: D.G. 449179-2 — Fono. 11/96; Gr. 12/96; Dp. 12/96

    CD: Musical Heritage Society 516171 — 2001

Edith Wiens (s), Andreas Schmidt (bar), Armin Jordan, Orch de la Suisse Romande (rec. 27 June to 1 July 1995) [11:41, 6:33, 7:38, 8:08, 2:02, 4:35, 8:14]

    CD: FNAC Aria 592011 — Dp. 2/97; Fa. 5/97

    CD: Virgin 5 62215 2 [2] — Dp. 7/04 [+ Mahler 3rd]

Anita Bader (s), Roland Fenes (bar), Christian Ehwald, Magdeburg Philharmonie (rec. 2000) [11:06, 6:25. 6:45, 8:16, 2:12, 4:45, 9:02]

   CD: Bella Musica BM 31 2340 — Klassik 11/01

Soile Isokoski (s), Bo Skovhus (bar), James Conlon, Cologne Gürzenich Orch (rec. 23–28 Aug. 2001) [10:34, 6:16, 6:10, 7:38, 2:02, 4:41, 7:44]

   CD: EMI 5 57307 2 — Dp. 5/02

   CD: EMI 3 72481 2 — 2007

Turid Karlsen (s), Franz Grundheber (bar), Antony Beaumont, Czech PO (rec. 14–19 May 2002) [10:01, 6:21, 6:30, 7:05, 1:58, 4:11, 7:34]

   CD: Chandos CHAN 10069 — Fa. 5/04

Christine Schäfer (s), Matthias Goerne (bar), Christoph Eschenbach, Orch de Paris (rec. 22, 26 May 2005) [10:48, 7:18, 7:12, 9:57, 2:02, 5:23, 9:09]

   SACD: Capriccio 71081 — Gr. 7/06; Fa. 9/06

Twyla Robinson (s), Roman Trekel (bar), Hans Graf, Houston SO (rec. 9–11 Nov. 2007) [11:13, 6:30, 6:06, 7:39, 2:07, 4:33, 8:20]

   CD: Naxos 8.572048 — Dp. 10/09; Fa. 11/09 [+ Berg]

Die Seejungfrau

Riccardo Chailly, Berlin Radio SO (rec. Mar. 1986) [15:19, 12:18, 12:31]

   LP: Decca 417450-1 — Gr. 6/87

   LP: Decca 6.43548 AZ — Fono. 7/87

   CD: Decca 417450-2 — Gr. 6/87; Dp. 6/87; Fono. 7/87; Fa. 11/87

   CD: Decca 444969-2 — Dp. 10/96

Zoltán Peskó, Baden-Baden Radio SO (rec. 10–11 May 1988) [17:00, 13:14, 14:11]

   CD: Wergo WER 6209-2 — Fono. 6/93; Fa. 9/93

Jacek Kaspszyk, North-Netherland Orch (rec. 30 June and 1–2 July 1994) [15:52, 13:36, 14:19]

   CD: Vanguard 99065 — Gr. 4/96; Dp. 7/96 [+ R. Stephan]

James Conlon, Cologne Gürzenich Orch (rec. Mar. 1995) [17:00, 13:27, 13:55]

   CD: EMI 5 55515 2 — Dp. 10/96; Fono. 12/96; Gr. 11/97; Fa. 9/98

   CD: EMI 5 75184 2 [2] — Biel. 10/03

Thomas Dausgaard, Danish Radio SO (rec. 21–22 Feb. 1997) [15:37, 13:42, 13:33]

   CD: Chandos CHAN 9601 — Fono. 8/98; Dp. 9/98; Gr. 9/98; Fa. 11/98

Antony Beaumont, Czech PO (rec. 12–14 and 22–23 Mar. 2003) [38:51]

   CD: Chandos CHAN 10138 — 2004

   SACD: Chandos CHSA 5022 — Dp. 2/04

JoAnn Falletta, Buffalo PO (rec. live 6 June 2004) [16:32, 16:43, 13:35]

   CD: Beau Fleuve Records 41267-CD — Fa. 7/05 www.bpo.org [+ Kodaly, Smetana]

Thomas Dausgaard, Danish Radio SO (rec. live 5 Nov. 2005) [14:26, 12:32, 13:08]

   CD: Dacapo 8226048 — Gr. 9/06; Dp. 10/06; Fa. 11/06 [+ A. Enna]

James Judd, New Zealand SO (rec. 6–8 June 2006) [15:30, 11:54, 13:27]

   CD: Naxos 8.570240 — Dp. 10/09; Fa. 1/10

Sinfonietta, op. 23

Dimitri Mitropoulos, PSO of New York (rec. 29 Dec. 1940) [17:12]
*Archival recordings of this broadcast are preserved at Yale Collection of Historical
    Sound Recordings and New York Philharmonic archives.*
Bernhard Klee, Berlin Radio SO (rec. 2–3 July or 15 Sept. 1980) [8:21, 7:31, 5:57]
    LP: Schwann VMS 1603 — Fono. 11/82; Fa. 11/82
    CD: Koch 311122 — Gr. 7/90; Fa. 9/90; Dp. 5/93 [+ Reger, R. Stephan]
James Conlon, Cologne Gürzenich Orch (rec. Mar. 1995) [8:21, 8:22, 5:52]
    CD: EMI 5 55515 2 — Dp. 10/96; Fono. 12/96; Gr. 11/97; Fa. 9/98
    CD: EMI 5 75184 2 [2] — Biel. 10/03
Thomas Dausgaard, Danish Radio SO (rec. 28–30 Apr. 1997) [7:01, 7:47, 5:29]
    CD: Chandos CHAN 9601 — Fono. 8/98; Dp. 9/98; Gr. 9/98; Fa. 11/98
Antony Beaumont, Czech PO (rec. 17–19 Jan. 2001) [6:58, 6:13, 5:33]
    CD: Nimbus NI 5682 — Gr. 11/01
    CD: Chandos CHAN 10204 — Dp. 7/04; Fa. 1/05
Mariss Jansons, Attersee Institute Orch (rec. live 31 Aug. 2003) [6:59, 6:22, 6:24]
    CD: Salzburger Festspiel SF 011 — issued 9/03 [+ Brahms, Ravel]
James Judd, New Zealand SO (rec. 6–8 June 2006) [9:02, 7:15, 5:29]
    CD: Naxos 8.570240 — Dp. 10/09; Fa. 1/10

Symphonische Gesänge, op. 20

Ortrun Wenkel (a), Vaclav Neumann, Baden-Baden Radio SO (rec. 28 June 1984) [3:10,
    3:26, 2:05, 2:24, 2:18, 1:18, 2:29]
    CD: Wergo WER 6209-2 — Fono. 6/93; Fa. 9/93
Franz Grundheber (bar), Gerd Albrecht, Hamburg State PO (rec. June 1992) [3:28,
    3:04, 2:12, 2:07, 2:30, 1:16, 2:24]
    CD: Capriccio 10448 — Fono. 10/93; Dp. 12/93; Fa. 1/94; Gr. 3/94
Willard White (bs-bar), Riccardo Chailly, Concertgebouw Orch of Amsterdam (rec.
    Oct. 1993) [3:35, 3:11, 2:27, 2:03, 2:42, 1:14, 2:22]
    CD: Decca 443569-2 — Gr. 12/94; Dp. 12/94; Fono. 1/95; Fa. 7/95
    CD: Decca 473734-2 [2] — Gr. 6/03
Michael Volle (bar), James Conlon, Cologne Gürzenich Orch (rec. live 15–17 Nov. 1998)
    [3:33, 3:06, 2:20, 2:07, 2:44, 1:22, 2:12]
    CD: EMI 5 57024 2 — Dp. 9/00; Gr. 11/00; Fa. 1/01
    CD: EMI 5 86079 2 [2] — Fa. 7/05

Symphony no. 1 in D minor

Ludovít Rajter, Bratislava RSO (rec. 12–15 Dec. 1989) (12:50, 5:34, 8:11; *finale lacking*]
    CD: Marco Polo 8.223166 — Gr. 12/91; Fono. 2/92; Fa. 3/92; Dp. 3/93
    CD: Naxos 8.557008 — Biel. 10/03
Antony Beaumont, Hamburg NDR SO (rec. 28–29 Nov. 1995) [11:06, 5:18, 7:52, 7:28]
    CD: Capriccio 10740 — Fono. 12/97; Dp. 6/98; Fa. 11/98

James Conlon, Cologne Gürzenich Orch (rec. 20–30 Jan. 1996) [9:13, 6:03, 9:10, 7:35]
    CD: EMI 5 56473 2 — Fono. 8/98; Fa. 9/98; Dp. 9/98
    CD: EMI. 41446 2 — Fa. 9/06
Antony Beaumont, Czech PO (rec. 12–14 and 22–23 Mar. 2003) [31:31]
    CD: Chandos CHAN 10138 — Gr. 2/04
    SACD: Chandos CHSA 5022 — Dp. 2/04

Symphony no. 2 in B-flat major

Edgar Seipenbusch, Slovak PO (rec. Nov. 1985) [14:14, 9:00, 8:22, 9:55]
    LP: Marco Polo 6.220391 — Gr. 9/86
    LP: Records International 7006-1 — Fa. 9/86
    LP: Opus 9310 1979 — P 1988
    CD: Marco Polo 8.220391 — Gr. 9/86; Fono. 11/86
    CD: Records International 7006-2 — Fa. 1/87
    CD: Opus 91 2670-2 — Dp. 10/99 [+ F. Schmidt]
    CD: Naxos 8.557008 — Biel. 10/03
Riccardo Chailly, Berlin Radio SO (rec. Sept. 1987) [14:48, 9:19, 9:21, 11:19]
    CD: Decca 421644-2 — Gr. 3/89; Dp. 3/89; Fono. 5/89; Fa. 9/89
James Conlon, Cologne Gürzenich Orch. (rec. 20–30 Jan. 1996) [12:07, 9:47, 10:15, 11:08]
    CD: EMI 5 56473 2 — Fono. 8/98; Fa. 9/98; Dp. 9/98
    CD: EMI. 41446 2 — Fa. 9/06
Antony Beaumont, Czech PO (rec. 17–19 Jan. 2001) [14:29, 8:59, 10:25, 11:37]
    CD: Nimbus NI 5682 — Gr. 11/01
    CD: Chandos CHAN 10204 — Dp. 7/04; Fa. 1/05

Der Triumph der Zeit

— *Drei Ballettstücke*
Gerd Albrecht, Hamburg State PO (rec. June 1992) [7:07, 4:46, 3:17]
    CD: Capriccio 10448 — Fono. 10/93; Dp. 12/93; Fa. 1/94; Gr. 3/94
    CD: Capriccio 67097 [3] — Biel. 3/04
Karl Anton Rickenbacker, Berlin Radio SO (rec. 8–10 Mar. 1994) [7:21, 4:50, 3:21]
    CD: Koch 3 1486 2; 231 486 2 — Gr. 7/99; Dp. 7/99

— *Ein Tanzpoem*
Ludovít Rajter, Bratislava Radio SO (rec. 17–21 Sept. 1990) [8:23, 7:33, 4:03, 17:16]
    CD: Marco Polo 8.223166 — Gr. 12/91; Fono. 2/92; Fa. 3/92; Dp. 3/93
James Conlon, Cologne Gürzenich Orch (rec. 20–22 Oct. 1996) [7:31, 7:26, 3:20, 17:03]
    CD: EMI 5 56474 2 — Dp. 12/97; Fa. 9/98
    CD: EMI 5 75184 2 [2] — Biel. 10/03

Select Bibliography

Abbreviations

AZ/AMW   Unpublished letters of Alexander Zemlinsky to Alma Schindler/Alma
Mahler/Alma Mahler Werfel. Van Pelt–Dietrich Library, University of
Pennsylvania

NLZ   Nachlass Louise Zemlinsky — personal documents, letters, photographs,
etc., of Alexander Zemlinsky and his second wife, Louise Sachsel. Archiv
der Gesellschaft der Musikfreunde, Vienna

Books, articles, dissertations

ADLER, Felix. 1917. "Alexander Zemlinskys 'Florentinische Tragödie'." Reprinted in
Eine florentinische Tragödie von Alexander Zemlinsky. Staatstheater Darmstadt
1987 Programmbuch nr. 54: 24–26.

——. 1923. "Zemlinsky." *Musikblätter des Anbruch*, no. 5: 144–46.

ADORNO, Theodor. 1978. "Zemlinsky." *Quasi una fantasia: Musikalische Schriften II.*
Gesammelte Schriften 16. Frankfurt am Main: Suhrkamp. 351–67.

——. 1992. *Quasi una Fantasia: Essays on Modern Music.* Trans. Rodney Livingstone.
London: Verso.

Akademie der Künste und Hochschule für Musik, Berlin. 1996. "Die Kunst hat nie ein
Mensch allein besessen." Eine Ausstellung der Akademie der Künste und Hochschule für Musik. Berlin, Ausstellungskatalog.

ANDRASCHKE, Peter. 1995. "Alexander Zemlinsky's Dehmel-Kompositionen." In Hartmut Krones, ed., *Alexander Zemlinsky: Ästhetik, Stil und Umfeld.* Vienna: Böhlau
Verlag.

ANTOLIK, Martha. 2000. *The Influence of Zemlinsky on Selected Jugenstil Song Composers.* Ph.D. dissertation. The University of Memphis.

AUNER, Joseph. 2003. *A Schoenberg Reader: Documents of a Life.* New Haven: Yale
University Press.

BACH, David Josef. 1924. "Aus der Jugendzeit." *Arnold Schönberg zum fünfzigsten Ge-
burtstage. Musikblätter des Anbruch*, no. 7–8: Sonderheft, 317–20.

BACHLER, Klaus, et al. 1998. *Die Volksoper: Das Wiener Musiktheater*. Vienna: Holzhausen.

BAILEY, Kathryn. 1998. *The Life of Webern*. Cambridge: Cambridge University Press.

BAILEY, Walter B., ed. 1998. *The Arnold Schoenberg Companion*. Connecticut: Greenwood Press.

BARRON, Stephanie, ed. (1991). *"Degenerate Art": The Fate of the Avant-Garde in Nazi Germany*. New York: Harry N. Abrams, Inc.

BEAUMONT, Antony. 1995. "Schicksalsakkord und Lebensmotiv." In Hartmut Krones, ed., *Alexander Zemlinsky: Ästhetik, Stil und Umfeld*. Vienna: Böhlau Verlag.

——. 2000. *Zemlinsky*. New York: Cornell University Press.

——, ed. 2006. *Zemlinsky Sonate in a-Moll für Violoncello und Klavier*. Munich: G. Ricordi & Co.

BEAUMONT, Antony, and Alfred CLAYTON. 1995. "Alexander Zemlinskys amerikanische Jahre." In Hartmut Krones, ed., *Alexander Zemlinsky: Ästhetik, Stil und Umfeld*. Vienna: Böhlau Verlag.

BEAUMONT, Antony, and Suzanne RODE-BREYMANN, eds. 1999. *Alma Mahler-Werfel: Diaries, 1898–1902*. Trans. Antony Beaumont. Cornell University Press.

BECHER, Christoph. 1992. "Sehnsucht zur Tat: Alexander Zemlinsky in Prag — Zur Lyrischen Symphonie." *Neue Zeitschrift für Musik*, 153, no. 12: 17–22.

BECKERMANN, Ruth. 1984. *Die Mazzesinsel: Juden in der Wiener Leopoldstadt, 1918–1938*. Vienna: Löcker Verlag.

BELLER, Steven. 1989. *Vienna and the Jews, 1867–1938: A Cultural History*. Cambridge: Cambridge University Press.

BERG, Alban. 1984. "Prospekt des Vereins für musikalische Privataufführungen." In Heinz-Klaus Metzger and Rainer Riehn, eds., *Schoenbergs Verein für musikalische Privataufführungen*. Musik-Konzept 36. Munich: Edition Text & Kritik.

BERKLEY, George E. 1988. *Vienna and Its Jews: The Tragedy of Success, 1880s–1980s*. Cambridge: Cambridge University Press.

BIBA, Otto, ed. 1992. *Bin ich kein Wiener? — Alexander Zemlinsky*. Vienna: Ausstellung im Archiv der Gesellschaft der Musikfreunde in Wien Katalog.

——. 1995. "Alexander Zemlinsky und die Gesellschaft der Musikfreunde in Wien." In Hartmut Krones, ed., *Alexander Zemlinsky: Ästhetik, Stil und Umfeld*. Vienna: Böhlau Verlag.

BLAUKOPF, Herta., ed. 1982. *Mahler: Briefe*. Vienna/Hamburg: Paul Zsolnay Verlag.

BLAUKOPF, Kurt, ed. 1976. *Mahler: A Documentary Study*. New York: Oxford University Press.

BRAND, Juliane, Christopher HAILEY and Donald HARRIS, eds. 1987. *The Berg–Schoenberg Correspondence: Selected Letters*. New York: W. W. Norton.

BRANDSTÄTTER, Christian. 2003. *Wiener Werkstättte*. New York: Abrams.

BREICHA, Otto. 1993. *Gerstl und Schönberg: Eine Beziehung*. Salzburg: Verlag Galerie Welz.

BREICHA, Otto, Renata KASSAL-MIKULA, and Wilhelm DEUTSCHMANN, eds. 1983. *Richard Gerstl (1883–1908)*. Vienna: Sonderausstellung des Historischen Museums der Stadt Wien.

CANETTI, Elias. 1999. *The Memoirs of Elias Canetti*. New York: Farrar/Straus/Giroux.

CARNER, Mosco, and Rudolf KLEIN. 1980. "Vienna." In *The New Grove Dictionary of Music and Musicians*, 19: 713. London: Macmillan.

———. 1983. Alban Berg: *The Man and The Work*. New York: Homes & Meier.

CHADWICK, Nicholas. 1980. "Schreker, Franz." In *The New Grove Dictionary of Music and Musicians*, 16: 740. London: Macmillan.

CLARE, George. 1980. *Last Waltz in Vienna: The Rise and Destruction of a Family, 1842–1942*. New York: Holt, Rinehart & Winston.

CLAYTON, Alfred. 1982. *The Operas of Alexander Zemlinsky*. Ph.D. dissertation. Oxford University.

———. 1983a. "Brahms und Zemlinsky." In Susanne Antonicek and Otto Biba, eds., *Brahms Kongress Wien 1983*. Congress Report. Tutzing: Hans Schneider. 1988. 81–93.

———. 1983b. "Zemlinsky's One-Act Operas." *Musical Times*, 124, no. 1686: 474–77.

———. 1985. "Weitere Anmerkungen zu Zemlinsky-Renaissance." *Die Musikforschung*, 38: 155–57.

———. 1995. "Alexander Zemlinskys künstlerische-pädagogische Beziehungen zu seinen Schülern." In Hartmut Krones, ed., *Alexander Zemlinsky: Ästhetick, Stil und Umfeld*. Vienna: Böhlau Verlag.

COHEN, Gary B. 2006. *The Politics of Ethnic Survival: Germans in Prague, 1861–1914*. West Lafayette: Purdue University Press.

COLE, Malcolm S. 1977. "Afrika singt: Austro-German Echoes of the Harlem Renaissance." *Journal of the American Musicological Society*, 30: 72–95.

COOKE, Deryck. 1980. "Bruckner, Anton." In *The New Grove Dictionary of Music and Musicians*, 3: 352–71. London: Macmillan.

CURJEL, Hans. 1975. *Experiment Krolloper (1927–1931): Aus dem Nachlass*. Ed. Eigel Kruttge. Munich: Prestel.

DANNENBERG, Peter. 1983. "Zeichenhafte Einfachheit: 'Der Kreidekreis' — Zentralwerk im Spätwerk Zemlinskys." *Oper in Hamburg, 1982/83*. Hamburg: Hans Chritians Verlag.

DAVIES, Norman. 1998. *Europe: A History*. New York: Harper Collins.

DAWIDOFF, Nicholas. 2003. *The Fly Swatter*. New York: Random House.

DEMETZ, Peter. 1997. *Prague in Black and Gold: Scenes from the Life of a European City*. New York: Hill & Wang.

Deutsches Bühnen-Jahrbuch. 1928. Berlin: Bühnenschriften-Vertrieb.

DREW, David, ed. 1975. *Über Kurt Weill*. Frankfurt: Suhrkamp.

ENGERTH, Ruediger. 1989. "Alexander von Zemlinsky." In Gottfried Kraus, ed., *Musik in Österreich*. Vienna: Verlag Christian Brandstätter.

ERICKSEN, Donald H. 1977. *Oscar Wilde*. New York: Twayne Publishers.

EVIDON, Richard. 1980. "Joseph Hellmesberger." In *The New Grove Dictionary of Music and Musicians*, 8: 463. London: Macmillan.

FINK, Fiedlio F. 1921. "Zemlinskys Kammerkunst." *Der Auftakt*, 14–15: 219–21.

FLEISCHMANN, H. R. 1921. "Zemlinsky und die neue Kunst." *Der Auftakt*, 14–15: 221–22.

FRAENKEL, Josef, ed. 1967. *The Jews of Austria: Essays on Their Life, History and Destruction*. London: Vallentine Mitchell.

FRAMPTON, Kenneth. 1985. *Modern Architecture: A Critical History*. London: Thames & Hudson.

FRIEDRICH, Otto. 1995. *Before the Deluge: A Portrait of Berlin in the 1920s*. New York: Harper Collins.

FRISCH, Walter. 1993. *The Early Works of Arnold Schoenberg, 1893–1908*. Berkeley: University of California Press.

GARTENBERG, Egon. 1978. *Mahler: The Man and His Music*. New York: Schirmer.

GAY, Peter. 1968. *Weimar Culture: The Insider as Outsider*. New York: Harper & Row.

——. 1978. *Freud, Jews and Other Germans*. New York: Oxford University Press.

——. 1988. *Freud: A Life for our Time*. New York: W. W. Norton.

GEEHR, Richard S. 1990. *Karl Lueger: Mayor of Fin de Siècle Vienna*. Detroit: Wayne State University Press.

GILL, Anton. 1993. *A Dance Between the Flames: Berlin Between the Wars*. New York: Carroll & Graf.

GIROUD, Françoise. 1991. *Alma Mahler, or The Art of Being Loved*. Trans. R. M. Stock. New York: Oxford University Press.

GLASS, Herbert. 2001. "LaSalle Quartet." In *The New Grove Dictionary of Music and Musicians*, 14: 290–91. London: Macmillan.

GOLDHAMMER, Leo. 1927. *Die Juden Wiens: Eine statistische Studie*. Vienna: R. Löwit Verlag.

GORRELL, Lorraine. 2002. *Discordant Melody: Alexander Zemlinsky, His Songs and the Second Viennese School*. Connecticut: Greenwood Press.

GRAF, Max. 1969. *Legend of a Musical City*. New York: Greenwood Press.

GREGOROVIUS, Ferdinand. 1892. *Gedichte von Ferdinand Gregorovius*. Ed. A. F. Graf von Schack. Leipzig: A. F. Brockhaus.

GROSS, Leonard. 1992. *The Last Jews in Berlin*. New York: Carroll & Graf .

GROSSMANN, Stefan. 1979. *Ich war begeistert: Eine Lebensgeschichte*. Königstein: Scriptor Verlag.

GRUN, Bernard, ed. and trans. 1971. *Alban Berg: Letters to his Wife*. New York: St. Martin's Press.

GRUŠA, Jiří. 1983. *Franz Kafka of Prague*. Trans. Eric Mosbacher. London: Secker & Warburg.

GÜLKE, Peter. 1995. "Zemlinskys 'Seejungfrau'." In Hartmut Krones, ed., *Alexander Zemlinsky: Ästhetik, Stil und Umfeld*. Vienna: Böhlau Verlag.

HAEFELI, Anton. 1980. "International Society for Contemporary Music." In *The New Grove Dictionary of Music and Musicians*, 9: 275. London: Macmillan.

HAILEY, Christopher. 1993. *Franz Schreker, 1878–1934: A Cultural Biography*. Cambridge: Cambridge University Press.

HAJEK, Christina. 1988. *Beiträge zur Rezeptionsgeschichte der Opern von Alexander Zemlinsky*. Ph.D. dissertation. Hochschule für Musik und darstellende Kunst Wien.

HAMANN, Brigitte. 1999. *Hitler's Vienna: A Dictator's Apprenticeship*. New York: Oxford University Press.

HANSLICK, Eduard. 1900. *Aus neuer und neuester Zeit*. Berlin: Allgemeiner Verein für deutsche Literatur.

HARDY, Charles O. 1934. *The Housing Program of the City of Vienna*. Washington, D.C.: The Brookings Institute.

HARRIS, E. Scott. 1993. *Formal Archetypes, Phrase Rhythm, and Motivic Design in the String Quartets of Alexander Zemlinsky*. Ph.D. dissertation. Indiana University.

HAYES, Malcolm. 1995. *Anton von Webern*. London: Phaidon Press.

HEILBUT, Anthony. 1983. *Exiled in Paradise*. Boston: Beacon Press.

HEINSHEIMER, Hans. 1987. "Die scharfe Brille über der Nase . . . : Meine Erinnerungen an Alexander Zemlinsky und eine Begegnung mit Louise Zemlinsky im Sommer 1981." In *Eine florentinische Tragödie von Alexander Zemlinsky*. Staatstheater Darmstadt Programmbuch Nr. 54: 9–21.

HEYWORTH, Peter. 1983. *Otto Klemperer: His Life and Times*, vol. 1 (1885–1933). Cambridge: Cambridge University Press.

——. 1985. *Conversations with Klemperer*. London: Faber & Faber.

HILMAR, Ernst. 1976. "Zemlinsky und Schoenberg." In Otto Kolleritsch, ed., *Alexander Zemlinsky: Tradition im Umkreis der Wiener Schule*. Graz: Studien zur Wertungsforschung.

——, ed. 1989. *40.000 Musikerbriefe auf Knopfdruck*. Tutzing: Hans Schneider.

——. 1990. "Alexander Zemlinsky: Die letzten Wiener Jahre." In *Beiträge der Österreichishen Gesellschaft für Musik*, 8: 111. Kassel: Bärenreiter.

——. 1995. "Text und Musik in einem Opernfragment Zemlinskys. In Hartmut Krones, ed., *Alexander Zemlinsky: Ästhetik, Stil und Umfeld*. Vienna: Böhlau Verlag.

HIRSBRUNNER, Theo. 1995. "Harmonie des Abends: Zemlinsky; Harmonie du soir: Debussy." In Hartmut Krones, ed., *Alexander Zemlinsky: Ästhetik, Stil und Umfeld*. Vienna: Böhlau Verlag.

HITLER, Adolf. 1971. *Mein Kampf*. Boston: Houghton Mifflin.

HOCHMAN, Elaine S. 1997. *Bauhaus: Crucible of Modernism*. New York: Fromm International.

HOFFMAN, Paul. 1988. *The Viennese: Splendor, Twilight and Exile*. New York: Doubleday.

HOFFMAN, Stanley. 1993. *Extended Tonality and Voice Leading in "Twelve Songs," Op. 27 by Alexander Zemlinsky*. Ph.D. dissertation. Brandeis University.

HOFFMANN, Rudolf Stephan. 1910. "Alexander Zemlinsky." *Der Merker*, 5: 193–97.

——. 1921. "Zemlinskys Opern." *Der Auftakt*, 14–15: 211–16.

——. 1924. "Zemlinskys Lyrische Symphonie." *Musikblätter des Anbruch*, no. 5: 198–200.

ISHERWOOD, Christopher. 1963. *The Berlin Stories*. New York: New Directions.

JALOWETZ, Heinrich. 1921. "Zemlinsky, Skizze zu einer Biographie." *Der Auftakt*, 14–15: 201–4.

——. 1922. "Der Dirigent." *Musikblätter des Anbruch*, no. 5–6: 77–78.

JANETSCHEK, Edwin. 1921. "Schönberg-Erstaufführung in Prag: Neues Deutsches Theater 9. und 10. Juni 1921." *Der Auftakt*, 11: 157–59.

JANIK, Allan, and Stephen TOULMIN. 1996. *Wittgenstein's Vienna*. New York: Ivan R. Dee, Inc.

Jahresbericht der k.k. Akademie für Musik und darstellende Kunst über das Schuljahr 1909–1910.

JOHNSTON, William M. 1972. *The Austrian Mind: An Intellectual and Social History, 1848–1938*. Berkeley: University of California Press.

JUNGK, Peter Stephan. 1987. *Franz Werfel: A Story in Prague, Vienna and Hollywood*. Trans. Anselm Hollo. New York: Grove Weidenfeld.

KALLIR, Jane. 1984. *Arnold Schoenberg's Vienna*. New York: Galerie St. Etienne/Rizzoli.

——. 1992. *Richard Gerstl/Oskar Kokoschka*. New York: Galerie St. Etienne/Rizzoli.

KAPP, Reinhard. 2001. "Zemlinsky als Dirigent." *Zeit-Wart Gegen-Geist: Beiträge über Phänomene der Kultur unserer Zeit* (Festschrift Sigrid Wiesmann). Vienna and Sidney: Verlag Reischl & Grossek. 171–201.

KATER, Michael H. 1997. *The Twisted Muse: Musicians and Their Music in the Third Reich*. New York: Oxford University Press.

KEANE, John. 2000. *Václav Havel: A Political Tragedy in Six Acts*. New York: Basic Books.

KELLER, Hans. 1994. *Essays on Music*. Ed. Christopher White. Cambridge: Cambridge University Press.

KERNER, Robert J., ed. 1945. *Czechoslovakia*. Berkeley: University of California Press.

KEYSERLINGK, Robert H. 1988. *Austria in World War II: An Anglo-American Dilemma*. Montreal: McGill Queen's University Press.

KIM, James. 2003. *Romantic Elements in Alexander Zemlinsky's Choral Music*. Ph.D. dissertation. University of Cincinnati.

KLAREN, Georg. 1921. "Zemlinsky vom Psychologischen Standpunkte." *Der Auftakt*, 14–15: 204–7.

KLEIN, Max. 1921. "Zemlinsky und die Künstler." *Der Auftakt*, 14–15: 225–26.

KLEMPERER, Otto. 1982. *Über Musik und Theater: Erinnerungen, Gespräche, Skizzen*. Wilhelmshaven: Heinrichshofen's Verlag.

KNEIF, Tibor. 1976. "Zemlinsky als Harmoniker." In Otto Kolleritsch, ed., *Alexander*

Zemlinsky: Tradition im Umkreis der Wiener Schule. Graz: Studien zur Wertungsforschung.

KOLLERITSCH, Otto, ed. 1976. *Alexander Zemlinsky: Tradition im Umkreis der Wiener
Schule*. Graz: Studien zur Wertungsforschung.

KONTA, Robert. 1921. "Zemlinsky als Lyriker." *Der Auftakt*, 14–15: 216–19.

———. 1923. "Zemlinskys 'Zwerg' in Der Wiener Oper." *Der Auftakt*, 2: 294.

KORNGOLD, Erich Wolfgang. 1921. "Aus meiner Lehrzeit bei Zemlinsky." *Der Auftakt*,
14–15: 230–32.

———. 1922. "Der Lehrer." *Musikblätter des Anbruch*, no. 5–6: 78–79.

KRAUS, Karl. 1901. *Die Fackel*, 90: 27.

KRONES, Hartmut. 1995b. "Tonale und Harmonische Semantik im Leidschaffen Alexander Zemlinsky's." In Hartmut Krones, ed., *Alexander Zemlinsky: Ästhetik, Stil
und Umfeld*. Vienna: Böhlau Verlag.

KRONES, Hartmut, ed. 1995a. *Alexander Zemlinsky: Ästhetik, Stil und Umfeld*. Vienna:
Böhlau Verlag.

LA GRANGE, Henry-Louis. 1976. *Gustav Mahler*, vol. 1. London: Victor Gollancz Ltd.

———. 1995. *Gustav Mahler*, vol. 2: *Vienna: The Years of Challenge* (1897–1904). New
York: Oxford University Press.

———. 1999. *Gustav Mahler*, vol. 3: *Triumph and Disillusion* (1904–1907). New York:
Oxford University Press.

LABER, Louis. 1921. "Zemlinsky auf dem Theater." *Der Auftakt*, 14–15: 223–24.

———. 1925. "Die Prager Deutsche Oper." *Musikblätter des Anbruch*, no. 5: Sonderheft,
262–66.

LEE, Sherry. 2003. *Opera, Narrative, and the Modernist Crisis of Historical Subjectiv-
ity*. Ph.D. dissertation. The University of British Columbia.

LEVI, Erik. 1994. *Music in the Third Reich*. New York: St. Martin's Press.

LICHTENFELD, Monika. 1976. "Zemlinsky und Mahler." In Otto Kolleritsch, ed., *Alexander Zemlinsky: Tradition im Umkreis der Wiener Schule*. Graz: Studien zur
Wertungsforschung.

LINDLAR, Heinrich. 1962. "Der Komponist Alexander Zemlinsky." *Neue Zeitschrift für
Musik*, 10: 452–54.

LOCKE, Brian. 2006. *Opera and Ideology in Prague*. Rochester: University of Rochester Press.

LOGAN HASTINGS, Mary. 1998. *Zemlinsky, Wilde: Values and Illusions*. Ph.D. dissertation. University of Maryland, College Park.

LOLL, Werner. 1990. *Zwischen Tradition und Avantgarde: Die Kammermusik Alexander Zemlinskys*. Kassel: Bärenreiter.

LUDVOVÁ, Jitka. 1983. *Německý hudební život v Praze, 1880–1939*. Prague: Uměnově
dné studie; sv. 4.

———. 1997. "Mahler, Zemlinsky and the Tchechische Philharmonie," *Nachrichten zur
Mahler-Forschung*, 36: 3–10.

MACARTNEY, C. A. 1968. *The Hapsburg Empire, 1790–1918*. London: Weidenfeld & Nicolson.

MAHLER, Arnošt. 1971. "Alexander Zemlinsky: Zu seinem 100. Geburtstag am 14. Oktober 1971." *Die Musikforschung* 24: 250–60.

———. 1972. "Alexander Zemlinskys Prager Jahre," *Hudební věeda*, 9: 237–48.

———. 1975. "Mahler–Schönberg–Zemlinsky." *Musica*, 29: 125–27.

———. 1976. "Alexander Zemlinsky: Das Porträt eines grossen Musikers." In Otto Kolleritsch, ed., *Alexander Zemlinsky: Tradition im Umkreis der Wiener Schule*. Graz: Studien zur Wertungsforschung.

MAHLER-WERFEL, Alma. 1958. *And the Bridge is Love*. New York: Harcourt & Brace.

———. *Mein Leben*. 1960. Frankfurt am Main: Fischer Taschenbuch Verlag GmbH.

———. 1969. *Gustav Mahler: Memories and Letters*. Ed. Donald Mitchell. Trans. Basil Creighton. New York: Viking Press.

MAHLER-WERFEL, Alma, ed. 1924. *Gustav Mahler: Briefe, 1879–1911*. Berlin: Paul Zsolnay Verlag.

MANSEL, Philip. 1995. *Constantinople: City of the World's Desire, 1453–1924*. New York: St. Martin's Griffen.

MARCUS, Leonard. 1979. "Who Are Zelenka and Zemlinsky and Why Is Everybody Voting for Them?" *High Fidelity* (Dec.): 69–70.

MARTNER, Knud, ed. 1979. *Selected Letters of Gustav Mahler*. Trans. Eithne Wilkins, Ernst Kaiser and Bill Hopkins. New York: Farrar/Straus/Giroux.

MARX, Karl, and Friedrich ENGELS. 1965. *The Communist Manifesto*. Trans. Samuel Moore. New York: Washington Square Press.

McCAGG, William O. 1989. *A History of Habsburg Jews, 1670–1918*. Bloomington: Indiana University Press.

McCOLL, Sandra. 1996. *Music Criticism in Vienna, 1896–1897*. Oxford: Oxford University Press.

METZ, Günther. 1988. "Alexander Zemlinsky: Lyrische Symphonie, op. 18." *Melos: Vierteljahresschrift für zeitgenössische Musik*, 50, no. 3: 81–114.

MEYER, Michael. 1991. *The Politics of Music in the Third Reich*. New York: Peter Lang.

MIEBACH, Judith Karen. 1984. *Schoenberg's "Society for Musical Private Performances," Vienna, 1918–1922: A Documentary Study*. Ph.D. dissertation. University of Pittsburgh.

MOLDENHAUER, Hans, and Rosaleen MOLDENHAUER. 1979. *Anton Von Webern: A Chronicle of His Life and Work*. New York: Alfred A. Knopf.

MONSON, Karen. 1979. *Alban Berg*. Boston: Houghton Mifflin.

———. 1983. *Alma Mahler; Muse to Genius*. Boston: Houghton Mifflin.

MOHOLY-NAGY, László. 1938. *The New Vision*. New York: W. W. Norton.

MUELLER, Kate Hevner. 1973. *Twenty-Seven Major American Symphony Orchestras: A History and Analysis of Their Repertoires, Seasons 1842–43 Through 1969–70*. Bloomington: Indiana University Press.

MÜLLER, Erich H., ed. 1929. *Deutsches Musiker-Lexikon*. Dresden: W. Limpert.

MUSIL, Robert. 1995. *The Man Without Qualities*. Trans. Sophie Wilkins. New York: Alfred A. Knopf.

NEIGHBOUR, O. W. 1980. "Schoenberg, Arnold." In *The New Grove Dictionary of Music and Musicians*, 16: 701–24. London: Macmillan.

NESTROY, Johann Nepomuk. 1970. *Komödien, 1846–1862*, vol. 3. Frankfurt am Main: Insel Verlag.

——. 1967. *Three Comedies*. Trans. Max Knight and Joseph Fabry. New York: Frederick Ungar.

NEUMANN, Angelo. 1907. *Erinnerungen an Richard Wagner*. Leipzig: L. Staackman.

NEUWIRTH, Gosta. 1959. *Franz Schreker*. Wien: Bergland Verlag.

——. 1976. "Alexander Zemlinskys 'Sechs Lieder für eine mittlere Stimme nach Texten von Maurice Maeterlinck' op. 13 und Franz Schrekers 'Fünf Gesänge für eine tiefe Stimme': Ein Vergleich." In Otto Kolleritsch, ed., *Alexander Zemlinsky: Tradition im Umkreis der Wiener Schule*. Graz: Studien zur Wertungsforschung.

NEWLIN, Dika. 1980. *Schoenberg Remembered: Diaries and Recollections* (1938–76). New York: Pendragon Press.

NEWMAN, Richard, and Karen KIRTLY. 2000. *Alma Rosé: Vienna to Auschwitz*. Portland: Amadeus Press.

NOTT, Carolyn. 1979. "The LaSalle Quartet." *Gramophone*, vol. 56, Nr. 671: 1686–91.

NUSSBAUM, Anna, Hermann Kesser, Josef Luitpold and Anna Siemsen, trans. 1929. *Afrika singt: Eine Auslese neuer Afro-Amerikanischer Lyrik*. Vienna: F. G. Speidel.

ONCLEY, Lawrence. 1975. *The Published Works of Alexander Zemlinsky*. Ph.D. dissertation. Indiana University.

——. 1977. "The Works of Alexander Zemlinsky: A Chronological List." *Notes*, 34, no. 2: 291–302.

OTTNER, Carmen. 1995. "Alexander Zemlinsky und die Wiener Hofoper." In Hartmut Krones, ed., *Alexander Zemlinsky: Ästhetik, Stil und Umfeld*. Vienna: Böhlau Verlag.

OXAAL, Ivar, Michael POLLAK and Gerhard BOTZ, eds. 1987. *Jews, Antisemitism and Culture in Vienna*. London: Routledge & Kegan Paul.

PALMER, R. R., and Joel COLTON. 1992. *A History of the Modern World*, 7th ed. New York: Alfred A. Knopf.

PARTSCH, Angelika. 1979. *Das opernschaffen Alexander Zemlinskys*. Ph.D. dissertation. Universität Wien.

PARTSCH, Erich Wolfgang. 1989. "Ergänzungen zur Verbreitungsgeschichte von Weberns Sechs Orchesterstücken op. 6." In *40.000 Musikerbriefe auf Knopfdruck*. Ernst Hilmar, ed. Tutzing: Hans Schneider.

PASCALL, Robert. 1977. "Robert Fuchs, 1847–1927." *The Musical Times*, 68: 115.

——. 1980. "Fuchs, Johann Nepomuk." In *The New Grove Dictionary of Music and Musicians*, 7: 3. London: Macmillan.

PASCALL, Robert. 1980. "Fuchs, Robert." In *The New Grove Dictionary of Music and Musicians*, 7: 4–5. London: Macmillan.

PASS, Walter. 1976. "Zemlinskys Wiener Presse bis zum Jahre 1911." In Otto Kolleritsch, ed., *Alexander Zemlinsky: Tradition im Umkreis der Wiener Schule*. Graz: Studien zur Wertungsforschung.

PAWEL, Ernst. 1984. *The Nightmare of Reason: A Life of Franz Kafka*. New York: Farrar/Straus/Giroux.

PEYSER, Joan. 1971. *The New Music: The Sense Behind the Sound*. New York: Delacorte Press.

PINE, Richard. 1995. *The Thief of Reason: Oscar Wilde and Modern Ireland*. New York: St. Martin's Press.

PISK, Paul A. 1933. "Zemlinsky's 'Der Kreidekreis'." *New York Times*, 5 November.

PLEASANTS, Henry, ed. 1950. *Hanslick's Music Criticisms*. New York: Dover Publications.

PORTER, Andrew. 1980. "A Great Composer?" *The New Yorker* (Jan. 14): 86–93.

POSEY, James. 1998. *A Forgotten Influence: The Songs of Alexander Zemlinsky*. Ph.D. dissertation. University of Maryland, College Park.

POTTER, William. 2005. *The Psalm Settings of Alexander Zemlinsky*. Ph.D. dissertation. University of North Carolina at Greensboro.

QUANDER, Georg. 1992. *250 Jahre Opernhaus Unter den Linden*. Berlin: Propyläen Verlag.

RADDATZ, Fritz Joachim. 1981. *Das Tage-Buch: Portrait einer Zeitschrift*. Königstein: Athenaum.

RADEMACHER, Udo. 1996. *Vokales Schaffen an der Schwelle zur Neuen Musik: Studien zum Klavierlied Alexander Zemlinskys*. Kassel: Gustav Bosse Verlag.

RATHGEBER, Eike. 1991. *Alexander von Zemlinsky: Der Komponist und seine Lieder op. 2*. Ph.D. dissertation. Universität Wien.

——. 1992. "Das Gläserne Herz." *Österreichesche Musik Zeitschrift*, 47/4: 199–206.

——. 1995. "Alexander Zemlinsky. Varianten zur Ruhelosigkeit." In Hartmut Krones, ed., *Alexander Zemlinsky: Ästhetik, Stil und Umfeld*. Vienna: Böhlau Verlag.

——. 2001. "Ein Souvenir aus *Mahagonny*: Von Zemlinsky, Weill und den Schwierigkeiten, die Moderne von der Postmoderne zu unterscheiden." In Alice Bolterauer and Elfriede Wiltschnigg, eds., *Kunstgrenzen: Funktionsräume der Ästhetik in Moderne und Postmoderne*. Vienna: Studien zur Moderne, 16: 83–95.

RATHGEBER, Eike and Christian HEITLER. 1999a. "In Zeiten des alterierten Tones: Ein Versuch über Alexander Zemlinskys nachgelassenen Liederzyklus 'Stromüber' nach Gedichten Richard Demels (1907)." In Rudolf Flotzinger, ed., *Fremdheit in der Moderne*. Vienna: Studien zur Moderne 3: 235–72.

——. 1999b. "Der Wiener Ansorge-Verein, 1903–1910 (Verein für Kunst und Kultur)." In Heidemarie Uhl, ed., *Kultur–Urbanität–Moderne: Differenzierungen der Moderne in Zentraleuropa um 1900*. Vienna: Studien zur Moderne, 4: 383–436.

REICH, Willi. 1971. *Schoenberg: A Critical Biography*. Trans. Leo Black. London: Longman.

RESCHKE, Claus, and Howard POLLACK, eds. 1992. *German Literature and Music: An Aesthetic Fusion: 1890–1989*. Munich: Wilhelm Fink Verlag.

RINGER, Alexander L. 1990. *Arnold Schoenberg: The Composer as Jew*. Oxford: Clarendon Press.

RODE, Susanne. 1992. "Alles wär schön auf der Welt — Wenn's keine Operetten gäbe: Zemlinskys Kapellmeisterzeit am Wiener Carltheater." *Österreichische Musikzeitschrift*, 4: 47.

RODE-BREYMANN, Susanne. 1995. "Zemlinsky Kompositionen und Entwürfe für das Musiktheater." In Hartmut Krones, ed., *Alexander Zemlinsky: Ästhetik, Stil und Umfeld*. Vienna: Böhlau Verlag.

ROOKE, Keith. 1981. "Alexander Zemlinskys 'Die Seejungfrau'." *Schweizerische Musikzeitung*, 121: 85–91.

ROTH, Joseph. 1976. *Juden auf Wanderschaft*. Amsterdam: Albert de Lange.

——. 1995. *The Radetzky March*. Trans. Joachim Neugroschel. New York: Overlook Press.

ROZENBLIT, Marsha L. 1983. *The Jews of Vienna, 1867–1914: Assimilation and Identity*. Albany: State University of New York Press.

RYCHNOVSKY, Ernst. 1924. "Alexander Zemlinsky." *Die Musik*, 16 (August): 792–97.

SAMS, Eric. 1980. "Wolf, Hugo." In *The New Grove Dictionary of Music and Musicians*, 20: 475–502. London: Macmillan.

SAX, Benjamin, and Dieter KUNTZ. 1992. *Inside Hitler's Germany*. Lexington, Mass.: D. C. Heath & Co.

SAYER, Derek. 1998. *The Coasts of Bohemia*. Trans. Alena Sayer. Princeton: Princeton University Press.

SCHEBERA, Jürgen. 1981. *Hanns Eisler*. Berlin: Henschelverlag Kunst und Gesellschaft.

——. 1995. *Kurt Weill: An Illustrated Life*. Trans. Caroline Murphy. New Haven: Yale University Press.

——. 2004. "Songspiel und Oper: Aufführungs- und Rezeptionsgeschichte, 1927–1933." *Brecht Yearbook*, vol. 29, ed. Marc Silberman and Florian Vassen. Pittsburgh: Carnegie Mellon University.

SCHLEISSNER, Leo von. 1925. "Aera Zemlinsky." *Der Auftakt*, 6: 193–95.

SCHNITZLER, Arthur. 1992. *The Road into the Open*. Trans. Roger Byers. Berkeley: University of California Press.

SCHOENBERG, Arnold. 1921. "Gedanken über Zemlinsky." *Der Auftakt*, 14–15: 228–30.

——. 1965. *Letters*. Ed. Erwin Stein. Trans. Eithne Wilkins and Ernst Kaiser. New York: St. Martin's Press.

——. 1974. *Berliner Tagebuch*. Ed. J. Rufer. Frankfurt am Main: Propyläen Verlag.

——. 1984. *Style and Idea*. Ed. Leonard Stein. Trans. Leo Black. Berkeley: University of California Press.

SCHÖNY, Heinz. 1978. "Alexander Zemlinsky." *Genealogie*, 14, no. 4: 97–101.

SCHORSKE, Carl E. 1981. *Fin-de-siècle Vienna: Politics and Culture*. New York: Vintage Books.

SCHRADER, Bärbel, and Jürgen SCHEBERA. 1988. *The "Golden" Twenties: Art and Literature in the Weimar Republic*. New Haven: Yale University Press.

SCHREKER, Franz. 1921. "Ein Gedenkblatt." *Der Auftakt*, 14–15: 232–33.

SCHRÖDER, Klaus Albricht. 1993. *Richard Gerstl, 1883–1908: Katalog zur Austellung, Wien und Zürich, 1993 und 1994*. Vienna: Kunstforum der Bank Austria.

SEGEL, Harold B. 1994. *The Vienna Coffeehouse Wits, 1890–1938*. West Lafayette, Ind.: Purdue University Press.

SELZ, Peter. 1957. *German Expressionist Painting*. Berkeley: University of California Press.

SHAWN, Allen. 2002. *Arnold Schoenberg's Journey*. New York: Farrar/Straus/Giroux.

SHIRER, William. 1960. *The Rise and Fall of the Third Reich*. New York: Simon & Schuster.

SKED, Alan. 1989. *The Decline and Fall of the Habsburg Empire, 1815–1918*. London: Longman.

SLONIMSKY, Nicolas. 1949. *Music Since 1900*, 3rd ed. New York: Coleman–Ross.

SMITH, Joan Allen. 1986. *Schoenberg and His Circle: A Viennese Portrait*. New York: Schirmer.

SPECHT, Richard. 1921. "Neue Musik in Wien." *Musikblätter des Anbruch*, no. 13–14: 245–56.

STEED, H. Wickham. 1910. "Austria-Hungary." *The Encyclopedia Britannica*, 11th ed., vol. 3: 2–39. New York: The Encyclopedia Britannica Company.

STEFAN, Paul. 1913. *Das Grab in Wien: Eine Chronik, 1903–1911*. Berlin: Erich Reiss.

——. 1921. "Aus Zemlinskys Wiener Zeit." *Der Auftakt*, 14–15: 227–28.

——. 1923. "Österreichische Musik seit Mahler." *Musikblätter des Anbruch*, no. 5: 131–33.

——. 1924. "Das Deutsche Theater beim Prager Musikfest." *Muskiblätter des Anbruch*, no. 6: 254–55.

——. 1932. "Zemlinsky." *Muskiblätter des Anbruch*, no. 7: 126–27.

STEINBERG, Michael. 1980. "Bodanzky, Artur." In *The New Grove Dictionary of Music and Musicians*, 2: 834–35. London: Macmillan.

STEINHARD, Erich. 1921. "Zemlinsky als Dirigent." *Der Auftakt*, 14–15: 207–11.

——. 1922. "Alexander Zemlinsky: Kleider machen Leute." *Der Auftakt*, 5–6: 152–53.

——. 1924. "Planlosigkeit der Prager Opernleitung." *Der Auftakt*, 4: 230–31.

——. 1925. "Aus Einem Prager Musikmilieu." *Musikblätter des Anbruch*, no. 5: Sonderheft, 259–62.

STENGEL, Theo, and Herbert GERIGK. 1941. *Lexikon der Juden in der Musik*. Berlin: Bernhard Hahnefeld Verlag.

STEPHAN, Rudolf. 1978. "Alexander Zemlinsky: Ein unbekannter Meister der Wiener Schule." In *Kieler Vorträge zum Theater*, vol. 4: 4–46.

STORM, Theodor. 1889. *Gedichte*, 8th ed. Berlin: Gebrüder Paetel.

STRAUSS, Franz and Alice STRAUSS, eds. 1952. *Strauss–Hofmannsthal Briefwechsel*. Zürich: Atlantis Verlag.

STRAVINSKY. Igor. 1964. "On Conductors and Conducting." *Show*, 28: 108.

STRAVINSKY, Vera, and Robert KRAFT. 1978. *Stravinsky in Pictures and Documents*. New York: Simon & Schuster.

STUCKENSCHMIDT, Hans H. 1976. *Die Musik eines halben Jahrhunderts*. Munich: R. Piper Verlag.

——. 1977. *Schoenberg: His Life, World and Work*. Trans. Humphrey Searle. New York: Schirmer.

——. 1979. *Arnold Schoenberg*. Trans. Edith Temple Roberts and Humphrey Searle. Westport, Ct.: Greenwood Press.

SWAFFORD, Jan. 1999. *Johannes Brahms*. New York: Vintage Books.

SZMOLYAN, Walter. 1974. "Schönbergs Wiener Verein für musikalische Privataufführungen." In Ernst Hilmar, ed., *Arnold Schönberg: Gedenkausstellung*. Vienna: Universal Edition.

——. 1976. "Schönbergs Wiener Skandalkonzert." *Österreichische Musik Zeitschrift*, 31: 298.

TAGORE, Rabindranath. 1941. *Collected Poems and Plays of Rabindranath Tagore*. New York: Macmillan.

TANAKH. 1985. *A New Translation of The Holy Scriptures*. Philadelphia: JPS.

TANCSIK, Pamela. 2000. *Die Prager Oper heisst Zemlinsky: Theatergeschichte des Neuen Deutschen Theaters Prag in der Ära Zemlinsky von 1911–1927*. Vienna: Böhlau Verlag.

TAPIÉ, Victor-L. 1971. *The Rise and Fall of the Habsburg Monarchy*. Trans. Stephen Hardman. New York: Praeger Publishers.

TAYLOR, Robert L. 1995. *The Completed Symphonic Compositions of Alexander Zemlinsky*. Ph.D. dissertation. The Ohio State University.

TAYLOR, Ronald. 1997. *Berlin and its Culture: A Historical Portrait*. New Haven: Yale University Press.

TRAUBNER, Richard. 1983. *Operetta: A Theatrical History*. New York: Doubleday & Co.

ULLMANN, Viktor. 1925. "Zemlinskys Konzerte." *Pult und Taktstock*, 5: 88–89.

UNGER, Max. 1922. "Alexander Zemlinsky: Der Zwerg." *Der Auftakt*, 7: 189–90.

United States Chief Counsel for Prosecution of Axis Criminality. 1946. "Nazi Conspiracy and Aggression," vol. 4, 1417-PS. Washington, D.C.: United States Government Printing Office.

VARNEDOE, Kirk. 1986. *Vienna 1900: Art, Architecture and Design*. New York: Museum of Modern Art.

VOJTECH, Ivan. 1974. "Der Verein für musikalische Privataufführungen in Prag." In Ernst Hilmar, ed., *Arnold Schönberg: Gedenkausstellung*. Vienna: Universal Edition.

VYSLOUZIL, Jiří. 1995. "Zemlinskys Prager Antrittsjahre." In Hartmut Krones, ed., *Alexander Zemlinsky: Ästhetik, Stil und Umfeld*. Vienna: Böhlau Verlag.

WALLACE, William V. 1976. *Czechoslovakia*. London: Ernest Benn, Ltd.

WANG, Pao-Hsiang. 1999. *Crisis of Identity of German Jews in Fin-de-Siècle Vienna: Operas and plays by Hofmannsthal, Schnitzler, Zemlinsky, and Schreker*. Ph.D. dissertation. University of California, Santa Barbara.

WEBER, Horst. 1971. "Zemlinsky in Wien, 1871–1911." *Archiv für Musikwissenschaft*, 28, no. 2: 77–96.

——. 1976. "Der retrospective Komponist: Alexander Zemlinsky." In Otto Kolleritsch, ed., *Alexander Zemlinsky: Tradition im Umkreis der Wiener Schule*. Graz: Studien zur Wertungsforschung.

——. 1977. *Alexander Zemlinsky*. Vienna: E. Lafite, Oesterreichischer Bundesverlag.

——. 1982. "The String Quartets of Zemlinsky." *Alexander Zemlinsky; Hans Erich Apostel; LaSalle Quartet* (liner notes). Hamburg : Deutsche Grammophon.

——. 1991. "Über Zemlinskys Oper Der Traumgörge." *Musik-Konzepte*, no. 74: 109–21.

——. 1995. *Zemlinskys Briefwechsel mit Schönberg, Webern, Berg und Schreker*. Ed. Horst Weber. Darmstadt: Wissenschaftliche Buchgesellschaft.

WECHSBERG, Joseph. 1971. *Prague: The Mystical City*. New York: Macmillan.

WEININGER, Otto. 1975. *Sex and Character*. New York: AMS Press.

WEISSWEILER, Eva. 1999. *Ausgemerzt! Das Lexikon der Juden in der Musik und seine mörderischen Folgen*. Cologne: Dittrich Verlag.

WELLESZ, Egon. 1926. *Arnold Schoenberg*. Trans. W. H. Kerridge. London: J. M. Dent & Sons, Ltd.

——. 1946. "E. J. Dent and the International Society for Contemporary Music." *The Music Review*, 7, no. 3: 2058.

WELLESZ, Egon, and Emmy WELLESZ. 1981. *Egon Wellesz: Leben und Werk*. Ed. Franz Endler. Vienna: Paul Zsolnay Verlag.

WERFEL, Franz. 1921. "Alexander Zemlinsky." *Der Auftakt*, 14–15: 197–200.

——. 1922. "Der Komponist." *Musikblätter des Anbruch*, no. 5–6: 74–77.

WERTHEIMER, Joseph Ritter von. 1842. *Die Juden in Oesterreich*, vol. 1. Leipzig: Mayer & Wigand.

WILLMOTT, H. P. 2003. *World War I*. New York: Dorling Kindersley.

WILLNAUER, Franz. 1979. *Gustav Mahler und die Wiener Oper*. Vienna: Jugend & Volk.

WINGLER, Hans M., ed. 1962. *Das Bauhaus, 1919–1933: Weimar, Dessau, Berlin*. Bramsche: Verlag Gebr. Rasch & Co.

WIRTH, Helmut. 1980. "Schmidt, Franz." In *The New Grove Dictionary of Music and Musicians*, 16: 672. London: Macmillan.

WISKEMANN, Elizabeth. 1938. *Czechs and Germans: A Study of the Struggle in the Historic Provinces of Bohemia and Moravia*. London: Oxford University Press.

WISTRICH, Robert S. 1989. *The Jews of Vienna in the Age of Franz Joseph*. New York: Oxford University Press.

WULF, Joseph. 1963. *Die Bildenden Künste im Dritten Reich*. Gütersloh: Sigbert Mohn Verlag.

WÜRFFEL, Stefan Bodo. 1984. ". . . und sage deine letzten Worte in Schweigen: Anmerkungen zur gegenwärtigen Zemlinsky-Renaissance." *Die Musikforschung*, 37: 191–206.

WURSTBAUER, Michael. 1984. "Uraufführung der Erwartung — Erwartung der Uraufführung." In *40.000 Musikerbriefe auf Knopfdruck*. Tutzing: Hans Schneider.

ZBAVITEL, Dusan. 1961. "Tagore and Czechoslovakia." *Rabindranath Tagore: A Centenary Volume*. Sahitya Akedemi. 365–66.

ZELLER, Kurt-Alexander. 1990. *Music for the Theater: Alexander Zemlinsky as Opera Composer*. Ph.D. dissertation. University of Cincinnati.

ZEMLINSKY, Alexander. 1915. [Observations by the musical director of the Deutschen Landestheater, Prague.] *Merkur* (March): 183–184.

——. 1922. "Brahms und die neuere Generation: Persönliche Erinnerungen." *Musikblätter des Anbruch*, no. 5–6: 69–70.

——. 1924. "Lyrische Symphonie." *Pult und Taktstock*, 1: 10–11.

——. 1927. "Einige Worte über das Studium von Schönbergs 'Erwartung'." *Pult und Taktstock*, 2, no. 4, 44–45.

——. 1934. "Jungenderinnerungen." *Arnold Schoenberg zum 60. Geburtstag*. Vienna: Universal Edition. 33–35.

ZEMLINSKY-SCHÜLER. 1922. "Aus einer modernen Dirigentenschule." *Der Auftakt*, 4: 121–23.

ZEMLINSZKY, Adolf von. 1888. *Geschichte der türkisch-israelitischen Gemeinde zu Wien von ihrer Gründung bis heute nach historischen Daten*. Vienna: Papo.

ZISCHLER, Hanns. 2003. *Kafka Goes To The Movies*. Chicago: University of Chicago Press.

ZIMMERMANN, Christian. 2000. *Klabautermann und Vagabund: Eine Einführung in Leben und Werke Klabunds (1890–1928)*. Begleitheft zur Kabinett-Ausstellung. Lübeck: Buddenbrookhaus.

ZWEIG, Stefan. 1964. *The World of Yesterday*. Lincoln: University of Nebraska Press.

Newspapers, journals

Allgemeine Musikzeitung (January, 1934)

Arbeiter Zeitung (April 1, 1913)

Der Auftakt: Musikblätter für die Tschechoslowakische Republik, ed. E. Steinhard (1921–25)

Berliner Börsen-Courier (1928–29)

Berliner Zeitung (February 13, 1929)

Die Fackel, 90 (1901)

Kölnische Zeitung (June 17, 1922; January 26, 1934)

Magdeburger Zeitung (November 25, 1926)

Der Merker (1910–15)

Monatsblätter für Musik, 1 Jg. (Berlin, 1949)

Münchener Post-und Augsburger Volkzeitung (October 13, 1897)

Münchner Zeitung (February 1, 1917)

The Musical Times, 68 (London, 1977)

Die Musik (February, 1928)

Musikblätter des Anbruch (1922–35; shortened to *Anbruch* from 1929)

Neue freie Presse (December 12, 1896)

Neue Musikalische Presse: Zeitschrift für Musik, Theater, Kunst, Sänger- und Vereins-wesen (1895–1909)

Neue Musik-Zeitung, 21 (1900)

Neue Wiener Journal (February 3, 1916)

Neues Wiener Tagblatt (1896–1917)

Neue Zürcher Nachrichten (October 17, 1933)

Neue Zürcher Zeitung (October 16, 1933)

New York Sun (December 30, 1940)

New York Times (1933–42)

Österreichische Musik und Theaterzeitung (December 15, 1896)

Österreichische Musikzeitschrift, 47, no. 4 (1992)

Prager Presse (1930)

Prager Tagblatt (March 5, 1917)

Pult und Taktstock (1924–27)

Der rote Fahne (November 29, 1927)

Schwäbische Merkur (January 31, 1917)

Vossische Zeitung Berlin, Nr. 279 (November 29, 1927)

Collections containing unpublished materials or manuscripts

Archive of the Gesellschaft der Musikfreunde, Vienna

Arnold Schönberg Center, Vienna

Israelitische Kultusgemeinde, Vienna

Library of Congress, Washington, D.C.

Moldenhauer Archive, The Houghton Library, Harvard University

Paul Sacher Stiftung, Basel, Switzerland

Universal Edition, Vienna

Van Pelt–Dietrich Library, University of Pennsylvania

Index

A Note on Typography

THIS BOOK has been designed to evoke (without slavishly reproducing) the flourishing of Central-European book design in the 1920s. The main typeface is Bauer Bodoni, a widely used German realization from 1926 of an influential early-nineteenth-century design by Giambattista Bodoni of Milan. The display type is Kabel, a pioneering geometric sans-serif designed by Rudolf Koch in 1927. The initials are in Prisma, an extra-heavy decorative variant of Kabel. The title on the dust jacket is in Vienna Black, inspired (like Koch's Neuland type of 1923) by poster lettering by Oskar Kokoschka and the Wiener Werkstätte before World War I. The ornaments on the title page and marking sections within chapters are taken from Caravan Decorations, designed by the American W. A. Dwiggins in 1940 after the style of Central-European abstractionism.